Air Fryer Cookbook for Beginners

1000 Quick & Easy Air Fryer Recipes with Tips & Tricks to
Fry, Grill, Roast, and Bake with Only 5 Ingredients.

By
Angela Spark

Table of Contents

Breakfast Recipes

Kale Omelet

Preparation time: 10 minutes **Cooking time:** 20 minutes
Servings: 4

1 eggplant, cubed	4 eggs, whisked
2 teaspoons cilantro, chopped Salt and black pepper to the taste	½ teaspoon Italian seasoning Cooking spray
½ cup kale, chopped	2 tablespoons cheddar, grated
2 tablespoons fresh basil, chopped	

1. In a bowl, mix all the ingredients except the cooking spray and whisk well. Grease a pan that fits your air fryer with the cooking spray, pour the eggs mix, spread, put the pan in the machine and cook at 370 degrees F for 20 minutes. Divide the mix between plates and serve for breakfast.

Nutrition:
Calories 241, fat 11, fiber 4, carbs 5, protein 12

Coconut Muffins

Prep time: 10 minutes **Cooking time:** 10 minutes **Servings:** 2

1/3 cup almond flour	2 tablespoons Erythritol
¼ teaspoon baking powder	1 teaspoon apple cider vinegar
1 tablespoon coconut milk	1 tablespoon coconut oil, softened
1 teaspoon ground cinnamon	Cooking spray

1. In the mixing bowl mix up almond flour. Erythritol, baking powder, and ground cinnamon. Add apple cider vinegar, coconut milk, and coconut oil. Stir the mixture until smooth. Spray the muffin molds with cooking spray. Scoop the muffin batter in the muffin molds. Spray the surface of every muffin with the help of the spatula. Preheat the air fryer to 365F. Insert the rack in the air fryer. Place the muffins on the rack and cook them for 10 minutes at 365F. Then cool the cooked muffins well and remove them from the molds.

Nutrition:
Calories 107, fat 10.9, fiber 1.3, carbs 2.7, protein 1.2

Coconut Veggie and Eggs Bake

Preparation time: 5 minutes **Cooking time:** 30 minutes
Servings: 6

Cooking spray	2 cups green and red bell pepper, chopped 2 spring onions, chopped
1 teaspoon thyme, chopped	Salt and black pepper to the taste 1 cup coconut cream
4 eggs, whisked	1 cup cheddar cheese, grated

1. In a bowl, mix all the ingredients except the cooking spray and the cheese and whisk well. Grease a pan that fits the air fryer with the cooking spray, pour the bell peppers and eggs mixture, spread, sprinkle the cheese on top, put the pan in the machine and cook at 350 degrees F for 30 minutes.
2. Divide between plates and serve for breakfast.

Nutrition:
Calories 251, fat 16, fiber 3, carbs 6, protein 11

Zucchini Cakes

Prep time: 10 minutes **Cooking time:** 8 minutes **Servings:** 4

2 zucchini, grated	3 tablespoons almond flour
1 medium egg, beaten	¼ teaspoon salt
¼ teaspoon ground black pepper	¼ teaspoon minced garlic
1 tablespoon spring onions, chopped	¼ teaspoon chili flakes

1. Put the grated zucchini in the bowl and add the almond flour. Then add egg, salt, ground black pepper, and minced garlic, onion, and chili flakes. Add green peas and stir the ingredients with the help of the fork until homogenous. Preheat the air fryer to 365F. With the help of the spoon make the fritters and put them on the baking paper. Place the baking paper with fritters in the air fryer and cook them for 4 minutes. Then flip the fritters on another side and cook them for 4 minutes more.

Nutrition:
Calories 160, fat 11.8, fiber 3.9, carbs 9.6, protein 7.6

Chives Yogurt Eggs

Preparation time: 5 minutes **Cooking time:** 20 minutes
Servings: 4

Cooking spray	Salt and black pepper to the taste 1 and ½ cups Greek yogurt
4 eggs, whisked	1 tablespoon chives, chopped 1 tablespoon cilantro, chopped

1. In a bowl, mix all the ingredients except the cooking spray and whisk well. Grease a pan that fits the air fryer with the cooking spray, pour the eggs mix, spread well, put the pan into the machine and cook the omelet at 360 degrees F for 20 minutes. Divide between plates and serve for breakfast.

Nutrition:
Calories 221, fat 14, fiber 4, carbs 6, protein 11

Hot Cups

Prep time: 10 minutes **Cooking time:** 3 minutes **Servings:** 6

6 eggs, beaten	2 jalapeno, sliced
2 oz bacon, chopped, cooked	½ teaspoon salt
½ teaspoon chili powder	Cooking spray

1. Spay the silicone egg molds with cooking spray from inside. In the mixing bowl mix up beaten eggs, sliced jalapeno, salt, bacon, and chili powder.
2. Stir the liquid gently and pour in the egg molds. Preheat the air fryer to 400F. Place the molds with the egg mixture in the air fryer. Cook the meal for 3 minutes. Then cool the cooked jalapeno & bacon cups for 2-3 minutes and remove from the silicone molds.

Nutrition:
Calories 116, fat 8.4, fiber 0.2, carbs 0.9, protein 9.1

Green Scramble

Preparation time: 5 minutes **Cooking time:** 20 minutes
Servings: 4

1 tablespoon olive oil	½ teaspoon smoked paprika 12 eggs, whisked
3 cups baby spinach	Salt and black pepper to the taste

1. In a bowl, mix all the ingredients except the oil and whisk them well. Heat up your air fryer at 360 degrees F, add the oil, heat it up, add the eggs and spinach mix, cover, cook for 20 minutes, divide between plates and serve.

Nutrition:
Calories 220, fat 11, fiber 3, carbs 4, protein 6

Creamy Veggie Omelet

Prep time: 10 minutes **Cooking time:** 14 minutes **Servings:** 4

4 eggs, beaten	1 tablespoon cream cheese
½ teaspoon chili flakes	½ cup broccoli florets, chopped
¼ teaspoon salt	¼ cup heavy cream
¼ teaspoon white pepper	Cooking spray

1. Put the beaten eggs in the big bowl. Add chili flakes, salt, and white pepper. With the help of the hand whisker stir the liquid until the salt is dissolved. Then add cream cheese and heavy cream. Stir the ingredients until you get the homogenous liquid. After this, add broccoli florets.
2. Preheat the air fryer to 375F. Spray the air fryer basket with cooking spray from inside. Pour the egg liquid in the air fryer basket. Cook the omelet for 14 minutes.

Nutrition:
Calories 102, fat 8.1, fiber 0.3, carbs 1.5, protein 6.2

Chicken Muffins

Prep time: 10 minutes **Cooking time:** 10 minutes **Servings:** 6

1 cup ground chicken	1 cup ground pork
½ cup Mozzarella, shredded	1 teaspoon dried oregano
½ teaspoon salt	1 teaspoon ground paprika
½ teaspoon white pepper	1 tablespoon ghee, melted
1 teaspoon dried dill	2 tablespoons almond flour
1 egg, beaten	

1. In the bowl mix up ground chicken, ground pork, dried oregano, salt, ground paprika, white pepper, dried dill, almond flour, and egg. When you get the homogenous texture of the mass, add ½ of all Mozzarella and mix up the mixture gently with the help of the spoon. Then brush the silicone muffin molds with melted ghee. Put the meat mixture in the muffin molds. Flatten the surface of every muffin with the help of the spoon and top with remaining Mozzarella. Preheat the air fryer to 375F. Then arrange the muffins in the air fryer basket and cook them for 10 minutes. Cool the cooked muffins to the room temperature and remove from the muffin molds.

Nutrition:
Calories 291, fat 20.6, fiber 1.3, carbs 2.7, protein 23.9

Cheddar Turkey Casserole

Preparation time: 5 minutes **Cooking time:** 25 minutes
Servings: 4

turkey breast, skinless, boneless, cut into strips and browned 2 teaspoons olive oil	cups almond milk
2 cups cheddar cheese, shredded 2 eggs, whisked	Salt and black pepper to the taste 1 tablespoon chives, chopped

1. In a bowl, mix the eggs with milk, cheese, salt, pepper and the chives and whisk well. Preheat the air fryer at 330 degrees F, add the oil, heat it up, add the turkey pieces and spread them well. Add the eggs mixture, toss a bit and cook for 25 minutes. Serve right away for breakfast.

Nutrition:
Calories 244, fat 11, fiber 4, carbs 5, protein 7

Eggs Ramekins

Prep time: 5 minutes **Cooking time:** 6 minutes **Servings:** 5

5 eggs	1 teaspoon coconut oil, melted
¼ teaspoon ground black pepper	

1. Brush the ramekins with coconut oil and crack the eggs inside. Then sprinkle the eggs with ground black pepper and transfer in the air fryer. Cook the baked eggs for 6 minutes at 355F.

Nutrition:
Calories 144, fat 8, fiber 4.5, carbs 9.1, protein 8.8

Spiced Baked Eggs

Prep time: 10 minutes **Cooking time:** 3 minutes **Servings:** 2
2 eggs

1 teaspoon mascarpone	¼ teaspoon ground nutmeg
¼ teaspoon dried basil	¼ teaspoon dried oregano
¼ teaspoon dried cilantro	¼ teaspoon ground turmeric
¼ teaspoon onion powder	¼ teaspoon salt

1. Crack the eggs in the mixing bowl and whisk them well. After this, add mascarpone and stir until you get a homogenous mixture. Then add all spices and mix up the liquid gently. Pour it in the silicone egg molds and transfer in the air fryer basket. Cook the egg cups for 3 minutes at 400F.

Nutrition:
Calories 72, fat 4.9, fiber 0.2, carbs 1.1, protein 5.9

Mixed Peppers Hash

Preparation time: 5 minutes **Cooking time:** 20 minutes
Servings: 4

1 red bell pepper, cut into strips	green bell pepper, cut into strips 1 orange bell pepper, cut into strips 4 eggs, whisked
Salt and black pepper to the taste	tablespoons mozzarella, shredded Cooking spray

1. In a bowl, mix the eggs with all the bell peppers, salt and pepper and toss. Preheat the air fryer at 350 degrees F, grease it with cooking spray, pour the eggs mixture, spread well, sprinkle the mozzarella on top and cook for 20 minutes. Divide between plates and serve for breakfast.

Nutrition:
Calories 229, fat 13, fiber 3, carbs 4, protein 7

Baked Eggs

Prep time: 10 minutes **Cooking time:** 10 minutes **Servings:** 3

> 3 eggs
> ¼ teaspoon salt
> 1 teaspoon butter, melted
>
> ½ teaspoon ground turmeric
> 3 bacon slices

1. Brush the muffin silicone molds with ½ teaspoon of melted butter. Then arrange the bacon in the silicone molds in the shape of circles. Preheat the air fryer to 400F. Cook the bacon for 7 minutes. After this, brush the center of every bacon circle with remaining butter. Then crack the eggs in every bacon circles, sprinkle with salt and ground turmeric. Cook the bacon cups for 3 minutes more.

Nutrition:
Calories 178, fat 13.6, fiber 0.1, carbs 0.9, protein 12.6

Paprika Cauliflower Bake

Preparation time: 5 minutes **Cooking time:** 20 minutes **Servings:** 4

> 2 cups cauliflower florets, separated 4 eggs, whisked
> tablespoons butter, melted
>
> teaspoon sweet paprika
> A pinch of salt and black pepper

1. Heat up your air fryer at 320 degrees F, grease with the butter, add cauliflower florets on the bottom, then add eggs whisked with paprika, salt and pepper, toss and cook for 20 minutes. Divide between plates and serve for breakfast.

Nutrition:
Calories 240, fat 9, fiber 2, carbs 4, protein 8

Cinnamon French Toast

Prep time: 12 minutes **Cooking time:** 9 minutes **Servings:** 2

> 1/3 cup almond flour
> ¼ teaspoon baking powder
> ¼ teaspoon vanilla extract
> ¼ teaspoon ground cinnamon
>
> 1 egg, beaten
> 2 teaspoons Erythritol
> 1 teaspoon cream cheese
> 1 teaspoon ghee, melted

1. In the mixing bowl mix up almond flour, baking powder, and ground cinnamon. Then add egg, vanilla extract, ghee, and cream cheese. Stir the mixture with the help of the fork until homogenous. Line the mugs bottom with baking paper. After this, transfer the almond flour mixture in the mugs and flatten well. Then preheat the air fryer to 355F. Place the mugs with toasts in the air fryer basket and cook them for 9 minutes. When the time is finished and the toasts are cooked, cool them little. Then sprinkle the toasts with Erythritol.

Nutrition:
Calories 85, fat 7.2, fiber 0.7, carbs 1.8, protein 3.9

Cheddar Tomatoes Hash

Preparation time: 5 minutes **Cooking time:** 25 minutes **Servings:** 4

> 2 tablespoons olive oil
> ½ pound cheddar, shredded
>
> pound tomatoes, chopped
> tablespoons chives, chopped Salt and black pepper to the taste 6 eggs, whisked

1. Add the oil to your air fryer, heat it up at 350 degrees F, add the tomatoes, eggs, salt and pepper and whisk. Also add the cheese on top and sprinkle the chives on top. Cook for 25 minutes, divide between plates and serve for breakfast.

Nutrition:
Calories 221, fat 8, fiber 3, carbs 4, protein 8

Scotch Eggs

Prep time: 15 minutes **Cooking time:** 13 minutes **Servings:** 4

> 4 medium eggs, hard-boiled, peeled
> 1 teaspoon garlic powder
>
> 1 oz coconut flakes
> 1 egg, beaten
> Cooking spray
>
> 9 oz ground beef
>
> ¼ teaspoon cayenne pepper
> ¼ teaspoon curry powder
> 1 tablespoon almond flour

1. In the mixing bowl combine together ground beef and garlic powder. Add cayenne pepper, almond flour, and curry powder. Stir the meat mixture until homogenous. After this, wrap the peeled eggs in the ground beef mixture. In the end, you should get meat balls. Coat every ball in the beaten egg and then sprinkle with coconut flakes. Preheat the air fryer to 400F. Then spray the air fryer basket with cooking spray and place the meat eggs inside. Cook the eggs for 13 minutes. Carefully flip the scotch eggs on another side after 7 minutes of cooking.

Nutrition:
Calories 272, fat 16, fiber 1.5, carbs 4.3, protein 28.6

Cheesy Frittata

Preparation time: 10 minutes **Cooking time:** 20 minutes **Servings:** 6

> 1 cup almond milk
> Cooking spray
> 1 cup cheddar cheese, shredded 6 spring onions, chopped
>
> 9 ounces cream cheese, soft
> Salt and black pepper to the taste 6 eggs, whisked

1. Heat up your air fryer with the oil at 350 degrees F and grease it with cooking spray. In a bowl, mix the eggs with the rest of the ingredients, whisk well, pour and spread into the air fryer and cook everything for 20 minutes. Divide everything between plates and serve.

Nutrition:
Calories 231, fat 11, fiber 3, carbs 5, protein 8

Herbed Omelet

Preparation time: 5 minutes **Cooking time:** 20 minutes **Servings:** 4

> 10 eggs, whisked
> 2 tablespoons parsley, chopped 2 tablespoons chives, chopped 2 tablespoons basil, chopped
> Cooking spray
>
> ½ cup cheddar, shredded
> Salt and black pepper to the taste

1. In a bowl, mix the eggs with all the ingredients except the cheese and the cooking spray and whisk well. Preheat the air fryer at 350 degrees F, grease it with the cooking spray, and pour the eggs mixture inside.
2. Sprinkle the cheese on top and cook for 20 minutes. Divide everything between plates and serve.

Nutrition:
Calories 232, fat 12, fiber 4, carbs 5, protein 7

Olives and Eggs Mix

Preparation time: 5 minutes **Cooking time:** 20 minutes
Servings: 4

2 cups black olives, pitted and chopped 4 eggs, whisked	¼ teaspoon sweet paprika
1 tablespoon cilantro, chopped	½ cup cheddar, shredded
A pinch of salt and black pepper Cooking spray	

1. In a bowl, mix the eggs with the olives and all the ingredients except the cooking spray and stir well. Heat up your air fryer at 350 degrees F, grease it with cooking spray, pour the olives and eggs mixture, spread and cook for 20 minutes. Divide between plates and serve for breakfast.

Nutrition:
Calories 240, fat 14, fiber 3, carbs 5, protein 8

Cheddar Biscuits

Prep time: 15 minutes **Cooking time:** 8 minutes **Servings:** 4

½ cup almond flour	¼ cup Cheddar cheese, shredded
¾ teaspoon salt	1 egg, beaten
1 tablespoon mascarpone	1 tablespoon coconut oil, melted
¾ teaspoon baking powder	½ teaspoon apple cider vinegar
¼ teaspoon ground nutmeg	

1. In the big bowl mix up ground nutmeg, almond flour, salt, and baking powder. After this, add egg, apple cider vinegar, coconut oil, and mascarpone. Add cheese and knead the soft dough. Then with the help of the fingertips make the small balls (biscuits). Preheat the air fryer to 400F. Then line the air fryer basket with parchment. Place the cheese biscuits on the parchment and cook them for 8 minutes at 400F. Shake the biscuits during the cooking to avoid burning. The cooked cheese biscuits will have a golden brown color.

Nutrition:
Calories 102, fat 9.1, fiber 0.4, carbs 1.6, protein 4.3

Eggplant Spread

Preparation time: 5 minutes **Cooking time:** 20 minutes
Servings: 4

3 eggplants	Salt and black pepper to the taste 2 tablespoons chives, chopped
2 tablespoons olive oil	2 teaspoons sweet paprika

1. Put the eggplants in your air fryer's basket and cook them for 20 minutes at 380 degrees F. Peel the eggplants, put them in a blender, add the rest of the ingredients, pulse well, divide into bowls and serve for breakfast.

Nutrition:
Calories 190, fat 7, fiber 3, carbs 5, protein 3

Fish Sticks

Prep time: 15 minutes **Cooking time:** 10 minutes **Servings:** 4

8 oz cod fillet	1 egg, beaten
¼ cup coconut flour	¼ teaspoon ground coriander
¼ teaspoon ground paprika	¼ teaspoon ground cumin
¼ teaspoon Pink salt	1/3 cup coconut flakes
1 tablespoon mascarpone Cooking spray	1 teaspoon heavy cream

1. Chop the cod fillet roughly and put it in the blender. Add egg, coconut flour ground coriander, paprika, cumin, salt, and blend the mixture until smooth. After this, transfer it in the bowl. Line the chopping board with parchment. Place the fish mixture over the parchment and flatten it in the shape of the flat square. Then cut the fish square into sticks. In the separated bowl whisk together heavy cream and mascarpone. Sprinkle every fish stick with mascarpone mixture and after this, coat in the coconut flakes. Preheat the air fryer to 400F. Spray the air fryer basket with cooking spray and arrange the fish sticks inside. Cook the fish sticks for 10 minutes. Flip them on another side in halfway of cooking.

Nutrition:
Calories 101, fat 5, fiber 1, carbs 1.9, protein 12.4

Sprouts Hash

Preparation time: 5 minutes **Cooking time:** 20 minutes
Servings: 4

1 tablespoon olive oil	1 pound Brussels sprouts, shredded 4 eggs, whisked
½ cup coconut cream	Salt and black pepper to the taste 1 tablespoon chives, chopped
¼ cup cheddar cheese, shredded	

1. Preheat the Air Fryer at 360 degrees F and grease it with the oil. Spread the Brussels sprouts on the bottom of the fryer, then add the eggs mixed with the rest of the ingredients, toss a bit and cook for 20 minutes. Divide between plates and serve.

Nutrition:
Calories 242, fat 12, fiber 3, carbs 5, protein 9

Fried Bacon

Prep time: 10 minutes **Cooking time:** 12 minutes **Servings:** 4

10 oz bacon	3 oz pork rinds
2 eggs, beaten	½ teaspoon salt
½ teaspoon ground black pepper	Cooking spray

1. Cut the bacon into 4 cubes and sprinkle with salt and ground black pepper. After this dip the bacon cubes in the beaten eggs and coat in the pork rinds. Preheat the air fryer to 395F. Spray the air fryer basket with cooking spray and put the bacon cubes inside. Cook them for 6 minutes. Then flip the bacon on another side and cook for 6 minutes more or until it is light brown.

Nutrition:
Calories 537, fat 39.4, fiber 0.1, carbs 1.4, protein 42.7

Broccoli Casserole

Preparation time: 5 minutes **Cooking time:** 25 minutes
Servings: 4

1 broccoli head, florets separated and roughly chopped 2 ounces cheddar cheese, grated	4 eggs, whisked
cup almond milk	teaspoons cilantro, chopped Salt and black pepper to the taste

1. In a bowl, mix the eggs with the milk, cilantro, salt and pepper and whisk. Put the broccoli in your air fryer, add the eggs mix over it, spread, sprinkle the cheese on top, cook at 350 degrees F for 25 minutes, divide between plates and serve for breakfast.

Nutrition:
Calories 214, fat 14, fiber 2, carbs 4, protein 9

Buttery Eggs

Preparation time: 5 minutes **Cooking time:** 20 minutes
Servings: 4

2 tablespoons butter, melted 6 teaspoons basil pesto	cup mozzarella cheese, grated 6 eggs, whisked
tablespoons basil, chopped	A pinch of salt and black pepper

1. In a bowl, mix all the ingredients except the butter and whisk them well. Preheat your Air Fryer at 360 degrees F, drizzle the butter on the bottom, spread the eggs mix, cook for 20 minutes and serve for breakfast.

Nutrition:
Calories 207, fat 14, fiber 3, carbs 4, protein 8

Sausage Bake

Prep time: 15 minutes **Cooking time:** 23 minutes **Servings:** 6

2 jalapeno peppers, sliced	7 oz ground sausages
1 teaspoon dill seeds	3 oz Colby Jack Cheese, shredded
4 eggs, beaten	1 tablespoon cream cheese
½ teaspoon salt	1 teaspoon butter, softened
1 teaspoon olive oil	

1. Preheat the skillet well and pour the olive oil inside. Then add ground sausages, salt, and cook the mixture for 5-8 minutes over the medium heat Stir it from time to time. Meanwhile, preheat the air fryer to 400F. Grease the air fryer basket with softened butter and place the cooked ground sausages inside. Flatten the mixture and top with the sliced jalapeno peppers. Then add shredded cheese. In the mixing bowl mix up eggs and cream cheese. Pour the liquid over the cheese. Sprinkle the casserole with dill seeds. The cooking time of the casserole is 16 minutes at 400F. You can increase the cooking time if you prefer the crunchy crust.

Nutrition:
Calories 230, fat 18.9, fiber 0.3, carbs 1.3, protein 13.4

Tomatoes Frittata

Preparation time: 5 minutes **Cooking time:** 20 minutes
Servings: 4

4 eggs	whisked
1 pound cherry tomatoes	halved 1 tablespoon parsley
chopped Cooking spray	
1 tablespoon cheddar	grated Salt and black pepper to the taste

1. Put the tomatoes in the air fryer's basket, cook at 360 degrees F for 5 minutes and transfer them to the baking pan that fits the machine greased with cooking spray. In a bowl, mix the eggs with the remaining ingredients, whisk, pour over the tomatoes an cook at 360 degrees F for 15 minutes. Serve right away for breakfast.

Nutrition:
Calories 230, fat 14, fiber 3, carbs 5, protein 11

French Frittata

Prep time: 10 minutes **Cooking time:** 18 minutes **Servings:** 3

3 eggs	1 tablespoon heavy cream
1 teaspoon Herbs de Provence	1 teaspoon almond butter, softened
2 oz Provolone cheese, grated	

1. Crack the eggs in the bowl and add heavy cream. Whisk the liquid with the help of the hand whisker. Then add herbs de Provence and grated cheese. Stir the egg liquid gently. Preheat the air fryer to 365F. Then grease the air fryer basket with almond butter. Pour the egg liquid in the air fryer basket and cook it for 18 minutes. When the frittata is cooked, cool it to the room temperature and then cut into servings.

Nutrition:
Calories 179, fat 14.3, fiber 0.5, carbs 1.9, protein 11.6

Paprika Zucchini Spread

Preparation time: 5 minutes **Cooking time:** 15 minutes
Servings: 4

4 zucchinis	roughly chopped 1 tablespoon sweet paprika
Salt and black pepper to the taste 1 tablespoon butter	melted

1. Grease a baking pan that fits the Air Fryer with the butter, add all the ingredients, toss, and cook at 360 degrees F for 15 minutes. Transfer to a blender, pulse well, divide into bowls and serve for breakfast.

Nutrition:
Calories 240, fat 14, fiber 2, carbs 5, protein 11

Creamy Parmesan Eggs

Prep time: 10 minutes **Cooking time:** 8 minutes **Servings:** 4

4 eggs	1 tablespoon heavy cream
1 oz Parmesan, grated	1 teaspoon dried parsley
3 oz kielbasa, chopped	1 teaspoon coconut oil

1. Toss the coconut oil in the air fryer basket and melt it at 385F. It will take about 2-3 minutes. Meanwhile, crack the eggs in the mixing bowl. Add heavy cream and dried parsley. Whisk the mixture. Put the chopped kielbasa in the melted coconut oil and cook it for 4 minutes at 385F. After this, add the whisked egg mixture, Parmesan, and stir with the help of the fork. Cook the eggs for 2 minutes. Then scramble them well and cook for 2 minutes more or until they get the desired texture.

Nutrition:
Calories 157, fat 12.2, fiber 0, carbs 1.5, protein 10.7

Dill Egg Rolls

Prep time: 10 minutes **Cooking time:** 4 minutes **Servings:** 4

2 eggs, hard-boiled, peeled	1 tablespoon cream cheese
1 tablespoon fresh dill, chopped	1 teaspoon ground black pepper
4 wontons wrap	1 egg white, whisked
1 teaspoon sesame oil	

1. Chop the eggs and mix them up with cream cheese, dill, and ground black pepper. Then place the egg mixture on the wonton wraps and roll them into the rolls. Brush every roll with whisked egg white. After this, preheat the air fryer to 395F and brush the air fryer basket with sesame oil.
2. Arrange the egg rolls in the hot air fryer and cook them for 2 minutes from each side or until the rolls are golden brown.

Nutrition:

Calories 81 fat 4.4, fiber 0.4, carbs 5.7, protein 4.9

Parsley Omelet

Preparation time: 5 minute **Cooking time:** 15 minutes **Servings:** 4

4 eggs	whisked
tablespoon parsley	chopped
½ teaspoons cheddar cheese	shredded 1 avocado
peeled	pitted and cubed Cooking spray

1. In a bowl, mix all the ingredients except the cooking spray and whisk well. Grease a baking pan that fits the Air Fryer with the cooking spray, pour the omelet mix, spread, introduce the pan in the machine and cook at 370 degrees F for 15 minutes. Serve for breakfast.

Nutrition:

Calories 240, fat 13, fiber 4, carbs 6, protein 9

Hard-Boiled Eggs

Prep time: 8 minutes **Cooking time:** 16 minutes **Servings:** 2

4 eggs	¼ teaspoon salt

1. Place the eggs in the air fryer and cook them for 16 minutes at 250F. When the eggs are cooked, cool them in the ice water. After this, peel the eggs and cut into halves. Sprinkle the eggs with salt.

Nutrition:

Calories 126, fat 8.8, fiber 0, carbs 0.7, protein 11.1

Spinach Spread

Preparation time: 5 minutes **Cooking time:** 10 minutes **Servings:** 4

tablespoons coconut cream 3 cups spinach leaves	2 tablespoons cilantro
2 tablespoons bacon, cooked and crumbled Salt and black pepper to the taste	

1. In a pan that fits the air fryer, combine all the ingredients except the bacon, put the pan in the machine and cook at 360 degrees F for 10 minutes. Transfer to a blender, pulse well, divide into bowls and serve with bacon sprinkled on top.

Nutrition:

Calories 200, fat 4, fiber 2, carbs 4, protein 4

Peppers Cups

Prep time: 10 minutes **Cooking time:** 12 minutes **Servings:** 12

6 green bell peppers	12 egg
½ teaspoon ground black pepper	½ teaspoon chili flakes

1. Cut the green bell peppers into halves and remove the seeds. Then crack the eggs in every bell pepper half and sprinkle with ground black pepper and chili flakes. After this, preheat the air fryer to 395F. Put the green bell pepper halves in the air fryer (cook for 2-3 halves per one time of cooking). Cook the egg peppers for 4 minutes. Repeat the same steps with remaining egg peppers.

Nutrition:

Calories 82, fat 4.5, fiber 0.8, carbs 4.9, protein 6.2

Chives Spinach Frittata

Preparation time: 5 minutes **Cooking time:** 20 minutes **Servings:** 4

1 tablespoon chives, chopped 1 eggplant, cubed	8 ounces spinach, torn Cooking spray
6 eggs, whisked	Salt and black pepper to the taste

1. In a bowl, mix the eggs with the rest of the ingredients except the cooking spray and whisk well. Grease a pan that fits your air fryer with the cooking spray, pour the frittata mix, spread and put the pan in the machine. Cook at 380 degrees F for 20 minutes, divide between plates and serve for breakfast.

Nutrition:

Calories 240, fat 8, fiber 3, carbs 6, protein 12

Mozzarella Rolls

Prep time: 15 minutes **Cooking time:** 6 minutes **Servings:** 6

6 wonton wrappers	1 tablespoon keto tomato sauce
½ cup Mozzarella, shredded	1 oz pepperoni, chopped
1 egg, beaten	Cooking spray

1. In the big bowl mix up together shredded Mozzarella, pepperoni, and tomato sauce. When the mixture is homogenous transfer it on the wonton wraps. Wrap the wonton wraps in the shape of sticks. Then brush them with beaten eggs. Preheat the air fryer to 400F. Spray the air fryer basket with cooking spray. Put the pizza sticks in the air fryer and cook them for 3 minutes from each side.

Nutrition:

Calories 65, fat 3.5, fiber 0.2, carbs 4.9, protein 3.5

Parmesan Muffins

Preparation time: 5 minutes **Cooking time:** 15 minutes **Servings:** 4

2 eggs, whisked Cooking spray	1 and ½ cups coconut milk
	1 tablespoon baking powder
4 ounces baby spinach, chopped	2 ounces parmesan cheese, grated 3 ounces almond flour

1. In a bowl, mix all the ingredients except the cooking spray and whisk really well. Grease a muffin pan that fits your air fryer with the cooking spray, divide the muffins mix, introduce the pan in the air fryer, cook at 380 degrees F for 15 minutes, divide between plates and serve.

Nutrition:

Calories 210, fat 12, fiber 3, carbs 5, protein 8

Cheese Eggs and Leeks

Prep time: 5 minutes **Cooking time:** 7 minutes **Servings:** 2

2 leeks, chopped	4 eggs, whisked
¼ cup Cheddar cheese, shredded	½ cup Mozzarella cheese, shredded
1 teaspoon avocado oil	

1. Preheat the air fryer to 400F. Then brush the air fryer basket with avocado oil and combine the eggs with the rest of the ingredients inside. Cook for 7 minutes and serve.

Nutrition:
Calories 160, fat 8.2, fiber 7.1, carbs 12.6, protein 8.6

Peppers Bowls

Preparation time: 5 minutes **Cooking time:** 20 minutes **Servings:** 4

½ cup cheddar cheese, shredded 2 tablespoons chives, chopped A pinch of salt and black pepper 1 cup red bell peppers, chopped Cooking spray	¼ cup coconut cream

1. In a bowl, mix all the ingredients except the cooking spray and whisk well. Pour the mix in a baking pan that fits the air fryer greased with cooking spray and place the pan in the machine. Cook at 360 degrees F for 20 minutes, divide between plates and serve for breakfast.

Nutrition:
Calories 220, fat 14, fiber 2, carbs 5, protein 11

Bacon Eggs

Prep time: 15 minutes **Cooking time:** 5 minutes **Servings:** 2

2 eggs, hard-boiled, peeled	4 bacon slices
½ teaspoon avocado oil	1 teaspoon mustard

1. Preheat the air fryer to 400F. Then sprinkle the air fryer basket with avocado oil and place the bacon slices inside. Flatten them in one layer and cook for 2 minutes from each side. After this, cool the bacon to the room temperature. Wrap every egg into 2 bacon slices. Secure the eggs with toothpicks and place them in the air fryer. Cook the wrapped eggs for 1 minute at 400F.

Nutrition:
Calories 278, fat 20.9, fiber 0.3, carbs 1.5, protein 20

Balsamic Asparagus Salad

Preparation time: 5 minutes **Cooking time:** 10 minutes **Servings:** 4

1 bunch asparagus, trimmed 1 cup baby arugula A pinch of salt and black pepper Cooking spray	tablespoon cheddar cheese, grated 1 tablespoon balsamic vinegar

1. Put the asparagus in your air fryer's basket, grease with cooking spray, season with salt and pepper and cook at 360 degrees F for 10 minutes. In a bowl, mix the asparagus with the arugula and the vinegar, toss, divide between plates and serve hot with cheese sprinkled on top

Nutrition:
Calories 200, fat 5, fiber 1, carbs 4, protein 5

Cheddar Pancakes

Prep time: 10 minutes **Cooking time:** 7 minutes **Servings:** 2

2 tablespoons almond flour	¼ teaspoon baking powder
1 teaspoon Erythritol	1 teaspoon cream cheese
1 teaspoon butter, melted	2 eggs, beaten
1 bacon slice, cooked, cut into halves	1 Cheddar cheese slice
1 teaspoon sesame oil	

1. Make the pancake batter: in the mixing bowl mix up baking powder, almond flour, Erythritol, cream cheese, and 1 beaten egg. Preheat the air fryer to 400F. Then line the air fryer with baking paper. Pour ¼ of the pancake batter in the air fryer in the shape of pancake and cook for 1 minute. Then flip the pancake on another side and cook for 1 minute more. Repeat the same steps with the remaining pancake batter. You should get 4 pancakes. After this, brush the air fryer basket with sesame oil. Pour the remaining beaten egg in the air fryer and cook it for 3 minutes at 390F. Cut the cooked egg into 2 parts. Place the 1 half of cooked egg on the one pancake. Top it with 1 half of the bacon and second pancake.

Nutrition:
Calories 374, fat 31.7, fiber 3, carbs 7, protein 18.7

Green Beans Salad

Preparation time: 5 minutes **Cooking time:** 20 minutes **Servings:** 4

cups green beans, cut into medium pieces 2 cups tomatoes, cubed 1 tablespoons cilantro, chopped Cooking spray	Salt and black pepper to the taste 1 teaspoon hot paprika

1. In a bowl, mix all the ingredients except the cooking spray and the cilantro and whisk them well. Grease a pan that fits the air fryer with the cooking spray, pour the green beans and tomatoes mix into the pan, sprinkle the cilantro on top, put the pan into the machine and cook at 360 degrees F for 20 minutes. Serve right away.

Nutrition:
Calories 222, fat 11, fiber 4, carbs 6, protein 12

Ground Pork Bake

Prep time: 10 minutes **Cooking time:** 12 minutes **Servings:** 2

8 oz ground pork	1 tablespoon keto tomato sauce
½ teaspoon dried basil	1/3 cup Mozzarella, shredded
½ teaspoon butter, melted Cooking spray	¼ teaspoon dried oregano

1. Preheat the air fryer to 365F. Then spray the air fryer basket with cooking spray. In the mixing bowl mix up ground pork, marinara sauce, dried basil, oregano, butter, and Mozzarella. Put the mixture in the air fryer basket and spread gently with the help of the spatula. Cook the morning pizza for 12 minutes.

Nutrition:
Calories 191, fat 6, fiber 0.3, carbs 1.4, protein 31.2

Chives Omelet

Preparation time: 5 minutes **Cooking time:** 20 minutes
Servings: 4

6 eggs, whisked	1 cup chives, chopped
	Cooking spray
1 cup mozzarella, shredded	Salt and black pepper to the taste

1. In a bowl, mix all the ingredients except the cooking spray and whisk well. Grease a pan that fits your air fryer with the cooking spray, pour the eggs mix, spread, put the pan into the machine and cook at 350 degrees F for 20 minutes. Divide the omelet between plates and serve for breakfast.

Nutrition:
Calories 270, fat 15, fiber 3, carbs 5, protein 9

Oregano Chicken Casserole

Preparation time: 5 minutes **Cooking time:** 25 minutes
Servings: 4

¼ cup almonds, chopped	½ cup almond milk 4 eggs, whisked
cup chicken meat, cooked and shredded	½ teaspoon oregano, dried
	Cooking spray
Salt and black pepper to the taste	

1. In a bowl, mix the eggs with the rest of the ingredients except the cooking spray and whisk well. Grease a baking pan with the cooking spray, pour the chicken mix into the pan, put the pan in the machine and cook the omelet at 350 degrees F for 25 minutes. Divide between plates and serve for breakfast.

Nutrition:
Calories 216, fat 11, fiber 3, carbs 5, protein 9

Beef and Cabbage Wrap

Prep time: 10 minutes **Cooking time:** 15 minutes **Servings:** 2

½ cup ground beef	½ jalapeno pepper, chopped
¼ teaspoon ground black pepper	½ teaspoon salt
1 teaspoon keto tomato sauce	1 teaspoon olive oil
¼ teaspoon minced garlic	¼ teaspoon onion powder
1 teaspoon dried cilantro	½ teaspoon ground cumin
2 oz avocado, chopped	2 big cabbage leaves, steamed
2 tablespoons water	

1. Preheat the air fryer to 360F. In the mixing bowl mix up ground beef, salt, ground black pepper, tomato sauce, olive oil, minced garlic, onion powder, dried cilantro, water, and ground cumin. Then add jalapeno and stir gently. Transfer the ground beef mixture in the preheated air fryer basket. Cook the meat mixture for 15 minutes. Stir it with the help of the spatula after 8 minutes of cooking. Then place the mixture over the cabbage leaves. Top the ground beef with chopped avocado and roll into the burritos.

Nutrition:
Calories 230, fat 15.9, fiber 9.3 carbs 15.9, protein 10.4

Cauliflower Rice and Spinach Mix

Preparation time: 5 minutes **Cooking time:** 15 minutes
Servings: 4

12 ounces cauliflower rice	3 tablespoons stevia
2 tablespoons olive oil	2 tablespoons lime juice
pound fresh spinach, torn	
1 red bell pepper, chopped	

1. In your air fryer, mix all the ingredients, toss, cook at 370 degrees F for 15 minutes, shaking halfway, divide between plates and serve for breakfast.

Nutrition:
Calories 219, fat 14, fiber 3, carbs 5, protein 7

Cheesy Sausage Sticks

Prep time: 15 minutes **Cooking time:** 8 minutes **Servings:** 3

6 small pork sausages	½ cup almond flour
½ cup Mozzarella cheese, shredded	2 eggs, beaten
1 tablespoon mascarpone	Cooking spray

1. Pierce the hot dogs with wooden coffee sticks to get the sausages on the sticks". Then in the bowl mix up almond flour, Mozzarella cheese, and mascarpone. Microwave the mixture for 15 seconds or until you get a melted mixture. Then stir the egg in the cheese mixture and whisk it until smooth. Coat every sausage stick in the cheese mixture. Then preheat the air fryer to 375F. Spray the air fryer basket with cooking spray. Place the sausage stock in the air fryer and cook them for 4 minutes from each side or until they are light brown.

Nutrition:
Calories 375, fat 32.2, fiber 0.5, carbs 5.1, protein 16.3

Avocado and Cabbage Salad

Preparation time: 5 minutes **Cooking time:** 15 minutes
Servings: 4

cups red cabbage, shredded A drizzle of olive oil	1 red bell pepper, sliced
small avocado, peeled, pitted and sliced	Salt and black pepper to the taste

1. Grease your air fryer with the oil, add all the ingredients, toss, cover and cook at 400 degrees F for 15 minutes. Divide into bowls and serve cold for breakfast.

Nutrition:
Calories 209, fat 8, fiber 2, carbs 4, protein 9

Mascarpone Eggs

Prep time: 8 minutes **Cooking time:** 5 minutes **Servings:** 6

7 eggs, beaten	¼ cup mascarpone
1 teaspoon ground paprika	½ teaspoon salt
1 teaspoon avocado oil	

1. Put eggs in the bowl and add mascarpone, salt, and ground paprika. With the help of the fork whisk the ingredients until homogenous. Then preheat the air fryer to 395F. Brush the air fryer basket with avocado oil. Pour the egg mixture in the air fryer basket. Cook the omelet for 5 minutes.

Nutrition:
Calories 93, fat 6.6, fiber 0.2, carbs 1, protein 7.7

Lemon and Almond Cookies

Prep time: 10 minutes **Cooking time:** 8 minutes **Servings:** 4

4 tablespoons coconut flour	½ teaspoon baking powder
1 teaspoon lemon juice	¼ teaspoon vanilla extract
¼ teaspoon lemon zest, grated	2 eggs, beaten
¼ cup of organic almond milk	1 teaspoon avocado oil
¼ teaspoon Himalayan pink salt	

1. In the big bowl mix up all ingredients from the list above. Knead the soft dough and cut it into 4 pieces. Preheat the air fryer to 400F. Then line the air fryer basket with baking paper. Roll the dough pieces in the balls and press them gently to get the shape of flat cookies. Place the cookies in the air fryer and cook them for 8 minutes.

Nutrition:

Calories 74, fat 3.8, fiber 3.1, carbs 5.6, protein 4.4

Mushroom Bake

Preparation time: 5 minutes **Cooking time:** 20 minutes **Servings:** 4

Garlic cloves, minced	1 teaspoon olive oil
2 celery stalks, chopped	½ cup white mushrooms, chopped
½ cup red bell pepper, chopped Salt and black pepper to the taste 1 teaspoon oregano, dried 1 tablespoon lemon juice	7 ounces mozzarella, shredded

1. Preheat the Air Fryer at 350 degrees F, add the oil and heat it up. Add garlic, celery, mushrooms, bell pepper, salt, pepper, oregano, mozzarella and the lemon juice, toss and cook for 20 minutes. Divide between plates and serve for breakfast.

Nutrition:

Calories 230, fat 11, fiber 2, carbs 4, protein 6

Spiced Cauliflower and Ham Quiche

Prep time: 10 minutes **Cooking time:** 15 minutes **Servings:** 4

5 eggs, beaten	½ cup heavy cream
1 teaspoon ground nutmeg	¼ teaspoon ground cardamom
¼ teaspoon salt	1 teaspoon ground black pepper
1 teaspoon butter, softened	¼ cup spring onions, chopped
¼ cup cauliflower florets	5 oz ham, chopped
3 oz Provolone cheese, grated	

1. Pour the beaten eggs in the bowl. Add heavy cream, ground nutmeg, ground cardamom, ground black pepper, and salt. After this, pour the liquid in the air fryer round pan. Add butter, onion, cauliflower florets, ham, and cheese. Gently stir the quiche liquid. Place it in the air fryer and cook the quiche for 15 minutes at 385F.

Nutrition:

Calories 280, fat 20.9, fiber 1.1, carbs 4.4, protein 18.9

Spiced Pudding

Preparation time: 4 minutes **Cooking time:** 12 minutes **Servings:** 2

½ teaspoon cinnamon powder	¼ teaspoon allspice, ground 4 tablespoons erythritol
4 eggs, whisked	2 tablespoons heavy cream Cooking spray

1. In a bowl, mix all the ingredients except the cooking spray, whisk well and pour into a ramekin greased with cooking spray. Add the basket to your Air Fryer, put the ramekin inside and cook at 400 degrees F for 12 minutes. Divide into bowls and serve for breakfast.

Nutrition.

Calories 201, fat 11, fiber 2, carbs 4, protein 6

Avocado and Spring Onions Frittata

Preparation time: 5 minutes **Cooking time:** 20 minutes **Servings:** 4

Eggs, whisked avocado, pitted, peeled and cubed 2 spring onions, chopped	1 tablespoon olive oil Salt and black pepper to the taste 1 ounce parmesan cheese, grated
½ cup coconut cream	

1. In a bowl, mix the eggs with the rest of the ingredients except the oil and whisk well. Grease a baking pan that fits the air fryer with the oil, pour the avocado mix, spread, put the pan in the machine and cook at 360 degrees F for 20 minutes. Divide between plates and serve for breakfast.

Nutrition:

Calories 271, fat 14, fiber 3, carbs 5, protein 11

Avocado Salad

Prep time: 10 minutes **Cooking time:** 3 minutes **Servings:** 4

1 avocado, peeled, pitted and roughly sliced	½ teaspoon minced garlic
¼ teaspoon chili flakes	½ teaspoon olive oil
1 tablespoon lime juice	¼ teaspoon salt
1 teaspoon cilantro, chopped	1 cup baby spinach
1 cup cherry tomatoes halved	Cooking spray

1. Preheat the air fryer to 400F. Then spray the air fryer basket with cooking spray from inside. Combine all the ingredients inside, cook for 3 minutes, divide into bowls and serve.

Nutrition:

Calories 142, fat 10.2, fiber 2.7, carbs 4.9, protein 8.8

Cheddar Kale Mix

Preparation time: 5 minutes **Cooking time:** 20 minutes **Servings:** 4

½ cup black olives, pitted and sliced 1 cup kale, chopped	tablespoons cheddar, grated 4 eggs, whisked
Cooking spray	A pinch of salt and black pepper

1. In a bowl, mix the eggs with the rest of the ingredients except the cooking spray and whisk well. Grease a pan that fits the air fryer with the cooking spray, pour the olives mixture inside, spread, put the pan into the machine, and cook at 360 degrees F for 20 minutes. Serve for breakfast hot.

Nutrition:

Calories 220, fat 13, fiber 4, carbs 6, protein 12

Mozzarella Swirls

Prep time: 15 minutes **Cooking time:** 12 minutes **Servings:** 6

2 tablespoons almond flour	1 tablespoon coconut flour
½ cup Mozzarella cheese, shredded	1 teaspoon Truvia
2 tablespoons butter, softened	¼ teaspoon baking powder
1 egg, beaten	Cooking spray

1. In the bowl mix up almond flour, coconut flour, Mozzarella cheese, Truvia, butter, baking powder, and egg. Knead the soft and non-sticky dough. Then preheat the air fryer to 355F. Meanwhile, roll up the cheese dough and cut it into 6 pieces. Make the swirl from every dough piece.
2. Spray the air fryer basket with cooking spray. Place the cheese swirls in the air fryer in one layer and cook them for 12 minutes or until they are light brown. Repeat the same step with remaining uncooked dough. It is recommended to serve the cheese Danish warm.

Nutrition:
Calories 115, fat 10, fiber 2, carbs 3.9, protein 4

Tomatoes Casserole

Preparation time: 5 minutes **Cooking time:** 15 minutes **Servings:** 4

4 eggs, whisked	1 teaspoon olive oil
3 ounces Swiss chard, chopped 1 cup tomatoes, cubed	Salt and black pepper to the taste

1. In a bowl, mix the eggs with the rest of the ingredients except the oil and whisk well. Grease a pan that fits the fryer with the oil, pour the swish chard mix and cook at 359 degrees F for 15 minutes. Divide between plates and serve for breakfast.

Nutrition:
Calories 202, fat 14, fiber 3, carbs 5, protein 12

Creamy Chives Muffins

Prep time: 15 minutes **Cooking time:** 12 minutes **Servings:** 4

4 slices of ham	¼ teaspoon baking powder
4 tablespoons coconut flour	4 teaspoons heavy cream
1 egg, beaten	1 teaspoon chives, chopped
1 teaspoon olive oil	½ teaspoon white pepper

1. Preheat the air fryer to 365F. Meanwhile, mix up baking powder, coconut flour, heavy cream, egg, chives, and white pepper. Stir the ingredients until getting a smooth mixture. Finely chop the ham and add it in the muffin liquid. Brush the air fryer muffin molds with olive oil. Then pour the muffin batter in the molds. Place the rack in the air fryer basket and place the molds on it. Cook the muffins for 12 minutes (365F). Cool the muffins to the room temperature and remove them from the molds.

Nutrition:
Calories 125, fat 7.8, fiber 3.5, carbs 6.1, protein 7.7

Salmon and Spinach Scramble

Preparation time: 5 minutes **Cooking time:** 20 minutes **Servings:** 4

A drizzle of olive oil	1 spring onion, chopped
1 cup smoked salmon, skinless, boneless and flaked 4 eggs, whisked	A pinch of salt and black pepper
¼ cup baby spinach	4 tablespoon parmesan, grated

1. In a bowl, mix the eggs with the rest of the ingredients except the oil and whisk well. Grease the Air Fryer with the oil, preheat it at 360 degrees F, pour the eggs and salmon mix and cook for 20 minutes. Divide between plates and serve for breakfast.

Nutrition:
Calories 230, fat 12, fiber 3, carbs 5, protein 12

Peppers and Cream Cheese Casserole

Prep time: 15 minutes **Cooking time:** 5 minutes **Servings:** 2

2 medium green peppers	1 chili pepper, chopped
4 oz chicken, shredded	1 tablespoon cream cheese
½ cup mozzarella, shredded	¼ teaspoon chili powder

1. Remove the seeds from the bell peppers. After this, preheat the air fryer to 375F. Meanwhile, in the bowl mix up chili pepper, shredded chicken, cream cheese, and shredded Mozzarella. Add chili powder and stir the mixture until homogenous. After this, fill the bell peppers with chicken mixture and wrap in the foil. Put the peppers in the preheated air fryer and cook for 5 minutes.

Nutrition:
Calories 137, fat 4.9, fiber 1.2, carbs 3.5, protein 19.4

Mushrooms Spread

Preparation time: 5 minutes **Cooking time:** 20 minutes **Servings:** 4

cup white mushrooms	¼ cup mozzarella, shredded
½ cup coconut cream	A pinch of salt and black pepper Cooking spray

1. Put the mushrooms in your air fryer's basket, grease with cooking spray and cook at 370 degrees F for 20 minutes. Transfer to a blender, add the remaining ingredients, pulse well, divide into bowls and serve as a spread.

Nutrition:
Calories 202, fat 12, fiber 2, carbs 5, protein 7

Chicken Bites

Prep time: 15 minutes **Cooking time:** 8 minutes **Servings:** 4

1 cup ground chicken, cooked	½ cup Cheddar cheese, shredded
1 egg, beaten	½ teaspoon salt
Cooking spray	

1. Put ground chicken and Cheddar cheese in the bowl. Add egg and salt and mix up the ingredients until you get a homogenous mixture. Preheat the air fryer to 390F. Spray the air fryer basket with the cooking spray from inside. Then make the small bites with the help of the scooper and place them in the air fryer basket. Cook the chicken and cheese bites for 4 minutes and then flip them on another side. Cook the bites for 4 minutes more.

Nutrition:
Calories 139, fat 8.4, fiber 0, carbs 0.3, protein 15

Tuna and Arugula Salad

Preparation time: 5 minutes **Cooking time:** 15 minutes
Servings: 4

½ pound smoked tuna, flaked 1 cup arugula	spring onions, chopped 1 tablespoon olive oil
A pinch of salt and black pepper	

1. In a bowl, all the ingredients except the oil and the arugula and whisk. Preheat the Air Fryer over 360 degrees F, add the oil and grease it. Pour the tuna mix, stir well, and cook for 15 minutes. In a salad bowl, combine the arugula with the tuna mix, toss and serve for breakfast.

Nutrition:
Calories 212, fat 8, fiber 3, carbs 5, protein 8

Cheddar and Ham Quiche

Prep time: 10 minutes **Cooking time:** 15 minutes **Servings:** 4

4 oz ham, chopped	1 cup Cheddar cheese, shredded
1 tablespoon chives, chopped	½ zucchini, grated
¼ cup heavy cream	1 tablespoon almond flour
½ teaspoon salt	½ teaspoon ground black pepper
½ teaspoon dried oregano	5 eggs, beaten
1 teaspoon coconut oil, softened	

1. In the big bowl mix up ham, cheese, chives, zucchini, heavy cream, almond flour, salt, ground black pepper, oregano, and eggs. Stir the ingredients with the help of the fork until you get a homogenous mixture. After this, preheat the air fryer to 365F. Then gently grease the air fryer basket with coconut oil. Pour the ham mixture in the air fryer basket.
2. Cook the quiche for 15 minutes. Then check if the quiche mixture is crusty, cook for extra 5 minutes if needed.

Nutrition:
Calories 320, fat 24.8, fiber 1.6, carbs 4.7, protein 20.7

Sausages Casserole

Prep time: 10 minutes **Cooking time:** 25 minutes **Servings:** 4

3 spring onions, chopped	1 green bell pepper, sliced
¼ teaspoon salt	¼ teaspoon ground turmeric
¼ teaspoon ground paprika	10 oz Italian sausages
1 teaspoon olive oil	4 eggs

1. Preheat the air fryer to 360F. Then pour olive oil in the air fryer basket. Add bell pepper and spring onions. Then sprinkle the vegetables with ground turmeric and salt. Cook them for 5 minutes. When the time is finished, shake the air fryer basket gently. Chop the sausages roughly and add in the air fryer basket. Cook the ingredients for 10 minutes. Then crack the eggs over the sausages and cook the casserole for 10 minutes more.

Nutrition:
Calories 342, fat 27.9, fiber 1.7, carbs 6.3, protein 16.5

Almond Oatmeal

Preparation time: 5 minutes **Cooking time:** 15 minutes
Servings: 4

cups almond milk	cup coconut, shredded 2 teaspoons stevia
teaspoons vanilla extract	

1. In a pan that fits your air fryer, mix all the ingredients, stir well, introduce the pan in the machine and cook at 360 degrees F for 15 minutes. Divide into bowls and serve for breakfast.

Nutrition:
Calories 201, fat 13, fiber 2, carbs 4, protein 7

Chicken and Cream Lasagna

Prep time: 10 minutes **Cooking time:** 25 minutes **Servings:** 2

1 egg, beaten	1 tablespoon heavy cream
1 teaspoon cream cheese	2 tablespoons almond flour
¼ teaspoon salt	¼ cup coconut cream
1 teaspoon dried basil	1 teaspoon keto tomato sauce
¼ cup Mozzarella, shredded	1 teaspoon butter, melted
½ cup ground chicken	

1. Make the lasagna batter: in the bowl mix up egg, heavy cream, cream cheese, and almond flour. Add coconut cream. Stir the liquid until smooth. Then preheat the air fryer to 355F. Brush the air fryer basket with butter.
2. Pour ½ part of lasagna batter in the air fryer basket and flatten it in one layer. Then in the separated bowl mix up tomato sauce, basil, salt, and ground chicken. Put the chicken mixture over the batter in the air fryer. Add beaten egg. Then top it with remaining lasagna batter and sprinkle with shredded Mozzarella. Cook the lasagna for 25 minutes.

Nutrition:
Calories 388, fat 31.8, fiber 3.8, carbs 8.7, protein 21

Okra Hash

Preparation time: 5 minutes **Cooking time:** 20 minutes
Servings: 4

2 cups okra	1 tablespoon butter, melted 4 eggs, whisked
A pinch of salt and black pepper	

1. Grease a pan that fits the air fryer with the butter. In a bowl, combine the okra with eggs, salt and pepper, whisk and pour into the pan. Introduce the pan in the air fryer and cook at 350 degrees F for 20 minutes. Divide the mix between plates and serve.

Nutrition:
Calories 220, fat 12, fiber 4, carbs 5, protein 8

Coconut Eggs Mix

Preparation time: 5 minutes **Cooking time:** 8 minutes
Servings: 4

1 tablespoon olive oil	and ½ cup coconut cream 8 eggs, whisked
½ cup mint, chopped	Salt and black pepper to the taste

1. In a bowl, mix the cream with salt, pepper, eggs and mint, whisk, pour into the air fryer greased with the oil, spread, cook at 350 degrees F for 8 minutes, divide between plates and serve.

Nutrition:
Calories 212, fat 9, fiber 4, carbs 5, protein 11

Mozzarella Cups

Prep time: 10 minutes **Cooking time:** 6 minutes **Servings:** 2

2 eggs	2 oz Mozzarella, grated
1 oz Parmesan, grated	1 teaspoon coconut oil, melted
¼ teaspoon chili powder	

1. Crack the eggs and separate egg yolks and egg whites. Then whisk the egg whites till the soft peaks. Separately whisk the egg yolks until smooth and add chili powder. Then carefully add egg whites, Parmesan, and Mozzarella. Stir the ingredients. Brush the silicone egg molds with coconut oil. Then put the cheese-egg mixture in the molds with the help of the spoon. Transfer the molds in the air fryer and cook at 385F for 6 minutes.

Nutrition:

Calories 209, fat 14.7, fiber 0.1, carbs 2, protein 18.1

Coconut Pudding

Preparation time: 5 minutes **Cooking time:** 20 minutes
Servings: 4

cup cauliflower rice	½ cup coconut, shredded
	3 cups coconut milk
tablespoons stevia	

1. In a pan that fits the air fryer, combine all the ingredients and whisk well. Introduce the in your air fryer and cook at 360 degrees F for 20 minutes. Divide into bowls and serve for breakfast.

Nutrition:

Calories 211, fat 11, fiber 3, carbs 4, protein 8

Cheesy Pancake

Prep time: 10 minutes **Cooking time:** 8 minutes **Servings:** 2

5 eggs, beaten	¼ cup almond flour
½ teaspoon baking powder	1 teaspoon apple cider vinegar
¼ cup Cheddar cheese, shredded	1 teaspoon butter
1 tablespoon mascarpone	½ teaspoon sesame oil

1. Brush the air fryer basket with sesame oil. Then in the mixing bowl mix up all remaining ingredients. Stir the liquid until homogenous. Pour it in the air fryer pan and place it in the air fryer. Cook the pancake for 8 minutes at 360F. Remove the cooked pancake from the air fryer pan and cut it into servings.

Nutrition:

Calories 276, fat 21.4, fiber 0.4, carbs 2.6, protein 19

Mozzarella Bell Peppers Mix

Preparation time: 5 minutes **Cooking time:** 15 minutes
Servings: 4

red bell pepper, roughly chopped	1 celery stalk, chopped
2 tablespoons butter, melted	green onions, sliced
	½ cup mozzarella cheese, shredded
A pinch of salt and black pepper	6 eggs, whisked

1. In a bowl, mix all the ingredients except the butter and whisk well. Preheat the air fryer at 360 degrees F, add the butter, heat it up, add the celery and bell peppers mix, and cook for 15 minutes, shaking the fryer once. Divide the mix between plates and serve for breakfast.

Nutrition:

Calories 222, fat 12, fiber 4, carbs 5, protein 7

Scallion Eggs Bake

Prep time: 10 minutes **Cooking time:** 20 minutes **Servings:** 2

2 eggs	4 oz double Gloucester cheese, grated'
1 teaspoon coconut flour	¼ cup heavy cream
1 tablespoon butter	1 tablespoon scallions, chopped

1. Place the eggs on the rack and insert the rack in the air fryer. Cook the eggs for 17 minutes at 250F. Then cool the eggs in cold water and peel. Cut the eggs into halves. In the bowl mix up cheese, heavy cream, butter, and coconut flour. Microwave the mixture for 1 minute or until it is liquid. Place the egg halves in the 2 ramekins. Pour the cheese mixture over the eggs and top with scallions. Place the ramekins in the air fryer and cook them for 3 minutes at 400F.

Nutrition:

Calories 395, fat 36.2, fiber 0.6, carbs 1.7, protein 20.4

Oregano and Coconut Scramble

Preparation time: 5 minutes **Cooking time:** 20 minutes
Servings: 4

8 eggs, whisked	2 tablespoons oregano, chopped Salt and black pepper to the taste 2 tablespoons parmesan, grated
¼ cup coconut cream	

1. In a bowl, mix the eggs with all the ingredients and whisk. Pour this into a pan that fits your air fryer, introduce it in the preheated fryer and cook at 350 degrees F for 20 minutes, stirring often. Divide the scramble between plates and serve for breakfast.

Nutrition:

Calories 221, fat 12, fiber 4, carbs 5, protein 9

Chia and Hemp Pudding

Prep time: 4 hours **Cooking time:** 2 minutes **Servings:** 2

1 teaspoon hemp seeds	1 teaspoon chia seeds
1 tablespoon almond flour	1 teaspoon coconut flakes
1 teaspoon walnuts, chopped	½ teaspoon flax meal
¼ teaspoon vanilla extract	½ teaspoon Erythritol
½ cup of coconut milk	¼ cup water, boiled

1. Put hemp seeds, chia seeds, almond flour, coconut flakes, walnuts, flax meal, vanilla extract, coconut milk, and water in the big bowl. Stir the mixture until homogenous and pour it into 2 mason jars. Leave the mason jars in the cold place for 4 hours. Then top the surface of the pudding with Erythritol. Place the mason jars in the air fryer and cook the pudding for 2 minutes at 400F or until you get the light brown crust.

Nutrition:

Calories 257, fat 24.2, fiber 4.4, carbs 8.4, protein 5.8

Zucchini Salad

Prep time: 4 minutes **Cooking time:** 15 minutes **Servings:** 2

cup watercress, torn	1 tablespoon olive oil
cups zucchini, roughly cubed	1 cup parmesan cheese, grated Cooking spray

1. Grease a pan that fits the air fryer with the cooking spray, add all the ingredients except the cheese, sprinkle the cheese on top and cook at 390 degrees F for 15 minutes. Divide into bowls and serve for breakfast.

Nutrition:

Calories 202, fat 11, fiber 3, carbs 5, protein 4

Sausages Squares

Prep time: 20 minutes **Cooking time:** 20 minutes **Servings:** 4

½ cup almond flour	¼ cup butter, melted
1 egg yolk	½ teaspoon baking powder
¼ teaspoon salt	6 oz sausage meat
¼ teaspoon ground black pepper	Cooking spray

1. Make the dough: in the mixing bowl mix up almond flour, butter, egg yolk, and baking powder. Add salt and knead the non-sticky dough. In the separated bowl mix up ground black pepper and sausage meat. Roll up the dough with the help of the rolling pin. Then cut the dough into squares.
2. Place the sausage meat in the center of dough squares and secure them in the shape of the puff. Then preheat the air fryer to 320F. Line the air fryer basket with baking paper. Put the sausage puffs over the baking paper and spray them with cooking spray. Cook the meal for 20 minutes at 325F.

Nutrition:

Calories 280, fat 26.5, fiber 0.4, carbs 1.3, protein 9.8

Cabbage and Pork Hash

Prep time: 15 minutes **Cooking time:** 20 minutes **Servings:** 4

1 Chinese cabbage, shredded	¼ cup chicken broth
½ teaspoon keto tomato sauce	1 green bell pepper, chopped
1 teaspoon salt	6 oz pork loin, chopped
1 tablespoon apple cider vinegar	1 teaspoon sesame oil
½ teaspoon chili flakes	½ teaspoon salt
¼ teaspoon ground black pepper	1 teaspoon ground turmeric

1. Put Chinese cabbage in the bowl. Add chicken broth, tomato sauce, bell pepper, and salt. Mix up the ingredients and transfer in the air fryer basket. Cook the cabbage for 5 minutes at 365F. Meanwhile, in the mixing bowl mix up ground black pepper, turmeric, salt, chili flakes, sesame oil, and apple cider vinegar. Add chopped pork loin and mix up the ingredients. Add the meat in the air fryer and cook the cabbage hash for 10 minutes at 385F. Then shake the hash well and cook it for 5 minutes more.

Nutrition:

Calories 131, fat 7.3, fiber 0.8, carbs 3.3, protein 12.6

Green Beans Salad

Preparation time: 5 minutes **Cooking time:** 15 minutes **Servings:** 4

1 and ¾ cups radishes, chopped	½ pound green beans, trimmed A pinch of salt and black pepper 4 eggs, whisked
Cooking spray	1 tablespoon cilantro, chopped

1. Grease a pan that fits the air fryer with the cooking spray, add all the ingredients, toss and cook at 360 degrees F for 15 minutes. Divide between plates and serve for breakfast.

Nutrition:

Calories 212, fat 12, fiber 3, carbs 4, protein 9

Coriander Sausages Muffins

Prep time: 10 minutes **Cooking time:** 12 minutes **Servings:** 4

4 teaspoons coconut flour	1 tablespoon coconut cream
1 egg, beaten	½ teaspoon baking powder
6 oz sausage meat	1 teaspoon spring onions, chopped
½ teaspoon ground coriander	1 teaspoon sesame oil
½ teaspoon salt	

1. In the mixing bowl mix up coconut flour, coconut cream, egg, baking powder, minced onion, and ground coriander. Add salt and whisk the mixture until smooth. After this, add the sausage meat and stir the muffin batter. Preheat the air tryer to 385F. Brush the muffin molds with sesame oil and pour the batter inside. Place the rack in the air fryer basket. Put the muffins on a rack. Cook the meal for 12 minutes.

Nutrition:

Calories 239, fat 17.2, fiber 5.1, carbs 8.7, protein 11.7

Cauliflower Rice and Spinach Mix

Preparation time: 5 minutes **Cooking time:** 15 minutes **Servings:** 4

12 ounces cauliflower rice	3 tablespoons stevia
2 tablespoons olive oil	2 tablespoons lime juice
pound fresh spinach, torn	1 red bell pepper, chopped

1. In your air fryer, mix all the ingredients, toss, cook at 370 degrees F for 15 minutes, shaking halfway, divide between plates and serve for breakfast.

Nutrition:

Calories 219, fat 14, fiber 3, carbs 5, protein 7

Cheesy Sausage Sticks

Prep time: 15 minutes **Cooking time:** 8 minutes **Servings:** 3

6 small pork sausages	½ cup almond flour
½ cup Mozzarella cheese, shredded	2 eggs, beaten
1 tablespoon mascarpone	Cooking spray

1. Pierce the hot dogs with wooden coffee sticks to get the sausages on the sticks". Then in the bowl mix up almond flour, Mozzarella cheese, and mascarpone. Microwave the mixture for 15 seconds or until you get a melted mixture. Then stir the egg in the cheese mixture and whisk it until smooth. Coat every sausage stick in the cheese mixture. Then preheat the air fryer to 375F. Spray the air fryer basket with cooking spray. Place the sausage stock in the air fryer and cook them for 4 minutes from each side or until they are light brown.

Nutrition:

Calories 375, fat 32.2, fiber 0.5, carbs 5.1, protein 16.3

Tomato and Greens Salad

Preparation time: 5 minutes **Cooking time:** 15 minutes **Servings:** 4

teaspoon olive oil	cups mustard greens
A pinch of salt and black pepper	½ pound cherry tomatoes, cubed 2 tablespoons chives, chopped

1. Heat up your air fryer with the oil at 360 degrees F, add all the ingredients, toss, cook for 15 minutes shaking halfway, divide into bowls and serve for breakfast.

Nutrition:

Calories 224, fat 8, fiber 2, carbs 3, protein 7

Lemon and Almond Cookies

Prep time: 10 minutes **Cooking time:** 8 minutes **Servings:** 4

4 tablespoons coconut flour	½ teaspoon baking powder
1 teaspoon lemon juice	¼ teaspoon vanilla extract
¼ teaspoon lemon zest, grated	2 eggs, beaten
¼ cup of organic almond milk	1 teaspoon avocado oil
¼ teaspoon Himalayan pink salt	

1. In the big bowl mix up all ingredients from the list above. Knead the soft dough and cut it into 4 pieces. Preheat the air fryer to 400F. Then line the air fryer basket with baking paper. Roll the dough pieces in the balls and press them gently to get the shape of flat cookies. Place the cookies in the air fryer and cook them for 8 minutes.

Nutrition:

Calories 74, fat 3.8, fiber 3.1, carbs 5.6, protein 4.4

Mushroom Bake

Preparation time: 5 minutes **Cooking time:** 20 minutes **Servings:** 4

garlic cloves, minced	1 teaspoon olive oil
2 celery stalks, chopped	½ cup white mushrooms, chopped
½ cup red bell pepper, chopped Salt and black pepper to the taste	1 teaspoon oregano, dried
7 ounces mozzarella, shredded	1 tablespoon lemon juice

1. Preheat the Air Fryer at 350 degrees F, add the oil and heat it up. Add garlic, celery, mushrooms, bell pepper, salt, pepper, oregano, mozzarella and the lemon juice, toss and cook for 20 minutes. Divide between plates and serve for breakfast.

Nutrition:

Calories 230, fat 11, fiber 2, carbs 4, protein 6

Spiced Cauliflower and Ham Quiche

Prep time: 10 minutes **Cooking time:** 15 minutes **Servings:** 4

5 eggs, beaten	½ cup heavy cream
1 teaspoon ground nutmeg	¼ teaspoon ground cardamom
¼ teaspoon salt	1 teaspoon ground black pepper
1 teaspoon butter, softened	¼ cup spring onions, chopped
¼ cup cauliflower florets	5 oz ham, chopped
3 oz Provolone cheese, grated	

1. Pour the beaten eggs in the bowl. Add heavy cream, ground nutmeg, ground cardamom, ground black pepper, and salt. After this, pour the liquid in the air fryer round pan. Add butter, onion, cauliflower florets, ham, and cheese. Gently stir the quiche liquid. Place it in the air fryer and cook the quiche for 15 minutes at 385F.

Nutrition:

Calories 280, fat 20.9, fiber 1.1, carbs 4.4, protein 18.9

Spiced Pudding

Preparation time: 4 minutes **Cooking time:** 12 minutes **Servings:** 2

½ teaspoon cinnamon powder	¼ teaspoon allspice, ground
4 tablespoons erythritol	4 eggs, whisked
2 tablespoons heavy cream	
Cooking spray	

1. In a bowl, mix all the ingredients except the cooking spray, whisk well and pour into a ramekin greased with cooking spray. Add the basket to your Air Fryer, put the ramekin inside and cook at 400 degrees F for 12 minutes. Divide into bowls and serve for breakfast.

Nutrition:

Calories 201, fat 11, fiber 2, carbs 4, protein 6

Bacon Pockets

Prep time: 15 minutes **Cooking time:** 4 minutes **Servings:** 6

6 wontons wrap	1 egg yolk, whisked
2 oz bacon, chopped, cooked	½ cup Edam cheese, shredded
1 teaspoon sesame oil	½ teaspoon ground black pepper

1. Put the chopped bacon in the bowl. Add Edam cheese and ground black pepper. Stir the ingredients gently with the help of the fork. After this, put the mixture on the wonton wrap and fold it in the shape of the pocket.
2. Repeat the steps with remaining filling and wonton wraps. Preheat the air fryer to 400F. Brush every wonton pocket with whisked egg yolk. Then brush the air fryer with sesame oil and arrange the pockets inside. Cook the meal for 2 minutes from each side.

Nutrition:

Calories 136, fat 10.1, fiber 0.1, carbs 2.6, protein 8.6

Green Beans and Eggs

Preparation time: 5 minutes **Cooking time:** 20 minutes **Servings:** 4

pound green beans, roughly chopped Cooking spray	eggs, whisked
Salt and black pepper to the taste	1 tablespoon sweet paprika ounces sour cream

1. Grease a pan that fits your air fryer with the cooking spray and mix all the ingredients inside. Put the pan in the Air Fryer and cook at 360 degrees F for 20 minutes. Divide between plates and serve.

Nutrition:

Calories 220, fat 14, fiber 2, carbs 3, protein 2

Basil Tomato Bowls

Preparation time: 5 minutes **Cooking time:** 15 minutes **Servings:** 4

1 pound cherry tomatoes, halved	1 cup mozzarella, shredded
	Cooking spray
Salt and black pepper to the taste	1 teaspoon basil, chopped

1. Grease the tomatoes with the cooking spray, season with salt and pepper, sprinkle the mozzarella on top, place them all in your air fryer's basket, cook at 330 degrees F for 15 minutes, divide into bowls, sprinkle the basil on top and serve.

Nutrition:

Calories 140, fat 7, fiber 3, carbs 4, protein 5

Tofu Wraps

Prep time: 15 minutes **Cooking time:** 9 minutes **Servings:** 4

4 low carb tortillas	5 oz tofu, cubed
1 teaspoon mustard	1 teaspoon avocado oil
1 teaspoon lemon juice	½ cup white cabbage, shredded
4 teaspoons cream cheese	2 chipotles, chopped

1. Preheat the air fryer to 400F. Meanwhile, mix up mustard with avocado oil and lemon juice. Place the tofu cubes in the mustard mixture and coat them well. Then put the tofu in the air fryer basket and cook for 9 minutes. Shake the tofu during cooking for 2-3 times to avoid burning. Then place the tofu on the tortillas. Add shredded cabbage, chipotles, and cream cheese. Fold the wraps.

Nutrition:
Calories 133, fat 5.1, fiber 8.1, carbs 15.7, protein 6.9

Coconut Berries Bowls

Preparation time: 5 minutes **Cooking time:** 15 minutes
Servings: 4

½ cups coconut milk	½ cup blackberries
2 teaspoon stevia	½ cup coconut, shredded

1. In your air fryer's pan, mix all the ingredients, stir, cover and cook at 360 degrees F for 15 minutes. Divide into bowls and serve for breakfast.

Nutrition:
Calories 171, fat 4, fiber 2, carbs 3, protein 5

Butter Donuts

Prep time: 20 minutes **Cooking time:** 10 minutes **Servings:** 4

1 cup almond flour	1 tablespoon flax meal
2 tablespoons Erythritol	2 eggs, beaten
1 teaspoon baking powder	1 teaspoon vanilla extract
1 teaspoon heavy cream	1 teaspoon butter, melted
1 tablespoon Psyllium husk powder	

1. Make the dough: mix up almond flour, flax meal, eggs, baking powder, vanilla extract, heavy cream, and butter. Add Psyllium husk and knead the soft but non-sticky dough. Then make the donuts balls and leave them for 10 minutes in a warm place. Preheat the air fryer to 355F. Line the air fryer basket with baking paper. Put the donuts inside and cook them for 10 minutes or until they are light brown. Then coat every donut in Erythritol.

Nutrition:
Calories 103, fat 7.8, fiber 3, carbs 4.9, protein 4.7

Almond Raspberries Bowls

Preparation time: 5 minutes **Cooking time:** 15 minutes
Servings: 4

cups almond milk and ½ cups coconut, shredded	½ cups raspberries
¼ teaspoon nutmeg, ground 2 teaspoons stevia	½ teaspoon cinnamon powder
	Cooking spray

1. Grease the air fryer's pan with cooking spray, mix all the ingredients inside, cover and cook at 360 degrees F for 15 minutes. Divide into bowls and serve for breakfast.

Nutrition:
Calories 172, fat 5, fiber 2, carbs 4, protein 6

Herbed Cheese Balls

Prep time: 20 minutes **Cooking time:** 9 minutes **Servings:** 3

1 teaspoon garlic powder	1 oz Parmesan, grated
½ cup Cheddar cheese, shredded	1 egg, beaten
1 tablespoon cream cheese	1 teaspoon dried dill
1 teaspoon dried cilantro	1 teaspoon dried parsley
Cooking spray	

1. Mix up Parmesan and Cheddar cheese. Add garlic powder, egg, cream cheese, dried dill, cilantro, and parsley. Stir the mixture until homogenous. With the help of the scoop make the cheese balls and put them in the freezer for 15 minutes. Preheat the air fryer to 400F. Then spray the air fryer basket with cooking spray. Put the frozen cheese balls in the air fryer basket. Cook them for 9 minutes or until they are golden brown.

Nutrition:
Calories 143, fat 10.9, fiber 0.1, carbs 1.7, protein 10.1

Zucchini and Spring Onions Cakes

Preparation time: 5 minutes **Cooking time:** 8 minutes
Servings: 4

8 ounces zucchinis, chopped	2 eggs, whisked
2 spring onions, chopped	
Salt and black pepper to the taste	¼ teaspoon sweet paprika, chopped Cooking spray

1. In a bowl, mix all the ingredients except the cooking spray, stir well and shape medium fritters out of this mix. Put the basket in the Air Fryer, add the fritters inside, grease them with cooking spray and cook at 400 degrees F for 8 minutes. Divide the fritters between plates and serve for breakfast.

Nutrition:
Calories 202, fat 10, fiber 2, carbs 4, protein 5

Peppers Rings

Prep time: 10 minutes **Cooking time:** 11 minutes **Servings:** 2

1 large green bell pepper	½ cup ground beef
1 egg, beaten	½ teaspoon salt
½ teaspoon ground black pepper	½ teaspoon Italian seasonings
1 teaspoon coconut oil, melted	

1. Remove the seeds from the pepper and wash it. Then cut the pepper into 2 rings. In the bowl combine together egg, ground beef, salt, ground black pepper, and Italian seasonings. Preheat the air fryer to 385F. Brush the air fryer basket with coconut oil. Place the pepper rings in the air fryer and fill them with ground beef mixture. Cook the meal at 385F for 11 minutes.

Nutrition:
Calories 140, fat 9.1, fiber 1.5, carbs 4.4, protein 10.1

Avocado and Cabbage Salad

Prep time: 5 minutes **Cooking time:** 15 minutes **Servings:** 4

Cups red cabbage	shredded A drizzle of olive oil
1 red bell pepper peeled	sliced small avocado
	pitted and sliced Salt and black pepper to the taste

1. Grease your air fryer with the oil, add all the ingredients, toss, cover and cook at 400 degrees F for 15 minutes. Divide into bowls and serve cold for breakfast.

Nutrition:
Calories 209, fat 8, fiber 2, carbs 4, protein 9

Artichokes and Parsley Frittata

Preparation time: 5 minutes **Cooking time:** 12 minutes
Servings: 4

1 pound artichoke hearts, steamed and chopped Salt and black pepper to the taste Tablespoons parsley, chopped Cooking spray	4 eggs, whisked green onion, chopped

1. Grease a pan that fits your air fryer with cooking spray. In a bowl, mix all the other ingredients, whisk well and pour evenly into the pan. Introduce the pan in the air fryer, cook at 390 degrees F for 12 minutes, divide between plates and serve for breakfast.

Nutrition:
Calories 185, fat 8, fiber 2, carbs 5, protein 8

Turmeric Mozzarella Sticks

Prep time: 15 minutes **Cooking time:** 7 minutes **Servings:** 2

4 oz Mozzarella	2 tablespoons coconut flakes
1 egg, beaten	1 teaspoon turmeric powder
1 tablespoon heavy cream	½ teaspoon ground black pepper
Cooking spray	

1. Cut Mozzarella into 2 sticks. Then in the mixing bowl mix up heavy cream, egg, and ground black pepper. Dip the cheese sticks in the liquid. After this, coat every cheese stick with coconut flakes. Preheat the air fryer to 400F. Then spray the air fryer basket with cooking spray. Put Mozzarella sticks in the air fryer and cook them for 7 minutes or until they are light brown.

Nutrition:
Calories 246, fat 19.3, fiber 0.6, carbs 2.7, protein 15.7

Endives Frittata

Preparation time: 5 minutes **Cooking time:** 15 minutes
Servings: 6

1 endive, shredded	6 eggs, whisked
A pinch of salt and black pepper	1 teaspoon sweet paprika
2 teaspoons cilantro, chopped Cooking spray	

1. In a bowl, mix all the ingredients except the cooking spray and stir well. Grease a baking pan with the cooking spray, pour the frittata mix and spread well. Put the pan in the Air Fryer and cook at 370 degrees F for 15 minutes. Divide between plates and serve them for breakfast.

Nutrition:
Calories 200, fat 12, fiber 1, carbs 5, protein 8

Eggs Salad

Preparation time: 5 minutes **Cooking time:** 10 minutes
Servings: 4

1 tablespoon lime juice	4 eggs, hard boiled, peeled and sliced
2 cups baby spinach	Salt and black pepper to the taste
3 tablespoons heavy cream	2 tablespoons olive oil

1. In your Air Fryer, mix the spinach with cream, eggs, salt and pepper, cover and cook at 360 degrees F for 6 minutes. Transfer this to a bowl, add the lime juice and oil, toss and serve for breakfast.

Nutrition:
Calories 200, fat 7, fiber 3, carbs 4, protein 7

Cod Sticks

Prep time: 15 minutes **Cooking time:** 6 minutes **Servings:** 2

10 oz cod fillet	¼ cup almond flour
1 tablespoon coconut flour	1 egg white
1 teaspoon dried oregano	½ teaspoon onion powder
½ teaspoon salt	1 teaspoon avocado oil

1. Chop the cod fillet and put it in the blender. Add coconut flour, egg white, dried oregano, salt, and onion powder. Blend the mixture until smooth.
2. Then make the medium sticks from the fish mixture and coat them in the almond flour. Brush the air fryer basket with avocado oil. Then place the cod sticks in the air fryer in one layer. Cook the fish sticks for 6 minutes at 400F. Flip the fish sticks after 3 minutes of cooking.

Nutrition:
Calories 167, fat 4.1, fiber 2.3, carbs 4.2, protein 28.8

Fish Meatballs

Prep time: 15 minutes **Cooking time:** 8 minutes **Servings:** 3

12 oz cod fillet, grinded	1 teaspoon ground coriander
½ teaspoon ground cumin	½ teaspoon salt
1 teaspoon dried dill	½ teaspoon lemon zest, grated
½ teaspoon ground paprika	1 egg, beaten
1 teaspoon chives, chopped Cooking spray	½ teaspoon lemon juice

1. In the bowl mix up grinded cod fillet, ground coriander, cumin, salt, dried dill, lemon zest, ground paprika, egg, chives, and lemon juice. Stir the mixture with the help of the spoon until homogenous. Preheat the air fryer to 400F. Spray the air fryer basket with cooking spray. Make the medium size meatballs from the fish mixture and put them in the air fryer in one layer. Cook the cod cakes for 4 minutes. Then flip them on another side and cook for 4 minutes more.

Nutrition:
Calories 116, fat 2.6, fiber 0.2, carbs 0.7, protein 22.3

Coconut Bok Choy Mix

Preparation time: 5 minutes **Cooking time:** 15 minutes
Servings: 4

7 ounces bok choy, torn	2 tablespoons olive oil
7 ounces baby spinach, torn	
2 eggs, whisked	2 tablespoons coconut cream
3 ounces mozzarella, shredded	Salt and black pepper to the taste

1. In your Air Fryer, combine all the ingredients except the mozzarella and toss them gently. Sprinkle the mozzarella on top, cook at 360 degrees F for 15 minutes, divide between plates and serve.

Nutrition:
Calories 200, fat 12, fiber 2, carbs 3, protein 8

Mascarpone Bites

Prep time: 20 minutes **Cooking time:** 3 minutes **Servings:** 4

4 tablespoons cream cheese	4 teaspoons Erythritol
¼ teaspoon vanilla extract	1 tablespoon mascarpone
4 tablespoons coconut milk	4 tablespoons almond flour

1. Mix up cream cheese with Erythritol, vanilla extract, and mascarpone. Make the cheesecake balls (bites) and put them on the baking paper.
2. Refrigerate the cheesecake balls for 10-15 minutes. Then preheat the air fryer to 300F. Dip the frozen bites in the coconut milk and coat in the almond flour. Cook them in the air fryer for 3 minutes.

Nutrition:

Calories 237, fat 21.6, fiber 3.3, carbs 7.3, protein 7.5

Artichoke Bowls

Preparation time: 5 minutes **Cooking time:** 20 minutes **Servings:** 4

½ pound artichokes, trimmed and chopped 2 zucchinis, sliced	4 spring onions, chopped
2 tomatoes, cut into quarters 4 eggs, whisked	Cooking spray
Salt and black pepper to the taste	

1. Grease a pan with cooking spray, and mix all the other ingredients inside. Put the pan in the Air Fryer and cook at 350 degrees F for 20 minutes.
2. Divide between plates and serve.

Nutrition:

Calories 210, fat 11, fiber 3, carbs 4, protein 6

Chicken Meatballs

Prep time: 15 minutes **Cooking time:** 9 minutes **Servings:** 6

1-pound chicken, minced	1 tablespoon minced onion
¼ teaspoon minced garlic	¼ teaspoon ground nutmeg
1 green bell pepper, diced	¼ teaspoon minced ginger
½ teaspoon salt	Cooking spray

1. Put the minced chicken in the bowl. Add minced onion, garlic, nutmeg, bell pepper, salt, and minced ginger. Stir the ingredients with the help of the spoon until homogenous. Make the chicken balls. Then insert the rack in the air fryer and place the chicken balls inside. Spray them with cooking spray and cook at 400F for 9 minutes. Shake the chicken balls after 5 minutes of cooking.

Nutrition:

Calories 122, fat 2.4, fiber 0.3, carbs 1.8, protein 22.2

Scallion Wontons

Prep time: 15 minutes **Cooking time:** 2 minutes **Servings:** 4

½ teaspoon garlic powder	1 oz scallions, chopped
1 teaspoon fresh dill, chopped	4 tablespoons cream cheese
8 wonton wraps	Cooking spray

1. In the mixing bowl mix up garlic powder, scallions, fresh dill, and cream cheese. Then fill the wonton wraps with cream cheese mixture and fold them. Preheat the air fryer to 355F. Place the wonton wraps in the air fryer basket and cook them for 2 minutes or until they are light brown.

Nutrition:

Calories 59, fat 3.5, fiber 0.2, carbs 5.2, protein 2

Strawberries and Coconut Mix

Preparation time: 5 minutes **cooking time:** 15 minutes **4**

cups coconut milk	¼ cup strawberries
¼ teaspoon vanilla extract	½ cup coconut, shredded
2 teaspoons stevia	
Cooking spray	

1. Grease the Air Fryer's pan with the cooking spray, add all the ingredients inside and toss. Cook at 365 degrees F for 15 minutes, divide into bowls and serve for breakfast.

Nutrition:

Calories 142, fat 7, fiber 2, carbs 3, protein 5

Tofu Scramble

Prep time: 10 minutes **Cooking time:** 12 minutes **Servings:** 3

3 eggs, beaten	3 oz tempeh
2 oz tofu	1 tablespoon mascarpone
1 teaspoon coconut oil, melted	¼ teaspoon chili flakes
1 teaspoon apple cider vinegar	½ teaspoon salt

1. Finely chop the tofu and tempeh and place it in the air fryer. Add chili flakes, apple cider vinegar, and coconut oil. Shake the ingredients gently and cook them for 8 minutes at 395F. Shake the ingredients after 4 minutes of cooking. After this, pour the beaten eggs over the tempeh and tofu and stir well. Cook the scramble for 2 minutes at 400F. Then scramble the mixture with the help of the fork and cook for 2 minutes more.

Nutrition:

Calories 153, fat 10.4, fiber 0.2, carbs 3.5, protein 12.9

Olives Eggs

Preparation time: 5 minutes **Cooking time:** 15 minutes **Servings:** 4

1 cup kalamata olives, pitted and sliced	1 cup cherry tomatoes, cubed
4 eggs, whisked	A pinch of salt and black pepper Cooking spray

1. Grease the air fryer with cooking spray, add all the ingredients, toss, cover and cook at 365 degrees F for 10 minutes. Divide between plates and serve for breakfast.

Nutrition:

Calories 182, fat 6, fiber 2, carbs 4, protein 8

Italian Pork Meatballs

Prep time: 15 minutes **Cooking time:** 10 minutes **Servings:** 4

12 oz ground pork	2 oz Parmesan, grated
1 teaspoon Italian seasonings	1 teaspoon ground black pepper
1 teaspoon chili flakes	1 teaspoon fresh parsley, chopped
1 teaspoon avocado oil	1 teaspoon salt

1. Mix up ground pork, Parmesan, Italian seasoning, ground black pepper, chili flakes, parsley, and salt. Make 4 balls from the mixture. Preheat the air fryer to 365F. Then brush the air fryer basket with avocado oil. Put the pork balls inside. Cook them at 365F for 10 minutes.

Nutrition:

Calories 174, fat 6.6, fiber 0.2, carbs 1.1, protein 26.9

Cheese Sandwich

Prep time: 15 minutes **Cooking time:** 3 minutes **Servings:** 2

2 low carb tortillas	2 Cheddar cheese slices
2 deli ham slices	2 lettuce leaves
2 teaspoons mascarpone	¼ teaspoon chives, chopped

1. Cut every tortilla into halves. In the shallow bowl mix up chives and mascarpone. Spread the tortilla halves with mascarpone mixture. Then place cheese and ham on 2 tortilla halves. Add leaves and top them with remaining tortilla halves. Preheat the air fryer to 400F. Place the tortilla sandwiches in the air fryer and cook them for 3 minutes at 400F.

Nutrition:

Calories 248, fat 14.4, fiber 8.4, carbs 13.8, protein 15.2

Lemony Raspberries

Preparation time: 5 minutes **Cooking time:** 12 minutes **Servings:** 2

cup raspberries	tablespoons lemon juice 2 tablespoons butter
teaspoon cinnamon powder	

1. In your air fryer, mix all the ingredients, toss, cover, cook at 350 degrees F for 12 minutes, divide into bowls and serve for breakfast.

Nutrition:

Calories 208, fat 6, fiber 9, carbs 14, protein 3

Spiced Crab Meatballs

Prep time: 10 minutes **Cooking time:** 9 minutes **Servings:** 2

10 oz crab meat	1 garlic clove, minced
1 tablespoon green onions, chopped	1 teaspoon ground nutmeg
½ teaspoon salt	½ teaspoon ground turmeric
2 tablespoons coconut flour	1 teaspoon coconut oil, melted

1. Put the crab meat in the bowl and churn it with the help of the fork. Then add minced garlic, green onion, ground nutmeg, salt, ground turmeric, and coconut flour. Stir the mixture until homogenous and make 4 crab meatballs preheat the air fryer to 375F. Put the meatballs in the air fryer and sprinkle them with coconut oil. Cook them for 5 minutes. Then flip them on another side and cook for 4 minutes more.

Nutrition:

Calories 192, fat 6.5, fiber 3.5, carbs 8.7, protein 19.5

Green Beans Bowls

Preparation time: 5 minutes **Cooking time:** 20 minutes **Servings:** 2

1 cup green beans, halved	Salt and black pepper to the taste
2 spring onions, chopped 4 eggs, whisked	
¼ teaspoon cumin, ground	

1. Preheat the air fryer at 360 degrees F, add all the ingredients, toss, cover, cook for 20 minutes, divide into bowls and serve for breakfast.

Nutrition:

Calories 183, fat 8, fiber 2, carbs 3, protein 7

Lunch Recipes

Coconut Tomato

Preparation time: 3 minutes **Cooking time:** 5 minutes
Servings: 4

1/3 cup coconut cream

½ pound cherry tomatoes, halved

avocados, pitted, peeled and cubed A pinch of salt and black pepper Cooking spray

1. Grease the air fryer with cooking spray, combine the tomatoes with avocados, and the other ingredients and cook at 350 degrees F for 5 minutes shaking once. Divide into bowls and serve

Nutrition:

Calories 226, fat 12, fiber 2, carbs 4, protein 8

Eggplant Lasagna

Prep time: 20 minutes **Cooking time:** 30 minutes **Servings:** 6

2 medium eggplants

½ cup keto tomato sauce

1 cup Cheddar cheese, shredded

½ cup Mozzarella cheese, shredded

1 cup ground pork

1 teaspoon Italian seasonings

1 teaspoon sesame oil

1. Slice the eggplants into the long slices. Then brush the air fryer pan with sesame oil. In the mixing bowl mix up ground pork and Italian seasonings. Then make the layer from the sliced eggplants in the air fryer pan. Top it with a small amount of ground pork and mozzarella cheese. Then sprinkle mozzarella with the tomato sauce Place the second eggplant layer over the sauce and repeat all the steps again. Cover the last layer with remaining eggplant and top with Cheddar cheese. Cover the lasagna with foil and place it in the air fryer. Cook the meal for 20 minutes at 365F. Then remove the foil from the lasagna and cook it for 10 minutes more. Let the cooked lasagna cool for 10 minutes before serving.

Nutrition:

Calories 260, fat 18.7, fiber 0.8, carbs 3, protein 19.6

Pork and Mushrooms Mix

Preparation time: 5 minutes **Cooking time:** 20 minutes
Servings: 4

pound pork stew meat, ground

1 cup mushrooms, sliced

spring onions, chopped

Salt and black pepper to the taste 1 teaspoon Italian seasoning

½ teaspoon garlic powder

1 tablespoon olive oil

1. Heat up a pan that fits the air fryer with the oil over medium high heat, add the meat and brown for 3-4 minutes. Add the rest of the ingredients, stir, put the pan in the Air Fryer, cover and cook at 360 degrees F for 15 minutes. Divide between plates and serve for lunch.

Nutrition:

Calories 220, fat 12, fiber 2, carbs 4, protein 7

Italian Sausages

Prep time: 10 minutes **Cooking time:** 12 minutes **Servings:** 4

4 pork Italian sausages

½ cup keto tomato sauce

4 Mozzarella sticks

1 teaspoon butter, softened

1. Make the cross-section in every sausage with the help of the knife. Then fill the cut with the Mozzarella stick. Brush the air fryer pan with butter. Put the stuffed sausages in the pan and sprinkle them with tomato sauce. Preheat the air fryer to 375F. Place the pan with sausages in the air fryer and cook them for 12 minutes or until the sausages are golden brown.

Nutrition:

Calories 383, fat 29, fiber 0.3, carbs 5.8, protein 23.9

Parmesan Chicken

Preparation time: 5 minutes **Cooking time:** 30 minutes
Servings: 4

1 teaspoon olive oil

4 spring onions, chopped and ½ cups parmesan cheese, grated

2 chicken breasts, skinless, boneless and cubed Salt and black pepper to the taste

½ cup keto tomato sauce

1. Preheat your air fryer at 400 degrees F, add half of the oil and the spring onions and fry them for 8 minutes, shaking the fryer halfway. Add the rest of the ingredients, toss, and cook at 370 degrees F for 22 minutes, shaking the fryer halfway as well. Divide between plates and serve for lunch.

Nutrition:

Calories 270, fat 14, fiber 2, carbs 6, protein 12

Chicken and Arugula Salad

Prep time: 15 minutes **Cooking time:** 12 minutes **Servings:** 2

2 bacon slices, cooked, chopped

2 cups arugula, chopped

10 oz chicken breast, skinless, boneless

1 teaspoon ground black pepper

½ teaspoon salt

1 teaspoon avocado oil

½ teaspoon ground cumin

½ teaspoon ground paprika

1 tablespoon olive oil

¼ teaspoon minced garlic

1 teaspoon fresh cilantro, chopped

1. Rub the chicken breast with ground black pepper, salt, ground cumin, ground paprika, and avocado oil. Then preheat the air fryer to 365F. Put the chicken breast in the preheated air fryer and cook for 12 minutes.

2. Meanwhile, in the salad bowl mix up chopped bacon, arugula, and fresh cilantro. In the shallow bowl mix up minced garlic and olive oil. Chop the cooked chicken breasts and add in the salad mixture. Sprinkle the salad with garlic oil and shake well.

Nutrition:

Calories 339, fat 19.1, fiber 1, carbs 2.5, protein 37.9

Pork and Eggs Bowls

Preparation time: 10 minutes **Cooking time:** 15 minutes
Servings: 4

eggs, whisked	1 and ½ pounds pork meat, ground 2 teaspoons olive oil
½ cup keto tomato sauce	Salt and black pepper to the taste

1. Heat up a pan that fits the Air Fryer with the oil over medium-high heat, add the meat and brown for 3-4 minutes. Add the rest of the ingredients, toss, put the pan in the machine and cook at 370 degrees F for 12 minutes. Divide into bowls and serve for lunch with a side salad.

Nutrition:

Calories 270, fat 13, fiber 2, carbs 6, protein 8

Beef Pie

Prep time: 25 minutes **Cooking time:** 6 minutes **Servings:** 4

2 cup cauliflower, boiled, mashed	2 oz celery stalk, chopped
1 cup ground beef	½ teaspoon salt
½ teaspoon ground turmeric	1 tablespoon coconut oil
½ teaspoon avocado oil	1 teaspoon dried parsley
1 tablespoon keto tomato sauce	1 garlic clove, diced

1. Toss the coconut oil in the skillet and melt it over the medium heat. Then add celery stalk. Cook the vegetables for 5 minutes. Stir them from time to time. Meanwhile, brush the air fryer pan with avocado oil. Transfer the cooked vegetables in the pan and flatten them in the shape of the layer.
2. Then put the ground beef in the pan. Add salt, parsley, and turmeric. Cook the ground meat for 10 minutes over the medium heat. Stir it from time to time. Add tomato sauce and stir well. After this, transfer the ground beef over the vegetables. Then add garlic and top the pie with mashed cauliflower mash. Preheat the air fryer to 360F. Put the pan with shepherd pie in the air fryer and cook for 6 minutes or until you get the crunchy crust.

Nutrition:

Calories 116, fat 7.7, fiber 1.9, carbs 4.5, protein 7.8

Paprika Chicken

Preparation time: 10 minutes **Cooking time:** 35 minutes
Servings: 6

3 pounds chicken thighs, bone-in	½ cup butter, melted
1 tablespoon smoked paprika 1 teaspoon lemon juice	

1. In a bowl, mix the chicken thighs with the paprika, toss, put all the pieces in your air fryer's basket and cook them at 360 degrees F for 25 minutes shaking the fryer from time to time and basting the meat with the butter. Divide between plates and serve.

Nutrition:

Calories 261, fat 16, fiber 3, carbs 5, protein 12

Creamy Zucchini Noodle Mix

Prep time: 10 minutes **Cooking time:** 9 minutes **Servings:** 2

1 zucchini, trimmed	4 oz chicken breast, skinless, boneless
¼ cup heavy cream	2 oz Parmesan, grated
½ teaspoon ground black pepper	¼ teaspoon ground paprika
½ teaspoon sesame oil	½ teaspoon dried basil

1. Make the zoodles from the zucchini with the help of the spiralizer. Then rub the chicken breast with ground black pepper, paprika, and basil.
2. Sprinkle the chicken breast with sesame oil and put it in the air fryer. Cook it for 8 minutes at 400F. Flip the chicken on another side after 4 minutes of cooking. When the chicken is cooked, remove it from the air fryer and place it on the plate. Then put the zucchini zoodles in the air fryer and cook then at 400F for 1 minute. Meanwhile, mix up parmesan and heavy cream and preheat the liquid over the medium heat until the cheese is melted. Then mix up heavy cream sauce and zucchini. Mix it up well. Chop the chicken roughly and top the zoodles with it.

Nutrition:

Calories 235, fat 14.4, fiber 1.3, carbs 5.2, protein 22.7

Tomato Cod Bake

Preparation time: 5 minutes **Cooking time:** 12 minutes
Servings: 4

tablespoons butter, melted	2 tablespoons parsley, chopped
¼ cup keto tomato sauce 8 cherry tomatoes, halved	2 cod fillets, boneless, skinless and cubed Salt and black pepper to the taste

1. In a baking pan that fits the air fryer, combine all the ingredients, toss, put the pan in the machine and cook the mix at 390 degrees F for 12 minutes. Divide the mix into bowls and serve for lunch.

Nutrition:

Calories 232, fat 8, fiber 2, carbs 5, protein 11

Parsley Turkey Stew

Preparation time: 5 minutes **Cooking time:** 25 minutes
Servings: 4

1 turkey breast, skinless, boneless and cubed 1 tablespoon olive oil Salt and black pepper to the taste 1 tablespoon parsley, chopped	1 broccoli head, florets separated 1 cup keto tomato sauce

1. In a baking dish that fits your air fryer, mix the turkey with the rest of the ingredients except the parsley, toss, introduce the dish in the fryer, bake at 380 degrees F for 25 minutes, divide into bowls, sprinkle the parsley on top and serve.

Nutrition:

Calories 250, fat 11, fiber 2, carbs 6, protein 12

Creamy Zucchini Noodle Mix

Prep time: 10 minutes **Cooking time:** 9 minutes **Servings:** 2

1 zucchini, trimmed	4 oz chicken breast, skinless, boneless
¼ cup heavy cream	2 oz Parmesan, grated
½ teaspoon ground black pepper	¼ teaspoon ground paprika
½ teaspoon sesame oil	½ teaspoon dried basil

1. Make the zoodles from the zucchini with the help of the spiralizer. Then rub the chicken breast with ground black pepper, paprika, and basil.
2. Sprinkle the chicken breast with sesame oil and put it in the air fryer. Cook it for 8 minutes at 400F. Flip the chicken on another side after 4 minutes of cooking. When the chicken is cooked, remove it from the air fryer and place it on the plate. Then put the zucchini zoodles in the air fryer and cook then at 400F for 1 minute. Meanwhile, mix up parmesan and heavy cream and preheat the liquid over the medium heat until the cheese is melted. Then mix up heavy cream sauce and zucchini. Mix it up well. Chop the chicken roughly and top the zoodles with it.

Nutrition:
Calories 235, fat 14.4, fiber 1.3, carbs 5.2, protein 22.7

Tomato Cod Bake

Preparation time: 5 minutes **Cooking time:** 12 minutes
Servings: 4

tablespoons butter, melted	2 tablespoons parsley, chopped
¼ cup keto tomato sauce 8 cherry tomatoes, halved	2 cod fillets, boneless, skinless and cubed Salt and black pepper to the taste

1. In a baking pan that fits the air fryer, combine all the ingredients, toss, put the pan in the machine and cook the mix at 390 degrees F for 12 minutes. Divide the mix into bowls and serve for lunch.

Nutrition:
Calories 232, fat 8, fiber 2, carbs 5, protein 11

Wrapped Zucchini

Prep time: 10 minutes **Cooking time:** 10 minutes **Servings:** 2

2 zucchinis, trimmed	8 bacon slices
1 teaspoon sesame oil	¼ teaspoon chili powder

1. Cut every zucchini into 4 sticks and sprinkle with chili powder. Then wrap every zucchini stick in bacon and sprinkle with sesame oil. Preheat the air fryer to 400F. Put the zucchini sticks in the air fryer in one layer and cook for 10 minutes. Flip the zucchini sticks after 5 minutes of cooking.

Nutrition:
Calories 464, fat 34.4, fiber 2.3, carbs 7.8, protein 30.6

Wrapped Zucchini

Prep time: 10 minutes **Cooking time:** 10 minutes **Servings:** 2

2 zucchinis, trimmed	8 bacon slices
1 teaspoon sesame oil	¼ teaspoon chili powder

1. Cut every zucchini into 4 sticks and sprinkle with chili powder. Then wrap every zucchini stick in bacon and sprinkle with sesame oil. Preheat the air fryer to 400F. Put the zucchini sticks in the air fryer in one layer and cook for 10 minutes. Flip the zucchini sticks after 5 minutes of cooking.

Nutrition:
Calories 464, fat 34.4, fiber 2.3, carbs 7.8, protein 30.6

Parsley Turkey Stew

Preparation time: 5 minutes **Cooking time:** 25 minutes
Servings: 4

1 turkey breast, skinless, boneless and cubed	1 tablespoon olive oil
1 broccoli head, florets separated	1 cup keto tomato sauce
Salt and black pepper to the taste	1 tablespoon parsley, chopped

1. In a baking dish that fits your air fryer, mix the turkey with the rest of the ingredients except the parsley, toss, introduce the dish in the fryer, bake at 380 degrees F for 25 minutes, divide into bowls, sprinkle the parsley on top and serve.

Nutrition:
Calories 250, fat 11, fiber 2, carbs 6, protein 12

Chicken, Eggs and Lettuce Salad

Prep time: 15 minutes **Cooking time:** 8 minutes **Servings:** 3

3 spring onions, sliced	8 oz chicken fillet, roughly chopped
1 bacon slice, cooked, crumbled	2 cherry tomatoes, halved
¼ avocado, chopped	2 eggs, hard-boiled, peeled, chopped
1 cup lettuce, roughly chopped	1 tablespoon sesame oil
½ teaspoon lemon juice	½ teaspoon avocado oil
½ teaspoon ground black pepper	½ teaspoon salt
1 egg, beaten	2 tablespoons coconut flakes

1. Sprinkle the chopped chicken fillets with salt and ground black pepper. Then dip the chicken in the egg and after this, coat in the coconut flakes. Preheat the air fryer to 385F. Place the chicken fillets inside and sprinkle them with avocado oil. Cook the chicken pieces for 8 minutes. Shake them after 4 minutes of cooking. After this, in the mixing bowl mix up spring onions, bacon, cherry tomatoes, hard-boiled eggs, lettuce, and lemon juice. Add sesame oil and shake the salad well. When the chicken is cooked, add it in the cobb salad and mix up gently with the help of the wooden spatulas.

Nutrition:
Calories 355, fat 22.5, fiber 2.8, carbs 7.2, protein 31.1

Pork and Spinach Stew

Preparation time: 5 minutes **Cooking time:** 25 minutes
Servings: 4

1 pound pork stew meat, cubed 3 garlic cloves, minced	¼ cup keto tomato sauce 1 cup spinach, torn
½ teaspoon olive oil	

1. In pan that fits your air fryer, mix the pork with the other ingredients except the spinach, toss, introduce in the fryer and cook at 370 degrees F for 15 minutes. Add the spinach, toss, cook for 10 minutes more, divide into bowls and serve for lunch.

Nutrition:
Calories 290, fat 14, fiber 3, carbs 5, protein 13

Chicken, Eggs and Lettuce Salad

Prep time: 15 minutes **Cooking time:** 8 minutes **Servings:** 3

3 spring onions, sliced	8 oz chicken fillet, roughly chopped
1 bacon slice, cooked, crumbled	2 cherry tomatoes, halved
¼ avocado, chopped	2 eggs, hard-boiled, peeled, chopped
1 cup lettuce, roughly chopped	1 tablespoon sesame oil
½ teaspoon lemon juice	½ teaspoon avocado oil
½ teaspoon ground black pepper	½ teaspoon salt
1 egg, beaten	2 tablespoons coconut flakes

1. Sprinkle the chopped chicken fillets with salt and ground black pepper. Then dip the chicken in the egg and after this, coat in the coconut flakes. Preheat the air fryer to 385F. Place the chicken fillets inside and sprinkle them with avocado oil. Cook the chicken pieces for 8 minutes. Shake them after 4 minutes of cooking. After this, in the mixing bowl mix up spring onions, bacon, cherry tomatoes, hard-boiled eggs, lettuce, and lemon juice. Add sesame oil and shake the salad well. When the chicken is cooked, add it in the cobb salad and mix up gently with the help of the wooden spatulas.

Nutrition:
Calories 355, fat 22.5, fiber 2.8, carbs 7.2, protein 31.1

Pork and Spinach Stew

Preparation time: 5 minutes **Cooking time:** 25 minutes **Servings:** 4

1 pound pork stew meat, cubed 3 garlic cloves, minced	¼ cup keto tomato sauce
1 cup spinach, torn	½ teaspoon olive oil

1. In pan that fits your air fryer, mix the pork with the other ingredients except the spinach, toss, introduce in the fryer and cook at 370 degrees F for 15 minutes. Add the spinach, toss, cook for 10 minutes more, divide into bowls and serve for lunch.

Nutrition:
Calories 290, fat 14, fiber 3, carbs 5, protein 13

Pancetta Salad

Prep time: 10 minutes **Cooking time:** 10 minutes **Servings:** 3

2 cups iceberg lettuce, chopped	6 oz pancetta, chopped
½ teaspoon ground black pepper	½ teaspoon olive oil
3 oz Parmesan, grated	

1. Mix up pancetta, ground black pepper, and olive oil. Preheat the air fryer to 365F. Put the chopped pancetta in the air fryer and cook for 10 minutes Shake the pancetta every 3 minutes to avoid burning. Meanwhile, in the salad bowl combine iceberg lettuce with grated parmesan. Then add cooked pancetta and mix up the salad.

Nutrition:
Calories 410, fat 30.6, fiber 0.3, carbs 3.2, protein 30.3

Mustard Chicken

Preparation time: 5 minutes **Cooking time:** 30 minutes **Servings:** 4

½ pounds chicken thighs, bone-in 2 tablespoons Dijon mustard	A pinch of salt and black pepper Cooking spray

1. In a bowl, mix the chicken thighs with all the other ingredients and toss. Put the chicken in your Air Fryer's basket and cook at 370 degrees F for 30 minutes shaking halfway. Serve these chicken thighs for lunch.

Nutrition:
Calories 253, fat 17, fiber 3, carbs 6, protein 12

Lemon Chicken Mix

Prep time: 15 minutes **Cooking time:** 15 minutes **Servings:** 3

4 chicken thighs, skinless, boneless	1 tablespoon lemon juice
1 teaspoon ground paprika	½ teaspoon salt
½ teaspoon ground black pepper	1 tablespoon sesame oil
½ teaspoon dried parsley	½ teaspoon keto tomato sauce

1. Cut the chicken thighs into halves and put them in the bowl. Add lemon juice, ground paprika, salt, ground black pepper, sesame oil, parsley, and tomato sauce. Mix up the chicken with the help of the fingertips and leave for 10-15 minutes to marinate. Then string the meat on the wooden skewers and put in the preheated to 375F air fryer. Cook the tavuk shish for 10 minutes at 375F. Then flip the meal on another side and cook for 5 minutes more.

Nutrition:
Calories 415, fat 19.1, fiber 0.4, carbs 0.9, protein 56.6

Tomato and Eggplant Casserole

Preparation time: 5 minutes **Cooking time:** 20 minutes **Servings:** 4

- eggplants, cubed
- 1 hot chili pepper, chopped 4 spring onions, chopped
- ½ pound cherry tomatoes, cubed Salt and black pepper to the taste 2 teaspoons olive oil
- ½ cup cilantro, chopped 4 garlic cloves, minced

1. Grease a baking pan that fits the air fryer with the oil, and mix all the ingredients in the pan. Put the pan in the preheated air fryer and cook at 380 degrees F for 20 minutes, divide into bowls and serve for lunch.

Nutrition:
Calories 232, fat 12, fiber 3, carbs 5, protein 10

Beef and Sauce

Preparation time: 5 minutes **Cooking time:** 20 minutes **Servings:** 4

1 pound lean beef meat, cubed and browned	2 garlic cloves, minced
Salt and black pepper to the taste Cooking spray	16 ounces keto tomato sauce

1. Preheat the Air Fryer at 400 degrees F, add the pan inside, grease it with cooking spray, add the meat and all the other ingredients, toss and cook for 20 minutes. Divide into bowls and serve for lunch.

Nutrition:
Calories 270, fat 15, fiber 3, carbs 6, protein 12

Masala Meatloaf

Prep time: 10 minutes **Cooking time:** 20 minutes **Servings:** 4

2 cups ground beef	1 large egg, beaten
2 spring onions, chopped	1 teaspoon garam masala
½ teaspoon ground ginger	1 teaspoon garlic powder
½ teaspoon salt	½ teaspoon ground turmeric
½ teaspoon cayenne pepper	1 teaspoon olive oil
¼ teaspoon ground nutmeg	

1. In the mixing bowl mix up ground beef, egg, onion, garam masala, ground ginger, garlic powder, salt, ground turmeric, cayenne pepper, and ground nutmeg. Stir the mass with the help of the spoon until homogenous. Then brush the round air fryer pan with olive oil and place the ground beef mixture inside. Press the meatloaf gently. Place the pan with meatloaf in the air fryer and cook for 20 minutes at 365F.

Nutrition:
Calories 174, fat 10.8, fiber 0.8, carbs 3.7, protein 15.1

Beef Burger

Prep time: 10 minutes **Cooking time:** 15 minutes **Servings:** 3

½ teaspoon salt	1 teaspoon cayenne pepper
1 teaspoon minced ginger	1 teaspoon minced garlic
2 tablespoons chives, chopped	6 lettuce leaves
10 oz ground beef	1 tablespoon avocado oil
1 teaspoon gochujang	

1. In the shallow bowl mix up gochujang, minced ginger, minced garlic, cayenne pepper, and salt. Then mix up ground beef and churned spices mixture. Add chives and stir the ground beef mass with the help of the fork until homogenous. Preheat the air fryer to 365F. Then make 3 burgers from the ground beef mixture and put them in the air fryer. Sprinkle the burgers with avocado oil and cook for 10 minutes at 365F. Then flip the burgers on another side and cook for 5 minutes more.

Nutrition:
Calories 195, fat 11.7, fiber 1.1, carbs 3.4, protein 18.1

Parmesan Beef Mix

Preparation time: 5 minutes **Cooking time:** 20 minutes **Servings:** 4

14 ounces beef, cubed	7 ounces keto tomato sauce
tablespoon chives, chopped	tablespoons parmesan cheese, grated 1 tablespoon oregano, chopped
1 tablespoon olive oil	Salt and black pepper to the taste

1. Grease a pan that fits the air fryer with the oil and mix all the ingredients except the parmesan. Sprinkle the parmesan on top, put the pan in the machine and cook at 380 degrees F for 20 minutes. Divide between plates and serve for lunch.

Nutrition:
Calories 280, fat 14, fiber 4, carbs 6, protein 15

Turmeric Chicken

Prep time: 10 minutes **Cooking time:** 14 minutes **Servings:** 2

2 chicken thighs, boneless, skinless	½ cup spring onions, chopped
1 green bell pepper, chopped	½ teaspoon chili powder
½ teaspoon ground turmeric	¼ teaspoon garam masala
¼ teaspoon salt	1 tablespoon olive oil
1 teaspoon keto tomato sauce	

1. Rub the chicken thighs with chili powder, ground turmeric, garam masala, salt, and tomato sauce. Then preheat the air fryer to 365F. Mix up spring onion and bell pepper and place the vegetables in the air fryer. Chop the chicken thighs roughly and put over the vegetables. Cook the meal for 7 minutes. Then shake the ingredients and cook the meal for 7 minutes more.

Nutrition:
Calories 363, fat 17.7, fiber 1.9, carbs 8.4, protein 41.7

Salmon Salad

Preparation time: 5 minutes **Cooking time:** 8 minutes **Servings:** 4

4 salmon fillets, boneless	2 tablespoons olive oil
Salt and black pepper to the taste 3 cups kale leaves, shredded	2 teaspoons balsamic vinegar

1. Put the fish in your air fryer's basket, season with salt and pepper, drizzle half of the oil over them, cook at 400 degrees F for 4 minutes on each side, cool down and cut into medium cubes. In a bowl, mix the kale with salt, pepper, vinegar, the rest of the oil and the salmon, toss gently and serve for lunch.

Nutrition:
Calories 240, fat 14, fiber 3, carbs 5, protein 10

Zucchini Pasta

Prep time: 15 minutes **Cooking time:** 14 minutes **Servings:** 4

½ cup ground beef	¼ teaspoon salt
½ teaspoon chili flakes	¼ teaspoon dried dill
2 zucchinis, trimmed	2 tablespoons mascarpone
1 teaspoon olive oil	½ teaspoon ground black pepper
Cooking spray	

1. In the mixing bowl mix up ground beef, salt, chili flakes, and dill. Then make the small meatballs. Preheat the air fryer to 365F. Spray the air fryer basket with cooking spray and place the meatballs inside in one layer.
2. Cook the meatballs for 12 minutes. Shake them after 6 minutes of cooking to avoid burning. Then remove the meatballs from the air fryer. With the help of the spiralizer make the zucchini noodles and sprinkle them with olive oil and ground black pepper. Place the zucchini noodles in the air fryer and cook them for 2 minutes at 400F. Then mix up zucchini noodles and mascarpone and transfer them in the serving plates. Top the noodles with cooked meatballs.

Nutrition:
Calories 145, fat 8.8, fiber 2.3, carbs 7.5, protein 10.7

Paprika Turkey Mix

Preparation time: 5 minutes **Cooking time:** 20 minutes
Servings: 4

turkey breast, boneless, skinless and cubed 2 teaspoons olive oil	½ teaspoon sweet paprika
Salt and black pepper to the taste	2 cups bok choy, torn and steamed 1 tablespoon balsamic vinegar

1. In a bowl, mix the turkey with the oil, paprika, salt and pepper, toss, transfer them to your Air Fryer's basket and cook at 350 degrees F for 20 minutes. In a salad, mix the turkey with all the other ingredients, toss and serve for lunch.

Nutrition:

Calories 250, fat 13, fiber 3, carbs 6, protein 14

Spiced Salmon and Cilantro Croquettes

Prep time: 10 minutes **Cooking time:** 8 minutes **Servings:** 4

1-pound smoked salmon, boneless and flaked	1 egg, beaten
1 tablespoon almond flour	½ teaspoon ground black pepper
¼ teaspoon ground cumin	½ teaspoon ground nutmeg
1 tablespoon fresh cilantro, chopped	1 teaspoon avocado oil

1. Put the salmon in the bowl and churn it with the help of the fork until you get the smooth mass. Then add an egg, almond flour, ground black pepper, cumin, nutmeg, and cilantro. Stir the ingredients until they are smooth. Preheat the air fryer to 365F. Wet your hands and make the croquettes. Then place them in the air fryer in one layer and sprinkle with avocado oil. Cook the croquettes for 5 minutes. Then flip them on another side and cook for 3 minutes more.

Nutrition:

Calories 210, fat 11.9, fiber 1, carbs 2, protein 25

Oregano Cod and Arugula Mix

Preparation time: 5 minutes **Cooking time:** 12 minutes
Servings: 4

tablespoons fresh cilantro, minced	pound cod fillets, boneless, skinless and cubed 1 spring onion, chopped
Salt and black pepper to the taste	½ teaspoon sweet paprika
½ teaspoon oregano, ground Λ drizzle of olive oil	cups baby arugula

1. In a bowl, mix the cod with salt, pepper, paprika, oregano and the oil, toss, transfer the cubes to your air fryer's basket and cook at 360 degrees F for 12 minutes. In a salad bowl, mix the cod with the remaining ingredients, toss, divide between plates and serve.

Nutrition:

Calories 240, fat 11, fiber 3, carbs 5, protein 8

Shrimp Salad

Prep time: 15 minutes **Cooking time:** 3 minutes **Servings:** 4

1-pound shrimps, peeled	1 tablespoon lemon juice
½ teaspoon ground cardamom	¼ teaspoon salt
½ teaspoon ground paprika	1 tablespoon olive oil
1 garlic clove, diced	1 avocado, peeled, pitted, chopped
1 teaspoon chives, chopped	

1. Put the shrimps in the big bowl. Add lemon juice, ground nutmeg, salt, and ground paprika. Mix up the shrimps and leave them for 10 minutes to marinate. Meanwhile, preheat the air fryer to 400F. Put the marinated shrimps in the air fryer and cook them for 3 minutes. It is recommended to arrange shrimps in one layer. Meanwhile, put the chopped avocado in the bowl and sprinkle it with diced garlic and chives. Cool the shrimps to the room temperature and add in the avocado bowl. Sprinkle the salad with olive oil. After this, gently mix the salad with the help of two spoons.

Nutrition:

Calories 271, fat 15.3, fiber 3.6, carbs 6.7, protein 26.9

Pork and Zucchinis

Preparation time: 5 minutes **Cooking time:** 30 minutes
Servings: 4

2 pounds pork stew meat, cubed 2 zucchinis, cubed	Salt and black pepper to the taste
½ cup beef stock	½ teaspoon smoked paprika Λ handful cilantro, chopped

1. In a pan that fits your air fryer, mix all the ingredients, toss, introduce in your air fryer and cook at 370 degrees F for 30 minutes. Divide into bowls and serve right away.

Nutrition:

Calories 245, fat 12, fiber 2, carbs 5, protein 14

Rosemary Salmon

Prep time: 10 minutes **Cooking time:** 7 minutes **Servings:** 2

4 oz Feta cheese, sliced	1 lemon slice, chopped
½ teaspoon dried rosemary	1 teaspoon apple cider vinegar
½ teaspoon ground paprika	1-pound salmon fillet
1 teaspoon olive oil	½ teaspoon salt
Cooking spray	

1. Rub the salmon with dried rosemary and salt. Then sprinkle the fish with ground paprika and apple cider vinegar. Preheat the air fryer to 395F. Line the air fryer basket with baking paper and put the salmon fillet on it. Spray it with cooking spray and cook for 3 minutes. Then flip the salmon on another side and cook it for 4 minutes more. After this, cut the cooked salmon into 2 servings and put it on the serving plate. Top the fish with sliced feta and chopped lemon slice. Sprinkle the meal with the olive oil before serving.

Nutrition:

Calories 596, fat 45, fiber 0.4, carbs 1.2, protein 47.4

Beef Chili

Prep time: 15 minutes **Cooking time:** 29 minutes **Servings:** 4

2 spring onions, chopped	2 medium green bell peppers, chopped
1 tablespoon avocado oil	½ teaspoon salt
½ teaspoon ground black pepper	2 cups ground beef
1 teaspoon ground paprika	1 teaspoon chili flakes
½ teaspoon white pepper	1 teaspoon ground cumin
½ teaspoon ground coriander	1 chili pepper, chopped
1 cup beef broth	1 tablespoon keto tomato sauce
1 cup lettuce leaves	

1. Put the spring onions in the air fryer pan. Add green bell peppers, avocado oil, salt, and ground black pepper. Stir the mixture gently. Preheat the air fryer to 365F and place the pan with vegetables inside. Cook them for 4 minutes. Then stir well. In the mixing bowl mix up ground beef, ground paprika, chili flakes, white pepper, ground cumin, ground coriander, and tomato sauce Put the meat mixture over the vegetables and carefully stir it with the help of the spoon. Add chili pepper and beef broth. Stir the chili gently. Cook it at 365F for 25 minutes. Stir the chili every 5 minutes of cooking. When the chili is cooked, cool it for 5-10 minutes. Then fill the lettuce leaves with chili and transfer in the serving plates.

Nutrition:
Calories 177, fat 9.3, fiber 2.4, carbs 7.7, protein 15.5

Chicken Rolls

Prep time: 15 minutes **Cooking time:** 18 minutes **Servings:** 4

2 large zucchini	½ cup Cheddar cheese, shredded
1-pound chicken breast, skinless, boneless	1 teaspoon dried oregano
½ teaspoon olive oil	1 teaspoon salt
2 spring onions, chopped	1 teaspoon ground paprika
½ teaspoon ground turmeric	½ cup keto tomato sauce

1. Preheat the skillet well and pour the olive oil inside. Put the onions in it and sprinkle with salt, ground paprika, and ground turmeric. Cook the onion for 5 minutes over the medium-high heat. Stir it from time to time. Meanwhile, shred the chicken. Add it in the skillet. Then add oregano. Stir well and cook the mixture for 2 minutes. After this, remove the skillet from the heat. Cut the zucchini into halves (lengthwise). Then make the zucchini slices with the help of the vegetable peeler. Put 3 zucchini slices on the chopping board overlapping each of them. Then spread the surface of them with the shredded chicken mixture. Roll the zucchini carefully in the shape of the roll. Repeat the same steps with remaining zucchini and shredded chicken mixture. Line the air fryer pan with parchment and put the enchilada rolls inside. Sprinkle them with tomato sauce Preheat the air fryer to 350F. Top the zucchini rolls (enchiladas) with Cheddar cheese and put in the air fryer basket. Cook the meal for 10 minutes.

Nutrition:
Calories 245, fat 9.3, fiber 3, carbs 10.3, protein 29.9

Seafood Bowls

Preparation time: 5 minutes **Cooking time:** 12 minutes **Servings:** 4

2 salmon fillets, boneless, skinless and cubed	8 ounces shrimp, peeled and deveined
Salt and black pepper to the taste 5 garlic cloves, minced	teaspoon sweet paprika 2 tablespoons olive oil

1. In a pan that fits the air fryer, combine all the ingredients, toss, cover and cook at 370 degrees F for 12 minutes. Divide into bowls and serve for lunch.

Nutrition:
Calories 270, fat 8, fiber 2, carbs 4, protein 7

Chicken and Asparagus

Preparation time: 5 minutes **Cooking time:** 20 minutes **Servings:** 4

4 chicken breasts, skinless, boneless and halved	1 tablespoon sweet paprika
bunch asparagus, trimmed and halved	1 tablespoon olive oil
Salt and black pepper to the taste	

1. In a bowl, mix all the ingredients, toss, put them in your Air Fryer's basket and cook at 390 degrees F for 20 minutes. Divide between plates and serve for lunch.

Nutrition:
Calories 230, fat 11, fiber 3, carbs 5, protein 12

Eggplant Bowls

Preparation time: 5 minutes **Cooking time:** 15 minutes **Servings:** 4

cups eggplants, cubed	1 cup keto tomato sauce
1 teaspoon olive oil	1 cup mozzarella, shredded

1. In a pan that fits the air fryer, combine all the ingredients except the mozzarella and toss. Sprinkle the cheese on top, introduce the pan in the machine and cook at 390 degrees F for 15 minutes. Divide between plates and serve for lunch.

Nutrition:
Calories 220, fat 9, fiber 2, carbs 6, protein 9

Cilantro Turkey Casserole

Preparation time: 5 minutes **Cooking time:** 25 minutes **Servings:** 4

tablespoons butter, melted	2 cups turkey breasts, skinless, boneless and cut into strips 1 cups zucchinis, sliced
12 ounces cream cheese, soft	
2 teaspoons sweet paprika	6 ounces cheddar cheese, grated
¼ cup cilantro, chopped	Salt and black pepper to the taste

1. In a baking dish that fits your air fryer, mix the butter with turkey, cream cheese and all the other ingredients except the cheddar cheese. Sprinkle the cheddar on top, put the dish in your air fryer and cook at 360 degrees F for 25 minutes. Divide between plates and serve for lunch.

Nutrition:
Calories 280, fat 10, fiber 2, carbs 4, protein 12

Cheesy Calzone

Prep time: 15 minutes **Cooking time:** 8 minutes **Servings:** 2

2 tablespoons almond flour	2 tablespoons flax meal
1 tablespoon coconut oil, softened	¼ teaspoon salt
¼ teaspoon baking powder	2 ham slices, chopped
1 oz Parmesan, grated	1 egg yolk, whisked
1 tablespoon spinach, chopped	Cooking spray

1. Make calzone dough: mix up almond flour, flax meal, coconut oil, salt, and baking powder. Knead the dough until soft and smooth. Then roll it up with the help of the rolling pin and cut into halves. Fill every dough half with chopped ham, grated Parmesan, and spinach. Fold the dough in the shape of calzones and secure the edges. Then brush calzones with the whisked egg yolk. Preheat the air fryer basket to 350F. Place the calzones in the air fryer basket and spray them with cooking spray. Cook them for 8 minutes or until they are light brown. Flip the calzones on another side after 4 minutes of cooking.

Nutrition:
Calories 368, fat 31, fiber 5.4, carbs 10.2, protein 18.1

Dill Egg Salad

Prep time: 10 minutes **Cooking time:** 17 minutes **Servings:** 3

1 avocado, peeled, pitted	5 eggs
1 tablespoon ricotta cheese	1 tablespoon heavy cream
1 teaspoon mascarpone cheese	½ teaspoon minced garlic
1 pickled cucumber	1 tablespoon fresh dill, chopped

1. Put the eggs in the air fryer basket and cook them for 17 minutes at 250F. Meanwhile, cut the avocado into cubes and put them in the salad bowl. In the shallow bowl whisk together ricotta cheese, mascarpone, and minced garlic. Grate the pickled cucumber and add it in the cheese mixture. Add dill and stir the mixture well. When the eggs are cooked, cool them in the ice water and peel. Cut the eggs into the cubes and add in the avocado.
2. Add cheese mixture and stir the salad well.

Nutrition:
Calories 275, fat 22.9, fiber 4.9, carbs 8.1, protein 11.7

Coconut Chicken

Preparation time: 4 minutes **Cooking time:** 20 minutes **Servings:** 4

- 4 chicken breasts, skinless, boneless and cubed Salt and black pepper to the taste
- ¼ cup coconut cream 1 teaspoon olive oil
- and ½ teaspoon sweet paprika

1. Grease a pan that fits your air fryer with the oil, mix all the ingredients inside, introduce the pan in the fryer and cook at 370 degrees F for 17 minutes. Divide between plates and serve for lunch.

Nutrition:
Calories 250, fat 12, fiber 2, carbs 5, protein 11

Radish and Tuna Salad

Prep time: 15 minutes **Cooking time:** 8 minutes **Servings:** 2

½ cup radish sprouts	8 oz tuna, smoked, boneless and shredded
1 egg, beaten	1 tablespoon coconut flour
½ teaspoon ground coriander	½ teaspoon lemon zest, grated
1 tablespoon olive oil	½ teaspoon salt
1 tablespoon lemon juice	½ cup radish, sliced

1. Mix up the tuna with coconut flour, ground coriander, lemon zest, and egg. Stir the mixture until homogenous. Preheat the air fryer to 400F. Then make the small tuna balls and put them in the hot air fryer. Sprinkle the tuna balls with ½ tablespoon of olive oil. Cook the tuna balls for 8 minutes. Flip the tuna balls on another side after 4 minutes of cooking.
2. Meanwhile, mix up together radish sprouts and radish. Sprinkle the mixture with remaining olive oil, salt, and lemon juice. Shake it well. Then top the salad with tuna balls.

Nutrition:
Calories 342, fat 18.9, fiber 1.8, carbs 5.4, protein 35.7

Pork Bowls

Preparation time: 5 minutes **Cooking time:** 20 minutes **Servings:** 4

½ pound pork stew meat, cubed	¼ cup keto tomato sauce 1 tablespoon olive oil
cups mustard greens	1 yellow bell pepper, chopped 2 green onions, chopped
Salt and black pepper to the taste	

1. In a pan that fits your air fryer, mix all the ingredients, toss, introduce the pan in the air fryer and cook at 370 degrees F for 20 minutes. Divide into bowls and serve for lunch.

Nutrition:
Calories 265, fat 12, fiber 3, carbs 5, protein 14

Broccoli Salad

Prep time: 10 minutes **Cooking time:** 18 minutes **Servings:** 2

1 cup broccoli florets	1 teaspoon olive oil
1 tablespoon hazelnuts, chopped	4 bacon slices
½ teaspoon salt	½ teaspoon lemon zest, grated
½ teaspoon sesame oil	

1. Mix up broccoli florets with olive oil, salt, and lemon zest. Shake the vegetables well. Preheat the air fryer to 385F. Put the broccoli in the air fryer basket and cook for 8 minutes. Shake the broccoli after 4 minutes of cooking. Then transfer the broccoli in the salad bowl. Place the bacon in the air fryer and cook it at 400F for 10 minutes or until it is crunchy. Chop the cooked bacon and add in the broccoli. After this, add hazelnuts and sesame oil. Stir the salad gently.

Nutrition:
Calories 266, fat 20.9, fiber 1.4, carbs 4.1, protein 15.7

Chicken Stew

Preparation time: 5 minutes **Cooking time:** 30 minutes
Servings: 6

tablespoon butter, soft 4 celery stalks, chopped

red bell peppers, chopped

1 pound chicken breasts, skinless, boneless and cubed 2 teaspoons garlic, minced

Salt and black pepper to the taste

½ cup coconut cream

1. Grease a baking dish that fits your air fryer with the butter, add all the ingredients in the pan and toss them. Introduce the dish in the fryer, cook at 360 degrees F for 30 minutes, divide into bowls and serve for lunch.

Nutrition:
Calories 246, fat 12, fiber 2, carbs 6, protein 12

Chives Chicken

Prep time: 10 minutes **Cooking time:** 12 minutes **Servings:** 4

4 chicken tenders

½ teaspoon ground paprika

½ teaspoon salt

½ cup coconut flakes

1 egg, beaten

1 tablespoon heavy cream

½ teaspoon dried dill

½ teaspoon onion powder

1 tablespoon chives, grinded

1 teaspoon sesame oil

1. Beat the chicken tenders gently with the help of the kitchen hammer. In the mixing bowl mix up salt, eggs heavy cream, dried dill, onion powder, and chives. Then dip the chicken tenders in the egg mixture and coat in the coconut flakes. Repeat the same steps one more time. Preheat the air fryer to 400F. Sprinkle the air fryer basket with sesame oil and place the chicken tenders inside. Cook the rack chicken for 6 minutes. Then flip it on another side and cook for 6 minutes more or until the chicken is light brown.

Nutrition:
Calories 354, fat 17.8, fiber 1.1, carbs 2.2, protein 44.2

Pork Casserole

Prep time: 15 minutes **Cooking time:** 30 minutes **Servings:** 6

1 teaspoon taco seasonings

1 teaspoon sesame oil

1 teaspoon salt

2 cups ground pork

½ cup keto tomato sauce

2 low carb tortillas

½ cup Cheddar cheese, shredded

¼ cup mozzarella cheese, shredded

1. Chop the tortillas roughly. Brush the air fryer pan with sesame oil and place ½ part of chopped tortilla in it. In the mixing bowl mix up taco seasonings, ground pork, and salt. Place ½ part of ground pork over the tortillas and top it with mozzarella cheese. Then cover the cheese with remaining tortillas, ground pork, and Cheddar cheese. Pour the marinara sauce over the cheese and cover the casserole with foil. Secure the edges. Preheat the air fryer to 395F. Put the casserole in the air fryer and cook it for 20 minutes. Then remove the foil and cook it for 10 minutes more.

Nutrition:
Calories 404, fat 27, fiber 2.9, carbs 7.4, protein 30.9

Turkey Stew

Preparation time: 5 minutes **Cooking time:** 25 minutes
Servings: 4

½ pound brown mushrooms, sliced Salt and black pepper to the taste

¼ cup keto tomato sauce

1 turkey breast, skinless, boneless, cubed and browned

1 tablespoon parsley, chopped

1. In a pan that fits your air fryer, mix the turkey with the mushrooms, salt, pepper and tomato sauce, toss, introduce in the fryer and cook at 350 degrees F for 25 minutes. Divide into bowls and serve for lunch with parsley sprinkled on top.

Nutrition:
Calories 220, fat 12, fiber 2, carbs 5, protein 12

Lime Cod

Prep time: 8 minutes **Cooking time:** 13 minutes **Servings:** 2

2 lime slices

1 tablespoon lime juice

1 teaspoon lime zest, grated

¼ teaspoon ground black pepper

1 teaspoon sesame oil

½ teaspoon chili flakes

1-pound cod fillets, boneless

1. Rub the fish with lime zest, ground black pepper, chili flakes, and lime juice. Then brush it with sesame oil. Preheat the air fryer to 400F. Put the cod in the air fryer basket and cook it for 13 minutes. Then cut the cooked fish into halves and top with the sliced lime.

Nutrition:
Calories 227, fat 4, fiber 0.5, carbs 4.8, protein 42.2

Pork Stew

Preparation time: 5 minutes **Cooking time:** 25 minutes
Servings: 4

and ½ pound pork stew meat, cubed

½ cup cilantro, chopped

½ cup green onions, chopped

½ cup keto tomato sauce

teaspoons chili powder

A drizzle of olive oil

1. Heat up a pan that fits the air fryer with the oil over medium-high heat, add the meat and brown for 5 minutes. Add the rest of the ingredients, toss, introduce the pan in the air fryer and cook at 370 degrees F for 20 minutes. Divide into and serve for lunch

Nutrition:
Calories 285, fat 14, fiber 4, carbs 6, protein 15

Rosemary Zucchini Mix

Preparation time: 5 minutes **Cooking time:** 12 minutes
Servings: 4

¼ cup keto tomato sauce 1 tablespoon olive oil

8 zucchinis, roughly cubed

Salt and black pepper to the taste

¼ teaspoon rosemary, dried

½ teaspoon basil, chopped

1. Grease a pan that fits your air fryer with the oil, add all the ingredients, toss, introduce the pan in the fryer and cook at 350 degrees F for 12 minutes. Divide into bowls and serve for lunch.

Nutrition:
Calories 200, fat 6, fiber 2, carbs 4, protein 6

Lemon Cauliflower and Spinach

Prep time: 15 minutes **Cooking time:** 20 minutes **Servings:** 4

1-pound cauliflower head	1 tablespoon olive oil
1 teaspoon lemon juice	1 teaspoon salt
1 teaspoon chili flakes	2 cups of water
6 bacon slices	½ cup spinach, chopped
½ cup Cheddar cheese, shredded	½ teaspoon minced garlic
1 egg, beaten	1 tablespoon mascarpone

1. Pour water in the saucepan and bring it to boil. Then add olive oil, lemon juice, salt, and chili flakes. Put the cauliflower head in the boiling water and simmer it for 10 minutes with the closed lid. Meanwhile, mix up minced ginger, egg, mascarpone, Cheddar cheese, and spinach. You should get a smooth and homogenous mixture. After this, cool the cooked cauliflower head and fill it with the spinach mixture. After this, wrap the cauliflower head in the bacon. Preheat the air fryer to 400F. Place the wrapped cauliflower head in the air fryer basket and cook it for 10 minutes or until bacon is light brown. Cut the cooked cauliflower head on 4 servings.

Nutrition:
Calories 294, fat 21.8, fiber 3, carbs 7.1, protein 18.3

Meat Bake

Preparation time: 5 minutes **Cooking time:** 30 minutes **Servings:** 4

1 pound lean beef, cubed	1 pound pork stew meat, cubed
1 tablespoon spring onions, chopped 2 tablespoons keto tomato sauce	A drizzle of olive oil
A pinch of salt and black pepper	¼ teaspoon sweet paprika

1. Heat up a pan that fits the air fryer with the oil over medium-high heat, add the pork and beef meat and brown for 5 minutes. Add the remaining ingredients, toss, introduce the pan in the air fryer and cook at 390 degrees F for 25 minutes. Divide the mix between plates and serve for lunch with a side salad.

Nutrition:
Calories 275, fat 14, fiber 2, carbs 6, protein 14

Shrimp and Spring Onions Stew

Preparation time: 5 minutes **Cooking time:** 12 minutes **Servings:** 4

red bell pepper, chopped	tablespoons keto tomato sauce 3 spring onions, chopped
14 ounces chicken stock	
1 and ½ pounds shrimp, peeled and deveined Salt and black pepper to the taste	1 tablespoon olive oil

1. In your air fryer's pan greased with the oil, mix the shrimp and the other ingredients, toss, introduce the pan in the machine, and cook at 360 degrees F for 12 minutes, stirring halfway. Divide into bowls and serve for lunch.

Nutrition:
Calories 223, fat 12, fiber 2, carbs 5, protein 9

Stuffed Avocado

Prep time: 15 minutes **Cooking time:** 10 minutes **Servings:** 2

1 avocado, peeled, pitted	2 tablespoons coconut flour
1 egg, beaten	1 tablespoon pork rinds, grinded
1 oz ground pork	1 oz Parmesan, grated
1 teaspoon avocado oil	Cooking spray

1. Heat up the skillet on the medium heat and add avocado oil. Add ground pork and cook it for 3 minutes. Stir it from time to time to avoid burning. Then add grated cheese and stir the mixture until cheese is melted.

2. Remove the mixture from the heat. After this, fill the avocado with the ground pork mixture and pork rinds. Secure two halves of avocado together and dip in the egg. Then coat the avocado in the coconut four and dip in the egg again. After this, coat the avocado in the coconut flour one more time. Preheat the air fryer to 400F. Place the avocado bomb in the air fryer and spray it with cooking spray. Cook the meal for 6 minutes at 400F. Cut the cooked avocado bomb into 2 servings and transfer in the serving plate.

Nutrition:
Calories 398, fat 31.4, fiber 9.7, carbs 13.8, protein 18.9

Seasoned Chicken Thighs

Prep time: 15 minutes **Cooking time:** 22 minutes **Servings:** 4

4 chicken thighs, skinless, boneless	1 teaspoon jerk seasonings
1 teaspoon Jerk sauce	Cooking spray

1. Sprinkle the chicken thighs with Jerk seasonings and Jerk sauce and leave them for 10 minutes to marinate. Meanwhile, preheat the air fryer to 385F. Place the marinated chicken thighs in the air fryer and spray them with the cooking spray. Cook the chicken thighs for 12 minutes. Then flip them on another side and cook for 10 minutes more.

Nutrition:
Calories 280, fat 10.8, fiber 0, carbs 0.8, protein 42.2

Rosemary Lamb

Preparation time: 5 minutes **Cooking time:** 30 minutes **Servings:** 4

1 tablespoon olive oil 2 garlic clove, minced	1 tablespoon rosemary, chopped
¼ cup keto tomato sauce	1 and ½ pounds lamb, cubed Salt and black pepper to the taste
1 cup baby spinach	

1. Heat up a pan that fits the air fryer with the oil over medium heat, add the lamb and garlic and brown for 5 minutes. Add the rest of the ingredients except the spinach, introduce the pan in the fryer and cook at 390 degrees F for 15 minutes, shaking the machine halfway. Add the spinach, cook for 10 minutes more, divide between plates and serve for lunch.

Nutrition:
Calories 257, fat 12, fiber 3, carbs 6, protein 14

Garlic Pork Stew

Prep time: 5 minutes **Cooking time:** 30 minutes **Servings:** 4

1 and ½ pounds pork stew meat, cubed 1 red cabbage, shredded	1 tablespoon olive oil
Salt and black pepper to the taste 2 chili peppers, chopped	4 garlic cloves, minced
½ cup veggie stock	¼ cup keto tomato sauce

1. Heat up a pan that fits the air fryer with the oil over medium heat, add the meat, chili peppers and the garlic, stir and brown for 5 minutes. Add the rest of the ingredients, toss, introduce the pan in the fryer and cook at 380 degrees F for 20 minutes. Divide the into bowls and serve for lunch.

Nutrition:

Calories 232, fat 11, fiber 3, carbs 5, protein 12

Chicken and Pepper Mix

Prep time: 15 minutes **Cooking time:** 20 minutes **Servings:** 6

3-pound chicken breast, skinless, boneless	1 tablespoon tikka seasonings
1 tomato, roughly chopped	1 green bell pepper, roughly chopped
1 tablespoon coconut oil	2 spring onions, chopped

1. Chop the chicken breast roughly and put it in the mixing bowl. Add tikka seasonings, bell pepper, and spring onion. Mix up the ingredients and leave for 10 minutes to marinate. Then preheat the air fryer to 360F. Put the chicken mixture and tomatoes in the air fryer basket. Cook the chicken tikkas for 20 minutes.

Nutrition:

Calories 290, fat 8, fiber 0.6, carbs 4.8, protein 48.5

Leeks Stew

Preparation time: 5 minutes **Cooking time:** 20 minutes **Servings:** 4

big eggplants, roughly cubed 1 cup veggie stock	leeks, sliced
2 tablespoons olive oil 1 tablespoon hot sauce	1 tablespoon sweet paprika
1 tablespoon keto tomato sauce Salt and black pepper to the taste	½ bunch cilantro, chopped 2 garlic cloves, minced

1. In a pan that fits the air fryer, mix all the ingredients, toss, introduce in the fryer and cook at 380 degrees F for 20 minutes. Divide the stew into bowls and serve for lunch.

Nutrition:

Calories 183, fat 4, fiber 2, carbs 4, protein 12

Cayenne Zucchini Mix

Prep time: 20 minutes **Cooking time:** 16 minutes **Servings:** 2

2 zucchini	½ cup Monterey jack cheese, shredded
¼ cup ground chicken	1 teaspoon salt
½ teaspoon cayenne pepper	1 teaspoon olive oil

1. Trim the zucchini and cut it into the Hasselback. In the mixing bowl mix up ground chicken, cheese, salt, and cayenne pepper. The fill the zucchini with chicken mixture and sprinkle with olive oil. Preheat the air fryer to 400F. Put the Hasselback zucchini in the air fryer and cook for 16 minutes at 400F.

Nutrition:

Calories 191, fat 12.6, fiber 2.3, carbs 7, protein 14.4

Ginger Pork

Prep time: 10 minutes **Cooking time:** 20 minutes **Servings:** 5

16 oz pork tenderloin	1 tablespoon fresh ginger, chopped
1 red bell pepper, cut into wedges	1 tablespoon lemon juice
1 teaspoon Erythritol	½ cup coconut flour
½ teaspoon salt	¼ teaspoon chili powder
½ teaspoon minced garlic	3 oz celery stalk
2 eggs, beaten	¼ cup beef broth
1 teaspoon apple cider vinegar	1 tablespoon butter

1. Chop the pork tenderloin into medium cubes and sprinkle with salt and chili powder. After this, dip the pork cubes in the beaten egg and coat in the coconut flour. Preheat the air fryer to 400F ad put the pork cubes in the air fryer basket. Cook them for 3 minutes. When the time is finished, flip the pork cubes on another side and cook for 3 minutes more.
2. Meanwhile, make the sweet-sour sauce. Put the butter in the pan. Add apple cider vinegar, chopped celery stalk, minced garlic, lemon juice, Erythritol, bell pepper, and fresh finger. Cook the mixture over the medium heat for 6 minutes. Stir the mixture from time to time. Then add beef broth and bring the mixture to boil. Add the cooked pork cubes and cook the meal for 4 minutes more.

Nutrition:

Calories 241, fat 8.7, fiber 5.6, carbs 11.5, protein 28.3

Lamb and Leeks

Preparation time: 5 minutes **Cooking time:** 30 minutes **Servings:** 4

1 pound lamb shoulder, trimmed and cubed 2 tablespoons olive oil	3 garlic cloves, minced 4 baby leeks, halved
1 cup okra	pound tomatoes, peeled and chopped Salt and black pepper to the taste
tablespoons tarragon, chopped	

1. Heat up a pan that fits your air fryer with the oil over medium-high heat, add the lamb, garlic, salt and pepper, toss and brown for 5 minutes. Add the remaining ingredients except the tarragon, toss, introduce the pan in the fryer and cook at 400 degrees F for 25 minutes. Divide everything into bowls and serve for lunch.

Nutrition:

Calories 235, fat 12, fiber 4, carbs 5, protein 15

Lamb Stew

Preparation time: 5 minutes **Cooking time:** 30 minutes **Servings:** 4

1 cup eggplant, cubed 2 garlic cloves, minced 3 celery ribs, chopped	½ cups keto tomato sauce
1 pound lamb stew meat, cubed 1 tablespoon olive oil	Salt and black pepper to the taste

1. Heat up a pan that fits the air fryer with the oil over medium-high heat, add the lamb, salt, pepper and the garlic and brown for 5 minutes. Add the rest of the ingredients, toss, introduce the pan in the machine and cook at 370 degrees F for 25 minutes. Divide into bowls and serve for lunch.

Nutrition:

Calories 235, fat 14, fiber 3, carbs 5, protein 14

Garlic Pork and Sprouts Stew

Preparation time: 5 minutes **Cooking time:** 25 minutes
Servings: 4

2 tablespoons olive oil 2 tomatoes, cubed	2 garlic cloves, minced
½ pound Brussels sprouts, halved 1 pound pork stew meat, cubed	¼ cup veggie stock
¼ cup keto tomato sauce	Salt and black pepper to the taste 1 tablespoon chives, chopped

1. Heat up a pan that fits the air fryer with the oil over medium-high heat, add the meat, garlic, salt and pepper, stir and brown for 5 minutes. Add all the other ingredients except the chives, toss, introduce in the fryer and cook at 380 degrees F for 20 minutes. Divide the stew into bowls and serve with chives sprinkled on top.

Nutrition:
Calories 200, fat 6, fiber 2, carbs 4, protein 13

Mozzarella Burger

Prep time: 15 minutes **Cooking time:** 12 minutes **Servings:** 2

4 sausage patties	1 teaspoon butter, softened
½ teaspoon ground black pepper	¼ teaspoon salt
1 oz Mozzarella, chopped Cooking spray	4 bacon slices

1. Sprinkle the sausage patties with ground black pepper and salt. Then put the cheese and butter on the patties. Make the balls from the sausage patties with the help of the fingertips. After this, roll them in the bacon. Preheat the air fryer to 390F. Put the bacon bombs in the air fryer and spray them with the cooking spray. Cook the bombs for 12 minutes – for 6 minutes from each side.

Nutrition:
Calories 564, fat 48.3, fiber 0.1, carbs 3.4, protein 30.2

Zucchini Casserole

Prep time: 15 minutes **Cooking time:** 30 minutes **Servings:** 4

1 cup ground chicken	½ cup ground pork
2 oz celery stalk, chopped	1 zucchini, grated
1 tablespoon coconut oil, melted	½ teaspoon salt
1 teaspoon ground black pepper	½ teaspoon chili flakes
1 teaspoon dried dill	½ teaspoon dried parsley
½ cup beef broth	

1. In the mixing bowl mix up ground chicken, ground pork, celery stalk, and salt. Add ground black pepper, chili flakes, dried dill, and dried parsley.
2. Stir the meat mixture until homogenous. Then brush the air fryer pan with coconut oil and put ½ part of all grated zucchini. Then spread it with all ground pork mixture. Sprinkle the meat with remaining grated zucchini and cover with foil. Preheat the air fryer to 375F. Place the pan with casserole in the air fryer and cook it for 25 minutes. When the time is finished, remove the foil and cook the casserole for 5 minutes more.

Nutrition:
Calories 229, fat 14.4, fiber 1, carbs 2.7, protein 21.6

Bacon Mushrooms

Prep time: 15 minutes **Cooking time:** 11 minutes **Servings:** 2

2 Portobello mushroom caps	2 eggs, beaten
½ cup coconut flakes	½ teaspoon chili flakes
½ teaspoon salt	½ teaspoon ground paprika
2 mozzarella slices	2 oz bacon, chopped
1 garlic clove, chopped	1 teaspoon olive oil

1. Mix up beaten egg, ground paprika, salt, and chili flakes. Then dip the mushroom caps in the beaten egg mixture and coat in the coconut flakes. After this, preheat the air fryer to 400F. Place the chopped bacon in the air fryer basket and add olive oil and garlic. Cook the ingredients for 6 minutes at 400F. Stir the mixture every 2 minutes. When the bacon is cooked, fill the mushrooms caps with it. Put the mushroom caps in the air fryer basket and cook them for 5 minutes at 400F.

Nutrition:
Calories 411, fat 30.3, fiber 3, carbs 8.6, protein 27.9

Okra Stew

Preparation time: 5 minutes **Cooking time:** 20 minutes
Servings: 4

1 cup okra	4 zucchinis, roughly cubed 1 teaspoon oregano, dried
2 green bell peppers, cut into strips 2 garlic cloves, minced	Salt and black pepper to the taste 7 ounces keto tomato sauce
2 tablespoons olive oil	2 tablespoons cilantro, chopped

1. In a pan that fits your air fryer, combine all the ingredients for the stew, toss, introduce the pan in the air fryer, cook the stew at 350 degrees F for 20 minutes, divide into bowls, and serve.

Nutrition:
Calories 230, fat 5, fiber 2, carbs 4, protein 8

Veggie Pizza

Prep time: 10 minutes **Cooking time:** 15 minutes **Servings:** 4

8 bacon slices	¼ cup black olives, sliced
¼ cup scallions, sliced	1 green bell pepper, sliced
1 cup Mozzarella, shredded	1 tablespoon keto tomato sauce
½ teaspoon dried basil	½ teaspoon sesame oil

1. Line the air fryer pan with baking paper. Then make the layer of the sliced bacon in the pan and sprinkle gently with sesame oil. Preheat the air fryer to 400F. Place the pan with the bacon in the air fryer basket and cook it for 9 minutes at 400F. After this, sprinkle the bacon with keto tomato sauce and top with Mozzarella. Then add bell pepper, spring onions, and black olives. Sprinkle the pizza with dried basil and cook for 6 minutes at 400F.

Nutrition:
Calories 255, fat 18.8, fiber 0.9, carbs 4.5, protein 16.5

Thyme Green Beans

Preparation time: 5 minutes **Cooking time:** 20 minutes
Servings: 6

1 pound green beans, trimmed and halved 2 eggplants, cubed	1 cup veggie stock
1 tablespoon olive oil 1 red chili pepper	red bell pepper, chopped
½ teaspoon thyme, dried	Salt and black pepper to the taste

1. In a pan that fits your air fryer, mix all the ingredients, toss, introduce the pan in the machine and cook at 350 degrees F for 20 minutes. Divide into bowls and serve for lunch.

Nutrition:

Calories 180, fat 3, fiber 2, carbs 5, protein 7

Chili Bell Peppers Stew

Preparation time: 5 minutes **Cooking time:** 15 minutes
Servings: 4

red bell peppers, cut into wedges	2 green bell peppers, cut into wedges 2 yellow bell peppers, cut into wedges
½ cup keto tomato sauce 1 tablespoon chili powder	2 teaspoons cumin, ground
¼ teaspoon sweet paprika	Salt and black pepper to the taste

1. In a pan that fits your air fryer, mix all the ingredients, toss, introduce the pan in the machine and cook at 370 degrees F for 15 minutes. Divide into bowls and serve for lunch.

Nutrition:

Calories 190, fat 4, fiber 2, carbs 4, protein 7

Salmon Skewers

Prep time: 15 minutes **Cooking time:** 10 minutes **Servings:** 4

1-pound salmon fillet	4 oz bacon, sliced
2 mozzarella balls, sliced	½ teaspoon avocado oil
½ teaspoon chili flakes	

1. Cut the salmon into the medium size cubes (4 cubes per serving) Then sprinkle salmon cubes with chili flakes and wrap in the sliced bacon.
2. String the wrapped salmon cubes on the skewers and sprinkle with avocado oil. After this, preheat the air fryer to 400F. Put the salmon skewers in the preheat air fryer basket and cook them at 400F for 4 minutes. Then flip the skewers on another side and cook them for 6 minutes at 385F.

Nutrition:

Calories 364, fat 23.4, fiber 0, carbs 0.5, protein 37.5

Pork and Okra Stew

Preparation time: 5 minutes **Cooking time:** 20 minutes
Servings: 4

1 and ½ pounds pork stew meat, cubed and browned	1 tablespoon olive oil 1 cup okra
2 teaspoons sweet paprika	
Salt and black pepper to the taste	3 garlic cloves, minced

1. In your air fryer's pan, combine the meat with the remaining ingredients, toss, cover and cook at 370 degrees F for 20 minutes. Divide the stew into bowls and serve.

Nutrition:

Calories 275, fat 12, fiber 4, carbs 6, protein 15

Spiced Beef Meatballs

Prep time: 15 minutes **Cooking time:** 10 minutes **Servings:** 2

1 oz pimiento jalapenos, pickled, chopped	½ teaspoon dried rosemary
½ teaspoon salt	9 oz ground beef
½ teaspoon ground coriander	¼ teaspoon ground nutmeg
1 egg, beaten	2 oz provolone cheese, shredded
2 teaspoons mascarpone	¼ teaspoon minced garlic
Cooking spray	

1. In the mixing bowl mix up pickled pimiento jalapenos, dried rosemary, salt, ground beef, coriander, nutmeg, egg, and make the medium-size meatballs. Preheat the air fryer to 365F. Then spray the air fryer basket with cooking spray and place the meatballs inside. Cook the meatballs for 6 minutes, Then carefully flip them on another side and cook for 4 minutes more. Meanwhile, churn together minced garlic and mascarpone. When the meatballs are cooked, transfer them in the serving plates andtop with garlic mascarpone.

Nutrition:

Calories 385, fat 18.5, fiber 0.7, carbs 2.3, protein 49.4

Green Beans Stew

Preparation time: 5 minutes **Cooking time:** 15 minutes
Servings: 4

1 pound green beans	halved 1 cup okra
1 tablespoon thyme	chopped
3 tablespoons keto tomato sauce Salt and black pepper to the taste 4 garlic cloves	minced

1. In a pan that fits your air fryer, mix all the ingredients, toss, introduce the pan in the air fryer and cook at 370 degrees F for 15 minutes. Divide the stew into bowls and serve.

Nutrition:

Calories 183, fat 5, fiber 2, carbs 4, protein 8

Rosemary Chicken Stew

Preparation time: 5 minutes **Cooking time:** 20 minutes
Servings: 4

2 cups okra	2 garlic cloves, minced
1 pound chicken breasts, skinless, boneless and cubed 4 tomatoes, cubed	1 tablespoon olive oil
teaspoon rosemary, dried	Salt and black pepper to the taste 1 tablespoon parsley, chopped

1. Heat up a pan that fits your air fryer with the oil over medium-high heat, add the chicken, garlic, rosemary, salt and pepper, toss and brown for 5 minutes. Add the remaining ingredients, toss again, place the pan in the air fryer and cook at 380 degrees F for 15 minutes more. Divide the stew into bowls and serve for lunch.

Nutrition:

Calories 220, fat 13, fiber 3, carbs 5, protein 11

Beef and Green Onions Casserole

Prep time: 15 minutes **Cooking time:** 21 minutes **Servings:** 4

10 oz lean ground beef	1 oz green onions, chopped
2 low carb tortillas	1 cup Mexican cheese blend, shredded
1 teaspoon fresh cilantro, chopped	1 teaspoon butter
1 tablespoon mascarpone	1 tablespoon heavy cream
¼ teaspoon garlic powder	1 teaspoon Mexican seasonings
1 teaspoon olive oil	

1. Pour olive oil in the skillet and heat it up over the medium heat. Then add ground beef and sprinkle it with garlic powder and Mexican seasonings. Cook the ground beef for 7 minutes over the medium heat. Stir it from time to time Then chop the low carb tortillas. Grease the air fryer pan with butter and put the tortillas in one layer inside. Put the ground beef mixture over the tortillas and spread it gently with the help of the spoon. Then sprinkle it with cilantro, green onions, mascarpone, and heavy cream. Top the casserole with Mexican cheese blend and cover with baking paper.
2. Secure the edges of the pan well. Preheat the air fryer to 360F. Cook the casserole for 10 minutes at 360F and then remove the baking paper and cook the meal for 5 minutes more to reach the crunchy crust.

Nutrition:
Calories 179, fat 14.7, fiber 3, carbs 6.6, protein 23.8

Cheese Quiche

Prep time: 20 minutes **Cooking time:** 19 minutes **Servings:** 5

½ cup almond flour	1 tablespoon Psyllium husk
½ teaspoon flax meal	¼ teaspoon baking powder
2 eggs, beaten	7 oz Feta cheese, crumbled
¼ cup scallions, diced	½ teaspoon ground black pepper
¼ teaspoon ground cardamom	1 oz Parmesan, grated
1 teaspoon coconut oil, melted	3 tablespoons almond butter

2. Make the quiche crust: mix up almond flour, Psyllium husk, flax meal, baking powder, and almond butter in the bowl. Stir the mixture until homogenous and knead the non-sticky dough. Then pour melted coconut oil in the skillet and bring it to boil. Add scallions and cook it for 3 minutes or until it is light brown. Then transfer the cooked onion in the mixing bowl. Add Parmesan, ground cardamom, and ground black pepper. After this, add Feta cheese and eggs. Stir the mass until homogenous. Cut the dough into 5 pieces. Place the dough in the quiche molds and flatten it in the shape of the pie crust with the help of the fingertips. Then fill every quiche crust with a Feta mixture. Preheat the air fryer to 365F. Put the molds with quiche in the air fryer basket and cook them for 15 minutes.

Nutrition:
Calories 254, fat 19.2, fiber 7.3, carbs 12.5, protein 12.5

Spring Onions and Shrimp Mix

Preparation time: 5 minutes **Cooking time:** 15 minutes **Servings:** 4

cups baby spinach	¼ cup veggie stock 2 tomatoes, cubed
1 tablespoon garlic, minced	15 ounces shrimp, peeled and deveined 4 spring onions, chopped
½ teaspoon cumin, ground	2 tablespoons cilantro, chopped Salt and black pepper to the taste
1 tablespoon lemon juice	

1. In a pan that fits your air fryer, mix all the ingredients except the cilantro, toss, introduce in the air fryer and cook at 360 degrees F for 15 minutes. Add the cilantro, stir, divide into bowls and serve for lunch.

Nutrition:
Calories 201, fat 8, fiber 2, carbs 4, protein 8

Chicken Stuffed Eggplants

Prep time: 20 minutes **Cooking time:** 20 minutes **Servings:** 4

1-pound mini eggplants	1 tomato, chopped
2 oz Feta cheese, crumbled	1 teaspoon fresh parsley, chopped
¼ teaspoon salt	9 oz ground chicken
½ teaspoon fennel seeds	1 teaspoon minced garlic
1 tablespoon ghee	1 teaspoon salt
1 cup of water	Cooking spray

1. Make the pockets in the eggplants by removing eggplant meat from them. Then sprinkle the eggplants with 1 teaspoon of salt and put in the water for 10-15 minutes. After this, preheat the air fryer to 365F. Dry the eggplants and place them in the air fryer in one layer. Spray them with the cooking spray and cook for 10 minutes at 365F. Meanwhile, put ghee in the skillet and melt it over the medium heat. Add parsley, tomato, ¼ teaspoon of salt, ground chicken, and minced garlic. Add fennel seeds and cook the ingredients for 10 minutes over the medium heat. When the eggplants are cooked, remove them from the air fryer and cool to the room temperature. Fill the eggplants with ground chicken mixture.

Nutrition:
Calories 229, fat 11.3, fiber 3.2, carbs 10.8, protein 21.6

Tomato and Peppers Stew

Preparation time: 5 minutes **Cooking time:** 15 minutes **Servings:** 4

4 spring onions, chopped 2 pound tormatoes, cubed 1 teaspoon sweet paprika tablespoon cilantro, chopped	Salt and black pepper to the taste 2 red bell peppers, cubed

1. In a pan that fits your air fryer, mix all the ingredients, toss, introduce the pan in the fryer and cook at 360 degrees F for 15 minutes. Divide into bowls and serve for lunch.

Nutrition:
Calories 185, fat 3, fiber 2, carbs 4, protein 9

Chili Sloppy Joes

Prep time: 10 minutes **Cooking time:** 20 minutes **Servings:** 3

1 cup ground pork	1 teaspoon sloppy Joes seasonings
1 teaspoon butter	1 tablespoon keto tomato sauce
1 teaspoon mustard	¼ cup beef broth
½ teaspoon chili flakes	½ bell pepper, chopped
½ teaspoon minced garlic	

1. In the bowl mix up chili flakes, beef broth, minced garlic, and tomato sauce. Add mustard and whisk the liquid until homogenous. After this, add ground pork and sloppy Joes seasonings. Stir the ingredients with the help of the spoon and transfer in the air fryer baking pan. Add butter.
2. Preheat the air fryer to 365F. Put the pan with sloppy Joe in the air fryer basket and cook the meal for 20 minutes. Stir the meal well after 10 minutes of cooking.

Nutrition:
Calories 344, fat 23.4, fiber 0.2, carbs 3.4, protein 27.8

Tuna Bake

Prep time: 15 minutes **Cooking time:** 15 minutes **Servings:** 6

2 spring onions, diced	1 pound smoked tuna, boneless
¼ cup ricotta cheese	3 oz celery stalk, diced
½ teaspoon celery seeds	1 tablespoon cream cheese
¼ teaspoon salt	½ teaspoon ground paprika
2 tablespoons lemon juice	1 tablespoon ghee
4 oz Edam cheese, shredded	

1. Mix up celery seeds, cream cheese, ground paprika, lemon juice, and ricotta cheese. Then shred the tuna until it is smooth and add it in the cream cheese mixture. Add onion and stir the mass with the help of the spoon. Grease the air fryer pan with ghee and put the tuna mixture inside. Flatten its surface gently with the help of the spoon and top with Edam cheese. Preheat the air fryer to 360F. Place the pan with tuna melt in the air fryer and cook it for 15 minutes.

Nutrition:
Calories 249, fat 14.3, fiber 1.1, carbs 5, protein 24.2

Fennel Stew

Preparation time: 5 minutes **Cooking time:** 15 minutes **Servings:** 4

cups tomatoes, cubed 2 fennel bulbs, shredded	½ cup chicken stock
2 tablespoons keto tomato puree 1 red bell pepper, chopped	2 garlic cloves, minced
1 teaspoon sweet paprika	Salt and black pepper to the taste
1 teaspoon rosemary, dried	

2. In a pan that fits your air fryer, mix all the ingredients, toss, introduce in the fryer and cook at 380 degrees F for 15 minutes. Divide the stew into bowls and serve for lunch.

Nutrition:
Calories 184, fat 7, fiber 2, carbs 3, protein 8

Bacon Pancetta Casserole

Prep time: 10 minutes **Cooking time:** 20 minutes **Servings:** 4

2 cups cauliflower, shredded	3 oz pancetta, chopped
2 oz bacon, chopped	1 cup Cheddar cheese, shredded
½ cup heavy cream	1 teaspoon salt
1 teaspoon cayenne pepper	1 teaspoon dried oregano

1. Put bacon and pancetta in the air fryer and cook it for 10 minutes at 400F. Stir the ingredients every 3 minutes to avoid burning. Then mix up shredded cauliflower and cooked pancetta and bacon. Add salt and cayenne pepper. Mix up the mixture. Add the dried oregano. Line the air fryer pan with baking paper and put the cauliflower mixture inside. Top it with Cheddar cheese and sprinkle with heavy cream. Cook the casserole for 10 minutes at 365F.

Nutrition:
Calories 381, fat 30.5, fiber 1.5, carbs 4.5, protein 22.1

Okra and Peppers Casserole

Preparation time: 5 minutes **Cooking time:** 20 minutes **Servings:** 4

teaspoon olive oil 3 cups okra	red bell peppers, cubed
Salt and black pepper to the taste 2 tomatoes, chopped	garlic cloves, minced
¼ cup keto tomato sauce	2 teaspoons coriander, ground 1 tablespoon cilantro, chopped
½ cup cheddar, shredded	

1. Grease a heat proof dish that fits your air fryer with the oil, add all the ingredients except the cilantro and the cheese and toss them really gently. Sprinkle the cheese and the cilantro on top, introduce the dish in the fryer and cook at 390 degrees F for 20 minutes. Divide between plates and serve for lunch.

Nutrition:
Calories 221, fat 7, fiber 2, carbs 4, protein 9

Cheese Pies

Prep time: 15 minutes **Cooking time:** 4 minutes **Servings:** 4

8 wonton wraps	1 egg, beaten
1 cup cottage cheese	1 tablespoon Erythritol
½ teaspoon vanilla extract	1 egg white, whisked
Cooking spray	

1. Mix up cottage cheese and Erythritol. Then add vanilla extract and egg. Stir the mixture well with the help of the fork. After this, put the cottage cheese mixture on the wonton wraps and fold them in the shape of pies. Then brush the pies with whisked egg white. Preheat the air fryer to 375F. Then put the cottage cheese pies in the air fryer and spray them with the cooking spray. Cook the meal for 2 minutes from each side.

Nutrition:
Calories 92, fat 2.2, fiber 0, carbs 6.3, protein 11

Tomato Casserole

Preparation time: 5 minutes **Cooking time:** 20 minutes
Servings: 4

tablespoon olive oil	spring onions, chopped 3 garlic cloves, minced
1 teaspoon smoked paprika 1 tablespoon thyme, dried 2 celery sticks, sliced	1 yellow bell pepper, chopped
14 ounces cherry tomatoes, cubed 2 courgettes, sliced	½ cup mozzarella, shredded

1. In a baking dish that fits your air fryer, mix all the ingredients except the cheese and toss. Sprinkle the cheese on top, introduce the dish in your air fryer and cook at 380 degrees F for 20 minutes. Divide between plates and serve for lunch.

Nutrition:
Calories 254, fat 12, fiber 2, carbs 4, protein 11

Smoked Chicken mix

Preparation time: 5 minutes **Cooking time:** 25 minutes
Servings: 4

½ pound chicken breasts, skinless, boneless and cubed Salt and black pepper to the taste teaspoons smoked paprika	½ cup chicken stock
	½ teaspoon basil, dried

1. In a pan that fits the air fryer, combine all the ingredients, toss, introduce the pan in the fryer and cook at 390 degrees F for 25 minutes. Divide between plates and serve for lunch with a side salad.

Nutrition:
Calories 223, fat 12, fiber 2, carbs 5, protein 13

Almond Chicken Curry

Prep time: 10 minutes
Cooking time: 15 minutes
Servings: 2

10 oz chicken fillet, chopped	1 teaspoon ground turmeric
½ cup spring onions, diced	1 teaspoon salt
½ teaspoon curry powder	½ teaspoon garlic, diced
½ teaspoon ground coriander	½ cup of organic almond milk
1 teaspoon Truvia	1 teaspoon olive oil

1. Put the chicken in the bowl. Add the ground turmeric, salt, curry powder, diced garlic, ground coriander, and almond Truvia. Then add olive oil and mix up the chicken. After this, add almond milk and transfer the chicken in the air fryer pan. Then preheat the air fryer to 375F and place the pan with korma curry inside. Top the chicken with diced onion. Cook the meal for 10 minutes. Stir it after 5 minutes of cooking. If the chicken is not cooked after 10 minutes, cook it for an additional 5 minutes.

Nutrition:
Calories 327, fat 14.5, fiber 1.5, carbs 5.6, protein 42

Cabbage Stew

Preparation time: 5 minutes **Cooking time:** 20 minutes
Servings: 4

14 ounces tomatoes, chopped	1 green cabbage head, shredded Salt and black pepper to the taste 1 tablespoon sweet paprika
4 ounces chicken stock	2 tablespoon dill, chopped

1. In a pan that fits your air fryer, mix the cabbage with the tomatoes and all the other ingredients except the dill, toss, introduce the pan in the fryer, and cook at 380 degrees F for 20 minutes. Divide into bowls and serve with dill sprinkled on top.

Nutrition:
Calories 200, fat 8, fiber 3, carbs 4, protein 6

Cheddar Beef Chili

Prep time: 15 minutes **Cooking time:** 20 minutes **Servings:** 2

1 cup ground beef	¼ cup Cheddar cheese, shredded
¼ cup green beans, trimmed and halved	¼ cup spring onion, diced
1 teaspoon fresh cilantro, chopped	2 chili pepper, chopped
1 teaspoon ghee	1 tablespoon keto tomato sauce
½ cup chicken broth	½ teaspoon salt
¼ teaspoon garlic powder	

1. Put ghee in the skillet and melt it. Put the ground beef in the skillet. Add spring onion, garlic powder, and salt. Stir the ground beef mixture and cook it over the medium heat for 5 minutes. Then transfer the mixture in the air fryer pan. Add tomato sauce and stir until homogenous. Add chicken broth, chili peppers, and cilantro. Then add green beans and cilantro. Mix up the chili gently and top with Cheddar cheese. Preheat the air fryer to 390F. Put the pan with chili con carne in the air fryer and cook it for 10 minutes.

Nutrition:
Calories 244, fat 15.5, fiber 1.7, carbs 6.4, protein 19.4

Sprouts and Chicken Casserole

Prep time: 15 minutes **Cooking time:** 25 minutes **Servings:** 2

1 cup Brussels sprouts	½ teaspoon salt
½ cup ground chicken	½ teaspoon ground black pepper
1 tablespoon coconut cream	1 teaspoon chili powder
1 tablespoon butter, melted	½ teaspoon ground paprika

1. Mix up ground chicken, ground black pepper, chili powder, ground paprika, and coconut cream. Add salt and stir the mixture. After this, grease the air fryer casserole mold with butter. Put Brussels sprouts in the casserole mold and flatten them in one layer. Then top the vegetables with ground chicken mixture. Cover the casserole with baking paper and secure the edges. Preheat the air fryer to 365F. Put the casserole mold in the air fryer basket and cook it for 25 minutes.

Nutrition:
Calories 170, fat 10.6, fiber 3.2, carbs 7.9, protein 12.5

Balsamic Cauliflower Stew

Preparation time: 5 minutes **Cooking time:** 20 minutes
Servings: 4

1 and ½ cups zucchinis, sliced	1 tablespoon olive oil
Salt and black pepper to the taste 1 tablespoon balsamic vinegar	1 cauliflower head, florets separated 2 green onions, chopped
handful parsley leaves, chopped	½ cup keto tomato sauce

1. In a pan that fits your air fryer, mix the zucchinis with the rest of the ingredients except the parsley, toss, introduce the pan in the air fryer and cook at 380 degrees F for 20 minutes. Divide into bowls and serve for lunch with parsley sprinkled on top.

Nutrition:
Calories 193, fat 5, fiber 2, carbs 4, protein 7

Chicken and Cucumber Salad

Prep time: 15 minutes **Cooking time:** 10 minutes **Servings:** 4

1 cucumber, chopped	1 tablespoon ricotta cheese
1 tablespoon mascarpone cheese	½ cup Monterey Jack cheese, grated
1-pound chicken breast, skinless, boneless	1 teaspoon avocado oil
½ teaspoon salt	1 teaspoon dried oregano
1 teaspoon ground black pepper	1 teaspoon ground paprika
1 oz bacon, chopped	

1. Rub the chicken breast with salt, dried oregano, ground black pepper, and ground paprika. Then put the chopped bacon in the air fryer basket. Place the chicken breast over the bacon and sprinkle with avocado oil. Cook the ingredients for 10 minutes at 395F. Meanwhile, in the shallow bowl mix up mascarpone cheese and ricotta cheese. Put the chopped cucumber in the salad bowl. Add grated Monterey jack cheese. When the chicken and bacon are cooked, remove them from the air fryer basket. Chop the chicken breast into tiny pieces and add in the salad bowl Add bacon and mascarpone mixture. Stir the salad with the help of the spatula.

Nutrition:
Calories 249, fat 11.3, fiber 0.9, carbs 4.2, protein 31.7

Olives Mix

Preparation time: 5 minutes **Cooking time:** 20 minutes
Servings: 4

cups black olives, pitted and halved 1 red bell pepper, chopped	celery stalks, chopped
Salt and black pepper to the taste 4 cups spinach, torn	2 tomatoes, chopped
½ cup keto tomato sauce	

1. In a pan that fits your air fryer, mix all the ingredients except the spinach, toss, introduce the pan in the air fryer and cook at 370 degrees F for 15 minutes. Add the spinach, toss, cook for 5-6 minutes more, divide into bowls and serve.

Nutrition:
Calories 193, fat 6, fiber 2, carbs 4, protein 6

Eggplant Sandwich

Prep time: 15 minutes **Cooking time:** 7 minutes **Servings:** 2

1 large eggplant	½ cup mozzarella, shredded
1 tablespoon fresh basil, chopped	1 teaspoon minced garlic
1 teaspoon salt	1 tablespoon nut oil
1 tomato	

1. Slice the tomato on 4 slices. Then slice along the eggplant on 4 slices. Then rub every eggplant slice with salt, minced garlic, and brush with nut oil. Preheat the air fryer to 400F. Put the eggplant slices in one layer and cook for 2 minutes at 400F. Then flip the vegetables on another side and cook for 2 minutes more. Transfer the cooked eggplant slices on the plate. Sprinkle 2 eggplant slices with basil and mozzarella. Then add 2 tomato slices on 2 eggplant slices. Cover the tomato slices with the remaining 2 eggplant slices and put in the air fryer basket. Cook the sandwich for 3 minutes at 400F.

Nutrition:
Calories 145, fat 8.5, fiber 8.5, carbs 15.4, protein 4.6

Chili Beef Bowl

Prep time: 25 minutes **Cooking time:** 18 minutes **Servings:** 3

9 oz beef sirloin	1 chili pepper
1 green bell pepper	½ teaspoon minced garlic
¼ teaspoon ground ginger	1 tablespoon apple cider vinegar
4 tablespoons water	½ teaspoon salt
3 spring onions, chopped	1 teaspoon avocado oil

1. Cut the beef sirloin into wedges. Then cut bell pepper and chili pepper into wedges. Put bell pepper, chili pepper, and beef sirloin in the bowl. Add minced garlic, ground ginger, apple cider vinegar, water, salt, and spring onions. Marinate the mixture for 15 minutes. Meanwhile, preheat the air fryer to 210F. Put the bell pepper, chili pepper, and onion in the air fryer basket. Sprinkle them with ½ teaspoon of avocado oil and cook them for 8 minutes. Transfer the cooked vegetables in 3 serving bowls. After this, put the beef wedges in the air fryer and sprinkle them with remaining avocado oil. Cook the meat for 10 minutes at 365F. Stir it from time to time to avoid burning. Meanwhile, pour the marinade from the beef and vegetables in the saucepan and bring it to boil. Simmer it for 2-3 minutes. Put the cooked beef in the serving bowls. Sprinkle the meal with hot marinade.

Nutrition:
Calories 19, 1 fat 5.7, fiber 1.5, carbs 7.1, protein .26.8

Broccoli and Spring Onions Stew

Prep time: 5 minutes **Cooking time:** 15 minutes **Servings:** 4

1 broccoli head, florets separated 3 tablespoons chicken stock	¾ cup keto tomato sauce 3 spring onions, chopped
¼ cup celery, chopped	Salt and black pepper to the taste

1. In a pan that fits your air fryer, mix all the ingredients, toss, introduce the pan in your fryer and cook at 380 degrees F for 15 minutes. Divide into bowls and serve for lunch.

Nutrition:
Calories 183, fat 4, fiber 2, carbs 4, protein 7

Beef and Tomato Mix

Preparation time: 5 minutes **Cooking time:** 25 minutes
Servings: 4

1 and ½ pounds beef stew meat, cubed	½ cup green onions, chopped 3 tablespoons butter, melted
½ cup celery stalks, chopped 1 garlic clove, minced	½ teaspoon Italian seasoning 15 ounces keto tomato sauce
Salt and black pepper to the taste	

1. Heat up a pan that fits your air fryer with the butter over medium heat, add the meat, toss and brown for 5 minutes. Add the rest of the ingredients, toss, introduce the pan in the fryer and cook at 390 degrees F for 20 minutes. Divide into bowls and serve for lunch.

Nutrition:
Calories 224, fat 14, fiber 3, carbs 5, protein 14

Shrimp and Mushroom Pie

Prep time: 15 minutes **Cooking time:** 15 minutes **Servings:** 4

10 oz shrimps, peeled	½ cup Cheddar cheese, shredded
3 tablespoons cream cheese	2 eggs, beaten
¼ cup cremini mushrooms, sliced	½ teaspoon salt
½ teaspoon ground black pepper	½ teaspoon seafood seasonings
1 teaspoon nut oil	

1. Mix up shrimps and seafood seasonings. Then brush the air fryer round pan with nut oil and put the shrimps inside. Flatten them gently with the help of the fork. After this, in the mixing bowl mix up shredded Cheddar cheese, cream cheese, mushrooms, salt, and ground black pepper. Add eggs and stir the mixture until homogenous. Pour the mixture over the shrimps and flatten the pie gently with the help of the fork or spoon.
2. Preheat the air fryer to 365F. Put the pan with the pie in the air fryer. Cook the shrimp pie for 15 minutes.

Nutrition:
Calories 211, fat 11.8, fiber 0.1, carbs 2, protein 23.1

Side Dish Recipes

Mozzarella Risotto

Preparation time: 5 minutes **Cooking time:** 20 minutes
Servings: 4

1 pound white mushrooms, sliced	¼ cup mozzarella, shredded
1 cauliflower head, florets separated and riced 1 cup chicken stock	1 tablespoon thyme, chopped 1 teaspoon Italian seasoning
A pinch of salt and black pepper 2 tablespoons olive oil	

1. Heat up a pan that fits the air fryer with the oil over medium heat, add the cauliflower rice and the mushrooms, toss and cook for a couple of minutes. Add the rest of the ingredients except the thyme, toss, put the pan in the air fryer and cook at 360 degrees F for 20 minutes. Divide the risotto between plates and serve with thyme sprinkled on top

Nutrition:
Calories 204, fat 12, fiber 3, carbs 4, protein 8

Creamy Cauliflower Tots

Prep time: 15 minutes **Cooking time:** 8 minutes **Servings:** 4

1 teaspoon cream cheese	5 oz Monterey Jack cheese, shredded
1 cup cauliflower, chopped, boiled	¼ teaspoon garlic powder
1 teaspoon sunflower oil	

1. Put the boiled cauliflower in the blender. Add garlic powder, cream cheese, and shredded Monterey Jack cheese. Blend the mixture until smooth. Make the cauliflower tots and refrigerate them for 10 minutes. Meanwhile, preheat the air fryer to 365F. Place the cauliflower inside the air fryer basket and sprinkle with sunflower oil. Cook the tots for 4 minutes from each side.

Nutrition:
Calories 152, fat 12.2, fiber 0.7, carbs 1.7, protein 9.3

Spinach Salad

Preparation time: 5 minutes **Cooking time:** 10 minutes
Servings: 4

1 pound baby spinach	Salt and black pepper to the taste 1 tablespoon mustard
Cooking spray	¼ cup apple cider vinegar
1 tablespoon chives, chopped	

1. Grease a pan that fits your air fryer with cooking spray, combine all the ingredients, introduce the pan in the fryer and cook at 350 degrees F for 10 minutes. Divide between plates and serve as a side dish.

Nutrition:
Calories 160, fat 3, fiber 2, carbs 4, protein 6

Turmeric Cauliflower Rice

Preparation time: 5 minutes **Cooking time:** 20 minutes
Servings: 4

1 big cauliflower, florets separated and riced 1 and ½ cups chicken stock	1 tablespoon olive oil
Salt and black pepper to the taste	½ teaspoon turmeric powder

1. In a pan that fits the air fryer, combine the cauliflower with the oil and the rest of the ingredients, toss, introduce in the air fryer and cook at 360 degrees F for 20 minutes. Divide between plates and serve as a side dish.

Nutrition:
Calories 193, fat 5, fiber 2, carbs 4, protein 6

Mushroom Cakes

Prep time: 10 minutes **Cooking time:** 8 minutes **Servings:** 4

9 oz mushrooms, finely chopped	¼ cup coconut flour
1 teaspoon salt	1 egg, beaten
3 oz Cheddar cheese, shredded	1 teaspoon dried parsley
½ teaspoon ground black pepper	1 teaspoon sesame oil
1 oz spring onion, chopped	

1. In the mixing bowl mix up chopped mushrooms, coconut flour, salt, egg, dried parsley, ground black pepper, and minced onion. Stir the mixture until smooth and add Cheddar cheese. Stir it with the help of the fork, Preheat the air fryer to 385F. Line the air fryer pan with baking paper.
2. With the help of the spoon make the medium size patties and put them in the pan. Sprinkle the patties with sesame oil and cook for 4 minutes from each side.

Nutrition:
Calories 164, fat 10.7, fiber 3.9, carbs 7.8, protein 10.3

Cauliflower and Tomato Bake

Preparation time: 5 minutes **Cooking time:** 20 minutes
Servings: 2

1 cup heavy whipping cream 2 tablespoons basil pesto	Salt and black pepper to the taste Juice of ½ lemon
1 pound cauliflower, florets separated 4 ounces cherry tomatoes, halved 7 ounces cheddar cheese, grated	3 tablespoons ghee, melted

1. Grease a baking pan that fits the air fryer with the ghee. Add the cauliflower, lemon juice, salt, pepper, the pesto and the cream and toss gently. Add the tomatoes, sprinkle the cheese on top, introduce the pan in the fryer and cook at 380 degrees F for 20 minutes. Divide between plates and serve as a side dish.

Nutrition:
Calories 200, fat 7, fiber 2, carbs 4, protein 7

Turmeric Tofu

Prep time: 10 minutes **Cooking time:** 9 minutes **Servings:** 2

6 oz tofu, cubed	1 teaspoon avocado oil
1 teaspoon apple cider vinegar	1 garlic clove, diced
¼ teaspoon ground turmeric	¼ teaspoon ground paprika
½ teaspoon dried cilantro	¼ teaspoon lemon zest, grated

1. In the bowl mix up avocado oil, apple cider vinegar, diced garlic, ground turmeric, paprika, cilantro, and lime zest. Coat the tofu cubes in the oil mixture. Preheat the air fryer to 400F. Put the tofu cubes in the air fryer and cook them for 9 minutes. Shake the tofu cubes from time to time during cooking.

Nutrition:
Calories 67, fat 3.9, fiber 1.1, carbs 2.5, protein 7.2

Mushroom Tots

Prep time: 15 minutes **Cooking time:** 6 minutes **Servings:** 2

1 cup white mushrooms, grinded	1 teaspoon onion powder
1 egg yolk	3 teaspoons flax meal
½ teaspoon ground black pepper	1 teaspoon avocado oil
1 tablespoon coconut flour	

1. Mix up grinded white mushrooms with onion powder, egg yolk, flax meal, ground black pepper, and coconut flour. When the mixture is smooth and homogenous, make the mushroom tots. Preheat the air fryer to 400F. Sprinkle the air fryer basket with melted coconut oil and put the mushroom tots inside. Cook them for 3 minutes. Then flip the mushroom tots on another side and cook them for 2-3 minutes more or until they are light brown.

Nutrition:
Calories 76, fat 4.6, fiber 3.2, carbs 6.2, protein 4.2

Chili Zucchini Balls

Prep time: 10 minutes **Cooking time:** 12 minutes **Servings:** 4

¼ teaspoon salt	¼ teaspoon ground cumin
1 zucchini, grated	2 oz Provolone cheese, grated
¼ teaspoon chili flakes	1 egg, beaten
¼ cup coconut flour	1 teaspoon sunflower oil

1. In the bowl mix up salt, ground cumin, zucchini, Provolone cheese, chili flakes, egg, and coconut flour. Stir the mass with the help of the spoon and make the small balls. Then line the air fryer basket with baking paper and sprinkle it with sunflower oil. Put the zucchini balls in the air fryer basket and cook them for 12 minutes at 375F. Shake the balls every 2 minutes to avoid burning.

Nutrition:
Calories 122, fat 7.4, fiber 3.7, carbs 7.3, protein 7.2

Coconut Chives Sprouts

Preparation time: 5 minutes **Cooking time:** 20 minutes **Servings:** 4

pound Brussels sprouts, trimmed and halved Salt and black pepper to the taste	tablespoons ghee, melted
½ cup coconut cream	2 tablespoons garlic, minced
1 tablespoon chives, chopped	

1. In your air fryer, mix the sprouts with the rest of the ingredients except the chives, toss well, introduce in the air fryer and cook them at 370 degrees F for 20 minutes. Divide the Brussels sprouts between plates, sprinkle the chives on top and serve as a side dish.

Nutrition:
Calories 194, fat 6, fiber 2, carbs 4, protein 8

Cheesy Zucchini Tots

Prep time: 15 minutes **Cooking time:** 6 minutes **Servings:** 4

1 zucchini, grated	½ cup Mozzarella, shredded
1 egg, beaten	2 tablespoons almond flour
½ teaspoon ground black pepper	1 teaspoon coconut oil, melted

1. Mix up grated zucchini, shredded Mozzarella, egg, almond flour, and ground black pepper. Then make the small zucchini tots with the help of the fingertips. Preheat the air fryer to 385F. Place the zucchini tots in the air fryer basket and cook for 3 minutes from each side or until the zucchini tots are golden brown.

Nutrition:
Calories 64, fat 4.7, fiber 1, carbs 2.8, protein 3.8

Creamy Broccoli and Cauliflower

Preparation time: 5 minutes **Cooking time:** 20 minutes **Servings:** 4

15 ounces broccoli florets	10 ounces cauliflower florets 1 leek, chopped
2 spring onions, chopped	Salt and black pepper to the taste 2 ounces butter, melted
2 tablespoons mustard 1 cup sour cream	5 ounces mozzarella cheese, shredded

1. In a baking pan that fits the air fryer, add the butter and spread it well. Add the broccoli, cauliflower and the rest of the ingredients except the mozzarella and toss. Sprinkle the cheese on top, introduce the pan in the air fryer and cook at 380 degrees F for 20 minutes. Divide between plates and serve as a side dish.

Nutrition:
Calories 242, fat 13, fiber 2, carbs 4, protein 8

Buttery Cauliflower Mix

Preparation time: 5 minutes **Cooking time:** 15 minutes
Servings: 4

1 pound cauliflower florets, roughly grated 3 eggs, whisked	3 tablespoons butter, melted
Salt and black pepper to the taste	1 tablespoon sweet paprika

1. Heat up a pan that fits the air fryer with the butter over high heat, add the cauliflower and brown for 5 minutes. Add whisked eggs, salt, pepper and the paprika, toss, introduce the pan in the fryer and cook at 400 degrees F for 10 minutes. Divide between plates and serve.

Nutrition:
Calories 153, fat 5, fiber 2, carbs 5, protein 5

Italian Eggplant Bites

Prep time: 10 minutes **Cooking time:** 10 minutes **Servings:** 5

2 medium eggplants, trimmed	1 tomato
1 teaspoon Italian seasonings	1 teaspoon avocado oil
3 oz Parmesan, sliced	

1. Slice the eggplants on 5 slices. Then thinly slice the tomato on 5 slices. Place the eggplants in the air fryer in one layer and cook for 3 minutes from every side at 400F. After this, top the sliced eggplants with tomato, sprinkle with avocado oil and Italian seasonings. Then top the eggplants with Parmesan. Cook the meal for 4 minutes at 400F.

Nutrition:
Calories 116, fat 4.5, fiber 7.9, carbs 14.1, protein 7.7

Bacon Cabbage

Prep time: 5 minutes **Cooking time:** 12 minutes **Servings:** 2

8 oz Chinese cabbage, roughly chopped	2 oz bacon, chopped
1 tablespoon sunflower oil	½ teaspoon onion powder
½ teaspoon salt	

1. Cook the bacon at 400F for 10 minutes. Stir it from time to time. Then sprinkle it with onion powder and salt. Add Chinese cabbage and shake the mixture well. Cook it for 2 minutes. Then add sunflower oil, stir the meal and place in the serving plates.

Nutrition:
Calories 232, fat 19.1, fiber 1.2, carbs 3.4, protein 12.3

Zucchinis and Arugula Mix

Preparation time: 5 minutes **Cooking time:** 20 minutes
Servings: 4

1 pound zucchinis, sliced	1 tablespoon olive oil
Salt and white pepper to the taste 4 ounces arugula leaves	¼ cup chives, chopped 1 cup walnuts, chopped

1. In a pan that fits the air fryer, combine all the ingredients except the arugula and walnuts, toss, put the pan in the machine and cook at 360 degrees F for 20 minutes. Transfer this to a salad bowl, add the arugula and the walnuts, toss and serve as a side salad.

Nutrition:
Calories 170, fat 4, fiber 1, carbs 4, protein 5

Garlic Bread

Prep time: 10 minutes **Cooking time:** 8 minutes **Servings:** 4

1 oz Mozzarella, shredded	2 tablespoons almond flour
1 teaspoon cream cheese	¼ teaspoon garlic powder
¼ teaspoon baking powder	1 egg, beaten
1 teaspoon coconut oil, melted	¼ teaspoon minced garlic
1 teaspoon dried dill	1 oz Provolone cheese, grated

1. In the mixing bowl mix up Mozzarella, almond flour, cream cheese, garlic powder, baking powder, egg, minced garlic, dried dill, and Provolone cheese. When the mixture is homogenous, transfer it on the baking paper and spread it in the shape of the bread. Sprinkle the garlic bread with coconut oil. Preheat the air fryer to 400F. Transfer the baking paper with garlic bread in the air fryer and cook for 8 minutes or until it is light brown. When the garlic bread is cooked, cut it on 4 servings and place it in the serving plates.

Nutrition:
Calories 155, fat 12.7, fiber 1.6, carbs 4, protein 8.3

Lemon Tempeh

Prep time: 8 minutes **Cooking time:** 12 minutes **Servings:** 4

1 teaspoon lemon juice	1 tablespoon sunflower oil
¼ teaspoon ground coriander	6 oz tempeh, chopped

1. Sprinkle the tempeh with lemon juice, sunflower oil, and ground coriander. Massage the tempeh gently with the help of the fingertips. After this, preheat the air fryer to 325F. Put the tempeh in the air fryer and cook it for 12 minutes. Flip the tempeh every 2 minutes during cooking.

Nutrition:
Calories 113, fat 8.1, fiber 0, carbs 4, protein 7.9

Cabbage Slaw

Preparation time: 5 minutes **Cooking time:** 20 minutes
Servings: 4

1 green cabbage head, shredded Juice of ½ lemon	A pinch of salt and black pepper
½ cup coconut cream	½ teaspoon fennel seeds 1 tablespoon mustard

1. In a pan that fits the air fryer, combine the cabbage with the rest of the ingredients, toss, introduce the pan in the machine and cook at 350 degrees F for 20 minutes. Divide between plates and serve right away as a side dish.

Nutrition:
Calories 202, fat 9, fiber 3, carbs 4, protein 7

Lemon Fennel

Preparation time: 5 minutes **Cooking time:** 15 minutes
Servings: 4

1 pound fennel, cut into small wedges A pinch of salt and black pepper	3 tablespoons olive oil
Salt and black pepper to the taste Juice of ½ lemon	2 tablespoons sunflower seeds

1. In a bowl, mix the fennel wedges with all the ingredients except the sunflower seeds, put them in your air fryer's basket and cook at 400 degrees F for 15 minutes. Divide the fennel between plates, sprinkle the sunflower seeds on top, and serve as a side dish.

Nutrition:
Calories 152, fat 4, fiber 2, carbs 4, protein 7

Cauliflower Mash

Preparation time: 5 minutes **Cooking time:** 20 minutes
Servings: 4

pounds cauliflower florets	ounces parmesan, grated 4
1 teaspoon olive oil	ounces butter, soft
Juice of ½ lemon	Zest of ½ lemon, grated
Salt and black pepper to the taste	

1. Preheated you air fryer at 380 degrees F, add the basket inside, add the cauliflower, also add the oil, rub well and cook for 20 minutes. Transfer the cauliflower to a bowl, mash well, add the rest of the ingredients, stir really well, divide between plates and serve as a side dish.

Nutrition:
Calories 174, fat 5, fiber 2, carbs 5, protein 8

Garlic Sprouts

Prep time: 15 minutes **Cooking time:** 13 minutes **Servings:** 6

1-pound Brussels sprouts	1 teaspoon minced garlic
2 oz celery stalks, minced	1 tablespoon butter, melted
1 teaspoon cayenne pepper	¼ teaspoon salt

1. Chop the Brussels sprouts roughly and sprinkle with minced garlic, celery, cayenne pepper, salt, and butter. Shake well and leave for 10 minutes to marinate. Meanwhile, preheat the air fryer to 385F. Put the marinated Brussels sprouts in the air fryer basket and cook them for 13 minutes.
2. Shake the vegetables from time to time during cooking.

Nutrition:
Calories 55, fat 2.3, fiber 3.1, carbs 8.1, protein 2.8

Cilantro Peppers Mix

Prep time: 5 minutes **Cooking time:** 20 minutes **Servings:** 4

8 ounces mini bell peppers, halved	1 tablespoon olive oil
1 tablespoon cilantro, chopped 8 ounces cream cheese, soft	1 cup cheddar cheese, shredded Salt and black pepper to the taste

1. Grease a baking dish that fits the air fryer with the oil and arrange the bell peppers inside. In a bowl, mix all the ingredients, whisk well, spread over the bell peppers, introduce the dish in the air fryer and cook at 370 degrees F for 20 minutes. Divide the peppers between plates and serve as a side dish.

Nutrition:
Calories 200, fat 8, fiber 2, carbs 5, protein 8

Parsley Cauliflower Puree

Prep time: 10 minutes **Cooking time:** 8 minutes **Servings:** 2

1 ½ cup cauliflower, chopped	1 tablespoon butter, melted
½ teaspoon salt	1 tablespoon fresh parsley, chopped
¼ cup heavy cream	Cooking spray

1. Put the cauliflower in the air fryer and spray with cooking spray. Cook it for 8 minutes at 400F. Stir the vegetables after 4 minutes of cooking. Then preheat the heavy cream until it is hot and pour it in the blender. Add cauliflower, parsley, salt, and butter. Blend the mixture until you get the smooth puree.

Nutrition:
Calories 122, fat 11.4, fiber 1.9, carbs 4.5, protein 1.9

Almond Brussels Sprouts

Prep time: 10 minutes **Cooking time:** 15 minutes **Servings:** 4

8 oz Brussels sprouts	2 tablespoons almonds, grinded
1 teaspoon coconut flakes	2 egg whites
½ teaspoon salt	½ teaspoon white pepper
Cooking spray	

1. Whisk the egg whites and add salt and white pepper. Then cut the Brussels sprouts into halves and put the egg white mixture. Shake the vegetables well and then coat in the grinded almonds and coconut flakes. Preheat the air fryer to 380F. Place the Brussels sprouts in the air fryer basket and cook them for 15 minutes. Shake the vegetables after 8 minutes of cooking.

Nutrition:
Calories 52, fat 1.9, fiber 2.6, carbs 6.1, protein 4.4

Lemon Cabbage

Preparation time: 4 minutes **Cooking time:** 25 minutes
Servings: 4

1 green cabbage head, shredded and cut into large wedges	2 tablespoons olive oil
1 tablespoon cilantro, chopped	1 tablespoon lemon juice
A pinch of salt and black pepper	

1. Preheat your air fryer at 370 degrees F, add the cabbage wedges mixed with all the ingredients in the basket and cook for 25 minutes. Divide between plates and serve as a side dish.

Nutrition:
Calories 185, fat 6, fiber 3, carbs 5, protein 4

Chili Rutabaga

Preparation time: 5 minutes **Cooking time:** 20 minutes
Servings: 4

15 ounces rutabaga, cut into fries	4 tablespoons olive oil
teaspoon chili powder	A pinch of salt and black pepper

1. In a bowl, mix the rutabaga fries with all the other ingredients, toss and put them in your air fryer's basket. Cook at 400 degrees F for 20 minutes, divide between plates and serve as a side dish.

Nutrition:
Calories 176, fat 8, fiber 2, carbs 4, protein 4

Cheddar Tomatillos

Prep time: 10 minutes **Cooking time:** 4 minutes **Servings:** 4

2 tomatillos	¼ cup coconut flour
2 eggs, beaten	¼ teaspoon ground nutmeg
¼ teaspoon chili flakes	1 oz Cheddar cheese, shredded
4 lettuce leaves	

1. Slice the tomatillos on 4 slices. Then mix up beaten eggs, ground nutmeg, and chili flakes. Dip the tomatillo slices in the egg mixture and after this, coat in coconut flour. Repeat the steps again. Meanwhile, preheat the air fryer to 400F. Place the coated tomatillos in the air fryer basket in one layer and cook them for 2 minutes from each side. Then place the cooked tomatillos on the lettuce leaves, Sprinkle them with shredded cheese.

Nutrition:
Calories 102, fat 6, fiber 3.4, carbs 6, protein 6.2

Roasted Sprouts and Mushrooms

Prep time: 5 minutes **Cooking time:** 20 minutes **Servings:** 4

1 pound Brussels sprouts, halved	1 tablespoon olive oil
8 ounces brown mushrooms, halved 8 ounces cherry tomatoes, halved	teaspoon rosemary, dried
A pinch of salt and black pepper Juice of 1 lime	

1. In a bowl, mix all the ingredients, toss, put them in your air fryer's basket, cook at 380 degrees F for 20 minutes, divide between plates and serve as a side dish.

Nutrition:
Calories 163, fat 4, fiber 2, carbs 4, protein 8

Lime and Mozzarella Eggplants

Prep 5 minutes **Cooking time:** 15 minutes **Servings:** 4

tablespoons olive oil	2 eggplants, roughly cubed
8 ounces mozzarella cheese, shredded 3 spring onions, chopped	Juice of 1 lime
2 tablespoons butter, melted 4 eggs, whisked	

1. Heat up a pan that fits the air fryer with the oil and the butter over medium-high heat, add the spring onions and the eggplants, stir and cook for 5 minutes. Add the eggs and lime juice and stir well. Sprinkle the cheese on top, introduce the pan in the fryer and cook at 380 degrees F for 10 minutes. Divide between plates and serve as a side dish.

Nutrition:
Calories 212, fat 9, fiber 2, carbs 4, protein 12

Garlic Asparagus

Prep time: 10 minutes **Cooking time:** 5 minutes **Servings:** 3

9 oz Asparagus	¼ teaspoon chili powder
¼ teaspoon garlic powder	1 teaspoon olive oil
4 Provolone cheese slices	

1. Trim the asparagus and sprinkle with chili powder and garlic powder. The preheat the air fryer to 400F. Put the asparagus in the air fryer basket and sprinkle with olive oil. Cook the vegetables for 3 minutes. Then top the asparagus with Provolone cheese and cook for 3 minutes more.

Nutrition:
Calories 163, fat 11.6, fiber 1.9, carbs 4.4, protein 11.5

Spinach Mash

Prep time: 10 minutes **Cooking time:** 13 minutes **Servings:** 4

3 cups spinach, chopped	½ cup Mozzarella, shredded
4 bacon slices, chopped	1 teaspoon butter
1 cup heavy cream	½ teaspoon salt
½ jalapeno pepper, chopped	

1. Place the bacon in the air fryer and cook it for 8 minutes at 400F. Stir it from time to time with the help of the spatula. After this, put the cooked bacon in the air fryer casserole mold. Add heavy cream spinach, jalapeno pepper, salt, butter, and Mozzarella. Stir it gently. Cook the mash for 5 minutes at 400F. Then stir the spinach mash carefully with the help of the spoon,

Nutrition:
Calories 230, fat 20.7, fiber 0.6, carbs 2.2, protein 9.3

Butter Cabbage

Preparation time: 5 minutes **Cooking time:** 20 minutes
Servings: 4

ounces butter, melted	1 green cabbage head, shredded 1 and ½ cups heavy cream
¼ cup parsley, chopped	1 tablespoon sweet paprika
1 teaspoon lemon zest, grated	

1. Heat up a pan that fits the air fryer with the butter, add the cabbage and sauté for 5 minutes. Add the remaining ingredients, toss, put the pan in the air fryer and cook at 380 degrees F for 15 minutes. Divide between plates and serve as a side dish.

Nutrition:
Calories 174, fat 4, fiber 3, carbs 5, protein 8

Cheese Broccoli

Prep time: 10 minutes **Cooking time:** 7 minutes **Servings:** 4

1 cup broccoli, chopped, boiled	1 teaspoon nut oil
1 teaspoon salt	1 teaspoon dried basil
½ cup Cheddar cheese, shredded	½ cup of coconut milk
½ teaspoon butter, softened	

1. Put broccoli in the air fryer pan. Add nut oil, salt, and dried dill. Stir the vegetables well and add coconut milk. Then add butter and top the meal with Cheddar cheese. Stir the meal gently. Preheat the air fryer to 400F and put the pan with the vegetable mixture inside. Cook it for 7 minutes.

Nutrition:
Calories 154, fat 13.6, fiber 1.9, carbs 4.7, protein 5.4

Turmeric Cauliflower

Prep time: 10 minutes **Cooking time:** 8 minutes **Servings:** 4

1-pound cauliflower head	1 tablespoon ground turmeric
1 tablespoon coconut oil	½ teaspoon dried cilantro
¼ teaspoon salt	

1. Slice the cauliflower head on 4 steaks. Then rub every cauliflower steak with dried cilantro, salt, and ground turmeric. Sprinkle the steaks with coconut oil. Preheat the air fryer to 400F. Place the cauliflower steaks in the air fryer basket and cook for 4 minutes from each side.

Nutrition:
Calories 64, fat 3.7, fiber 3.2, carbs 7.1, protein 2.4

Butter Green Beans

Prep time: 5 minutes **Cooking time:** 20 minutes **Servings:** 4

10 ounces green beans, trimmed A pinch of salt and black pepper 3 ounces butter, melted
¼ cup parsley, chopped 2 garlic cloves, minced

1 cup coconut cream Zest of ½ lemon, grated

1. In a bowl, the butter with all the ingredients except the green beans and whisk really well. Put the green beans in a pan that fits the air fryer, drizzle the buttery sauce all over, introduce the pan in the machine and cook at 370 degrees F for 20 minutes. Divide between plates and serve as a side dish.

Nutrition:

Calories 200, fat 9, fiber 2, carbs 4, protein 9

Zucchini Nests

Prep time: 15 minutes **Cooking time:** 6 minutes **Servings:** 6

10 oz zucchini, grated
1 tablespoon coconut flour
¼ teaspoon cayenne pepper

4 quail eggs
1 oz Parmesan, grated
1 teaspoon butter, melted

1. Brush the muffin molds with butter. Then mix up cayenne pepper and grated zucchini. Put the vegetable mixture in the muffin molds and flatten it in the shape of the nests. After this, crack the quail eggs in the nests and sprinkle with grated Parmesan. Preheat the air fryer to 390F. Put the muffin molds with nests in the air fryer basket and cook for 6 minutes.

Nutrition:

Calories 44, fat 2.6, fiber 1, carbs 2.6, protein 3.1

Curry Cabbage Sauté

Prep time: 5 minutes **Cooking time:** 20 minutes **Servings:** 4

30 ounces green cabbage, shredded
3 tablespoons coconut oil, melted

1 tablespoon red curry paste
A pinch of salt and black pepper

1. In a pan that fits the air fryer, combine the cabbage with the rest of the ingredients, toss, introduce the pan in the machine and cook at 380 degrees F for 20 minutes. Divide between plates and serve as a side dish.

Nutrition:

Calories 180, fat 14, fiber 4, carbs 6, protein 8

Jalapeno Clouds

Prep time: 10 minutes **Cooking time:** 4 minutes **Servings:** 4

2 egg whites
1 teaspoon almond flour

1 jalapeno pepper
1 oz Jarlsberg cheese, grated

1. Whisk the egg whites until you get the strong peaks. After this, carefully mix up egg white peaks, almond flour, and Jarlsberg cheese. Slice the jalapeno pepper on 4 slices. Preheat the air fryer to 385F. Line the air fryer basket with baking paper. With the help of the spoon make the egg white clouds on the baking paper. Top the clouds with sliced jalapeno.
2. Cook them for 4 minutes or until the clouds are light brown.

Nutrition:

Calories 75, fat 5.6, fiber 0.9, carbs 1.8, protein 5.1

Broccoli Puree

Prep time: 5 minutes **Cooking time:** 20 minutes **Servings:** 4

20 ounces broccoli florets
A drizzle of olive oil

1 garlic clove, minced

4 tablespoons basil, chopped 3 ounces butter, melted
A pinch of salt and black pepper

1. In a bowl, mix the broccoli with the oil, salt and pepper, toss and transfer to your air fryer's basket. Cook at 380 degrees F for 20 minutes, cool the broccoli down and put it in a blender. Add the rest of the ingredients, pulse, divide the mash between plates and serve as a side dish.

Nutrition:

Calories 200, fat 14, fiber 3, carbs 6, protein 7

Dill Cabbage Sauté

Prep time: 5 minutes **Cooking time:** 20 minutes **Servings:** 4

30 ounces red cabbage, shredded
A pinch of salt and black pepper
1 tablespoon red wine vinegar

4 ounces butter, melted

1 teaspoon cinnamon powder
2 tablespoons dill, chopped

1. In a pan that fits your air fryer, mix the cabbage with the rest of the ingredients, toss, put the pan in the machine and cook at 390 degrees F for 20 minutes. Divide between plates and serve as a side dish.

Nutrition:

Calories 201, fat 17, fiber 2, carbs 5, protein 5

Coconut Celery and Broccoli Mash

Prep time: 10 minutes **Cooking time:** 5 minutes **Servings:** 2

7 oz broccoli florets

½ teaspoon salt
2 tablespoons coconut cream

1 tablespoon almond butter
2 oz celery stalk, chopped
Cooking spray

1. Preheat the air fryer to 400F. Then put the broccoli florets and celery stalk in the air fryer basket and spray them with cooking spray. Cook the vegetables for 5 minutes at 400F. Then put the cooked vegetables in the blender and blend them until you get a puree. After this, put the puree in the bowl. Add salt, almond butter, and coconut cream. Stir the puree with the help of the spoon.

Nutrition:

Calories 122, fat 8.5, fiber 4.2, carbs 9.8, protein 5

Cumin Brussels Sprouts

Prep time: 5 minutes **Cooking time:** 15 minutes **Servings:** 4

1 pound Brussels sprouts, trimmed and shredded
Zest of 1 lemon, grated

¼ cup almonds, toasted and chopped
1 teaspoon chili paste

½ cup olive oil Juice of 1 lemon
A pinch of salt and black pepper

½ teaspoon cumin, crushed

1. In a pan that fits the air fryer, combine the Brussels sprouts with all the other ingredients, toss, put the pan in the fryer and cook at 390 degrees F for 15 minutes. Divide between plates and serve as a side dish.

Nutrition:

Calories 200, fat 9, fiber 2, carbs 6, protein 9

Collard Greens with Peanuts

Prep time: 10 minutes **Cooking time:** 10 minutes **Servings:** 4

2 cups collard greens, chopped	3 oz bacon, chopped
1 teaspoon butter, melted	1 oz peanuts, chopped
¼ teaspoon salt	

1. Preheat the air fryer to 400F. Put the bacon in the air fryer basket and cook for 8 minutes. Stir it from time to time. After this, add collard greens and salt. Mix up the mixture and cook for 2 minutes more. Transfer the cooked meal in the serving plates and top with butter and peanuts.

Nutrition:
Calories 170, fat 13.5, fiber 1.4, carbs 2.7, protein 10.2

Parsley Zucchini Spaghetti

Prep time: 5 minutes **Cooking time:** 15 minutes **Servings:** 4

1 pound zucchinis, cut with a spiralizer	¼ cup olive oil
Salt and black pepper to the taste	6 garlic cloves, minced
½ teaspoon red pepper flakes	1 cup parmesan, grated
¼ cup parsley, chopped	

1. In a pan that fits your air fryer, mix all the ingredients, toss, introduce in the fryer and cook at 370 degrees F for 15 minutes. Divide between plates and serve as a side dish.

Nutrition:
Calories 200, fat 6, fiber 3, carbs 4, protein 5

Garlic Broccoli Rabe

Prep time: 10 minutes **Cooking time:** 20 minutes **Servings:** 4

7 oz broccoli rabe, roughly chopped	2 tablespoons almond flour
1 teaspoon coconut oil, melted	¼ teaspoon salt
1 tablespoon avocado oil	1 teaspoon garlic powder

1. Preheat the air fryer to 355F. In the mixing bowl, mix up broccoli rabe, salt, garlic powder, and melted coconut oil. Mix up the greens and sprinkle them with almond flour. Shake them well. After this, sprinkle the broccoli rabe with avocado oil and transfer in the air fryer. Cook the greens for 20 minutes. Shake them every 5 minutes to avoid burning.

Nutrition:
Calories 108, fat 8.6, fiber 1.7, carbs 5.5, protein 4.3

Coconut Risotto

Preparation time: 5 minutes **Cooking time:** 20 minutes **Servings:** 4

cups cauliflower rice 1 cup coconut milk	2 tablespoons coconut oil, melted 1 tablespoon cilantro, chopped
1 tablespoon olive oil tablespoons parmesan, grated	teaspoon lime zest, grated

1. In a pan that fits your air fryer, mix all the ingredients, stir, introduce in the fryer and cook at 360 degrees F for 20 minutes. Divide between plates and serve as a side dish.

Nutrition:
Calories 193, fat 4, fiber 3, carbs 5, protein 6

Creamy Cauliflower

Prep time: 10 minutes **Cooking time:** 25 minutes **Servings:** 4

8 oz cauliflower florets, boiled	½ cup ground chicken
1 tablespoon keto tomato sauce	1 tablespoon coconut oil
2 tablespoons cream cheese	½ cup Mozzarella cheese, shredded
1 teaspoon fresh parsley, chopped	1 teaspoon salt
1 teaspoon cayenne pepper	½ teaspoon basil

1. Put the coconut oil in the skillet and melt it over the medium heat. Then add ground chicken, salt, cayenne pepper, and parsley. Add basil and mix up the ground chicken mixture. Cook it for 5 minutes. Then stir well and add tomato sauce. Mix up the mixture well. Put the ½ part of cauliflower florets in the air fryer pan. Then top them with ground chicken mixture.
2. Cover this layer with remaining cauliflower, cream cheese, and Mozzarella cheese. Cook the meal at 375F for 10 minutes.

Nutrition:
Calories 109, fat 7.2, fiber 1.7, carbs 4.3, protein 7.8

Goat Cheese Cauliflower and Bacon

Preparation time: 5 minutes **Cooking time:** 20 minutes **Servings:** 4

8 cups cauliflower florets, roughly chopped 4 bacon strips, chopped	Salt and black pepper to the taste
½ cup spring onions, chopped	1 tablespoon garlic, minced
10 ounces goat cheese, crumbled	¼ cup soft cream cheese Cooking spray

1. Grease a baking pan that fits the air fryer with the cooking spray and mix all the ingredients except the goat cheese into the pan. Sprinkle the cheese on top, introduce the pan in the machine and cook at 400 degrees F for 20 minutes. Divide between plates and serve as a side dish.

Nutrition:
Calories 203, fat 13, fiber 2, carbs 5, protein 9

Asparagus and Green Beans Salad

Prep time: 15 minutes **Cooking time:** 6 minutes **Servings:** 3

3 oz asparagus, chopped	2 oz green beans, chopped
1 cup arugula, chopped	1 tablespoon hazelnuts, chopped
1 teaspoon flax seeds	2 oz Mozzarella, chopped
1 tablespoon olive oil	½ teaspoon salt
½ teaspoon ground paprika	½ teaspoon ground black pepper
Cooking spray	

1. Preheat the air fryer to 400F. Put the asparagus and green beans in the air fryer and spray them with cooking spray. Cook the vegetables for 6 minutes at 400F. Shake the vegetables after 3 minutes of cooking. Then cool them to the room temperature and put in the salad bowl. Add hazelnuts, flax seeds, chopped Mozzarella, salt, ground paprika, and ground black pepper. Sprinkle the salad with olive oil and shake well.

Nutrition:
Calories 122, fat 9.4, fiber 1.9, carbs 4.3, protein 6.9

Cinnamon Cauliflower

Prep time: 5 minutes **Cooking time:** 15 minutes **Servings:** 4

1 cauliflower head, florets separated 1 tablespoon butter, melted	A pinch of salt and black pepper 1 tablespoon olive oil
¼ teaspoon turmeric powder	½ teaspoon cumin, ground
¼ teaspoon cinnamon powder	¼ teaspoon cloves, ground

1. In a bowl, mix cauliflower florets with the rest of the ingredients and toss. Put the cauliflower in your air fryer's basket and cook at 390 degrees F for 15 minutes. Divide between plates and serve as a side dish.

Nutrition:
Calories 182, fat 8, fiber 2, carbs 4, protein 8

Lemongrass Cauliflower

Prep time: 10 minutes **Cooking time:** 12 minutes **Servings:** 4

2 cups cauliflower florets	1 teaspoon curry paste
¼ teaspoon lemongrass, chopped	2 tablespoons heavy cream
1 tablespoon avocado oil	1 teaspoon fresh cilantro, chopped
Cooking spray	

1. In the bowl whisk together curry paste, lemongrass, heavy cream, avocado oil, and fresh cilantro. Then sprinkle the cauliflower florets with curry mixture and shake well. Preheat the air fryer to 395F and place the cauliflower florets in the air fryer basket. Cook the vegetables for 7 minutes. Then flip them on another side and cook for 5 minutes more.

Nutrition:
Calories 52, fat 4, fiber 1.4, carbs 3.4, protein 1.2

Kale Mash

Prep time: 5 minutes **Cooking time:** 20 minutes **Servings:** 4

1 cauliflower head, florets separated 4 teaspoons butter, melted	4 garlic cloves, minced 3 cups kale, chopped
2 scallions, chopped	A pinch of salt and black pepper 1/3 cup coconut cream
tablespoon parsley, chopped	

1. In a pan that fits the air fryer, combine the cauliflower with the butter, garlic, scallions, salt, pepper and the cream, toss, introduce the pan in the machine and cook at 380 degrees F for 20 minutes. Mash the mix well, add the remaining ingredients, whisk, divide between plates and serve.

Nutrition:
Calories 198, fat 9, fiber 2, carbs 6, protein 8

Leeks and Spring Onions

Prep time: 10 minutes **Cooking time:** 6 minutes **Servings:** 4

1 cup spring onions, chopped	3 leeks, sliced
2 oz Parmesan, grated	1 egg, beaten
½ teaspoon ground black pepper	1 teaspoon dried parsley

1. Preheat the air fryer to 400F. Combine all the ingredients inside and cook for 6 minutes.
2. Divide between plates and serve.

Nutrition:
Calories 91, fat 4.5, fiber 2, carbs 6.6, protein 6.9

Chives Cauliflower and Kale Puree

Prep time: 10 minutes **Cooking time:** 5 minutes **Servings:** 2

1 cup kale, chopped	1 cup cauliflower, chopped, boiled
2 tablespoons butter	½ teaspoon salt
1 teaspoon olive oil	1 tablespoon chives
1 tablespoon ricotta cheese	

1. Preheat the air fryer to 400F. Mash the cauliflower. In the air fryer pan mix up chopped kale, mashed cauliflower, butter, salt, olive oil, and ricotta cheese. Place the mixture in the air fryer and cook for 5 minutes. Then stir the mixture until smooth and transfer in the serving plates.

Nutrition:
Calories 162, fat 14.5, fiber 1.8, carbs 6.6, protein 3

Chili Cauliflower

Preparation time: 5 minutes **Cooking time:** 20 minutes **Servings:** 4

cups cauliflower florets, roughly chopped	1 tablespoon olive oil
Salt and black pepper to the taste 4 garlic cloves, minced	1 red chili pepper, chopped 2 tomatoes, cubed
1 teaspoon cumin powder	½ teaspoon chili powder
1 tablespoon coriander, chopped	avocado, peeled, pitted and sliced
1 tablespoon lime juice	

1. In a pan that fits the air fryer, combine the cauliflower with the other ingredients except the coriander, avocado and lime juice, toss, introduce the pan in the machine and cook at 380 degrees F for 20 minutes. Divide between plates, top each serving with coriander, avocado and lime juice and serve as a side dish.

Nutrition:
Calories 187, fat 8, fiber 2, carbs 5, protein 7

Parmesan Cauliflower Risotto

Prep time: 10 minutes **Cooking time:** 18 minutes **Servings:** 4

1 cup cauliflower, shredded	4 oz cremini mushrooms, sliced
2 oz Parmesan, grated	1 teaspoon ground black pepper
1 tablespoon heavy cream	¼ teaspoon garlic powder
3 spring onions, diced	1 tablespoon olive oil
½ teaspoon Italian seasonings	

1. Preheat the air fryer to 400f. Then sprinkle the air fryer basket with olive oil. Place the mushrooms inside and sprinkle them with ground black pepper. Cook them at 400F for 4 minutes. Then stir them well and add the spring onion. Cook the vegetables for 4 minutes more. Then shake them well and sprinkle with garlic powder and Italian seasonings. Mix up well and transfer in the air fryer mold. Add heavy cream and shredded cauliflower. Then add parmesan and mix up. Place the mold in the air fryer and cook for 10 minutes at 375F. Then mix up risotto and transfer in the serving plates.

Nutrition:
Calories 112 fat 8.2, fiber 1.3, carbs 5, protein 6.2

Green Celery Puree

Prep time: 10 minutes **Cooking time:** 6 minutes **Servings:** 6

1-pound celery stalks, chopped	½ cup spinach, chopped
2 oz Parmesan, grated	¼ cup chicken broth
½ teaspoon cayenne pepper	

1. In the air fryer pan, mix celery stalk with chopped spinach, chicken broth, and cayenne pepper. Blend the mixture until homogenous. After this, top the puree with Parmesan. Preheat the air fryer to 400F. Put the pan with puree in the air fryer basket and cook the meal for 6 minutes.

Nutrition:

Calories 65, fat 2.4, fiber 1.5, carbs 7.5, protein 4.5

Butter Risotto

Prep time: 5 minutes **Cooking time:** 20 minutes **Servings:** 6

2 tablespoons butter, melted 1 pound cauliflower, riced 2 garlic cloves, minced	½ cup chicken stock 1 cup heavy cream
1 cup parmesan, grated	3 tablespoons sun-dried tomatoes
½ teaspoon nutmeg, ground	

1. Heat up a pan that fits your air fryer with the butter over medium heat, add cauliflower rice, stir and cook for 2 minutes. Add the rest of the ingredients, toss, introduce the pan in the fryer and cook at 360 degrees F for 20 minutes. Divide between plates and serve as a side dish.

Nutrition:

Calories 193, fat 8, fiber 2, carbs 5, protein 9

Harissa Cauliflower

Prep time: 10 minutes **Cooking time:** 11 minutes **Servings:** 3

1 cup cauliflower, chopped	1 teaspoon harissa
1 teaspoon tahini	3 tablespoons olive oil
¼ teaspoon ground paprika	1 garlic clove
Cooking spray	

1. Preheat the air fryer to 400F. Then put the cauliflower and garlic clove in the air fryer and sprinkle with 1 teaspoon of olive oil. Cook the vegetables for 11 minutes. Then transfer the cooked cauliflower in the food processor. Add tahini, harissa, remaining olive oil, and ground paprika.
2. Blend the mixture until smooth. Transfer the hummus in the serving bowl.

Nutrition:

Calories 146, fat 15.2, fiber 1.1, carbs 3.2, protein 1.1

Basil Squash

Prep time: 5 minutes **Cooking time:** 10 minutes **Servings:** 4

1 teaspoon sesame oil	1 teaspoon dried basil
6 oz Kabocha squash, roughly chopped	

1. Sprinkle the squash with dried basil and sesame oil and place it in the air fryer basket. Cook the vegetables at 400F for 4 minutes. Then shake them well and cook for 6 minutes more. The time of cooking depends on kabocha squash size.

Nutrition:

Calories 25, fat 1.1, fiber 0.5, carbs 3.5, protein 0.5

Mashed Chives Celery

Preparation time: 5 minutes **Cooking time:** 20 minutes **Servings:** 4

14 ounces celery stalks 1 cup cauliflower florets	Salt and black pepper to the taste 2 garlic cloves, minced
1/3 cup heavy cream tablespoon chives, chopped Zest of 1 lemon, grated	4 ounces butter, melted

1. In a pan that fits your air fryer, mix all the ingredients except the chives and the cream, stir, introduce the pan in the machine and cook at 360 degrees F for 20 minutes. Mash the mix, add the rest of the ingredients, whisk well, divide between plates and serve as a side dish.

Nutrition:

Calories 201, fat 9, fiber 2, carbs 6, protein 9

Mixed Veggies

Prep time: 10 minutes **Cooking time:** 5 minutes **Servings:** 4

½ cup cauliflower, diced	½ cup zucchini, diced
1/3 cup cherry tomatoes, chopped	¼ cup black olives, chopped
3 oz halloumi cheese, chopped	1 tablespoon olive oil
½ teaspoon chili flakes	½ teaspoon dried basil
½ teaspoon salt	Cooking spray

1. Put the diced cauliflower in the air fryer pan. Spray them with cooking spray and then add zucchini. Preheat the air fryer to 395F and put the pan with vegetables inside it. Cook the vegetables for 5 minutes. Then shake them well and transfer in the salad bowl. Add cherry tomatoes, black olives, chopped halloumi, chili flakes, basil, and salt. Then add olive oil and mix up the anti-pasta.

Nutrition:

Calories 125, fat 25.8, fiber 0.9, carbs 2.8, protein 5.2

Balsamic Zucchinis

Preparation time: 5 minutes **Cooking time:** 20 minutes **Servings:** 4

pounds zucchinis, sliced	2 ounces feta cheese, crumbled
1 tablespoon parsley, chopped	¼ cup olive oil
2 tablespoons balsamic vinegar	1 teaspoon thyme, dried
A pinch of salt and black pepper	

1. In a pan that fits your air fryer, mix the zucchini slices with the other ingredients except the cheese and toss. Sprinkle the cheese on top, introduce the pan in the fryer and cook at 400 degrees F for 20 minutes. Divide between plates and serve as a side dish.

Nutrition:

Calories 203, fat 9, fiber 3, carbs 6, protein 5

Basil Zucchini Noodles

Preparation time: 5 minutes **Cooking time:** 15 minutes
Servings: 4

4 zucchinis, cut with a spiralizer	1 tablespoon olive oil
4 garlic cloves, minced	1 and ½ cups tomatoes, crushed Salt and black pepper to the taste 1 tablespoon basil, chopped
¼ cup green onions, chopped	

1. In a pan that fits your air fryer, mix zucchini noodles with the other ingredients, toss, introduce in the fryer and cook at 380 degrees F for 15 minutes. Divide between plates and serve as a side dish.

Nutrition:
Calories 194, fat 7, fiber 2, carbs 4, protein 9

Ricotta Asparagus Mix

Prep time: 10 minutes **Cooking time:** 5 minutes **Servings:** 4

11 oz asparagus, trimmed	5 oz gouda cheese, grated
1 teaspoon ground paprika	¼ teaspoon salt
1 teaspoon olive oil	¼ tablespoon ricotta cheese

1. Slice the asparagus and sprinkle it with ground paprika, salt, and olive oil. Then place it in the air fryer mold and top with grated gouda cheese and ricotta cheese. Preheat the air fryer to 400F. Insert the mold in the air fryer basket and cook the meal for 5 minutes.

Nutrition:
Calories 155, fat 11.1, fiber 1.8, carbs 4.2, protein 10.8Zucchini Fritters

Prep time: 10 minutes **Cooking time:** 10 minutes **Servings:** 4

2 zucchinis, grated	4 oz Blue cheese
1 egg, beaten	1 tablespoon flax meal
1 teaspoon dried cilantro	¼ teaspoon salt
¼ cup spring onions, chopped	1 teaspoon olive oil
3 oz celery stalk, diced	1 tablespoon coconut flour

1. Crumble Blue cheese and mix it up with grated zucchini. Add egg, flax meal, dried cilantro, salt, spring onions, diced celery stalk, and coconut flour. Then stir the ingredients with the help of the spoon until homogenous. Make the fritters and sprinkle them with olive oil. After this, preheat the air fryer to 400F. Place the zucchini fritters in the air fryer and cook them for 5 minutes. Then flip the fritters on another side and cook for 5 minutes more or until they are golden brown.

Nutrition:
Calories 164, fat 11.6, fiber 2.8, carbs 6.9, protein 9.6

Lemon Squash

Preparation time: 5 minutes **Cooking time:** 25 minutes
Servings: 4

4 summer squash, cut into wedges	¼ cup olive oil
¼ cup lemon juice	½ cup mint, chopped
cup mozzarella, shredded	Salt and black pepper to the taste

1. In a pan that fits your air fryer, mix the squash with the rest of the ingredients, toss, introduce the pan in the air fryer and cook at 370 degrees F for 25 minutes. Divide between plates and serve as a side dish.

Nutrition:
Calories 201, fat 7, fiber 2, carbs 4, protein 9

Coconut Zucchini Gratin

Preparation time: 5 minutes **Cooking time:** 25 minutes
Servings: 4

4 cups zucchinis, sliced	1 and ½ cups mozzarella, shredded 2 tablespoons butter, melted
½ teaspoon garlic powder	½ cup coconut cream
½ tablespoon parsley, chopped	

1. In a baking pan that fits the air fryer, mix all the ingredients except the mozzarella and the parsley, and toss. Sprinkle the mozzarella and parsley, introduce in the air fryer and cook at 370 degrees F for 25 minutes. Divide between plates and serve as a side dish.

Nutrition:
Calories 220, fat 14, fiber 2, carbs 5, protein 9

Parmesan Artichokes and Cauliflower

Prep time: 5 minutes **Cooking time:** 20 minutes **Servings:** 4

1 tablespoon olive oil	1 cup cauliflower florets 2 garlic cloves, minced
½ cup chicken stock	1 pound artichoke hearts, chopped 1 tablespoon parmesan, grated
1 and ½ tablespoons parsley, chopped Salt and black pepper to the taste	

1. In a pan that fits your air fryer, mix all the ingredients except the parmesan and toss. Sprinkle the parmesan on top, introduce the pan in the air fryer and cook at 380 degrees F for 20 minutes. Divide between plates and serve as a side dish.

Nutrition:
Calories 195, fat 6, fiber 2, carbs 4, protein 8

Zucchini Latkes

Prep time: 15 minutes **Cooking time:** 12 minutes **Servings:** 6

7 oz zucchini, grated	1 egg, beaten
1 teaspoon salt	2 spring onions, chopped
2 tablespoons almond flour	1 teaspoon avocado oil
½ teaspoon ground black pepper	

1. In the mixing bowl mix up grated zucchini, egg, salt, chopped onion, almond flour, and ground black pepper. With the help of the spoon make medium-sized latkes. Preheat the air fryer to 390F. Place the latkes in the air fryer in one layer and sprinkle with avocado oil. Cook the side dish for 6 minutes from each side.

Nutrition:
Calories 72, fat 5.6, fiber 1.5, carbs 3.8, protein 3.4

Hot Broccoli

Prep time: 10 minutes **Cooking time:** 5 minutes **Servings:** 4

11 oz broccoli stems	1 tablespoon olive oil
¼ teaspoon chili powder	

1. Preheat the air fryer to 400F. Then chop the broccoli stems roughly and sprinkle with chili powder and olive oil. Transfer the greens in the preheated air fryer and cook them for 5 minutes.

Nutrition:
Calories 57, fat 3.8, fiber 2.1, carbs 5.3, protein 2.2

Pesto Pasta

Prep time: 5 minutes **Cooking time:** 15 minutes **Servings:** 4

cups zucchinis, cut with a spiralizer Salt and black pepper to the taste	1 tablespoon olive oil
½ cup coconut cream	4 ounces mozzarella, shredded
¼ cup basil pesto	

1. In a pan that fits your air fryer, mix the zucchini noodles with the pesto and the rest of the ingredients, toss, introduce the pan in the fryer and cook at 370 degrees F for 15 minutes. Divide between plates and serve as a side dish.

Nutrition:

Calories 200, fat 8, fiber 2, carbs 4, protein 10

Parm Squash

Prep time: 10 minutes **Cooking time:** 25 minutes **Servings:** 4

1 medium spaghetti squash	2 oz Mozzarella, shredded
1 oz Parmesan, shredded	1 teaspoon avocado oil
½ teaspoon dried oregano	½ teaspoon dried cilantro
½ teaspoon ground nutmeg	2 teaspoons butter

1. Cut the spaghetti squash into halves and remove the seeds. Then sprinkle it with avocado oil, dried oregano, dried cilantro, and ground nutmeg. Put 1 teaspoon of butter in every spaghetti squash half and transfer the vegetables in the air fryer. Cook them for 15 minutes at 365F. After this, fill the squash with Mozzarella and Parmesan and cook for 10 minutes more at the same temperature.

Nutrition:

Calories 91, fat 6.3, fiber 0.2, carbs 2.8, protein 6.5

Paprika Green Beans

Prep time: 5 minutes **Cooking time:** 20 minutes **Servings:** 4

6 cups green beans, trimmed	2 tablespoons olive oil
1 tablespoon hot paprika	A pinch of salt and black pepper

1. In a bowl, mix the green beans with the other ingredients, toss, put them in the air fryer's basket and cook at 370 degrees F for 20 minutes. Divide between plates and serve as a side dish.

Nutrition:

Calories 120, fat 5, fiber 1, carbs 4, protein 2

Garlic Lemony Asparagus

Preparation time: 5 minutes **Cooking time:** 15 minutes **Servings:** 4

1 bunch asparagus, trimmed	Salt and black pepper to the taste 4 tablespoons olive oil
4 garlic cloves, minced	3 tablespoons parmesan, grated
Juice of ½ lemon	

1. In a bowl, mix the asparagus with all the ingredients except the parmesan, toss, transfer it to your air fryer's basket and cook at 400 degrees F for 15 minutes. Divide between plates, sprinkle the parmesan on top and serve as a side dish.

Nutrition:

Calories 173, fat 12, fiber 2, carbs 5, protein 7

Pecorino Zucchini

Prep time: 15 minutes **Cooking time:** 5 minutes **Servings:** 5

1 large zucchini	2 cherry tomatoes, chopped
1 bell pepper, diced	3 spring onions, diced
1 tablespoon sesame oil	4 oz Pecorino cheese, grated
½ teaspoon chili flakes	¼ teaspoon minced garlic
1 teaspoon flax seeds	

1. Make the spirals from the zucchini with the help of the spiralizer and sprinkle with sesame oil. Then place them in the air fryer, add diced bell pepper, and cook for 5 minutes at 355F. After this, transfer the cooked vegetables in the big bowl. Add cherry tomatoes, spring onions, Pecorino, chili flakes, minced garlic, and flax seeds. Mix up zucchini Primavera with the help of 2 spatulas.

Nutrition:

Calories 169, fat 12.2, fiber 1.9, carbs 6.6, protein 10.7

Swiss Chard Mix

Prep time: 10 minutes **Cooking time:** 15 minutes **Servings:** 5

7 oz Swiss chard, chopped	4 oz Swiss cheese, grated
4 teaspoons almond flour	½ cup heavy cream
½ teaspoon ground black pepper	

1. Mix up Swiss chard and Swiss cheese. Add almond flour, heavy cream, and ground black pepper. Stir the mixture until homogenous. After this, transfer it in 5 small ramekins. Preheat the air fryer to 365F. Place the ramekins with gratin in the air fryer basket and cook them for 15 minutes.

Nutrition:

Calories 264, fat 22.1, fiber 3.1, carbs 8, protein 11.9

Balsamic Greens Sauté

Prep time: 5 minutes **Cooking time:** 15 minutes **Servings:** 4

1 pound collard greens	¼ cup cherry tomatoes, halved
1 tablespoon balsamic vinegar	A pinch of salt and black pepper
2 tablespoons chicken stock	

1. In a pan that fits your air fryer, mix the collard greens with the other ingredients, toss gently, introduce in the air fryer and cook at 360 degrees F for 15 minutes. Divide between plates and serve as a side dish.

Nutrition:

Calories 121, fat 3, fiber 4, carbs 6, protein 5

Butter Zucchini Noodles

Prep time: 5 minutes **Cooking time:** 15 minutes **Servings:** 4

1 pound zucchinis, cut with a spiralizer 2 tomatoes, cubed	3 tablespoons butter, melted 4 garlic cloves, minced
3 tablespoons parsley, chopped Salt and black pepper to the taste	

1. In a pan that fits your air fryer, mix all the ingredients, toss, introduce in the fryer and cook at 350 degrees F for 15 minutes. Divide between plates and serve as a side dish.

Nutrition:

Calories 170, fat 6, fiber 2, carbs 5, protein 6

Smoked Asparagus

Prep time: 5 minutes **Cooking time:** 20 minutes **Servings:** 4

pound asparagus stalks	Salt and black pepper to the taste
¼ cup olive oil+ 1 teaspoon 1 tablespoon smoked paprika	tablespoons balsamic vinegar
1 tablespoon lime juice	

1. In a bowl, mix the asparagus with salt, pepper and 1 teaspoon oil, toss, transfer to your air fryer's basket and cook at 370 degrees F for 20 minutes. Meanwhile, in a bowl, mix all the other ingredients and whisk them well. Divide the asparagus between plates, drizzle the balsamic vinaigrette all over and serve as a side dish.

Nutrition:

Calories 187, fat 6, fiber 2, carbs 4, protein 9

Dill Bok Choy

Prep time: 20 minutes **Cooking time:** 5 minutes **Servings:** 2

6 oz bok choy	1 teaspoon sesame seeds
1 garlic clove, diced	1 tablespoon olive oil
1 teaspoon fresh dill, chopped	1 teaspoon apple cider vinegar

1. Preheat the air fryer to 350F. Then chop the bok choy roughly and sprinkle with olive oil, diced garlic, olive oil, fresh dill, and apple cider vinegar. Mix up the bok choy and leave to marinate for 15 minutes. Then transfer the marinated bok choy in the air fryer basket and cook for 5 minutes. Shake it after 3 minutes of cooking. Transfer the cooked vegetables in the bowl and sprinkle with sesame seeds. Shake the meal gently before serving.

Nutrition:

Calories 84, fat 8, fiber 1.1, carbs 3, protein 1.8

Bacon Green Beans Mix

Prep time: 15 minutes **Cooking time:** 13 minutes **Servings:** 4

1 cup green beans, trimmed	4 oz bacon, sliced
¼ teaspoon salt	1 tablespoon avocado oil

1. Wrap the green beans in the sliced bacon. After this, sprinkle the vegetables with salt and avocado oil. Preheat the air fryer to 385F. Carefully arrange the green beans in the air fryer in one layer and cook them for 5 minutes. Then flip the green beans on another side and cook for 8 minutes more.

Nutrition:

Calories 167, fat 12.3, fiber 0.9, carbs 2.6, protein 10.5

Garlic Endives and Scallions

Preparation time: 5 minutes **Cooking time:** 20 minutes **Servings:** 4

scallions, chopped	garlic cloves, minced 1 tablespoon olive oil
Salt and black pepper to the taste 1 teaspoon chili sauce	endives, trimmed and roughly shredded

1. Grease a pan that fits your air fryer with the oil, add all the ingredients, toss, introduce in the air fryer and cook at 370 degrees F for 20 minutes. Divide everything between plates and serve.

Nutrition:

Calories 184, fat 2, fiber 2, carbs 3, protein 5

Nutmeg and Dill Ravioli

Prep time: 20 minutes **Cooking time:** 8 minutes **Servings:** 6

4 tablespoons almond flour	2 tablespoons coconut flour
1 tablespoon xanthan gum	½ teaspoon baking powder
1 egg, beaten	1 tablespoon water
1 teaspoon apple cider vinegar	4 tablespoons ricotta cheese
½ teaspoon minced garlic	¼ teaspoon ground nutmeg
½ teaspoon dried dill Cooking spray	1 egg yolk, whisked

1. Make the dough: mix up almond flour, coconut flour, xanthan gum, baking powder, egg, water, and apple cider vinegar. Then knead the dough with the help of the fingertips until it is soft and non-sticky. Roll up the dough and cut it on the ravioli squares. Make the ravioli filling: mix up dried ill, ground nutmeg, minced garlic, and ricotta cheese. Then fill the dough squats with ricotta cheese. Top the cheese with another ravioli dough squares. Secure the edges. Brush the ravioli with egg yolk. Preheat the air fryer to 375F. Then spray the air fryer basket with cooking spray and place the ravioli inside in one layer. Cook the meal for 4 minutes from each side or until they are light brown.

Nutrition:

Calories 165, fat 12, fiber 6.2, carbs 9.7, protein 6.9

Parmesan Artichokes

Preparation time: 5 minutes **Cooking time:** 15 minutes **Servings:** 4

2 tablespoon olive oil	12 ounces artichoke hearts
	4 spring onions, chopped
Salt and black pepper to the taste	½ cup parmesan, grated

1. In a bowl, mix artichoke hearts with the oil, salt, pepper and spring onions and toss. Put the artichokes in your air fryer's basket, sprinkle the parmesan all over and cook at 370 degrees F for 15 minutes. Divide between plates and serve as a side dish.

Nutrition:

Calories 208, fat 8, fiber 3, carbs 5, protein 8

Parmesan Cherry Tomatoes

Preparation time: 5 minutes **Cooking time:** 15 minutes **Servings:** 4

tablespoon ghee, melted	cups cherry tomatoes, halved
3 tablespoons scallions, chopped	1 teaspoon lemon zest, grated
2 tablespoons parsley, chopped	¼ cup parmesan, grated

1. In a pan that fits the air fryer, combine all the ingredients except the parmesan, and toss. Sprinkle the parmesan on top, introduce the pan in the machine and cook at 360 degrees F for 10 minutes. Divide between plates and serve.

Nutrition:

Calories 141, fat 6, fiber 2, carbs 4, protein 7

Spinach Samosa

Prep time: 25 minutes **Cooking time:** 20 minutes **Servings:** 6

1 teaspoon garlic, diced	¼ teaspoon ground ginger
1 teaspoon olive oil	1 teaspoon ground turmeric
½ teaspoon garam masala	½ teaspoon ground coriander
½ teaspoon chili flakes	1 cup spinach, chopped
3 spring onions, chopped	1 teaspoon keto tomato sauce
1 cup Mozzarella, shredded	½ cup almond flour
½ teaspoon baking powder	Cooking spray

1. Preheat the olive oil in the skillet. Add garlic and ground ginger. Cook the ingredients for 2 minutes over the medium heat. Stir them well. Then add 1 teaspoon of ground turmeric, garam masala, ground coriander, and chili flakes. Add spinach and stir the mixture well. Add spring onions and tomato sauce. Stir the mixture well and cook it with the closed lid for 10 minutes over the low heat. The cooked spinach mixture should be very soft. Cool the spinach mixture. Meanwhile, make the samosa dough: microwave the cheese until it is melted. Then mix it up with almond flour and baking powder. Knead the soft dough and put it on the baking paper. Cover the dough with the second baking paper and roll-up. Then cut the flat dough on the triangles. Place the spinach mixture on every triangle and fold them in the shape of the samosa. Secure the edges of samosa well. Preheat the air fryer to 375F. Spray the air fryer basket with cooking spray. Put the samosa in the air fryer in one layer and cook for 5 minutes. Then flip samosa on another side and cook it for 5 minutes or until the meal is light brown.

Nutrition:
Calories 42, fat 2.8, fiber 0.7, carbs 2.6, protein 2.2

Radicchio and Cauliflower Mix

Prep time: 10 minutes **Cooking time:** 15 minutes **Servings:** 4

2 cups radicchio	2 eggs, beaten
2 oz Parmesan, grated	½ cup cauliflower, shredded
1 tablespoon butter, softened	½ teaspoon ground black pepper
¼ cup coconut cream	

1. Chop radicchio roughly and sprinkle it with ground black pepper. After this, grease the air fryer gratin mold with butter and put the radicchio inside. Top it with beaten egg, coconut cream, and Parmesan. Then add cauliflower. Mix up the mixture gently. Preheat the air fryer to 375F. Put the gratin in the air fryer basket and cover with the foil. Cook the gratin for 10 minutes. Then remove the foil from the gratin. Cook the meal for 5 minutes more.

Nutrition:
Calories 145, fat 11.8, fiber 0.9, carbs 3.2, protein 8.3

Butter Fennel

Preparation time: 5 minutes **Cooking time:** 12 minutes **Servings:** 4

2 big fennel bulbs, sliced	2 tablespoons butter, melted
Salt and black pepper to the taste	½ cup coconut cream

1. In a pan that fits the air fryer, combine all the ingredients, toss, introduce in the machine and cook at 370 degrees F for 12 minutes. Divide between plates and serve as a side dish.

Nutrition:
Calories 151, fat 3, fiber 2, carbs 4, protein 6

Thyme Zucchinis

Prep time: 10 minutes **Cooking time:** 12 minutes **Servings:** 8

12 oz zucchini, cubed	1/3 cup spring onions, chopped
1 teaspoon fresh thyme	2 eggs, beaten
3 tablespoons coconut milk	1 teaspoon olive oil

1. In the air fryer pan, mix the zucchinis with spring onions and the other ingredients and cook for 12 minutes at 400F. Divide between plates and serve.

Nutrition:
Calories 54, fat 2.3, fiber 2, carbs 6.2, protein 2.6

Cream Cheese Zucchini

Preparation time: 5 minutes **Cooking time:** 15 minutes **Servings:** 4

1 pound zucchinis, cut into wedges	1 cup cream cheese, soft
1 green onion, sliced	teaspoon garlic powder
tablespoons basil, chopped	A pinch of salt and black pepper
1 tablespoon butter, melted	

1. In a pan that fits your air fryer, mix the zucchinis with all the other ingredients, toss, introduce in the air fryer and cook at 370 degrees F for 15 minutes. Divide between plates and serve as a side dish.

Nutrition:
Calories 129, fat 6, fiber 2, carbs 5, protein 8

Balsamic Okra

Prep time: 10 minutes **Cooking time:** 6 minutes **Servings:** 2

1 teaspoon balsamic vinegar	1 teaspoon avocado oil
8 oz okra, sliced	½ teaspoon salt
½ teaspoon white pepper	

1. Sprinkle the sliced okra with avocado oil, salt, and white pepper. Then preheat the air fryer to 360F. Put the okra in the air fryer basket and cook it for 3 minutes. Then shake the sliced vegetables well and cook for 3 minutes more. Transfer the cooked okra in the serving bowl and sprinkle with balsamic vinegar.

Nutrition:
Calories 50, fat 0.5, fiber 3.9, carbs 8.9, protein 2.3

Parsley Zucchini Rounds

Preptime: 5 minutes **Cooking time:** 20 minutes **Servings:** 4

4 zucchinis, sliced	1 egg, whisked
1 egg white, whisked	1 and ½ cups parmesan, grated
¼ cup parsley, chopped	½ teaspoon garlic powder
	Cooking spray

1. In a bowl, mix the egg with egg whites, parmesan, parsley and garlic powder and whisk. Dredge each zucchini slice in this mix, place them all in your air fryer's basket, grease them with cooking spray and cook at 370 degrees F for 20 minutes. Divide between plates and serve as a side dish.

Nutrition:

Calories 183, fat 6, fiber 2, carbs 3, protein 8

Sage Artichoke

Prep time: 10 minutes **Cooking time:** 12 minutes **Servings:** 4

4 artichokes	1 tablespoon sage
4 teaspoons avocado oil	1 teaspoon chives, chopped
½ teaspoon salt	

1. Cut the artichoke into halves and rub them with sage avocado oil, minced garlic, and salt. Preheat the air fryer to 375F. Place the artichoke halves in the air fryer basket and cook them for 12 minutes.

Nutrition:

Calories 84, fat 0.9, fiber 9, carbs 17.6, protein 5.5

Nutmeg Kale

Prep time: 5 minutes **Cooking time:** 15 minutes **Servings:** 4

1 tablespoon butter, melted	½ cup almond milk
Salt and black pepper to the taste 3 garlic cloves	10 cups kale, roughly chopped
¼ teaspoon nutmeg, ground	¼ cup walnuts, chopped
1/3 cup parmesan, grated	

1. In a pan that fits the air fryer, combine all the ingredients, toss, introduce the pan in the machine and cook at 360 degrees F for 15 minutes. Divide between plates and serve.

Nutrition:

Calories 160, fat 7, fiber 2, carbs 4, protein 5

Nutmeg Muffins

Prep time: 10 minutes **Cooking time:** 15 minutes **Servings:** 4

4 tablespoons almond flour	¼ teaspoon baking powder
¼ teaspoon salt	1 tablespoon butter, softened
2 tablespoons heavy cream	¼ teaspoon ground nutmeg
Cooking spray	

1. In the mixing bowl make the batter: mix up almond flour, baking powder, salt, butter, heavy cream, and nutmeg. In the end, you should get a smooth batter. Preheat the air fryer to 365F. Spray the muffin mold with cooking spray. Then fill every muffin mold with muffin batter (fill ½ part of every muffin mold) and place them in the air fryer basket. Cook English muffins for 15 minutes.

Nutrition:

Calories 212, fat 9.7, fiber 3, carbs 6.4, protein 6.2

Lemon Kale

Preparation time: 5 minutes **Cooking time:** 15 minutes **Servings:** 4

10 cups kale, torn	2 tablespoons olive oil
Salt and black pepper to the taste	2 tablespoons lemon zest, grated
1 tablespoon lemon juice	1/3 cup pine nuts

1. In a pan that fits the air fryer, combine all the ingredients, toss, introduce the pan in the machine and cook at 380 degrees F for 15 minutes. Divide between plates and serve as a side dish.

Nutrition:

Calories 121, fat 9, fiber 2, carbs 4, protein 5

Keto Tortillas

Prep time: 20 minutes **Cooking time:** 16 minutes **Servings:** 4

½ teaspoon Psyllium husk powder	¼ cup almond flour
1/3 teaspoon baking powder	1 egg white
4 tablespoons water	1 teaspoon sesame oil

1. In the mixing bowl mix up Psyllium husk, almond flour, baking powder, egg white, and water. Knead the soft non-sticky dough. Then cut the dough on 4 pieces. Roll them up with the help of the rolling pin in the shape of tortillas. Preheat the air fryer to 400F. Place the first tortilla in the air fryer and gently sprinkle with sesame oil. Cook it for 2 minutes from each side or until it is light brown. Repeat the same steps with all remaining tortillas.

Nutrition:

Calories 27, fat 2.1, fiber 0.2, carbs 0.6, protein 1.3

Bok Choy Sauté

Prep time: 5 minutes **Cooking time:** 15 minutes **Servings:** 4

2 tablespoons chicken stock 1 tablespoon olive oil	2 bok choy heads, trimmed and cut into strips 1 tablespoon butter, melted
A pinch of salt and black pepper	1 teaspoon lemon juice

1. In a pan that fits your air fryer, mix all the ingredients, toss, introduce the pan in the air fryer and cook at 380 degrees F for 15 minutes. Divide between plates and serve as a side dish.

Nutrition:

Calories 141, fat 3, fiber 2, carbs 4, protein 3

Artichoke Sauté

Prep time: 15 minutes **Cooking time:** 10 minutes **Servings:** 4

4 artichoke hearts, chopped	4 teaspoons lemon juice
2 teaspoons avocado oil	¼ teaspoon lemon zest, grated

1. Preheat the air fryer to 360F. Meanwhile, sprinkle the chopped artichoke hearts with lemon juice, avocado oil, and lemon zest. Shake them well and leave for 10 minutes to marinate. After this, put the artichoke hearts in the preheated air fryer and cook them for 8 minutes. Shake them well and cook for an additional 2 minutes.

Nutrition:

Calories 64, fat 0.5, fiber 7.1, carbs 13.8, protein 4.3

Balsamic and Garlic Cabbage Mix

Preparation time: 10 minutes **Cooking time:** 15 minutes
Servings: 4

4 garlic cloves, minced 1 tablespoon olive oil	6 cups red cabbage, shredded
1 tablespoon balsamic vinegar	Salt and black pepper to the taste

1. In a pan that fits the air fryer, combine all the ingredients, toss, introduce the pan in the air fryer and cook at 380 degrees F for 15 minutes. Divide between plates and serve as a side dish.

Nutrition:
Calories 151, fat 2, fiber 3, carbs 5, protein 5

Macadamia and Cauliflower Rice

Prep time: 15 minutes **Cooking time:** 8 minutes **Servings:** 4

9 oz cauliflower	1 tablespoon butter
1 oz macadamia nuts, grinded	3 tablespoons chicken broth

1. Cut the cauliflower on the florets. Then grate the cauliflower with the help of the grater. Grease the air fryer pan with butter and put the cauliflower rice inside. Add grinded macadamia nuts and chicken broth. Gently stir the vegetable mixture. Cook the cauliflower rice at 365F for 8 minutes.
2. Stir the vegetables after 4 minutes of cooking.

Nutrition:
Calories 94, fat 8.4, fiber 2.2, carbs 4.4, protein 2.1

Radishes and Spring Onions Mix

Preparation time: 5 minutes **Cooking time:** 15 minutes
Servings: 4

20 radishes, halved	1 tablespoon olive oil
3 green onions, chopped	Salt and black pepper to the taste
3 teaspoons black sesame seeds	2 tablespoons olive oil

1. In a bowl, mix all the ingredients and toss well. Put the radishes in your air fryer's basket, cook at 400 degrees F for 15 minutes, divide between plates and serve as a side dish.

Nutrition:
Calories 150, fat 4, fiber 2, carbs 3, protein 5

Almond Cabbage

Prep time: 10 minutes **Cooking time:** 13 minutes **Servings:** 4

10 oz white cabbage	½ cup chicken broth
½ teaspoon salt	½ teaspoon ground paprika
1 teaspoon almond butter	4 oz Mozzarella, sliced

1. Preheat the air fryer to 400F. Then insert the air fryer pan in the air fryer basket. Cut the white cabbage on the small patties and sprinkle them with salt. Crackle the cabbage to get juice from it. Then place it in the air fryer pan and sprinkle with ground paprika. Add almond butter and chicken broth. After this, cook the cabbage for 3 minutes. Then shake it well and top with Mozzarella. Cook the side dish for 10 minutes at 375F.

Nutrition:
Calories 128, fat 7.5, fiber 2.3, carbs 6.1, protein 10.4

Balsamic Radishes

Preparation time: 5 minutes **Cooking time:** 15 minutes
Servings: 4

2 bunches red radishes, halved	1 tablespoon olive oil
2 tablespoons balsamic vinegar	2 tablespoons parsley, chopped Salt and black pepper to the taste

1. In a bowl, mix the radishes with the remaining ingredients except the parsley, toss and put them in your air fryer's basket. Cook at 400 degrees F for 15 minutes, divide between plates, sprinkle the parsley on top and serve as a side dish.

Nutrition:
Calories 180, fat 4, fiber 2, carbs 3, protein 5

Coriander Leeks

Prep time: 5 minutes **Cooking time:** 10 minutes **Servings:** 6

10 oz leek, chopped	2 tablespoons ricotta
1 tablespoon butter, melted	1 teaspoon ground coriander
¼ teaspoon salt	

1. Sprinkle the leek with salt and ground coriander and transfer in the air fryer. Add butter and gently stir the ingredients. After this, cook the leek for 5 minutes at 375F. Stir the vegetables well and add ricotta. Cook the meal for 5 minutes more. Serve the cooked leek with ricotta gravy.

Nutrition:
Calories 64, fat 3, fiber 1, carbs 8.3, protein 1.6

Balsamic Cabbage Mix

Prep time: 5 minutes **Cooking time:** 15 minutes **Servings:** 4

6 cups green cabbage, shredded 6 radishes, sliced	½ cup celery leaves, chopped
¼ cup green onions, chopped	tablespoons balsamic vinegar 1 teaspoon lemon juice
tablespoons olive oil	½ teaspoon hot paprika

1. In your air fryer's pan, combine all the ingredients and toss well. Introduce the pan in the fryer and cook at 380 degrees F for 15 minutes. Divide between plates and serve as a side dish.

Nutrition:
Calories 130, fat 4, fiber 3, carbs 4, protein 7

Greek Bread

Prep time: 15 minutes **Cooking time:** 4 minutes **Servings:** 6

1 cup Mozzarella, shredded	2 tablespoons Greek yogurt
1 egg, beaten	½ teaspoon baking powder
½ cup almond flour	1 teaspoon butter, melted

1. In the glass bowl mix up Mozzarella and yogurt. Microwave the mixture for 2 minutes. After this, mix up baking powder, almond flour, and egg. Combine together the almond flour mixture and melted Mozzarella mixture. Stir it with the help of the spatula until smooth. Refrigerate the dough for 10 minutes. Then cut it on 6 pieces and roll up to get the flatbread pieces. Air fryer the bread for 3 minutes at 400F. Then brush it with melted butter and cook for 1 minute more or until the bread is light brown.

Nutrition:
Calories 43, fat 3.4, fiber 0.3, carbs 0.9, protein 2.8

Garlic Radishes

Preparation time: 5 minutes **Cooking time:** 15 minutes
Servings: 4

20 radishes, halved	1 teaspoon chives, chopped
1 tablespoon garlic, minced	Salt and black pepper to the taste
2 tablespoons olive oil	

2. In your air fryer's pan, combine all the ingredients and toss. Introduce the pan in the machine and cook at 370 degrees F for 15 minutes. Divide between plates and serve as a side dish.

Nutrition:
Calories 160, fat 2, fiber 3, carbs 4, protein 6

Cauliflower Bites

Prep time: 15 minutes **Cooking time:** 4 minutes **Servings:** 2

1 egg	1 cup cauliflower, shredded
1 teaspoon chives, chopped	1 tablespoon almond flour
¼ teaspoon salt	1 teaspoon ground turmeric
2 oz Pecorino cheese, grated	Cooking spray

1. Crack the egg in the bowl and whisk it. Add shredded cauliflower, chives, almond flour, and salt. Mix up the mixture until it is homogenous. Then add Pecorino cheese and turmeric, and stir it until smooth. Make the small balls and press them gently with the help of the fingertips in the shape of nuggets. Preheat the air fryer to 395F. Place the cauli nuggets in the air fryer basket and spray them with cooking spray. Cook the nuggets for 2 minutes from each side. Cook the nuggets for 2 extra minutes for a saturated golden color.

Nutrition:
Calories 211, fat 15.4, fiber 1.9, carbs 4.3, protein 16

Ginger Paneer

Prep time: 10 minutes **Cooking time:** 6 minutes **Servings:** 4

1 cup paneer, cubed	1 tomato
2 spring onions, chopped	½ teaspoon ground coriander
1 tablespoon lemon juice	½ teaspoon fresh cilantro, chopped
1 tablespoon mustard oil	¼ teaspoon ginger paste
½ teaspoon minced garlic	½ teaspoon red chili powder
¼ teaspoon garam masala powder	¼ teaspoon salt

1. Chop the tomato on 4 cubes. Then chop the onion on 4 cubes too. Sprinkle the paneer with ground coriander, lemon juice, cilantro, mustard oil, ginger paste, minced garlic, red chili powder, garam masala, and salt.
2. Massage the paneer cubes with the help of the fingertips to coat them well. After this, string the paneer cubes, tomato, and onion on the skewers. Preheat the air fryer to 385F. Place the paneer tikka skewers in the air fryer basket and cook them for 3 minutes from each side.

Nutrition:
Calories 84, fat 4.2, fiber 0.7, carbs 4.2, protein 7.4

Basil Tomatoes

Preparation time: 5 minutes **Cooking time:** 15 minutes
Servings: 4

4 tomatoes, halved	½ teaspoon smoked paprika
½ teaspoon garlic powder	½ teaspoon onion powder
½ teaspoon oregano, dried	½ cup parmesan, grated
1 tablespoon basil, chopped	Cooking spray

1. In a bowl, mix all the ingredients except the cooking spray and the parmesan. Arrange the tomatoes in your air fryer's pan, sprinkle the parmesan on top and grease with cooking spray. Cook at 370 degrees F for 15 minutes, divide between plates and serve.

Nutrition:
Calories 200, fat 7, fiber 2, carbs 4, protein 6

Lemon and Butter Artichokes

Preparation time: 5 minutes **Cooking time:** 15 minutes
Servings: 4

12 ounces artichoke hearts	4 tablespoons butter, melted
Juice of ½ lemon	
2 tablespoons tarragon, chopped Salt and black pepper to the taste	

1. In a bowl, mix all the ingredients, toss, transfer the artichokes to your air fryer's basket and cook at 370 degrees F for 15 minutes. Divide between plates and serve as a side dish.

Nutrition:
Calories 200, fat 7, fiber 2, carbs 3, protein 7

Cumin Artichokes

Preparation time: 5 minutes **Cooking time:** 15 minutes
Servings: 4

12 ounces artichoke hearts	½ teaspoon olive oil
1 teaspoon coriander, ground	½ teaspoon cumin seeds
Salt and black pepper to the taste	1 tablespoon lemon juice

1. In a pan that fits your air fryer, mix all the ingredients, toss, introduce the pan in the fryer and cook at 370 degrees F for 15 minutes. Divide the mix between plates and serve as a side dish.

Nutrition:
Calories 200, fat 7, fiber 2, carbs 5, protein 8

Cumin Tofu

Prep time: 10 minutes **Cooking time:** 7 minutes **Servings:** 3

1 cup tofu, cubed	1 tablespoon lime juice
2 tablespoons avocado oil	¼ teaspoon ground coriander
¼ teaspoon ground cumin	¼ teaspoon chili flakes

1. In the mixing bowl mix up lime juice, avocado oil, ground coriander, cumin, and chili flakes. Then coat the tofu in the lime juice mixture well. Preheat the air fryer to 400F. Put the tofu cubes and all the oily liquid in the air fryer. Cook the tofu for 5 minutes. Then shake it well and cook for 2 minutes more.

Nutrition:
Calories 72, fat 4.7, fiber 1.2, carbs 2, protein 7

Cinnamon Mushroom

Prep time: 5 minutes **Cooking time:** 15 minutes **Servings:** 4

1 pound brown mushrooms	4 garlic cloves, minced
1 teaspoon olive oil	
½ teaspoon turmeric powder	¼ teaspoon cinnamon powder Salt and black pepper to the taste

1. In a bowl, combine all the ingredients and toss. Put the mushrooms in your air fryer's basket and cook at 370 degrees F for 15 minutes. Divide the mix between plates and serve as a side dish.

Nutrition:

Calories 208, fat 7, fiber 3, carbs 5, protein 7

Cauliflower Patties

Prep time: 15 minutes **Cooking time:** 10 minutes **Servings:** 2

¼ cup cauliflower, shredded	1 egg yolk
½ teaspoon ground turmeric	¼ teaspoon onion powder
¼ teaspoon salt	2 oz Cheddar cheese, shredded
¼ teaspoon baking powder	1 teaspoon heavy cream
1 tablespoon coconut flakes	Cooking spray

1. Squeeze the shredded cauliflower and put it in the bowl. Add egg yolk, ground turmeric, onion powder, baking powder, salt, heavy cream, and coconut flakes. Then melt Cheddar cheese and add it in the cauliflower mixture. Stir the ingredients until you get the smooth mass. After this, make the medium size cauliflower patties. Preheat the air fryer to 365F. Spray the air fryer basket with cooking spray and put the patties inside. Cook them for 5 minutes from each side.

Nutrition:

Calories 165, fat 13.5, fiber 0.7, carbs 2.7, protein 8.9

Artichokes Sauté

Preparation time: 5 minutes **Cooking time:** 15 minutes **Servings:** 4

10 ounces artichoke hearts, halved 3 garlic cloves	2 cups baby spinach
¼ cup veggie stock	2 teaspoons lime juice
Salt and black pepper to the taste	

1. In a pan that fits your air fryer, mix all the ingredients, toss, introduce in the fryer and cook at 370 degrees F for 15 minutes. Divide between plates and serve as a side dish.

Nutrition:

Calories 209, fat 6, fiber 2, carbs 4, protein 8

Almond Broccoli Rice

Prep time: 10 minutes **Cooking time:** 8 minutes **Servings:** 4

2 cup broccoli, shredded	½ teaspoon apple cider vinegar
¼ teaspoon salt	1 tablespoon cream cheese
½ teaspoon pumpkin seeds, crushed	1 tablespoon organic almond milk
1 teaspoon butter, melted	

1. In the bowl mix up butter, broccoli, apple cider vinegar, salt, and pumpkin seeds. Transfer the mixture in the baking pan for the air fryer. Add almond milk and mix up the vegetable mixture until homogenous. Cover it with the foil. Preheat the air fryer to 375F. Place the pan in the preheated air fryer and cook for 8 minutes. Then remove the pan from the air fryer and add cream cheese. Stir the cooked broccoli rice well.

Nutrition:

Calories 43, fat 3, fiber 1.3, carbs 3.4, protein 1.7

Snack and Appetizer Recipes

Sprouts Wraps

Preparation time: 5 minutes **Cooking time:** 20 minutes
Servings: 12

12 bacon strips | 12 Brussels sprouts A drizzle of olive oil

1. Wrap each Brussels sprouts in a bacon strip, brush them with some oil, put them in your air fryer's basket and cook at 350 degrees F for 20 minutes. Serve as an appetizer.

Nutrition:

Calories 140, fat 5, fiber 2, carbs 4, protein 4

Pickled Bacon Bowls

Preparation time: 5 minutes **Cooking time:** 20 minutes
Servings: 4

4 dill pickle spears, sliced in half and quartered 8 bacon slices, halved | 1 cup avocado mayonnaise

1. Wrap each pickle spear in a bacon slice, put them in your air fryer's basket and cook at 400 degrees F for 20 minutes. Divide into bowls and serve as a snack with the mayonnaise.

Nutrition:

Calories 100, fat 4, fiber 2, carbs 3, protein 4

Cheese Zucchini Chips

Prep time: 10 minutes **Cooking time:** 13 minutes **Servings:**8

2 zucchinis, thinly sliced | 4 tablespoons almond flour
2 oz Parmesan | 2 eggs, beaten
½ teaspoon white pepper | Cooking spray

1. In the big bowl mix up almond flour, Parmesan, and white pepper. Then dip the zucchini slices in the egg and coat in the almond flour mixture.
2. Preheat the air fryer to 355F. Place the prepared zucchini slices in the air fryer in one layer and cook them for 10 minutes. Then flip the vegetables on another side and cook them for 3 minutes more or until crispy.

Nutrition:

Calories 127, fat 9.7, fiber 2.1, carbs 5.1, protein 7.3

Coconut Chicken Bites

Preparation time: 5 minutes **Cooking time:** 20 minutes
Servings: 4

2 teaspoons garlic powder | Salt and black pepper to the taste
2 eggs |
¾ cup coconut flakes | pound chicken breasts, skinless, boneless and cubed
Cooking spray |

1. Put the coconut in a bowl and mix the eggs with garlic powder, salt and pepper in a second one. Dredge the chicken cubes in eggs and then in coconut and arrange them all in your air fryer's basket. Grease with cooking spray, cook at 370 degrees F for 20 minutes. Arrange the chicken bites on a platter and serve as an appetizer.

Nutrition:

Calories 202, fat 12, fiber 2, carbs 4, protein 7

Chocolate Bacon Bites

Preparation time: 5 minutes **Cooking time:** 10 minutes
Servings: 4

4 bacon slices, halved | 1 cup dark chocolate, melted A pinch of pink salt

1. Dip each bacon slice in some chocolate, sprinkle pink salt over them, put them in your air fryer's basket and cook at 350 degrees F for 10 minutes. Serve as a snack.

Nutrition:

Calories 151, fat 4, fiber 2, carbs 4, protein 8

Almond Coconut Granola

Prep time: 10 minutes **Cooking time:** 12 minutes **Servings:**4

1 teaspoon monk fruit | 1 teaspoon almond butter
1 teaspoon coconut oil | 2 tablespoons almonds, chopped
1 teaspoon pumpkin puree | ½ teaspoon pumpkin pie spices
2 tablespoons coconut flakes | 2 tablespoons pumpkin seeds, crushed
1 teaspoon hemp seeds | 1 teaspoon flax seeds
Cooking spray |

1. In the big bowl mix up almond butter and coconut oil. Microwave the mixture until it is melted. After this, in the separated bowl mix up monk fruit, pumpkin spices, coconut flakes, pumpkin seeds, hemp seeds, and flax seeds. Add the melted coconut oil and pumpkin puree. Then stir the mixture until it is homogenous. Preheat the air fryer to 350F. Then put the pumpkin mixture on the baking paper and make the shape of the square.
2. After this, cut the square on the serving bars and transfer in the preheated air fryer. Cook the pumpkin granola for 12 minutes.

Nutrition:

Calories 91, fat 8.2, fiber 1.4, carbs 3, protein 3

Tomato Smokies

Prep time: 15 minutes **Cooking time:** 10 minutes **Servings:**10

12 oz pork and beef smokies | 3 oz bacon, sliced
1 teaspoon keto tomato sauce | 1 teaspoon Erythritol
1 teaspoon avocado oil | ½ teaspoon cayenne pepper

1. Sprinkle the smokies with cayenne pepper and tomato sauce. Then sprinkle them with Erythritol and olive oil. After this, wrap every smokie in the bacon and secure it with the toothpick. Preheat the air fryer to 400F. Place the bacon smokies in the air fryer and cook them for 10 minutes.
2. Shake them gently during cooking to avoid burning.

Nutrition:

Calories 126, fat 9.7, fiber 0.1, carbs 1.4, protein 8.7

Pizza Bites

Prep time: 15 minutes **Cooking time:** 3 minutes **Servings:** 10

    10 Mozzarella cheese slices   10 pepperoni slices

1. Preheat the air fryer to 400F. Line the air fryer pan with baking paper and put Mozzarella in it in one layer. After this, place the pan in the air fryer basket and cook the cheese for 3 minutes or until it is melted. After this, remove the cheese from the air fryer and cool it to room temperature.
2. Then remove the melted cheese from the baking paper and put the pepperoni slices on it. Fold the cheese in the shape of turnovers.

Nutrition:

Calories 117, fat 10.4, fiber 0, carbs 0, protein 8.3

Mozzarella Snack

Preparation time: 5 minutes **Cooking time:** 5 minutes **Servings:** 8

    cups mozzarella, shredded   ¾ cup almond flour
    2 teaspoons psyllium husk   ¼ teaspoon sweet paprika
    powder

1. Put the mozzarella in a bowl, melt it in the microwave for 2 minutes, add all the other ingredients quickly and stir really until you obtain a dough. Divide the dough into 2 balls, roll them on 2 baking sheets and cut into triangles. Arrange the tortillas in your air fryer's basket and bake at 370 degrees F for 5 minutes. Transfer to bowls and serve as a snack.

Nutrition:

Calories 170, fat 2, fiber 3, carbs 4, protein 6

Mushroom Pizza Bites

Prep time: 10 minutes **Cooking time:** 7 minutes **Servings:** 6

    6 cremini mushroom caps   3 oz Parmesan, grated
    1 tablespoon olive oil   ½ tomato, chopped
    ½ teaspoon dried basil   1 teaspoon ricotta cheese

1. Preheat the air fryer to 400F. Sprinkle the mushroom caps with olive oil and put in the air fryer basket in one layer. Cook them for 3 minutes. After this, mix up tomato and ricotta cheese. Fill the mushroom caps with tomato mixture. Then top them with parmesan and sprinkle with dried basil. Cook the mushroom pizzas for 4 minutes at 400F.

Nutrition:

Calories 73, fat 5.5, fiber 0.2, carbs 1.6, protein 5.2

Paprika Chips

Preparation time: 2 minutes **Cooking time:** 5 minutes **Servings:** 4

    8 ounces cheddar cheese,   1 teaspoon sweet paprika
    shredded

1. Divide the cheese in small heaps in a pan that fits the air fryer, sprinkle the paprika on top, introduce the pan in the machine and cook at 400 degrees F for 5 minutes. Cool the chips down and serve them.

Nutrition:

Calories 150, fat 4, fiber 3, carbs 4, protein 6

Zucchini Crackers

Prep time: 15 minutes **Cooking time:** 20 minutes **Servings:** 16

    1 cup zucchini, grated   2 tablespoons flax meal
    1 teaspoon salt   3 tablespoons almond flour
    ¼ teaspoon baking powder   ¼ teaspoon chili flakes
    1 tablespoon xanthan gum   1 tablespoon butter, softened
    1 egg, beaten   Cooking spray

1. Squeeze the zucchini to get rid of vegetable juice and transfer in the big bowl. Add flax meal, salt, almond flour, baking powder, chili flakes, xanthan gum, and stir well. After this, add butter and egg. Knead the non-sticky dough. Place it on the baking paper and cover with the second sheet of baking paper. Roll up the dough into the flat square. After this, remove the baking paper from the dough surface. Cut it on medium size crackers. Line the air fryer basket with baking paper and put the crackers inside in one layer. Spray them with cooking spray. Cook them at 355F for 20 minutes.

Nutrition:

Calories 46, fat 3.9, fiber 1.3, carbs 2.1, protein 1.8

Olives Fritters

Preparation time: 5 minutes **Cooking time:** 12 minutes **Servings:** 6

    Cooking spray   ½ cup parsley, chopped 1 egg
    ½ cup almond flour   Salt and black pepper to the taste 3 spring onions, chopped
    ½ cup kalamata olives, pitted and minced 3 zucchinis, grated

1. In a bowl, mix all the ingredients except the cooking spray, stir well and shape medium fritters out of this mixture. Place the fritters in your air fryer's basket, grease them with cooking spray and cook at 380 degrees F for 6 minutes on each side. Serve them as an appetizer.

Nutrition:

Calories 165, fat 5, fiber 2, carbs 3, protein 7

Mexican Muffins

Prep time: 10 minutes **Cooking time:** 15 minutes **Servings:** 4

    1 cup ground beef   1 teaspoon taco seasonings
    2 oz Mexican blend cheese, shredded   1 teaspoon keto tomato sauce
    Cooking spray

1. Preheat the air fryer to 375F. Meanwhile, in the mixing bowl mix up ground beef and taco seasonings. Spray the muffin molds with cooking spray. Then transfer the ground beef mixture in the muffin molds and top them with cheese and tomato sauce. Transfer the muffin molds in the preheated air fryer and cook them for 15 minutes.

Nutrition:

Calories 123, fat 8.3, fiber 0, carbs 1.7, protein 9.6

Mushroom Bites

Preparation time: 5 minutes **Cooking time:** 12 minutes
Servings: 6

Salt and black pepper to the taste 1 and ¼ cups coconut flour	2 garlic clove, minced
tablespoons basil, minced	½ pound mushrooms, minced 1 egg, whisked

1. In a bowl, mix all the ingredients except the cooking spray, stir well and shape medium balls out of this mix. Arrange the balls in your air fryer's basket, grease them with cooking spray and bake at 350 degrees F for 6 minutes on each side. Serve as an appetizer.

Nutrition:
Calories 151, fat 2, fiber 1, carbs 3, protein 6

Chaffle

Prep time: 10 minutes **Cooking time:** 25 minutes **Servings:**4

4 eggs, beaten	2 oz bacon, chopped, cooked
1 cucumber, pickled, grated	2 oz Cheddar cheese, shredded
¼ teaspoon salt	½ teaspoon ground black pepper
Cooking spray	

1. In the mixing bowl mix up eggs, bacon, pickled cucumber, cheese, salt, and ground black pepper. Whisk the mixture gently. The chaffle batter is cooked. Then spray the air fryer pan with cooking spray. Pour ¼ part of the liquid inside. Preheat the air fryer to 400F. Put the pan with chaffle in the air fryer basket and cook it for 6 minutes. Then transfer the cooked chaffle in the plate. Repeat the same steps with the remaining chaffle batter. In the end, you should get 4 chaffles.

Nutrition:
Calories 209, fat 15.1, fiber 0.5, carbs 3.6, protein 14.8

Zucchini Chips

Preparation time: 5 minutes **Cooking time:** 15 minutes
Servings: 6

zucchinis, thinly sliced	Salt and black pepper to the taste 2 eggs, whisked
cup almond flour	

1. In a bowl, mix the eggs with salt and pepper. Put the flour in a second bowl. Dredge the zucchinis in flour and then in eggs. Arrange the chips in your air fryer's basket, cook at 350 degrees F for 15 minutes and serve as a snack.

Nutrition:
Calories 120, fat 4, fiber 2, carbs 3, protein 5

Cheese Rounds

Prep time: 10 minutes **Cooking time:** 6 minutes **Servings:**4

1 cup Cheddar cheese, shredded

1. Preheat the air fryer to 400F. Then line the air fryer basket with baking paper. Sprinkle the cheese on the baking paper in the shape of small rounds. Cook them for 6 minutes or until the cheese is melted and starts to be crispy.

Nutrition:
Calories 114, fat 9.4, fiber 0, carbs 0.4, protein 7

Bacon Avocado Wraps

Preparation time: 5 minutes **Cooking time:** 15 minutes
Servings: 4

avocados, peeled, pitted and cut into 12 wedges 12 bacon strips	1 tablespoon ghee, melted

1. Wrap each avocado wedge in a bacon strip, brush them with the ghee, put them in your air fryer's basket and cook at 360 degrees F for 15 minutes. Serve as an appetizer.

Nutrition:
Calories 161, fat 4, fiber 2, carbs 4, protein 6

Coconut Cheese Sticks

Prep time: 10 minutes **Cooking time:** 4 minutes **Servings:**4

1 egg, beaten	4 tablespoons coconut flakes
1 teaspoon ground paprika Cooking spray	6 oz Provolone cheese

1. Cut the cheese into sticks. Then dip every cheese stick in the beaten egg. After this, mix up coconut flakes and ground paprika. Coat the cheese sticks in the coconut mixture. Preheat the air fryer to 400F. Put the cheese sticks in the air fryer and spray them with cooking spray. Cook the meal for 2 minutes from each side. Cool them well before serving.

Nutrition:
Calories 184, fat 14.2, fiber 0.7, carbs 2.1, protein 12.5

Garlic Avocado Balls

Preparation time: 5 minutes **Cooking time:** 5 minutes
Servings: 4

avocado, peeled, pitted and mashed	¼ cup ghee, melted
garlic cloves, minced 2 spring onions, minced	1 chili pepper, chopped
1 tablespoon lime juice	2 tablespoons cilantro
A pinch of salt and black pepper	4 bacon slices, cooked and crumbled Cooking spray

1. In a bowl, mix all the ingredients except the cooking spray, stir well and shape medium balls out of this mix. Place them in your air fryer's basket, grease with cooking spray and cook at 370 degrees F for 5 minutes. Serve as a snack.

Nutrition:
Calories 160, fat 6, fiber 3, carbs 4, protein 6

Pork Rinds

Prep time: 10 minutes **Cooking time:** 10 minutes **Servings:**3

6 oz pork skin	1 tablespoon keto tomato sauce
1 teaspoon olive oil	

1. Chop the pork skin into the rinds and sprinkle with the sauce and olive oil. Mix up well. Then preheat the air fryer to 400F. Place the pork skin rinds in the air fryer basket in one layer and cook for 10 minutes. Flip the rinds on another side after 5 minutes of cooking.

Nutrition:
Calories 324, fat 19.3, fiber 0.2, carbs 0.3, protein 34.8

Cilantro Shrimp Balls

Prep time: 5 minutes **Cooking time:** 15 minutes **Servings:** 4

1 pound shrimp, peeled, deveined and minced 1 egg, whisked	3 tablespoons coconut, shredded
½ cup coconut flour tablespoon cilantro, chopped	1 tablespoon avocado oil

1. In a bowl, mix all the ingredients, stir well and shape medium balls out of this mix Place the balls in your lined air fryer's basket, cook at 350 degrees F for 15 minutes and serve as an appetizer.

Nutrition:
Calories 184, fat 5, fiber 2, carbs 4, protein 7

Coconut Salmon Bites

Preparation time: 5 minutes **Cooking time:** 10 minutes **Servings:** 12

2 avocados, peeled, pitted and mashed	4 ounces smoked salmon, skinless, boneless and chopped 2 tablespoons coconut cream
1 teaspoon avocado oil 1 teaspoon dill, chopped	A pinch of salt and black pepper

1. In a bowl, mix all the ingredients, stir well and shape medium balls out of this mix. Place them in your air fryer's basket and cook at 350 degrees F for 10 minutes. Serve as an appetizer.

Nutrition:
Calories 100, fat 2, fiber 1, carbs 2, protein 2

Cashew Dip

Preparation time: 5 minutes **Cooking time:** 8 minutes **Servings:** 6

½ cup cashews, soaked in water for 4 hours and drained 3 tablespoons cilantro, chopped	garlic cloves, minced 1 teaspoon lime juice
A pinch of salt and black pepper	2 tablespoons coconut milk

1. In a blender, combine all the ingredients, pulse well and transfer to a ramekin. Put the ramekin in your air fryer's basket and cook at 350 degrees F for 8 minutes. Serve as a party dip.

Nutrition:
Calories 144, fat 2, fiber 1, carbs 3, protein 4

Mascarpone Duck Wraps

Prep time: 15 minutes **Cooking time:** 6 minutes **Servings:** 6

1-pound duck fillet, boiled	1 tablespoon mascarpone
1 teaspoon chili flakes	1 teaspoon onion powder
6 wonton wraps	1 egg yolk, whisked
Cooking spray	

1. Shred the boiled duck fillet and mix it up with mascarpone, chili flakes, and onion powder. After this, fill the wonton wraps with the duck mixture and roll them in the shape of pies. Brush the duck pies with the egg yolk. Preheat the air fryer to 385F. Put the duck pies in the air fryer and spray them with the cooking spray. Cook the snack for 3 minutes from each side.

Nutrition:
Calories 119, fat 1.5, fiber 0, carbs 2.5, protein 23.6

Turmeric Chicken Cubes

Prep time: 10 minutes **Cooking time:** 12 minutes **Servings:** 6

8 oz chicken fillet	½ teaspoon ground black pepper
½ teaspoon ground turmeric	¼ teaspoon ground coriander
½ teaspoon ground paprika	3 egg whites, whisked
4 tablespoons almond flour	Cooking spray

1. In the shallow bowl mix up ground black pepper, turmeric, coriander, and paprika. Then chop the chicken fillet on the small cubes and sprinkle them with spice mixture. Stir well and ad egg white. Mix up the chicken and egg whites well. After this, coat every chicken cube in the almond flour.
2. Preheat the air fryer to 375F. Put the chicken cubes in the air fryer basket in one layer and gently spray with cooking spray. Cook the chicken popcorn for 7 minutes. Then shake the chicken popcorn well and cook it for 5 minutes more.

Nutrition:
Calories 189, fat 12.2, fiber 2.2, carbs 4.5, protein 16.8

Garlic Eggplant Chips

Prep time: 10 minutes **Cooking time:** 25 minutes **Servings:** 4

1 eggplant, sliced	1 teaspoon garlic powder
1 tablespoon olive oil	

1. Mix up olive oil and garlic powder. Then brush every eggplant slice with a garlic powder mixture. Preheat the air fryer to 400F. Place the eggplant slices in the air fryer basket in one layer and cook them for 15 minutes.
2. Then flip the eggplant slices on another side and cook for 10 minutes.

Nutrition:
Calories 61, fat 3.7, fiber 4.1, carbs 7.2, protein 1.2

Chives Meatballs

Preparation time: 5 minutes **Cooking time:** 20 minutes **Servings:** 6

pound beef meat, ground	1 teaspoon onion powder
1 teaspoon garlic powder	A pinch of salt and black pepper
2 tablespoons chives, chopped Cooking spray	

1. In a bowl, mix all the ingredients except the cooking spray, stir well and shape medium meatballs out of this mix. Pace them in your lined air fryer's basket, grease with cooking spray and cook at 360 degrees F for 20 minutes. Serve as an appetizer.

Nutrition:
Calories 180, fat 5, fiber 2, carbs 5, protein 7

Pickled Fries

Prep time: 10 minutes **Cooking time:** 8 minutes **Servings:** 4

2 pickles, sliced	1 tablespoon dried dill
1 egg, beaten	2 tablespoons flax meal

1. Dip the sliced pickles in the egg and then sprinkle with dried ill and flax meal. Place them in the air fryer basket in one layer and cook at 400F for 8 minutes.

Nutrition:
Calories 36, fat 2.4, fiber 1.5, carbs 2.3, protein 2.4

Basil Pork Bites

Preparation time: 10 minutes **Cooking time:** 25 minutes
Servings: 6

2 pounds pork belly, cut into strips	2 tablespoons olive oil
2 teaspoons fennel seeds	A pinch of salt and black pepper A pinch of basil, dried

1. In a bowl, mix all the ingredients, toss and put the pork strips in your air fryer's basket and cook at 425 degrees F for 25 minutes. Divide into bowls and serve as a snack.

Nutrition:
Calories 251, fat 14, fiber 3, carbs 5, protein 18

Tomato Platter

Preparation time: 5 minutes **Cooking time:** 20 minutes
Servings: 6

6 tomatoes, halved	3 teaspoons sugar-free apricot jam 2 ounces watercress
2 teaspoons oregano, dried	A pinch of salt and black pepper 3 ounces cheddar cheese, grated
1 tablespoon olive oil	

1. Spread the jam on each tomato half, sprinkle oregano, salt and pepper, and drizzle the oil all over them Introduce them in the fryer's basket, sprinkle the cheese on top and cook at 360 degrees F for 20 minutes. Arrange the tomatoes on a platter, top each half with some watercress and serve as an appetizer.

Nutrition:
Calories 131, fat 7, fiber 2, carbs 4, protein 7

Mixed Veggie Bites

Prep time: 10 minutes **Cooking time:** 20 minutes **Servings:** 6

1 cup zucchinis, cubed	1 cup eggplant, cubed
3 oz Parmesan	1 tablespoon coconut cream
1 egg, beaten	½ tablespoon avocado oil

1. In the mixing bowl mix up beaten egg and coconut cream. Then dip the veggie cubes in the egg mixture and sprinkle with Parmesan. Place the vegetables in the air fryer basket in one layer and cook at 400F for 10 minutes. Serve as a snack.

Nutrition:
Calories 75, fat 4.6, fiber 0.9, carbs 3.6, protein 5.9

Parmesan Green Beans Sticks

Preparation time: 5 minutes **Cooking time:** 12 minutes
Servings: 4

12 ounces green beans, trimmed 1 cup parmesan, grated	1 egg, whisked
A pinch of salt and black pepper	¼ teaspoon sweet paprika

1. In a bowl, mix the parmesan with salt, pepper and the paprika and stir. Put the egg in a separate bowl, Dredge the green beans in egg and then in the parmesan mix. Arrange the green beans in your air fryer's basket and cook at 380 degrees F for 12 minutes. Serve as a snack.

Nutrition:
Calories 112, fat 6, fiber 1, carbs 2, protein 9

Chili Calamari Rings

Prep time: 10 minutes **Cooking time:** 15 minutes **Servings:** 2

1 pound calamari rings	1 teaspoon black pepper
½ teaspoon avocado oil	¼ teaspoon chili powder

1. In the air fryer, mix the calamari with black pepper and the other ingredients and toss. Cook the onion rings at 400F for 10 minutes.

Nutrition:
Calories 127, fat 8.2, fiber 1.3, carbs 5.7, protein 7.7

Lemon Shrimp Bowls

Preparation time: 5 minutes **Cooking time:** 10 minutes
Servings: 4

pound shrimp, peeled and deveined 3 garlic cloves, minced	¼ cup olive oil Juice of ½ lemon
A pinch of salt and black pepper	¼ teaspoon cayenne pepper

1. In a pan that fits your air fryer, mix all the ingredients, toss, introduce in the fryer and cook at 370 degrees F for 10 minutes. Serve as a snack.

Nutrition:
Calories 242, fat 14, fiber 2, carbs 3, protein 17

Cucumber Sushi

Prep time: 10 minutes **Cooking time:** 10 minutes **Servings:** 10

10 bacon slices	2 tablespoons cream cheese
1 cucumber	

1. Place the bacon slices in the air fryer in one layer and cook for 10 minutes at 400F. Meanwhile, cut the cucumber into small wedges. When the bacon is cooked, cool it to the room temperature and spread with cream cheese.
2. Then place the cucumber wedges over the cream cheese and roll the bacon into the sushi.

Nutrition:
Calories 114, fat 8.7, fiber 0.2, carbs 1.4, protein 7.4

Garlic Chicken Meatballs

Preparation time: 5 minutes **Cooking time:** 20 minutes
Servings: 12

pound chicken breast, skinless, boneless and ground A pinch of salt and black pepper	2 garlic cloves, minced
2 spring onions, chopped	2 tablespoons ghee, melted 6 tablespoons keto hot sauce
¾ cup almond meal Cooking spray	

1. In a bowl, mix all the ingredients except the cooking spray, stir well and shape medium meatballs out of this mix. Arrange the meatballs in your air fryer's basket, grease them with cooking spray and cook at 360 degrees F for 20 minutes. Serve as an appetizer.

Nutrition:
Calories 257, fat 14, fiber 1, carbs 3, protein 17

Hot Dogs

Prep time: 15 minutes **Cooking time:** 5 minutes **Servings:** 4

4 hot dogs	1 egg, beaten
1/3 cup coconut flour	½ teaspoon ground turmeric

1. In the bowl mix up egg, coconut flour, and ground turmeric. Then dip the hot dogs in the mixture. Transfer the hot dogs in the freezer and freeze them for 5 minutes. Meanwhile, preheat the air fryer to 400F. Place the frozen hot dogs in the air fryer basket and cook them for 6 minutes or until they are light brown.

Nutrition:

Calories 205, fat 15.5, fiber 4.1, carbs 8, protein 8.2

Cilantro Pork Meatballs

Preparation time: 5 minutes **Cooking time:** 20 minutes **Servings:** 12

1 pound pork meat, ground 3 spring onions, minced	3 tablespoons cilantro, chopped 1 tablespoon ginger, grated
2 garlic cloves, minced 1 chili pepper, minced	A pinch of salt and black pepper
1 and ½ tablespoons coconut aminos Cooking spray	

1. In a bowl, mix all the ingredients except the cooking spray, stir really well and shape medium meatballs out of this mix. Arrange them in your air fryer's basket, grease with cooking spray and cook at 380 degrees F for 20 minutes. Serve as an appetizer.

Nutrition:

Calories 200, fat 12, fiber 2, carbs 3, protein 14

Harissa Deviled Eggs

Prep time: 10 minutes **Cooking time:** 17 minutes **Servings:** 4

2 eggs	½ teaspoon harissa
½ teaspoon chili flakes	¼ teaspoon chili powder
1 teaspoon ricotta cheese	½ teaspoon dried thyme

1. Preheat the air fryer to 250F. Place the eggs in the air fryer basket and cook them for 17 minutes. Then cool and peel the eggs. Cut the peeled eggs into halves and remove the egg yolks. Stir the egg yolks with the help of the fork until they are smooth. After this, add chili flakes, harissa, chili powder, ricotta cheese, and dried thyme. Stir the mass until smooth. Fill the egg whites with hot egg yolk mixture.

Nutrition:

Calories 72, fat 4.9, fiber 0.2. carbs 1.3, protein 6

Coconut Radish Chips

Preparation time: 5 minutes **Cooking time:** 15 minutes **Servings:** 4

16 ounces radishes, thinly sliced A pinch of salt and black pepper	2 tablespoons coconut oil, melted

1. In a bowl, mix the radish slices with salt, pepper and the oil, toss well, place them in your air fryer's basket and cook at 400 degrees F for 15 minutes, flipping them halfway. Serve as a snack.

Nutrition:

Calories 174, fat 5, fiber 1, carbs 3, protein 6

Bacon Asparagus Wraps

Preparation time: 5 minutes **Cooking time:** 15 minutes **Servings:** 8

16 asparagus spears, trimmed 16 bacon strips	2 tablespoons olive oil
1 tablespoon lemon juice	1 teaspoon thyme, chopped
1 teaspoon oregano, chopped	A pinch of salt and black pepper

1. In a bowl, mix the oil with lemon juice, the herbs, salt and pepper and whisk well. Brush the asparagus spears with this mix and wrap each in a bacon strip. Arrange the asparagus wraps in your air fryer's basket and cook at 390 degrees F for 15 minutes. Serve as an appetizer.

Nutrition:

Calories 173, fat 4, fiber 2, carbs 3, protein 6

Pickled Chips

Prep time: 10 minutes **Cooking time:** 10 minutes **Servings:** 4

1 cup pickles, sliced	2 eggs, beaten
½ cup coconut flakes	1 teaspoon dried cilantro
¼ cup Provolone cheese, grated	

1. Mix up coconut flakes, dried cilantro, and Provolone cheese. Then dip the sliced pickles in the egg and coat in coconut flakes mixture. Preheat the air fryer to 400F. Arrange the pickles in the air fryer in one layer and cook them for 5 minutes. Then flip the pickles on another side and cook for another 5 minutes.

Nutrition:

Calories 100, fat 7.8, fiber 1.4, carbs 2.8, protein 5.4

Cashew Bowls

Prep time: 5 minutes **Cooking time:** 5 minutes **Servings:** 4

4 oz cashew	1 teaspoon ranch seasoning
1 teaspoon sesame oil	

1. Preheat the air fryer to 375F. Mix up cashew with ranch seasoning and sesame oil and put in the preheated air fryer. Cook the cashew for 4 minutes. Then shake well and cook for 1 minute more.

Nutrition:

Calories 6, fat 117, fiber 9.5, carbs 6.2, protein 2.9

Lemon Olives Dip

Preparation time: 5 minutes **Cooking time:** 5 minutes **Servings:** 6

1 cup black olives, pitted and chopped	¼ cup capers
½ cup olive oil	3 tablespoons lemon juice
	2 garlic cloves, minced
2 teaspoon apple cider vinegar 1 cup parsley leaves	1 cup basil leaves
A pinch of salt and black pepper	

1. In a blender, combine all the ingredients, pulse well and transfer to a ramekin. Place the ramekin in your air fryer's basket and cook at 350 degrees F for 5 minutes. Serve as a snack.

Nutrition:

Calories 120, fat 5, fiber 2, carbs 3, protein 7

Scallions Spinach Pie

Prep time: 15 minutes **Cooking time:** 15 minutes **Servings:** 6

½ cup almond flour	6 eggs
2 cup spinach, chopped	1 oz scallions, chopped
1 teaspoon sesame oil	1 tablespoon cream cheese
½ teaspoon baking powder	1 tablespoon butter, softened
1 teaspoon ground black pepper	

1. In the mixing bowl put almond flour, baking powder, and butter. Then crack 2 eggs and mix up the mixture gently. After this, knead the non- sticky dough. Transfer the dough in the air fryer baking pan and flatten well to get the shape of the pie crust. After this, preheat the air fryer to 365F and put the pan with the pie crust inside. Cook it for 10 minutes. Meanwhile, pour sesame oil in the skillet and preheat it over the medium heat. Add scallions and cook them for 2 minutes. Then stir the vegetables and add chopped spinach and cream cheese. Cook the greens for 5 minutes over the medium heat. Then sprinkle it with ground black pepper. Transfer the spinach mixture in the pie crust and flatten gently. Bake the pie for 5 minutes at 365F in the air fryer.

Nutrition:
Calories 111, fat 8.9, fiber 0.7, carbs 2, protein 6.6

Lime Tomato Salsa

Prep time: 5 minutes **Cooking time:** 8 minutes **Servings:** 4

4 tomatoes, cubed	3 chili peppers, minced 2 spring onions, chopped
1 garlic clove, minced	2 tablespoons lime juice
2 teaspoons cilantro, chopped	2 teaspoons parsley, chopped Cooking spray

1. Grease a pan that fits your air fryer with the cooking spray, and mix all the ingredients inside. Introduce the pan in the machine and cook at 360 degrees F for 8 minutes. Divide into bowls and serve as an appetizer.

Nutrition:
Calories 148, fat 1, fiber 2, carbs 3, protein 5

Beet Chips

Prep time: 5 minutes **Cooking time:** 30 minutes **Servings:**4

6 oz beetroot, sliced	1 teaspoon salt

1. Sprinkle the beetroot slices with salt and mix up well. Then preheat the air fryer to 320F and put the beetroot slices in the air fryer basket. Cook them for 30 minutes. Shake the beetroot chips every 5 minutes.

Nutrition:
Calories 19, fat 0.1, fiber 0.9, carbs 4.2, protein 0.7

Chili Kale Chips

Prep time: 5 minutes **Cooking time:** 5 minutes **Servings:**4

1 teaspoon nutritional yeast	1 teaspoon salt
2 cups kale, chopped	½ teaspoon chili flakes
1 teaspoon sesame oil	

1. Mix up kale leaves with nutritional yeast, salt, chili flakes, and sesame oil. Shake the greens well. Preheat the air fryer to 400F and put the kale leaves in the air fryer basket. Cook them for 3 minutes and then give a good shake. Cook the kale leaves for 2 minutes more.

Nutrition:
Calories 30, fat 1.2, fiber 0.7, carbs 3.9, protein 1.4

Chives Salmon Dip

Preparation time: 5 minutes **Cooking time:** 6 minutes **Servings:** 4

8 ounces cream cheese, soft	2 tablespoons lemon juice
½ cup coconut cream	4 ounces smoked salmon, skinless, boneless and minced A pinch of salt and black pepper
1 tablespoon chives, chopped	

1. In a bowl, mix all the ingredients and whisk them really well. Transfer the mix to a ramekin, place it in your air fryer's basket and cook at 360 degrees F for 6 minutes. Serve as a party spread.

Nutrition:
Calories 180, fat 7, fiber 1, carbs 5, protein 7

Herbed Pork Skewers

Prep time: 10 minutes **Cooking time:** 20 minutes **Servings:** 4

½ pound pork shoulder, cubed	¼ teaspoon sweet paprika
1 tablespoon coconut oil, melted	¼ teaspoon cumin, ground
¼ cup olive oil	¼ cup green bell peppers, chopped 1 and ½ tablespoons lemon juice
1 tablespoon cilantro, chopped 2 tablespoons parsley, chopped 2 garlic cloves, minced	A pinch of salt and black pepper

1. In a blender, combine the olive oil with bell peppers, lemon juice, cilantro, parsley, garlic, salt and pepper and pulse well. Thread the meat onto the skewers, sprinkle cumin and paprika all over and rub with the coconut oil. In a bowl mix the pork skewers with the herbed mix and rub well. Place the skewers in your air fryer's basket, cook at 370 degrees F for 10 minutes on each side and serve as an appetizer.

Nutrition:
Calories 249, fat 16, fiber 2, carbs 3, protein 17

Cheesy Spinach Triangles

Prep time: 6 minutes **Cooking time:** 20 minutes **Servings:** 6

cups mozzarella, shredded	½ cup almond flour 2 eggs, whisked
4 tablespoons coconut flour	
A pinch of salt and black pepper 6 ounces spinach, chopped	¼ cup parmesan, grated
ounces cream cheese, soft	2 tablespoons ghee, melted

1. In a bowl, mix the mozzarella with coconut and almond flour, eggs, salt and pepper, stir well until you obtain a dough and roll it well on a parchment paper. Cut into triangles and leave them aside for now. In a bowl, mix the spinach with parmesan, cream cheese, salt and pepper and stir really well. Divide this into the center of each dough triangle, roll and seal the edges. Brush the rolls with the ghee, place them in your air fryer's basket and cook at 360 degrees F for 20 minutes. Serve as an appetizer.

Nutrition:
Calories 210, fat 8, fiber 1, carbs 3, protein 8

Turmeric Jicama Bites

Prep time: 10 minutes **Cooking time:** 3 minutes **Servings:**4

8 oz Jicama, peeled	½ teaspoon ground turmeric
¼ teaspoon dried dill	1 tablespoon avocado oil

1. Cut the Jicama on the wedges and sprinkle them with turmeric and dried dill. Then sprinkle the vegetables with avocado oil. Preheat the air fryer to 400F. Place the Jicama wedges in the air fryer basket in one layer and cook them for 3 minutes.

Nutrition:

Calories 27, fat 0.5, fiber 3, carbs 5.4, protein 0.5

Cheese Bites

Prep time: 10 minutes **Cooking time:** 6 minutes **Servings:**4

8 oz goat cheese	1 egg, beaten
1 tablespoon heavy cream	¼ cup coconut flour
¼ cup almond flour	1 teaspoon sesame oil

1. Slice the goat cheese on 4 slices. Then mix up beaten egg and heavy cream. In the separated bowl mix up coconut flour and almond flour. Preheat the air fryer to 400F. Dip the goat cheese slices in the egg mixture and then coat in the almond flour mixture. Repeat the last 2 steps two times. Transfer the goat cheese slices in the air fryer basket and cook them for 3 minutes from each side or until the cheese slices are light brown.

Nutrition:

Calories 340, fat 25.9, fiber 3.2, carbs 6.3, protein 20.6

Eggplant Dip

Prep time: 10 minutes **Cooking time:** 15 minutes **Servings:**4

1 eggplant, peeled	1 garlic clove, peeled
1 tablespoon sesame oil	¼ teaspoon ginger, grated
1 chili pepper, minced	½ tablespoon spring onions, chopped
½ teaspoon chili powder	¼ teaspoon ground coriander
¼ teaspoon turmeric	½ teaspoon fresh cilantro, chopped

1. Chop the eggplant into the cubes and put it in the air fryer. Add garlic and cook the vegetables at 400F for 15 minutes. Shake the vegetables every 5 minutes. After this, transfer the soft eggplants and garlic in the bowl and mash them with the help of the fork. Add sesame oil, ginger, minced chili pepper, onion, chili powder, ground coriander, and turmeric. Stir the mixture until homogenous and top with cilantro.

Nutrition:

Calories 63, fat 3.7, fiber 4.3, carbs 7.5, protein 1.3

Bacon Butter

Prep time: 30 minutes **Cooking time:** 2 minutes **Servings:**5

½ cup butter	3 oz bacon, chopped

1. Preheat the air fryer to 400F and put the bacon inside. Cook it for 8 minutes. Stir the bacon every 2 minutes. Meanwhile, soften the butter in the oven and put it in the butter mold. Add cooked bacon and churn the butter. Refrigerate the butter for 30 minutes.

Nutrition:

Calories 255, fat 25.5, fiber 0, carbs 0.3, protein 6.5

Balsamic Mushroom Platter

Preparation time: 5 minutes **Cooking time:** 12 minutes **Servings:** 4

tablespoons balsamic vinegar 2 tablespoons olive oil	½ teaspoon basil, dried
½ teaspoon tarragon, dried	½ teaspoon rosemary, dried
½ teaspoon thyme, dried	A pinch of salt and black pepper
12 ounces Portobello mushrooms, sliced	

1. In a bowl, mix all the ingredients and toss well. Arrange the mushroom slices in your air fryer's basket and cook at 380 degrees F for 12 minutes. Arrange the mushroom slices on a platter and serve.

Nutrition:

Calories 147, fat 8, fiber 2, carbs 3, protein 3

Turkey Balls

Prep time: 5 minutes **Cooking time:** 20 minutes **Servings:** 8

2 cups mozzarella, grated	1 pound turkey breast, skinless, boneless and ground
½ cup almond meal	½ cup coconut milk
3 tablespoons ghee, melted	tablespoon Italian seasoning
1 teaspoon garlic powder	½ cup parmesan, grated Cooking spray

1. In a bowl, mix all the ingredients except the parmesan and the cooking spray and stir well. Shape medium balls out of this mix, coat each in the parmesan, and arrange them in your air fryer. Grease the balls with cooking spray and cook at 380 degrees F for 20 minutes. Serve as an appetizer.

Nutrition:

Calories 210, fat 12, fiber 2, carbs 4, protein 14

Cucumber Bites

Prep time: 10 minutes **Cooking time:** 7 minutes **Servings:**4

1 teaspoon cream cheese	½ teaspoon cumin seeds
1 cucumber	4 oz salmon fillet
¼ teaspoon lemon juice	¼ teaspoon olive oil
¼ teaspoon salt	

1. Sprinkle the salmon fillet with lemon juice, olive oil, and salt, Place it in the air fryer and cook for 7 minutes at 385F. Then chop it and mix up with cumin seeds and cream cheese. Cut the cucumber into 4 slices. Top every cucumber slice with salmon mixture.

Nutrition:

Calories 55, fat 2.5, fiber 0.4, carbs 2.9, protein 6.1

Sage Radish Chips

Prep time: 10 minutes **Cooking time:** 35 minutes **Servings:**6

2 cups radish, sliced	½ teaspoon sage
2 teaspoons avocado oil	½ teaspoon salt

1. In the mixing bowl mix up radish, sage, avocado oil, and salt. Preheat the air fryer to 320F. Put the sliced radish in the air fryer basket and cook it for 35 minutes. Shake the vegetables every 10 minutes.

Nutrition:

Calories 8, fat 0.3, fiber 0.7, carbs 1.4, protein 0.3

Lemon Tofu Cubes

Prep time: 10 minutes **Cooking time:** 7 minutes **Servings:** 2

½ teaspoon ground coriander	1 tablespoon avocado oil
1 teaspoon lemon juice	½ teaspoon chili flakes
6 oz tofu	

1. In the shallow bowl mix up ground coriander, avocado oil, lemon juice, and chili flakes. Chop the tofu into cubes and sprinkle with coriander mixture. Shake the tofu. After this, preheat the air fryer to 400F and put the tofu cubes in it. Cook the tofu for 4 minutes. Then flip the tofu on another side and cook for 3 minutes more.

Nutrition:
Calories 70, fat 4.5, fiber 1.1, carbs 1.9, protein 7.1

Crab and Chives Balls

Prep time: 5 minutes **Cooking time:** 20 minutes **Servings:** 8

½ cup coconut cream	tablespoons chives, mined 1 egg, whisked
1 teaspoon mustard	1 teaspoon lemon juice
16 ounces lump crabmeat, chopped 2/3 cup almond meal	A pinch of salt and black pepper Cooking spray

1. In a bowl, mix all the ingredients except the cooking spray and stir well. Shape medium balls out of this mix, place them in the fryer and cook at 390 degrees F for 20 minutes. Serve as an appetizer.

Nutrition:
Calories 141, fat 7, fiber 2, carbs 4, protein 9

Creamy Sausage Bites

Prep time: 10 minutes **Cooking time:** 9 minutes **Servings:** 6

1 cup ground pork sausages	¼ cup almond flour
¼ teaspoon baking powder	¼ teaspoon salt
1 teaspoon flax meal	1 egg, beaten
½ teaspoon dried dill	2 tablespoons heavy cream
1 teaspoon sunflower oil	

1. In the bowl mix up ground pork sausages, almond flour, baking powder, salt, flax meal, egg, dried dill, and heavy cream. Make the small balls from the mixture. Preheat the air fryer to 400F. Place the sausage balls in the air fryer in one layer and cook them for 9 minutes. Flip the balls on another side after 5 minutes of cooking.

Nutrition:
Calories 67, fat 4.9, fiber 0.3, carbs 0.9, protein 5.4

Shrimp Dip

Prep time: 5 minutes **Cooking time:** 20 minutes **Servings:** 4

1 pound shrimp, peeled, deveined and minced 2 tablespoons ghee, melted	¼ pound mushrooms, minced
½ cup mozzarella, shredded 4 garlic cloves, minced	1 tablespoon parsley, chopped Salt and black pepper to the taste

1. In a bowl, mix all the ingredients, stir well, divide into small ramekins and place them in your air fryer's basket. Cook at 360 degrees F for 20 minutes and serve as a party dip.

Nutrition:
Calories 271, fat 15, fiber 3, carbs 4, protein 14

Stuffed Eggs

Prep time: 10 minutes **Cooking time:** 17 minutes **Servings:** 4

4 eggs	2 oz avocado, peeled, mashed
1 teaspoon lemon juice	¼ teaspoon butter, melted

1. Place the eggs in the air fryer and cook them at 250F for 17 minutes. Then cool and peel the eggs. Cut the eggs into halves and remove the egg yolk. Churn the egg yolks with the help of the fork. Add butter, mashed avocado, and lemon juice. Stir the mixture until smooth. Fill the egg whites with the avocado mixture.

Nutrition:
Calories 94, fat 7.4, fiber 1, carbs 1.6, protein 5.8

Tuna Bowls

Prep time: 5 minutes **Cooking time:** 10 minutes **Servings:** 2

1 pound tuna, skinless, boneless and cubed 3 scallion stalks, minced	1 chili pepper, minced 2 tablespoon olive oil
1 tablespoon coconut cream	1 tablespoon coconut aminos 2 tomatoes, cubed
1 teaspoon sesame seeds	

1. In a pan that fits your air fryer, mix all the ingredients except the sesame seeds, toss, introduce in the fryer and cook at 360 degrees F for 10 minutes. Divide into bowls and serve as an appetizer with sesame seeds sprinkled on top.

Nutrition:
Calories 231, fat 18, fiber 3, carbs 4, protein 18

Avocado Wedges

Prep time: 5 minutes **Cooking time:** 8 minutes **Servings:** 4

4 avocados, peeled, pitted and cut into wedges 1 egg, whisked	and ½ cups almond meal
A pinch of salt and black pepper Cooking spray	

1. Put the egg in a bowl, and the almond meal in another. Season avocado wedges with salt and pepper, coat them in egg and then in meal almond. Arrange the avocado bites in your air fryer's basket, grease them with cooking spray and cook at 400 degrees F for 8 minutes. Serve as a snack right away.

Nutrition:
Calories 200, fat 12, fiber 3, carbs 5, protein 16

Bacon Dip

Prep time: 5 minutes **Cooking time:** 20 minutes **Servings:** 12

tablespoons ghee, melted	cups spring onions, chopped A pinch of salt and black pepper
2 ounces cheddar cheese, shredded 1/3 cup coconut cream	6 bacon slices, cooked and crumbled

1. Heat up a pan that fits the fryer with the ghee over medium-high heat, add the onions, stir and sauté for 7 minutes. Add the remaining ingredients, except the bacon and stir well. Sprinkle the bacon on top, introduce the pan in the machine and cook at and 380 degrees F for 13 minutes. Divide into bowls and serve as a party dip.

Nutrition:
Calories 220, fat 12, fiber 2, carbs 4, protein 15

Eggplant Sticks

Prep time: 10 minutes **Cooking time:** 8 minutes **Servings:** 3

6 oz eggplant, trimmed	½ teaspoon dried oregano
½ teaspoon dried cilantro	½ teaspoon dried thyme
½ teaspoon ground cumin	½ teaspoon salt
1 tablespoon olive oil	¼ teaspoon garlic powder

1. Cut the eggplant into the fries and sprinkle with dried oregano, cilantro, thyme, cumin, salt, and garlic powder. Then sprinkle the eggplant fries with olive oil and shake well. Preheat the air fryer to 400F. Place the eggplant fries in the air fryer and cook them for 4 minutes from each side.

Nutrition:

Calories 58, fat 4.9, fiber 2.2, carbs 3.9, protein 0.7

Crab Dip

Prep time: 5 minutes **Cooking time:** 20 minutes **Servings:** 4

8 ounces cream cheese, soft 1 tablespoon lemon juice	1 cup coconut cream
1 tablespoon lemon juice	1 bunch green onions, minced
1 pound artichoke hearts, drained and chopped 12 ounces jumbo crab meat	A pinch of salt and black pepper
1 and ½ cups mozzarella, shredded	

1. In a bowl, combine all the ingredients except half of the cheese and whisk them really well. Transfer this to a pan that fits your air fryer, introduce in the machine and cook at 400 degrees F for 15 minutes. Sprinkle the rest of the mozzarella on top and cook for 5 minutes more. Divide the mix into bowls and serve as a party dip.

Nutrition:

Calories 240, fat 8, fiber 2, carbs 4, protein 14

Coconut Chicken Wings

Prep time: 10 minutes **Cooking time:** 10 minutes **Servings:** 4

4 chicken wings	1 teaspoon keto tomato sauce
2 tablespoons coconut cream	1 teaspoon nut oil
¼ teaspoon salt	

1. Sprinkle the chicken wings with tomato sauce, nut oil, coconut cream, and salt. Massage the chicken wings with the help of the fingertips and put in the air fryer. Cook the chicken at 400f for 6 minutes. Then flip the wings on another side and cook for 4 minutes more.

Nutrition:

Calories 53, fat 4.6, fiber 0.2, carbs 0.7, protein 2.5

Chicken Wraps

Prep time: 10 minutes **Cooking time:** 10 minutes **Servings:** 2

6 oz chicken fillet	2 oz bacon, sliced
1 teaspoon avocado oil	¼ teaspoon ground black pepper

1. Chop the chicken fillets into cubes and wrap in the bacon. Then slice the wrapped chicken nuggets with ground black pepper and avocado oil and place in the air fryer. Cook the nuggets for 10 minutes at 400F.

Nutrition:

Calories 319, fat 18.5, fiber 0.2, carbs 0.7, protein 35.2

Chicken and Berries Bowls

Preparation time: 5 minutes **Cooking time:** 20 minutes **Servings:** 2

1 chicken breast, skinless, boneless and cut into strips 2 cups baby spinach	1 cup blueberries
6 strawberries, chopped	½ cup walnuts, chopped
3 tablespoons balsamic vinegar 1 tablespoon olive oil	3 tablespoons feta cheese, crumbled

1. Heat up a pan that fits the air fryer with the oil over medium heat, add the meat and brown it for 5 minutes. Add the rest of the ingredients except the spinach, toss, introduce in the fryer and cook at 370 degrees F for 15 minutes. Add the spinach, toss, cook for another 5 minutes, divide into bowls and serve.

Nutrition:

Calories 240, fat 14, fiber 2, carbs 3, protein 12

Tomato Salad

Preparation time: 5 minutes **Cooking time:** 12 minutes **Servings:** 6

1 pound tomatoes, sliced	1 tablespoon balsamic vinegar 1 tablespoon ginger, grated
½ teaspoon coriander, ground 1 teaspoon sweet paprika	1 teaspoon chili powder
1 cup mozzarella, shredded	

1. In a pan that fits your air fryer, mix all the ingredients except the mozzarella, toss, introduce the pan in the air fryer and cook at 360 degrees F for 12 minutes. Divide into bowls and serve cold as an appetizer with the mozzarella sprinkled all over.

Nutrition:

Calories 185, fat 8, fiber 2, carbs 4, protein 8

Turmeric Cauliflower Popcorn

Prep time: 10 minutes **Cooking time:** 11 minutes **Servings:** 4

1 cup cauliflower florets	1 teaspoon ground turmeric
2 eggs, beaten	2 tablespoons almond flour
1 teaspoon salt	Cooking spray

1. Cut the cauliflower florets into small pieces and sprinkle with ground turmeric and salt. Then dip the vegetables in the eggs and coat in the almond flour. Preheat the air fryer to 400F. Place the cauliflower popcorn in the air fryer in one layer and cook for 7 minutes. Give a good shake to the vegetables and cook them for 4 minutes more.

Nutrition:

Calories 120, fat 9.3, fiber 2.3, carbs 4.9, protein 6.3

Beef Bites

Prep time: 10 minutes **Cooking time:** 15 minutes **Servings:** 2

1 teaspoon cayenne pepper	8 oz beef loin, chopped
1 tablespoon coconut flour	1 teaspoon nut oil
¼ teaspoon salt	1 teaspoon apple cider vinegar

1. Sprinkle the beef with apple cider vinegar and salt. Then sprinkle it with cayenne pepper and coconut flour. Shake the meat well and transfer in the air fryer. Sprinkle it with nut oil and cook at 365F for 15 minutes. Shake the beef popcorn every 5 minutes to avoid burning.

Nutrition:

Calories 222, fat 11.5, fiber 2.7, carbs 5.9, protein 22

Zucchini and Tomato Salsa

Preparation time: 5 minutes **Cooking time:** 15 minutes
Servings: 6

½ pounds zucchinis, roughly cubed	2 spring onions, chopped tomatoes, cubed
Salt and black pepper to the taste	1 tablespoon balsamic vinegar

1. In a pan that fits your air fryer, mix all the ingredients, toss, introduce the pan in the fryer and cook at 360 degrees F for 15 minutes. Divide the salsa into cups and serve cold.

Nutrition:

Calories 164, fat 6, fiber 2, carbs 3, protein 8

Cumin Pork Sticks

Prep time: 10 minutes **Cooking time:** 12 minutes **Servings:** 4

2 eggs, beaten	4 tablespoons flax meal
½ teaspoon chili powder	¼ teaspoon ground cumin
8 oz pork loin	1 teaspoon sunflower oil

1. Cut the pork loin into the sticks and sprinkle with chili powder and cumin powder. Then dip the pork sticks in the eggs and coat in the flax meal.
2. Place the meat in the air fryer and sprinkle with sunflower oil. Cook the snack at 400F for 6 minutes. Then flip the pork sticks on another side and cook for 6 minutes more.

Nutrition:

Calories 211, fat 13.8, fiber 2.1, carbs 2.4, protein 19.8

Cucumber and Spring Onions Salsa

Preparation time: 5 minutes **Cooking time:** 5 minutes
Servings: 4

½ pounds cucumbers, sliced 2 spring onions, chopped	tomatoes cubed
2 red chili peppers, chopped 2 tablespoons ginger, grated	1 tablespoon balsamic vinegar A drizzle of olive oil

1. In a pan that fits your air fryer, mix all the ingredients, toss, introduce in the fryer and cook at 340 degrees F for 5 minutes. Divide into bowls and serve cold as an appetizer.

Nutrition:

Calories 150, fat 2, fiber 1, carbs 2, protein 4

Cucumber Chips

Prep time: 10 minutes **Cooking time:** 30 minutes **Servings:** 2

1 cucumber, thinly sliced	1 teaspoon butter, melted
½ teaspoon Truvia	

1. Sprinkle the cucumber chips with Truvia and melted butter. After this, preheat the air fryer to 335F. Put the cucumber chips in the air fryerbasket and cook them for 30 minutes. Shake the chips every 5 minutes during cooking.

Nutrition:

Calories 29, fat 1.9, fiber 1, carbs 3.5, protein 0.3

Spinach Dip

Preparation time: 5 minutes **Cooking time:** 20 minutes
Servings: 6

6 tablespoons ghee, melted	4 spring onions, chopped
1 pound spinach, torn	
1 cup mozzarella, shredded	Salt and black pepper to
1 cup coconut cream	the taste

1. In a pan that fits the air fryer, combine all the ingredients and whisk them really well. Introduce the pan in your air fryer and cook at 370 degrees F for 20 minutes. Divide into bowls and serve.

Nutrition:

Calories 184, fat 12, fiber 2, carbs 3, protein 9

Coconut Celery Stalks

Prep time: 10 minutes **Cooking time:** 4 minutes **Servings:** 4

4 celery stalks	1 teaspoon flax meal
1 egg, beaten	1 teaspoon coconut flour
1 teaspoon sunflower oil	

1. In the bowl mix up flax meal and coconut flour. Then dip the celery stalks in the egg and coat in the flax meal mixture. Sprinkle the celery stalks with sunflower oil and place in the air fryer basket. Cook for 4 minutes at 400F.

Nutrition:

Calories 34, fat 2.6, fiber 0.7, carbs 1.1, protein 1.8

Cheese Dip

Preparation time: 5 minutes **Cooking time:** 10 minutes
Servings: 10

1 pound mozzarella, shredded	1 tablespoon thyme, chopped 6 garlic cloves, minced
3 tablespoons olive oil	teaspoon rosemary, chopped A pinch of salt and black pepper

1. In a pan that fits your air fryer, mix all the ingredients, whisk really well, introduce in the air fryer and cook at 370 degrees F for 10 minutes. Divide into bowls and serve right away.

Nutrition:

Calories 184, fat 11, fiber 3, carbs 5, protein 7

Pepperoni Chips

Prep time: 5 minutes **Cooking time:** 10 minutes **Servings:** 4

10 oz pepperoni, sliced	Cooking spray

1. Preheat the air fryer to 375F. Place the pepperoni chips in the air fryer basket in one layer and cook them for 10 minutes – for 5 minutes from each side.

Nutrition:

Calories 350, fat 31.2, fiber 0, carbs 0, protein 16.1

Zucchini Fries

Prep time: 15 minutes **Cooking time:** 4 minutes **Servings:** 4

1 large zucchini, trimmed	3 tablespoon coconut flakes
1 tablespoon coconut flour	1 teaspoon salt
1 teaspoon dried oregano	1 tablespoon cream cheese
Cooking spray	

1. Cut the zucchini into the fries and sprinkle them with salt and dried oregano. Then mix up coconut flakes and coconut flour. Sprinkle the zucchini fries with the cream cheese and then coat vegetables in the coconut flour mixture. Preheat the air fryer to 400F. Place the zucchini fries in one layer and cook them for 4 minutes.

Nutrition:
Calories 44, fat 2.6, fiber 2, carbs 4.6, protein 1.6

Artichokes and Cream Cheese Dip

Prep time: 5 minutes **Cooking time:** 25 minutes **Servings:** 6

teaspoons olive oil	2 spring onions, minced
1 pound artichoke hearts, steamed and chopped 2 garlic cloves, minced	6 ounces cream cheese, soft
½ cup almond milk	cup mozzarella, shredded
A pinch of salt and black pepper	

1. Grease a baking pan that fits the air fryer with the oil and mix all the ingredients except the mozzarella inside. Sprinkle the cheese all over, introduce the pan in the air fryer and cook at 370 degrees F for 25 minutes. Divide into bowls and serve as a party dip.

Nutrition:
Calories 231, fat 11, fiber 2, carbs 4, protein 8

Avocado and Feta Dip

Prep time: 5 minutes **Cooking time:** 5 minutes **Servings:** 6

avocados, peeled, pitted and mashed	½ cup feta cheese, crumbled
¼ cup spring onion, chopped	¼ cup parsley, chopped
1 tablespoon jalapeno, minced 1 garlic clove, minced	Juice of 1 lime

1. In a ramekin, mix all the ingredients and whisk them well. Introduce in the fryer and cook at 380 degrees F for 5 minutes. Serve as a party dip right away.

Nutrition:
Calories 200, fat 12, fiber 2, carbs 4, protein 9

Avocado Fries

Prep time: 15 minutes **Cooking time:** 8 minutes **Servings:** 6

1 avocado, pitted, peeled	1 egg, beaten
¼ teaspoon salt	4 tablespoons almond flour
Cooking spray	

1. Cut the avocado on 6 fries and sprinkle them with salt. Then dip the fries in the egg and coat in the almond flour. Preheat the air fryer to 395F. Place the avocado fries in one layer in the air fryer basket, spray with the cooking spray. and cook them for 4 minutes from each side.

Nutrition:
Calories 185, fat 16.6, fiber 4.2, carbs 6.9, protein 5.6

Broccoli Coconut Dip

Preparation time: 10 minutes **Cooking time:** 15 minutes **Servings:** 4

½ cups veggie stock 3 cups broccoli florets	garlic cloves, minced
Salt and black pepper to the taste 1/3 cup coconut milk	1 tablespoon balsamic vinegar 1 tablespoon olive oil

1. In a pan that fits your air fryer, mix all the ingredients, toss, introduce in the fryer and cook at 390 degrees F for 15 minutes. Divide into bowls and serve.

Nutrition:
Calories 163, fat 4, fiber 2, carbs 4, protein 5

Shrimps Cakes

Prep time: 10 minutes **Cooking time:** 5 minutes **Servings:** 4

10 oz shrimps, chopped	1 egg, beaten
1 teaspoon dill, chopped	1 teaspoon Psyllium husk
2 tablespoons almond flour	1 teaspoon olive oil
1 teaspoon chives	

1. In the mixing bowl mix up shrimps, egg, dill, Psyllium husk, almond flour, and chives. When the mixture is homogenous, make 4 cakes.
2. Preheat the air fryer to 400F. Put the cakes in the air fryer and sprinkle with olive oil. Cook the meal for 5 minutes.

Nutrition:
Calories 198, fat 10.5, fiber 3.9, carbs 7.1, protein 20.6

Tomatoes and Cheese Dip

Prep time: 5 minutes **Cooking time:** 20 minutes **Servings:** 6

1 pint grape tomatoes, halved	A pinch of salt and black pepper 1 teaspoon olive oil
12 ounces cream cheese, soft	8 ounces mozzarella cheese, grated
¼ cup parmesan, grated 4 garlic cloves, minced	tablespoons thyme, chopped
¼ cup basil, chopped	½ tablespoon oregano, chopped

1. Put the tomatoes in your air fryer's basket and cook them at 400 degrees F for 15 minutes. In a blender, combine the fried tomatoes with the rest of the ingredients and pulse well. Transfer this to a ramekin, place it in the air fryer and cook at 400 degrees F for 5-6 minutes more. Serve as a snack.

Nutrition:
Calories 184, fat 8, fiber 3, carbs 4, protein 8

Fennel and Parmesan Dip

Prep time: 5 minutes **Cooking time:** 25 minutes **Servings:** 8

tablespoons olive oil	fennel bulbs, trimmed and cut into wedges A pinch of salt and black pepper
garlic cloves, minced	¼ cup parmesan, grated

1. Put the fennel in the air fryer's basket and bake at 380 degrees F for 20 minutes. In a blender, combine the roasted fennel with the rest of the ingredients and pulse well. Put the spread in a ramekin, introduce it in the fryer and cook at 380 degrees F for 5 minutes more. Divide into bowls and serve as a dip.

Nutrition:
Calories 240, fat 11, fiber 3, carbs 4, protein 12

Sesame Tortilla Chips

Prep time: 10 minutes **Cooking time:** 4 minutes **Servings:** 4

4 low carb tortillas
1 teaspoon sesame oil

½ teaspoon salt

1. Cut the tortillas into the strips. Preheat the air fryer to 365F. Place the tortilla strips in the air fryer basket and sprinkle with sesame oil. Cook them for 3 minutes. Then give a shake to the chips and sprinkle with salt. Cook the chips for 1 minute more.

Nutrition:

Calories 90, fat 3.1, fiber 7, carbs 12, protein 3

Hot Cheesy Dip

Preparation time: 5 minutes **Cooking time:** 12 minutes
Servings: 6

12 ounces coconut cream
8 ounces cheddar cheese, grated

2 teaspoons keto hot sauce

1. In ramekin, mix the cream with hot sauce and cheese and whisk. Put the ramekin in the fryer and cook at 390 degrees F for 12 minutes. Whisk, divide into bowls and serve as a dip.

Nutrition:

Calories 170, fat 9, fiber 2, carbs 4, protein 12

Stuffed Mushrooms

Prep time: 10 minutes **Cooking time:** 15 minutes **Servings:** 4

1 cup cremini mushroom caps
1 teaspoon butter, melted

5 oz ground sausages

Cooking spray

1. Mix up ground sausages and butter. Fill the mushroom caps with the ground sausage mixture. Transfer the vegetables in the air fryer basket in one layer and spray with the cooking spray. Cook the meal at 365F for 15 minutes.

Nutrition:

Calories 133, fat 11, fiber 0.1, carbs 0.7, protein 7.4

Peppers Dip

Preparation time: 5 minutes **Cooking time:** 20 minutes
Servings: 6

8 ounces cream cheese, soft 4 ounces parmesan, grated 4 ounces mozzarella, grated
2 bacon slices, cooked and crumbled A pinch of salt and black pepper

2 roasted red peppers, chopped

1. In a pan that fits your air fryer, mix all the ingredients and whisk really well. Introduce the pan in the fryer and cook at 400 degrees F for 20 minutes. Divide into bowls and serve cold.

Nutrition:

Calories 173, fat 8, fiber 2, carbs 4, protein 11

Creamy Cheddar Eggs

Prep time: 10 minutes **Cooking time:** 16 minutes **Servings:** 8

4 eggs
¼ cup Cheddar cheese, shredded
1 teaspoon fresh dill, chopped

2 oz pork rinds
1 tablespoon heavy cream

1. Place the eggs in the air fryer and cook them at 255F for 16 minutes. Then cool the eggs in the cold water and peel. Cut every egg into the halves and remove the egg yolks. Transfer the egg yolks in the mixing bowl. Add shredded cheese, heavy cream, and fresh dill. Stir the mixture with the help of the fork until smooth and add pork rinds. Mix it up. Fill the egg whites with the egg yolk mixture.

Nutrition:

Calories 93, fat 6.6, fiber 0, carbs 0.3, protein 8.3

Leeks Dip

Preparation time: 5 minutes **Cooking time:** 12 minutes
Servings: 6

2 spring onions, minced

3 tablespoons coconut milk 4 leeks, sliced
Salt and white pepper to the taste

2 tablespoons butter, melted

¼ cup coconut cream

1. In a pan that fits your air fryer, mix all the ingredients and whisk them well. Introduce the pan in the fryer and cook at 390 degrees F for 12 minutes. Divide into bowls and serve.

Nutrition:

Calories 204, fat 12, fiber 2, carbs 4, protein 14

Thyme Fat Bombs

Prep time: 10 minutes **Cooking time:** 8 minutes **Servings:** 4

1 teaspoon Bagel seasonings
2 tablespoons cream cheese
1 bacon slice, chopped

½ teaspoon dried thyme

1 cup Cheddar cheese, shredded
½ teaspoon avocado oil

1. Preheat the air fryer to 400F and put the bacon inside. Sprinkle it with avocado oil. Cook it for 4 minutes. Then shake it well and cook for 4 minutes more. After this, transfer the bacon in the bowl and cool it to the room temperature. Add cream cheese, dried thyme, Bagel seasonings, and Cheddar cheese. Stir it until homogenous. With the help of the scooper make 4 fat bombs. Store them in the fridge for up to 2 days.

Nutrition:

Calories 158, fat 13.2, fiber 0.1, carbs 0.7, protein 9.2

Fish and Seafood Recipes

Shrimp and Celery Salad

Prep time: 10 minutes **Cooking time:** 5 minutes **Servings:** 4

3 oz chevre	1 teaspoon avocado oil
½ teaspoon dried oregano	8 oz shrimps, peeled
1 teaspoon butter, melted	½ teaspoon salt
½ teaspoon chili flakes	4 oz celery stalk, chopped

1. Sprinkle the shrimps with dried oregano and melted butter and put in the air fryer. Cook the seafood at 400F for 5 minutes. Meanwhile, crumble the chevre. Put the chopped celery stalk in the salad bowl, Add crumbled chevre, chili flakes, salt, and avocado oil. Mix up the salad well and top it with cooked shrimps.

Nutrition:

Calories 158, fat 7.5, fiber 0.6, carbs 4.2, protein 17.7

Basil and Paprika Cod

Prep time: 5 minutes **Cooking time:** 15 minutes **Servings:** 4

4 cod fillets, boneless	1 teaspoon red pepper flakes
½ teaspoon hot paprika 2 tablespoon olive oil 1 teaspoon basil, dried	Salt and black pepper to the taste

1. In a bowl, mix the cod with all the other ingredients and toss. Put the fish in your air fryer's basket and cook at 380 degrees F for 15 minutes.
2. Divide the cod between plates and serve.

Nutrition:

Calories 194, fat 7, fiber 2, carbs 4, protein 12

Cajun Shrimps

Prep time: 10 minutes **Cooking time:** 6 minutes **Servings:** 4

8 oz shrimps, peeled	1 teaspoon Cajun spices
1 teaspoon cream cheese	1 egg, beaten
½ teaspoon salt	1 teaspoon avocado oil

1. Sprinkle the shrimps with Cajun spices and salt. In the mixing bowl mix up cream cheese and egg, Dip every shrimp in the egg mixture. Preheat the air fryer to 400F. Place the shrimps in the air fryer and sprinkle with avocado oil. Cook the popcorn shrimps for 6 minutes. Shake them well after 3 minutes of cooking.

Nutrition:

Calories 88, fat 2.5, fiber 0.1, carbs 1, protein 14.4

Balsamic Cod

Prep time: 5 minutes **Cooking time:** 15 minutes **Servings:** 4

4 cod fillets, boneless	Salt and black pepper to the taste 1 cup parmesan
4 tablespoons balsamic vinegar A drizzle of olive oil	3 spring onions, chopped

1. Season fish with salt, pepper, grease with the oil, and coat it in parmesan. Put the fillets in your air fryer's basket and cook at 370 degrees F for 14 minutes. Meanwhile, in a bowl, mix the spring onions with salt, pepper and the vinegar and whisk. Divide the cod between plates, drizzle the spring onions mix all over and serve with a side salad.

Nutrition:

Calories 220, fat 12, fiber 2, carbs 5, protein 13

Wrapped Scallops

Prep time: 15 minutes **Cooking time:** 7 minutes **Servings:** 4

1 teaspoon ground coriander	½ teaspoon ground paprika
¼ teaspoon salt	16 oz scallops
4 oz bacon, sliced	1 teaspoon sesame oil

1. Sprinkle the scallops with ground coriander, ground paprika, and salt. Then wrap the scallops in the bacon slices and secure with toothpicks. Sprinkle the scallops with sesame oil. Preheat the air fryer to 400F. Put the scallops in the air fryer basket and cook them for 7 minutes.

Nutrition:

Calories 264, fat 13.9, fiber 0.1, carbs 3.2, protein 29.6

Cod and Sauce

Prep time: 5 minutes **Cooking time:** 15 minutes **Servings:** 2

2 cod fillets, boneless	Salt and black pepper to the taste
1 bunch spring onions, chopped	3 tablespoons ghee, melted

1. In a pan that fits the air fryer, combine all the ingredients, toss gently, introduce in the air fryer and cook at 360 degrees F for 15 minutes. Divide the fish and sauce between plates and serve.

Nutrition:

Calories 240, fat 12, fiber 2, carbs 5, protein 11

Thyme Catfish

Prep time: 10 minutes **Cooking time:** 12 minutes **Servings:** 4

20 oz catfish fillet (4 oz each fillet)	2 eggs, beaten
1 teaspoon dried thyme	½ teaspoon salt
1 teaspoon apple cider vinegar	1 teaspoon avocado oil
¼ teaspoon cayenne pepper	1/3 cup coconut flour

1. Sprinkle the catfish fillets with dried thyme, salt, apple cider vinegar, cayenne pepper, and coconut flour. Then sprinkle the fish fillets with avocado oil. Preheat the air fryer to 385F. Put the catfish fillets in the air fryer basket and cook them for 8 minutes. Then flip the fish on another side and cook for 4 minutes more.

Nutrition:

Calories 198, fat 10.7, fiber 4.2, carbs 6.5, protein 18.3

Garlic Shrimp Mix

Prep time: 10 minutes **Cooking time:** 5 minutes **Servings:** 3

1-pound shrimps, peeled	½ teaspoon garlic powder
¼ teaspoon minced garlic	1 teaspoon ground cumin
¼ teaspoon lemon zest, grated	½ tablespoon avocado oil
½ teaspoon dried parsley	

1. In the mixing bowl mix up shrimps, garlic powder, minced garlic, ground cumin, lemon zest, and dried parsley. Then add avocado oil and mix up the shrimps well. Preheat the air fryer to 400F. Put the shrimps in the preheated air fryer basket and cook for 5 minutes.

Nutrition:

Calories 187, fat 3, fiber 0.2, carbs 3.2, protein 34.7

Salmon and Creamy Chives Sauce

Preparation time: 5 minutes **Cooking time:** 20 minutes
Servings: 4

4 salmon fillets, boneless	A pinch of salt and black pepper
½ cup heavy cream	1 tablespoon chives, chopped 1 teaspoon lemon juice
1 teaspoon dill, chopped 2 garlic cloves, minced	¼ cup ghee, melted

1. In a bowl, mix all the ingredients except the salmon and whisk well. Arrange the salmon in a pan that fits the air fryer, drizzle the sauce all over, introduce the pan in the machine and cook at 360 degrees F for 20 minutes. Divide everything between plates and serve.

Nutrition:
Calories 220, fat 14, fiber 2, carbs 5, protein 12

Tilapia and Tomato Salsa

Preparation time: 5 minutes **Cooking time:** 15 minutes
Servings: 4

4 tilapia fillets, boneless 1 tablespoon olive oil	A pinch of salt and black pepper 12 ounces tomatoes, chopped
2 tablespoons green onions, chopped	2 tablespoons sweet red pepper, chopped 1 tablespoon balsamic vinegar

1. Arrange the tilapia in a baking sheet that fits the air fryer and season with salt and pepper. In a bowl, combine all the other ingredients, toss and spread over the fish. Introduce the pan in the fryer and cook at 350 degrees F for 15 minutes. Divide the mix between plates and serve.

Nutrition:
Calories 221, fat 12, fiber 2, carbs 5, protein 14

Crusted Turmeric Salmon

Prep time: 15 minutes **Cooking time:** 8 minutes **Servings:** 4

12 oz salmon fillet	¼ cup pistachios, grinded
1 teaspoon cream cheese	½ teaspoon ground nutmeg
2 tablespoons coconut flour	½ teaspoon ground turmeric
¼ teaspoon sage	½ teaspoon salt
1 tablespoon heavy cream	Cooking spray

1. Cut the salmon fillet on 4 servings. In the mixing bowl mix up cream cheese, ground turmeric, sage, salt, and heavy cream. Then in the separated bowl mix up coconut flour and pistachios. Dip the salmon fillets in the cream cheese mixture and then coat in the pistachio mixture.
2. Preheat the air fryer to 380F. Place the coated salmon fillets in the air fryer and spray them with the cooking spray. Cook the fish for 8 minutes.

Nutrition:
Calories 168, fat 9.5, fiber 2, carbs 3.7, protein 18.2

Catfish with Spring Onions and Avocado

Preparation time: 5 minutes **Cooking time:** 15 minutes
Servings: 4

2 teaspoons oregano, dried 2 teaspoons cumin, ground	2 teaspoons sweet paprika
A pinch of salt and black pepper 4 catfish fillets	avocado, peeled and cubed
½ cup spring onions, chopped 2 tablespoons cilantro, chopped 2 teaspoons olive oil	tablespoons lemon juice

1. In a bowl, mix all the ingredients except the fish and toss. Arrange this in a baking pan that fits the air fryer, top with the fish, introduce the pan in the machine and cook at 360 degrees F for 15 minutes, flipping the fish halfway. Divide between plates and serve.

Nutrition:
Calories 280, fat 14, fiber 3, carbs 5, protein 14

Ginger Cod

Prep time: 10 minutes **Cooking time:** 8 minutes **Servings:** 2

10 oz cod fillet	½ teaspoon cayenne pepper
¼ teaspoon ground coriander	½ teaspoon ground ginger
½ teaspoon ground black pepper	1 tablespoon sunflower oil
½ teaspoon salt	½ teaspoon dried rosemary
½ teaspoon ground paprika	

1. In the shallow bowl mix up cayenne pepper, ground coriander, ginger, ground black pepper, salt, dried rosemary, and ground paprika. Then rub the cod fillet with the spice mixture. After this, sprinkle it with sunflower oil. Preheat the air fryer to 390F. Place the cod fillet in the air fryer and cook it for 4 minutes. Then carefully flip the fish on another side and cook for 4 minutes more.

Nutrition:
Calories 183, fat 8.5, fiber 0.7, carbs 1.4, protein 25.6

Paprika Tilapia

Preparation time: 5 minutes **Cooking time:** 20 minutes
Servings: 4

4 tilapia fillets, boneless	3 tablespoons ghee, melted
A pinch of salt and black pepper	2 tablespoons capers
teaspoon garlic powder	½ teaspoon smoked paprika
½ teaspoon oregano, dried	2 tablespoons lemon juice

1. In a bowl, mix all the ingredients except the fish and toss. Arrange the fish in a pan that fits the air fryer, pour the capers mix all over, put the pan in the air fryer and cook 360 degrees F for 20 minutes, shaking halfway.
2. Divide between plates and serve hot.

Nutrition:
Calories 224, fat 10, fiber 0, carbs 2, protein 18

Shrimp Skewers

Prep time: 10 minutes **Cooking time:** 5 minutes **Servings:** 5

4-pounds shrimps, peeled	2 tablespoons fresh cilantro, chopped
2 tablespoons apple cider vinegar	1 teaspoon ground coriander
1 tablespoon avocado oil	Cooking spray

1. In the shallow bowl mix up avocado oil, ground coriander, apple cider vinegar, and fresh cilantro. Then put the shrimps in the big bowl and sprinkle with avocado oil mixture. Mix them well and leave for 10 minutes to marinate. After this, string the shrimps on the skewers. Preheat the air fryer to 400F. Arrange the shrimp skewers in the air fryer and cook them for 5 minutes.

Nutrition:
Calories 223, fat 14.9, fiber 3.1, carbs 5.5, protein 17.4

Stevia Cod

Preparation time: 5 minutes **Cooking time:** 14 minutes **Servings:** 4

1/3 cup stevia	tablespoons coconut aminos
4 cod fillets, boneless	A pinch of salt and black pepper

1. In a pan that fits the air fryer, combine all the ingredients and toss gently. Introduce the pan in the fryer and cook at 350 degrees F for 14 minutes, flipping the fish halfway. Divide everything between plates and serve.

Nutrition:
Calories 267, fat 18, fiber 2, carbs 5, protein 20

Lime Cod

Preparation time: 5 minutes **Cooking time:** 14 minutes **Servings:** 4

cod fillets, boneless	1 tablespoon olive oil
Salt and black pepper to the taste	2 teaspoons sweet paprika
Juice of 1 lime	

1. In a bowl, mix all the ingredients, transfer the fish to your air fryer's basket and cook 350 degrees F for 7 minutes on each side. Divide the fish between plates and serve with a side salad.

Nutrition:
Calories 240, fat 14, fiber 2, carbs 4, protein 16

Chili Haddock

Prep time: 10 minutes **Cooking time:** 8 minutes **Servings:** 4

12 oz haddock fillet	1 egg, beaten
1 teaspoon cream cheese	1 teaspoon chili flakes
½ teaspoon salt	1 tablespoon flax meal
Cooking spray	

1. Cut the haddock on 4 pieces and sprinkle with chili flakes and salt. After this, in the small bowl mix up egg and cream cheese. Dip the haddock pieces in the egg mixture and generously sprinkle with flax meal. Preheat the air fryer to 400F. Put the prepared haddock pieces in the air fryer in one layer and cook them for 4 minutes from each side or until they are golden brown.

Nutrition:
Calories 122, fat 2.8, fiber 0.5, carbs 0.6, protein 22.5

Butter Crab Muffins

Prep time: 15 minutes **Cooking time:** 20 minutes **Servings:** 2

5 oz crab meat, chopped	2 eggs, beaten
2 tablespoons almond flour	¼ teaspoon baking powder
½ teaspoon apple cider vinegar	½ teaspoon ground paprika
1 tablespoon butter, softened	Cooking spray

1. Grind the chopped crab meat and put it in the bowl. Add eggs, almond flour, baking powder, apple cider vinegar, ground paprika, and butter. Stir the mixture until homogenous. Preheat the air fryer to 365F. Spray the muffin molds with cooking spray. Then pour the crab meat batter in the muffin molds and place them in the preheated air fryer. Cook the crab muffins for 20 minutes or until they are light brown. Cool the cooked muffins to the room temperature and remove from the muffin mold.

Nutrition:
Calories 340, fat 25.5, fiber 3.2, carbs 8.2, protein 20.5

Tilapia and Kale

Preparation time: 5 minutes **Cooking time:** 20 minutes **Servings:** 4

4 tilapia fillets, boneless	Salt and black pepper to the taste 2 garlic cloves, minced
1 teaspoon fennel seeds	½ teaspoon red pepper flakes, crushed
1 bunch kale, chopped	Table9spoons olive oil

1. In a pan that fits the fryer, combine all the ingredients, put the pan in the fryer and cook at 360 degrees F for 20 minutes. Divide everything between plates and serve.

Nutrition:
Calories 240, fat 12, fiber 2, carbs 4, protein 12

Mackerel with Spring Onions and Peppers

Prep time: 15 minutes **Cooking time:** 20 minutes **Servings:** 5

1-pound mackerel, trimmed	1 tablespoon ground paprika
1 green bell pepper	½ cup spring onions, chopped
1 tablespoon avocado oil	1 teaspoon apple cider vinegar
½ teaspoon salt	

1. Wash the mackerel if needed and sprinkle with ground paprika. Chop the green bell pepper. Then fill the mackerel with bell pepper and spring onion. After this, sprinkle the fish with avocado oil, apple cider vinegar, and salt. Preheat the air fryer to 375F. Place the mackerel in the air fryer basket and cook it for 20 minutes.

Nutrition:
Calories 258, fat 16.8, fiber 1.2, carbs 3.8, protein 22.2

Ginger Salmon

Preparation time: 5 minutes **Cooking time:** 12 minutes
Servings: 4

2 tablespoons lime juice	1 pound salmon fillets, boneless, skinless and cubed
	1 tablespoon ginger, grated
4 teaspoons olive oil	1 tablespoon coconut aminos
1 tablespoon sesame seeds, toasted 1 tablespoon chives, chopped	

1. In a pan that fits the air fryer, combine all the ingredients, toss, introduce in the fryer and cook at 360 degrees F for 12 minutes. Divide into bowls and serve.

Nutrition:
Calories 206, fat 8, fiber 1, carbs 4, protein 13

Sardine Cakes

Prep time: 15 minutes **Cooking time:** 10 minutes **Servings:** 5

12 oz sardines, trimmed, cleaned	¼ cup coconut flour
1 egg, beaten	2 tablespoons flax meal
1 teaspoon ground black pepper	1 teaspoon salt
Cooking spray	

1. Chop the sardines roughly and put them in the bowl. Add coconut flour, egg, flax meal, ground black pepper, and salt. Mix up the mixture with the help of the fork. Then make 5 cakes from the sardine mixture. Preheat the air fryer to 390F. Spray the air fryer basket with cooking spray and place the cakes inside. Cook them for 5 minutes from each side.

Nutrition:
Calories 1700, fat 9.8, fiber 1.2, carbs 1.5, protein 18.6

Coconut Shrimp

Preparation time: 5 minutes **Cooking time:** 12 minutes
Servings: 4

1 tablespoon ghee, melted	1 pound shrimp, peeled and deveined
¼ cup coconut cream	A pinch of red pepper flakes
A pinch of salt and black pepper	1 tablespoon parsley, chopped
1 tablespoon chives, chopped	

1. In a pan that fits the fryer, combine all the ingredients except the parsley, put the pan in the fryer and cook at 360 degrees F for 12 minutes. Divide the mix into bowls, sprinkle the parsley on top and serve.

Nutrition:
Calories 195, fat 11, fiber 2, carbs 4, protein 11

Parmesan Salmon Fillets

Prep time: 5 minutes **Cooking time:** 15 minutes **Servings:** 4

4 salmon fillets, skinless 1 teaspoon mustard	A pinch of salt and black pepper
½ cup coconut flakes	1 tablespoon parmesan, grated Cooking spray

1. In a bowl, mix the parmesan with the other ingredients except the fish and cooking spray and stir well. Coat the fish in this mix, grease it with cooking spray and arrange in the air fryer's basket. Cook at 400 degrees F for 15 minutes, divide between plates and serve with a side salad.

Nutrition:
Calories 240, fat 13, fiber 3, carbs 6, protein 15

Halibut Steaks

Prep time: 15 minutes **Cooking time:** 10 minutes **Servings:** 4

24 oz halibut steaks (6 oz each fillet)	½ teaspoon salt
½ teaspoon ground black pepper	4 oz bacon, sliced
1 tablespoon sunflower oil	

1. Cut every halibut fillet on 2 parts and sprinkle with salt and ground black pepper. Then wrap the fish fillets in the sliced bacon. Preheat the air fryer to 400F. Sprinkle the halibut bites with sunflower oil and put in the air fryer basket. Cook the meal for 5 minutes. Then flip the fish bites on another side and cook them for 5 minutes more.

Nutrition:
Calories 375, fat 19.4, fiber 0.1, carbs 0.6, protein 46.5

Tuna Skewers

Prep time: 5 minutes **Cooking time:** 12 minutes **Servings:** 4

1 pound tuna steaks, boneless and cubed	1 chili pepper, minced
4 green onions, chopped	2 tablespoons lime juice A drizzle of olive oil
Salt and black pepper to the taste	

1. In a bowl mix all the ingredients and toss them. Thread the tuna cubes on skewers, arrange them in your air fryer's basket and cook at 370 degrees F for 12 minutes. Divide between plates and serve with a side salad.

Nutrition:
Calories 226, fat 12, fiber 2, carbs 4, protein 15

Cheesy Shrimps

Prep time: 15 minutes **Cooking time:** 5 minutes **Servings:** 4

14 oz shrimps, peeled	2 eggs, beaten
¼ cup heavy cream	1 teaspoon salt
1 teaspoon ground black pepper	4 oz Monterey jack cheese, shredded
5 tablespoons coconut flour	1 tablespoon lemon juice, for garnish

1. In the mixing bowl mix up heavy cream, salt, and ground black pepper. Add eggs and whisk the mixture until homogenous. After this, mix up coconut flour and Monterey jack cheese. Dip the shrimps in the heavy cream mixture and coat in the coconut flour mixture. Then dip the shrimps in the egg mixture again and coat in the coconut flour. Preheat the air fryer to 400F. Arrange the shrimps in the air fryer in one layer and cook them for 5 minutes. Repeat the same step with remaining shrimps. Sprinkle the bang-bang shrimps with lemon juice.

Nutrition:
Calories 327, fat 16.8, fiber 3.9, carbs 8.1, protein 34.4

Mustard Cod

Prep time: 10 minutes **Cooking time:** 14 minutes **Servings:** 4

1 cup parmesan, grated 4 cod fillets, boneless	Salt and black pepper to the taste
1 tablespoon mustard	

1. In a bowl, mix the parmesan with salt, pepper and the mustard and stir. Spread this over the cod, arrange the fish in the air fryer's basket and cook at 370 degrees F for 7 minutes on each side. Divide between plates and serve with a side salad.

Nutrition:
Calories 270, fat 14, fiber 3, carbs 5, protein 12

Salmon and Lime Sauce

Prep time: 5 minutes **Cooking time:** 20 minutes **Servings:** 4

4 salmon fillets, boneless	¼ cup coconut cream
1 teaspoon lime zest, grated 1/3 cup heavy cream	¼ cup lime juice
½ cup coconut, shredded	A pinch of salt and black pepper

1. In a bowl, mix all the ingredients except the salmon and whisk. Arrange the fish in a pan that fits your air fryer, drizzle the coconut sauce all over, put the pan in the machine and cook at 360 degrees F for 20 minutes.
2. Divide between plates and serve.

Nutrition:

Calories 227, fat 12, fiber 2, carbs 1, protein 9

Catfish Bites

Prep time: 10 minutes **Cooking time:** 10 minutes **Servings:** 4

¼ cup coconut flakes	3 tablespoons coconut flour
1 teaspoon salt	3 eggs, beaten
10 oz catfish fillet	Cooking spray

1. Cut the catfish fillet on the small pieces (nuggets) and sprinkle with salt. After this, dip the catfish pieces in the egg and coat in the coconut flour. Then dip the fish pieces in the egg again and coat in the coconut flakes. Preheat the air fryer to 385F. Place the catfish nuggets in the air fryer basket and cook them for 6 minutes. Then flip the nuggets on another side and cook them for 4 minutes more.

Nutrition:

Calories 187, fat 11.3, fiber 2.7, carbs 4.4, protein 16.5

Turmeric Salmon

Prep time: 10 minutes **Cooking time:** 7 minutes **Servings:** 2

8 oz salmon fillet	2 tablespoons coconut flakes
1 tablespoon coconut cream	½ teaspoon salt
½ teaspoon ground turmeric	½ teaspoon onion powder
1 teaspoon nut oil	

1. Cut the salmon fillet into halves and sprinkle with salt, ground turmeric, and onion powder. After this, dip the fish fillets in the coconut cream and coat in the coconut flakes. Sprinkle the salmon fillets with nut oil. Preheat the air fryer to 380F. Arrange the salmon fillets in the air fryer basket and cook for 7 minutes.

Nutrition:

Calories 209, fat 12.8, fiber 0.8, carbs 0.2, protein 22.4

Salmon and Garlic Sauce

Prep time: 5 minutes **Cooking time:** 15 minutes **Servings:** 4

3 tablespoons parsley, chopped 4 salmon fillets, boneless	¼ cup ghee, melted
2 garlic cloves, minced 4 shallots, chopped	Salt and black pepper to the taste

1. Heat up a pan that fits the air fryer with the ghee over medium-high heat, add the garlic, shallots, salt, pepper and the parsley, stir and cook for 5 minutes. Add the salmon fillets, toss gently, introduce the pan in the air fryer and cook at 380 degrees F for 15 minutes. Divide between plates and serve.

Nutrition:

Calories 270, fat 12, fiber 2, carbs 4, protein 17

Hot Tilapia

Prep time: 15 minutes **Cooking time:** 9 minutes **Servings:** 2

1 chili pepper, chopped	1 teaspoon chili flakes
1 tablespoon sesame oil	½ teaspoon salt
10 oz tilapia fillet	¼ teaspoon onion powder

1. In the shallow bowl mix up chili pepper, chili flakes, salt, and onion powder. Gently churn the mixture and add sesame oil. After this, slice the tilapia fillet and sprinkle with chili mixture. Massage the fish with the help of the fingertips gently and leave for 10 minutes to marinate. Preheat the air fryer to 390F. Put the tilapia fillets in the air fryer basket and cook for 5 minutes. Then flip the fish on another side and cook for 4 minutes more.

Nutrition.

Calories 179, fat 8.1, fiber 0.1, carbs 0.5, protein 26.4

Paprika Cod and Endives

Prep time: 5 minutes **Cooking time:** 20 minutes **Servings:** 4

2 endives, shredded	2 tablespoons olive oil
Salt and back pepper to the taste	4 salmon fillets, boneless
½ teaspoon sweet paprika	

2. In a pan that fits the air fryer, combine the fish with the rest of the ingredients, toss, introduce in the fryer and cook at 350 degrees F for 20 minutes, flipping the fish halfway. Divide between plates and serve right away.

Nutrition:

Calories 243, fat 13, fiber 3, carbs 6, protein 14

Sesame Salmon

Prep time: 10 minutes **Cooking time:** 9 minutes **Servings:** 6

18 oz salmon fillet	2 tablespoons swerve
1 tablespoon apple cider vinegar	6 teaspoons liquid aminos
1 teaspoon minced ginger	1 tablespoon sesame seeds
2 tablespoons lemon juice	½ teaspoon minced garlic
1 tablespoon avocado oil	

1. Cut the salmon fillet on 8 servings and sprinkle with apple cider vinegar, minced ginger, lemon juice, minced garlic, and liquid aminos. Leave the fish for 10-15 minutes to marinate. After this, sprinkle the fish with avocado oil and put in the preheated to 380F air fryer in one layer. Cook the fish fillets for 7 minutes. Then sprinkle them with swerve and sesame seeds and cook for 2 minutes more at 400F.

Nutrition:

Calories 127, fat 6.4, fiber 0.3, carbs 6.1, protein 17.5

Butter Mussels

Prep time: 10 minutes **Cooking time:** 2 minutes **Servings:** 5

2-pounds mussels	1 shallot, chopped
1 tablespoon minced garlic	1 tablespoon butter, melted
1 teaspoon sunflower oil	1 teaspoon salt
1 tablespoon fresh parsley, chopped	½ teaspoon chili flakes

1. Clean and wash mussels and put them in the big bowl. Add shallot, minced garlic, butter, sunflower oil, salt, and chili flakes. Shake the mussels well. Preheat the air fryer to 390F. Put the mussels in the air fryer basket and cook for 2 minutes. Then transfer the cooked meal in the serving bowl and top it with chopped fresh parsley.

Nutrition:

Calories 192, fat 7.3, fiber 0.1, carbs 8.3, protein 21.9

Cilantro Cod Mix

Preparation time: 5 minutes **Cooking time:** 15 minutes
Servings: 4

1 cup cherry tomatoes, halved Salt and black pepper to the taste	2 tablespoons olive oil
4 cod fillets, skinless and boneless	2 tablespoons cilantro, chopped

1. In a baking dish that fits your air fryer, mix all the ingredients, toss gently, introduce in your air fryer and cook at 370 degrees F for 15 minutes.
2. Divide everything between plates and serve right away.

Nutrition:
Calories 248, fat 11, fiber 2, carbs 5, protein 11

Cayenne Salmon

Prep time: 10 minutes **Cooking time:** 9 minutes **Servings:** 3

1-pound salmon	1 tablespoon Erythritol
1 tablespoon coconut oil, melted	½ teaspoon cayenne pepper
1 teaspoon water	¼ teaspoon ground nutmeg

1. In the small bowl mix up Erythritol and water. Then rub the salmon with ground nutmeg and cayenne pepper. After this, brush the fish with Erythritol liquid and sprinkle with melted coconut oil. Put the salmon on the foil. Preheat the air fryer to 385F. Transfer the foil with salmon in the air fryer basket and cook for 9 minutes.

Nutrition:
Calories 241, fat 14, fiber 0.1, carbs 5.3, protein 29.4

Lemon and Oregano Tilapia Mix

Preparation time: 5 minutes **Cooking time:** 20 minutes
Servings: 4

4 tilapia fillets, boneless and halved Salt and black pepper to the taste	1 cup roasted peppers, chopped
¼ cup keto tomato sauce	1 cup tomatoes, cubed
1 tablespoon lemon juice	2 tablespoons olive oil
1 teaspoon garlic powder	1 teaspoon oregano, dried

1. In a baking dish that fits your air fryer, mix the fish with all the other ingredients, toss, introduce in your air fryer and cook at 380 degrees F for 20 minutes. Divide into bowls and serve.

Nutrition:
Calories 250, fat 9, fiber 2, carbs 5, protein 14

Butter Lobster

Prep time: 10 minutes **Cooking time:** 6 minutes **Servings:** 4

4 lobster tails, peeled	4 teaspoons almond butter
½ teaspoon salt	½ teaspoon dried thyme
1 tablespoon avocado oil	

1. Make the cut on the back of every lobster tail and sprinkle them with dried thyme and salt. After this, sprinkle the lobster tails with avocado oil.
2. Preheat the air fryer to 380F. Place the lobster tails in the air fryer basket and cook them for 5 minutes. After this, gently spread the lobster tails with almond butter and cook for 1 minute more.

Nutrition:
Calories 183, fat 10, fiber 1.8, carbs 4.,3, protein 20.5

Lemony Mustard Shrimp

Prep time: 5 minutes **Cooking time:** 12 minutes **Servings:** 4

½ pounds shrimp, peeled and deveined Zest of ½ lemon, grated	Juice of ½ lemon
A pinch of salt and black pepper	2 tablespoons mustard
tablespoons olive oil	2 tablespoons parsley, chopped

1. In a bowl, mix all the ingredients and toss well. Put the shrimp in your air fryer's basket and reserve the lemon vinaigrette. Cook at 350 degrees F for 12 minutes, flipping the shrimp halfway, divide between plates and serve with reserved vinaigrette drizzled on top.

Nutrition:
Calories 202, fat 8, fiber 2, carbs 5, protein 14

Turmeric Fish Fingers

Prep time: 15 minutes **Cooking time:** 9 minutes **Servings:**4

1-pound cod fillet	½ cup almond flour
2 eggs, beaten	½ teaspoon ground turmeric
1 tablespoon flax meal	1 teaspoon salt
1 teaspoon avocado oil	

1. Slice the cod fillets into the strips (fingers). In the mixing bowl, mix up eggs, ground turmeric, and salt. Stir the liquid until salt is dissolved. Then in the separated bowl mix up almond flour and flax meal. Dip the cod fingers in the egg mixture and coat in the almond flour mixture. Preheat the air fryer to 400F. Place the fish fingers in the air fryer basket in one layer and sprinkle with avocado oil. Cook the fish fingers for 4 minutes.
2. Then flip them on another side and cook for 5 minutes more or until the fish fingers are golden brown.

Nutrition:
Calories 153, fat 5.8, fiber 1, carbs 1.7, protein 24.2

Parsley Shrimp

Prep time: 5 minutes **Cooking time:** 12 minutes **Servings:** 4

pound shrimp, peeled and deveined 1 teaspoon cumin, ground	tablespoons parsley, chopped 2 tablespoons olive oil
A pinch of salt and black pepper 4 garlic cloves, minced	1 tablespoon lime juice

1. In a pan that fits your air fryer, mix all the ingredients, toss, put the pan in your air fryer and cook at 370 degrees F and cook for 12 minutes, shaking the fryer halfway. Divide into bowls and serve.

Nutrition:
Calories 220, fat 11, fiber 2, carbs 5, protein 12

Fried Crawfish

Prep time: 10 minutes **Cooking time:** 5 minutes **Servings:** 4

1-pound crawfish	1 tablespoon avocado oil
1 teaspoon onion powder	1 tablespoon rosemary, chopped

1. Preheat the air fryer to 340F. Place the crawfish in the air fryer basket and sprinkle with avocado oil and rosemary. Add the onion powder and stir the crawfish gently. Cook the meal for 5 minutes.

Nutrition:
Calories 108, fat 2.1, fiber 0.5, carbs 1.2, protein 20

Herbed Salmon

Prep time: 10 minutes **Cooking time:** 15 minutes **Servings:** 4

½ teaspoon dried rosemary	½ teaspoon dried thyme
½ teaspoon dried basil	½ teaspoon ground coriander
½ teaspoon ground cumin	½ teaspoon ground paprika
½ teaspoon salt	1-pound salmon
1 tablespoon olive oil	

1. In the bowl mix up spices: dried rosemary, thyme, basil, coriander, cumin, paprika, and salt. After this, gently rub the salmon with the spice mixture and sprinkle with olive oil. Preheat the air fryer to 375F. Line the air fryer with baking paper and put the prepared salmon inside. Cook the fish for 15 minutes or until you get the light crunchy crust.

Nutrition:
Calories 183, fat 10.6, fiber 0.2, carbs 0.4, protein 22.1

Ghee Shrimp and Green Beans

Prep time: 5 minutes **Cooking time:** 15 minutes **Servings:** 4

pound shrimp, peeled and deveined A pinch of salt and black pepper tablespoons cilantro, chopped	½ pound green beans, trimmed and halved Juice of 1 lime
	¼ cup ghee, melted

1. In a pan that fits your air fryer, mix all the ingredients, toss, introduce in the fryer and cook at 360 degrees F for 15 minutes shaking the fryer halfway. Divide into bowls and serve.

Nutrition:
Calories 222, fat 8, fiber 3, carbs 5, protein 10

Basil Scallops

Prep time: 15 minutes **Cooking time:** 6 minutes **Servings:** 4

12 oz scallops	1 tablespoon dried basil
½ teaspoon salt	1 tablespoon coconut oil, melted

1. Mix up salt, coconut oil, and dried basil. Brush the scallops with basil mixture and leave for 5 minutes to marinate. Meanwhile, preheat the air fryer to 400F. Put the marinated scallops in the air fryer and sprinkle them with remaining coconut oil and basil mixture. Cook the scallops for 4 minutes. Then flip them on another side and cook for 2 minutes more.

Nutrition:
Calories 104, fat 4.1, fiber 0, carbs 2, protein 14.3

Italian Shrimp

Preparation time: 3 minutes **Cooking time:** 12 minutes **Servings:** 4

1 pound shrimp, peeled and deveined A pinch of salt and black pepper	1 tablespoon sesame seeds, toasted
½ teaspoon Italian seasoning	1 tablespoon olive oil

1. In a bowl, mix the shrimp with the rest of the ingredients and toss well. Put the shrimp in the air fryer's basket, cook at 370 degrees F for 12 minutes, divide into bowls and serve,

Nutrition:
Calories 199, fat 11, fiber 2, carbs 4, protein 11

Rosemary Shrimp

Preparation time: 5 minutes **Cooking time:** 12 minutes **Servings:** 4

1 pound shrimp, peeled and deveined	1 cup cherry tomatoes, halved
4 garlic cloves, minced	Salt and black pepper to the taste
1 tablespoon rosemary, chopped	2 tablespoons ghee, melted

1. In a pan that fits the air fryer, mix all the ingredients, toss, put the pan in the fryer and cook at 380 degrees F for 12 minutes. Divide into bowls and serve hot.

Nutrition:
Calories 220, fat 14, fiber 2, carbs 6, protein 15

Cod and Cauliflower Patties

Prep time: 15 minutes **Cooking time:** 12 minutes **Servings:** 4

½ cup cauliflower, shredded	4 oz cod fillet, chopped
1 egg, beaten	1 teaspoon chives, chopped
¼ teaspoon chili flakes	1 teaspoon salt
½ teaspoon ground cumin	2 tablespoons coconut flour
1 spring onion, chopped	1 tablespoon sesame oil

1. Grind the chopped cod fillet and put it in the mixing bowl. Add shredded cauliflower, egg, chives, chili flakes, salt, ground cumin, and chopped onion. Stir the mixture until homogenous and add coconut flour. Stir it again. After this, make the medium size patties. Preheat the air fryer to 385F. Place the patties in the air fryer basket and sprinkle with sesame oil. Cook the fish patties for 8 minutes. Then flip them on another side and cook for 4 minutes more or until the patties are light brown.

Nutrition:
Calories 91, fat 5.4, fiber 1.9, carbs 3.4, protein 7.5

Sea Bass and Coconut Sauce

Preparation time: 5 minutes **Cooking time:** 20 minutes **Servings:** 4

4 sea bass fillets, boneless	A pinch of salt and black pepper 2 spring onions, chopped
Juice of 1 lime	garlic clove, minced 2 tomatoes, cubed
cups coconut cream A handful coriander, chopped 2 red chilies, minced	½ cup okra

1. Put the coconut cream in a pan that fits the air fryer, add garlic, spring onions, lime juice, tomatoes, okra, chilies and the coriander, toss, bring to a simmer and cook for 5-6 minutes. Add the fish, toss gently, introduce in the fryer and cook at 380 degrees F for 15 minutes. Divide between plates and serve.

Nutrition:
Calories 261, fat 12, fiber 5, carbs 6, protein 11

Shrimp and Sausage Gumbo

Prep time: 10 minutes **Cooking time:** 12 minutes **Servings:** 4

10 oz shrimps, peeled	5 oz smoked sausages, chopped
1 teaspoon olive oil	1 teaspoon ground black pepper
3 spring onions, diced	1 jalapeno pepper, chopped
½ cup chicken broth	1 teaspoon chili flakes
½ teaspoon dried cilantro	½ teaspoon salt

1. Preheat the air fryer to 400F. In the mixing bowl mix up smoked sausages, ground black pepper, and chili flakes. Put the smoked sausages in the air fryer and cook them for 4 minutes. Meanwhile, in the mixing bowl mix up onion, jalapeno pepper, and salt. Put the ingredients in the air fryer baking pan and sprinkle with olive oil. After this, remove the sausages from the air fryer. Put the pan with onion in the air fryer and cook it for 2 minutes. After this, add smoked sausages, dried cilantro, and shrimps. Add chicken broth. Stir the ingredients gently and cook the meal for 6 minutes at 400F.

Nutrition:
Calories 233, fat 12.7, fiber 0.8, carbs 4.3, protein 24.1

Clams and Sauce

Preparation time: 5 minutes **Cooking time:** 20 minutes **Servings:** 4

15 small clams	1 tablespoon spring onions, chopped Juice of 1 lime
10 ounces coconut cream	2 tablespoons cilantro, chopped 1 teaspoon olive oil

1. Heat up a pan that fits your air fryer with the oil over medium heat, add the spring onions and sauté for 2 minutes. Add lime juice, coconut cream and the cilantro, stir and cook for 2 minutes more. Add the clams, toss, introduce in the fryer and cook at 390 degrees F for 15 minutes. Divide into bowls and serve hot.

Nutrition:
Calories 231, fat 6, fiber 2, carbs 6, protein 10

Creamy Tilapia

Prep time: 10 minutes **Cooking time:** 12 minutes **Servings:** 2

8 oz tilapia fillet	1 teaspoon coconut cream
1 teaspoon coconut flour	½ teaspoon salt
¼ teaspoon smoked paprika	½ teaspoon dried oregano
½ teaspoon coconut oil, melted	¼ teaspoon ground cumin

1. Rub the tilapia fillet with ground cumin, dried oregano, smoked paprika, and salt. Then dip it in the coconut cream. Cut the tilapia fillet on 2 servings. After this, sprinkle every tilapia fillet with coconut flour gently. Preheat the air fryer to 385F. Sprinkle the air fryer basket with coconut oil and put the tilapia fillets inside. Cook the fillets for 6 minutes from every side.

Nutrition:
Calories 117, fat 3.1, fiber 0.8, carbs 1.3, protein 21.5

Shrimp and Pine Nuts Mix

Preparation time: 5 minutes **Cooking time:** 12 minutes **Servings:** 4

½ cup parsley leaves	½ cup basil leaves
2 tablespoons lemon juice	¼ cup parmesan, grated
1/3 cup pine nuts	
A pinch of salt and black pepper	½ cup olive oil
1 and ½ pounds shrimp, peeled and deveined	¼ teaspoon lemon zest, grated

1. In a blender, combine all the ingredients except the shrimp and pulse well. In a bowl, mix the shrimp with the pesto and toss. Put the shrimp in your air fryer's basket and cook at 360 degrees F for 12 minutes, flipping the shrimp halfway. Divide the shrimp into bowls and serve.

Nutrition:
Calories 240, fat 10, fiber 1, carbs 4, protein 12

Coconut Calamari

Prep time: 10 minutes **Cooking time:** 6 minutes **Servings:** 2

6 oz calamari, trimmed	2 tablespoons coconut flakes
1 egg, beaten	1 teaspoon Italian seasonings
Cooking spray	

1. Slice the calamari into the rings and sprinkle them with Italian seasonings. Then transfer the calamari rings in the bowl with a beaten egg and stir them gently. After this, sprinkle the calamari rings with coconut flakes and shake well. Preheat the air fryer to 400F. Put the calamari rings in the air fryer basket and spray them with cooking spray. Cook the meal for 3 minutes. Then gently stir the calamari and cook them for 3 minutes more.

Nutrition:
Calories 135, fat 5.6, fiber ,0.5 carbs 4.2, protein 18.1

Salmon and Olives

Prep time: 5 minutes **Cooking time:** 15 minutes **Servings:** 4

1 tablespoon lemon zest, grated 1/3 cup olive oil	4 salmon fillets, boneless
1 cup green olives, pitted and sliced Juice of 2 limes	Salt and black pepper to the taste

1. In a baking dish that fits your air fryer, mix all the ingredients, toss, put the pan in the fryer and cook at 370 degrees F for 15 minutes. Divide everything between plates and serve.

Nutrition:
Calories 204, fat 12, fiber 3, carbs 5, protein 15

Oregano Salmon

Prep time: 10 minutes **Cooking time:** 7 minutes **Servings:** 2

10 oz salmon fillet	1 teaspoon dried oregano
1 teaspoon sesame oil	2 oz Parmesan, grated
¼ teaspoon chili flakes	

1. Sprinkle the salmon fillet with dried oregano and chili flakes. Then brush it with sesame oil. Preheat the air fryer to 385F. Place the salmon in the air fryer basket and cook it for 5 minutes. Then flip the fish on another side and top with Parmesan. Cook the fish for 2 minutes more.

Nutrition:
Calories 301, fat 17.2, fiber 0.3, carbs 1.5, protein 36.7

Lemon Shrimp and Zucchinis

Preparation time: 5 minutes **Cooking time:** 15 minutes
Servings: 4

pound shrimp, peeled and deveined	A pinch of salt and black pepper
zucchinis, cut into medium cubes	1 tablespoon lemon juice
1 tablespoon olive oil	1 tablespoon garlic, minced

1. In a pan that fits the air fryer, combine all the ingredients, toss, put the pan in the machine and cook at 370 degrees F for 15 minutes. Divide between plates and serve right away.

Nutrition:
Calories 221, fat 9, fiber 2, carbs 15, protein 11

Tuna Stuffed Avocado

Prep time: 15 minutes **Cooking time:** 12 minutes **Servings:** 2

1 avocado, pitted, halved	½ pound smoked tuna, boneless and shredded
1 egg, beaten	½ teaspoon salt
½ teaspoon chili powder	½ teaspoon ground nutmeg
1 teaspoon dried parsley	Cooking spray

1. Scoop ½ part of the avocado meat from the avocado to get the avocado boats. Use the scooper for this step. After this, in the mixing bowl mix up tuna and egg. Shred the mixture with the help of the fork. Add salt, chili powder, ground nutmeg, and dried parsley. Stir the tuna mixture until homogenous. Add the scooped avocado meat and mix up the mixture well. Fill the avocado boats with tuna mixture. Preheat the air fryer to 385F. Arrange the tuna boats in the air fryer basket and cook them for 12 minutes.

Nutrition:
Calories 400, fat 29, fiber 7.1, carbs 9.5, protein 27.4

Paprika and Cumin Shrimp

Prep time: 10 minutes **Cooking time:** 10 minutes **Servings:** 4

1 teaspoon chili flakes	1 teaspoon ground cumin
½ teaspoon salt	½ teaspoon dried oregano
10 oz shrimps, peeled	1 green bell pepper
2 spring onions, chopped	1 teaspoon apple cider vinegar
1 tablespoon olive oil	1 teaspoon smoked paprika

1. In the mixing bowl mix up chili flakes, ground cumin, salt, dried oregano, and shrimps. Shake the mixture well. After this, preheat the air fryer to 400F. Put the spring onions in the air fryer and cook it for 3 minutes.
2. Meanwhile, slice the bell pepper. Add it in the air fryer and cook the vegetables for 2 minutes more. Then add shrimps and sprinkle the mixture with smoked paprika, olive oil, and apple cider vinegar. Shake it gently and cook for 5 minutes more. Transfer the cooked fajita in the serving plates.

Nutrition:
Calories 139, fat 5, fiber 1.3, carbs 6.6, protein 16.9

Turmeric Salmon and Cauliflower Rice

Preparation time: 5 minutes **Cooking time:** 25 minutes
Servings: 4

4 salmon fillets, boneless	Salt and black pepper to the taste
1 cup cauliflower, riced	½ cup chicken stock
1 teaspoon turmeric powder	1 tablespoon butter, melted

1. In a pan that fits your air fryer, mix the cauliflower rice with the other ingredients except the salmon and toss. Arrange the salmon fillets over the cauliflower rice, put the pan in the fryer and cook at 360 degrees F for 25 minutes, flipping the fish after 15 minutes. Divide everything between plates and serve.

Nutrition:
Calories 241, fat 12, fiber 2, carbs 6, protein 12

Minty Trout and Pine Nuts

Preparation time: 5 minutes **Cooking time:** 16 minutes
Servings: 4

4 rainbow trout	1 cup olive oil + 3 tablespoons Juice of 1 lemon
A pinch of salt and black pepper 1 cup parsley, chopped	3 garlic cloves, minced
½ cup mint, chopped Zest of 1 lemon	1/3 pine nuts
1 avocado, peeled, pitted and roughly chopped	

1. Pat dry the trout, season with salt and pepper and rub with 3 tablespoons oil. Put the fish in your air fryer's basket and cook for 8 minutes on each side. Divide the fish between plates and drizzle half of the lemon juice all over. In a blender, combine the rest of the oil with the remaining lemon juice, parsley, garlic, mint, lemon zest, pine nuts and the avocado and pulse well. Spread this over the trout and serve.

Nutrition:
Calories 240, fat 12, fiber 4, carbs 6, protein 9

Fried Anchovies

Prep time: 20 minutes **Cooking time:** 6 minutes **Servings:** 4

1-pound anchovies	¼ cup coconut flour
2 eggs, beaten	1 teaspoon salt
1 teaspoon ground black pepper	1 tablespoon lemon juice
1 tablespoon sesame oil	

1. Trim and wash anchovies if needed and put in the big bowl. Add salt and ground black pepper. Mix up the anchovies. Then add eggs and stir the fish until you get a homogenous mixture. After this coat every anchovies fish in the coconut flour. Brush the air fryer pan with sesame oil. Place the anchovies in the pan in one layer. Preheat the air fryer to 400F. Put the pan with anchovies in the air fryer and cook them for 6 minutes or until anchovies are golden brown.

Nutrition:
Calories 332, fat 17.7, fiber 2.7, carbs 4.6, protein 36.6

Herbed Trout Mix

Preparation time: 5 minutes **Cooking time:** 20 minutes
Servings: 4

4 trout fillets, boneless and skinless	1 tablespoon lemon juice
2 tablespoons olive oil	A pinch of salt and black pepper
1 bunch asparagus, trimmed	2 tablespoons ghee, melted
¼ cup mixed chives and tarragon	

1. Mix the asparagus with half of the oil, salt and pepper, put it in your air fryer's basket, cook at 380 degrees F for 6 minutes and divide between plates. In a bowl, mix the trout with salt, pepper, lemon juice, the rest of the oil and the herbes and toss, Put the fillets in your air fryer's basket and cook at 380 degrees F for 7 minutes on each side. Divide the fish next to the asparagus, drizzle the melted ghee all over and serve.

Nutrition:
Calories 240, fat 12, fiber 4, carbs 6, protein 9

Tilapia Bowls

Prep time: 15 minutes **Cooking time:** 10 minutes **Servings:** 4

7 oz tilapia fillet or flathead fish	1 teaspoon arrowroot powder
1 teaspoon ground paprika	½ teaspoon salt
½ teaspoon ground black pepper	¼ teaspoon ground cumin
½ teaspoon garlic powder	1 teaspoon lemon juice
4 oz purple cabbage, shredded	1 jalapeno, sliced
1 tablespoon heavy cream	½ teaspoon minced garlic
Cooking spray	

1. Sprinkle the tilapia fillet with arrowroot powder, ground paprika, salt, ground black pepper, ground cumin, and garlic powder. Preheat the air fryer to 385F. Spray the tilapia fillet with cooking spray and place it in the air fryer. Cook the fish for 10 minutes. Meanwhile, in the bowl mix up shredded cabbage, jalapeno pepper, and lemon juice. When the tilapia fillet is cooked, chop it roughly. Put the shredded cabbage mixture in the serving bowls. Top them with chopped tilapia. After this, in the shallow bowl mix up minced garlic and heavy cream. Sprinkle the meal with a heavy cream mixture.

Nutrition:
Calories 69, fat 2, fiber 1.1, carbs 3.6, protein 9.9

Cilantro Salmon

Preparation time: 5 minutes **Cooking time:** 12 minutes
Servings: 4

4 salmon fillets, boneless	¼ cup chives, chopped
Juice of ½ lemon	
4 cilantro springs, chopped	Salt and black pepper to the taste
3 tablespoons olive oil	

1. In a bowl, mix the salmon with all the other ingredients and toss. Put the fillets in your air fryer's basket and cook at 370 degrees F for 12 minutes, flipping the fish halfway. Divide everything between plates and serve with a side salad.

Nutrition:
Calories 240, fat 12, fiber 5, carbs 6, protein 14

Mahi Mahi and Broccoli Cakes

Prep time: 15 minutes **Cooking time:** 11 minutes **Servings:** 4

½ cup broccoli, shredded	1 tablespoon flax meal
1 egg, beaten	1 teaspoon ground coriander
1 oz Monterey Jack cheese, shredded	½ teaspoon salt
6 oz Mahi Mahi, chopped	Cooking spray

1. In the mixing bowl mix up flax meal, egg, ground coriander, salt, broccoli, and chopped Mahi Mahi. Stir the ingredients gently with the help of the fork and add shredded Monterey Jack cheese. Stir the mixture until homogenous. Then make 4 cakes. Preheat the air fryer to 390F. Place the Mahi Mahi cakes in the air fryer and spray them gently with cooking spray. Cook the fish cakes for 5 minutes and then flip on another side.
2. Cook the fish cakes for 6 minutes more.

Nutrition:
Calories 90, fat 4.2, fiber 0.8, carbs 1.4, protein 11.7

Balsamic Trouts with Tomatoes and Pepper

Preparation time: 5 minutes **Cooking time:** 16 minutes
Servings: 2

2 trout fillets, boneless 2 tomatoes, cubed	1 red bell pepper, chopped
1 tablespoon olive oil	2 garlic cloves, minced tablespoon balsamic vinegar A pinch of salt and black pepper 2 tablespoon almond flakes

1. Arrange the fish in a pan that fits your air fryer, add the rest of the ingredients and toss gently. Cook at 370 degrees F for 16 minutes, divide between plates and serve.

Nutrition:
Calories 261, fat 14, fiber 5, carbs 6, protein 14

Squid Stuffed with Cauliflower Mix

Prep time: 20 minutes **Cooking time:** 6 minutes **Servings:** 4

4 squid tubes, trimmed	1 teaspoon ground paprika
½ teaspoon ground turmeric	½ teaspoon garlic, diced
½ cup cauliflower, shredded	1 egg, beaten
½ teaspoon salt	½ teaspoon ground ginger
Cooking spray	

1. Clean the squid tubes if needed. After this, in the mixing bowl mix up ground paprika, turmeric, garlic, shredded cauliflower, salt, and ground ginger. Stir the mixture gently and add a beaten egg. Mix the mixture up. Then fill the squid tubes with shredded cauliflower mixture. Secure the edges of the squid tubes with toothpicks. Preheat the air fryer to 390F. Place the stuffed squid tubes in the air fryer and spray with cooking spray. Cook the meal for 6 minutes.

Nutrition:
Calories 8., fat 2.7, fiber 0.6, carbs 1.5, protein 13.8

Almond and Ghee Trout

Prep time: 5 minutes **Cooking time:** 15 minutes **Servings:** 2

trout fillets, boneless	2 tablespoons almonds, crushed Zest of ½ lemon, grated
1 tablespoon olive oil	tablespoon ghee, melted
A pinch of salt and black pepper	1 tablespoon parsley, chopped

1. In a bowl, mix the trout with all the other ingredients except the parsley and toss. Put the fish in your air fryer's basket and cook at 370 degrees F for 15 minutes, flipping the fillets halfway. Divide between plates, sprinkle the parsley on top and serve.

Nutrition:

Calories 271, fat 13, fiber 4, carbs 6, protein 12.

Herbed Calamari Rings

Prep time: 10 minutes **Cooking time:** 4 minutes **Servings:** 4

1 chili pepper, chopped	¼ teaspoon salt
10 oz calamari	½ teaspoon dried cilantro
½ teaspoon dried parsley	1 teaspoon apple cider vinegar
1 teaspoon butter, melted	¼ teaspoon ground coriander
1 teaspoon sesame oil	

1. Trimmed and wash the calamari. Then slice it into rings and sprinkle with salt, dried cilantro, ground coriander, and apple cider vinegar. Add sesame oil and stir the calamari rings. Preheat the air fryer to 400F. Put the calamari rings in the air fryer basket and cook them for 2 minutes. When the time is finished, shake them well and cook for 2 minutes more.
2. Transfer the calamari rings in the big bowl and sprinkle with butter.

Nutrition:

Calories 84, fat 3.1, fiber 0.1, carbs 2.3, protein 11.1

Shrimp and Parsley Olives

Prep time: 5 minutes **Cooking time:** 12 minutes **Servings:** 4

1 pound shrimp, peeled and deveined	4 garlic clove, minced
1 cup black olives, pitted and chopped	3 tablespoons parsley
1 tablespoon olive oil	

1. In a pan that fits the air fryer, combine all the ingredients, toss, put the pan in the machine and cook at 380 degrees F for 12 minutes. Divide between plates and serve.

Nutrition:

Calories 251, fat 12, fiber 3, carbs 6, protein 15

Sea Bass and Olives Mix

Prep time: 5 minutes **Cooking time:** 20 minutes **Servings:** 2

sea bass, fillets	1 fennel bulb, sliced Juice of 1 lemon
¼ cup black olives, pitted and sliced	1 tablespoon olive oil
A pinch of salt and black pepper	¼ cup basil, chopped

1. In a pan that fits the air fryer, combine all the ingredients, introduce the pan in the machine and cook at 380 degrees F from 20 minutes, shaking the fryer halfway. Divide between plates and serve.

Nutrition:

Calories 254, fat 10, fiber 4, carbs 6, protein 11

Creole Crab

Prep time: 15 minutes **Cooking time:** 6 minutes **Servings:** 6

1 teaspoon Creole seasonings	4 tablespoons almond flour
¼ teaspoon baking powder	1 teaspoon apple cider vinegar
¼ teaspoon onion powder	1 teaspoon dried dill
1 teaspoon ghee	13 oz crab meat, finely chopped
1 egg, beaten	Cooking spray

1. In the mixing bowl mix up crab meat, egg, dried dill, ghee, onion powder, apple cider vinegar, baking powder, and Creole seasonings. Then add almond flour and stir the mixture with the help of the fork until it is homogenous. Make the small balls (hushpuppies). Preheat the air fryer to 390F. Put the hushpuppies in the air fryer basket and spray with cooking spray. Cook them for 3 minutes. Then flip them on another side and cook for 3 minutes more or until the hushpuppies are golden brown.

Nutrition:

Calories 179, fat 11.9, fiber 2, carbs 5.4, protein 12.6

Tarragon Sea Bass and Risotto

Preparation time: 5 minutes **Cooking time:** 25 minutes **Servings:** 4

4 sea bass fillets, boneless	A pinch of salt and black pepper
1 tablespoon ghee, melted	1 garlic clove, minced
1 cup cauliflower rice	½ cup chicken stock
1 tablespoon parmesan, grated	1 tablespoon chervil, chopped
1 tablespoon parsley, chopped	1 tablespoon tarragon, chopped

1. In a pan that fits your air fryer, mix the cauliflower rice with the stock, parmesan, chervil, tarragon and parsley, toss, introduce the pan in the air fryer and cook at 380 degrees F for 12 minutes. In a bowl, mix the fish with salt, pepper, garlic and melted ghee and toss gently. Put the fish over the cauliflower rice, cook at 380 degrees F for 12 minutes more, divide everything between plates and serve.

Nutrition:

Calories 261, fat 12, fiber 4, carbs 6, protein 11

Taco Lobster

Prep time: 10 minutes **Cooking time:** 6 minutes **Servings:** 4

4 lettuce leaves	½ teaspoon taco seasonings
4 lobster tails	1 teaspoon Splenda
½ teaspoon ground cumin	½ teaspoon chili flakes
1 tablespoon ricotta cheese	1 teaspoon avocado oil

1. Peel the lobster tails and sprinkle with ground cumin, taco seasonings, and chili flakes. Arrange the lobster tails in the air fryer basket and sprinkle with avocado oil. Cook them for 6 minutes at 380F. After this, remove the cooked lobster tails from the air fryer and chop them roughly. Transfer the lobster tails into the bowl. Add ricotta cheese and Splenda. Mix them up. Place the lobster mixture on the lettuce leaves and fold them.

Nutrition:

Calories 92, fat 1.2, fiber 0.1, carbs 2.1, protein 16.7

Peppercorn Cod

Preparation time: 5 minutes **Cooking time:** 15 minutes
Servings: 4

4 cod fillets, boneless	A pinch of salt and black pepper
1 tablespoon thyme, chopped	½ teaspoon black peppercorns
2 tablespoons olive oil	fennel, sliced
garlic cloves, minced	red bell pepper, chopped
teaspoons Italian seasoning	

1. In a bowl, mix the fennel with bell pepper and the other ingredients except the fish fillets and toss. Put this into a pan that fits the air fryer, add the fish on top, introduce the pan in your air fryer and cook at 380 degrees F for 15 minutes. Divide between plates and serve.

Nutrition:
Calories 241, fat 12, fiber 4, carbs 7, protein 11

Creamy Cod Strips

Prep time: 10 minutes **Cooking time:** 6 minutes **Servings:** 4

10 oz cod fillet	1 tablespoon coconut flour
1 tablespoon coconut flakes	1 egg, beaten
1 teaspoon ground turmeric	½ teaspoon salt
1 tablespoon heavy cream	1 teaspoon olive oil

1. Cut the cod fillets on the fries strips. After this, in the mixing bowl mix up coconut flour, coconut flakes, ground turmeric, and salt. In the other bowl mix up egg and heavy cream. After this, dip the fish fries in the egg mixture. Then coat them in the coconut flour mixture. Repeat the steps again. Preheat the air fryer to 400F. Put the fish fries in the air fryer basket in one layer and sprinkle them with olive oil. Cook the meal for 3 minutes. Then flip the fish fries on another side and cook for 3 minutes more.

Nutrition:
Calories 111, fat 5.1, fiber 1, carbs 1.9, protein 14.6

Chili Sea Bass Mix

Preparation time: 5 minutes **Cooking time:** 15 minutes
Servings: 4

4 sea bass fillets, boneless	1 cup veggie stock
4 garlic cloves, minced	
Juice of 1 lime	
A pinch of salt and black pepper	1 tablespoon black peppercorns, crushed 1-inch ginger, grated
4 lemongrass, chopped 4 small chilies, minced	bunch coriander, chopped

1. In a blender, combine all the ingredients except the fish and pulse well. Pour the mix in a pan that fits the air fryer, add the fish, toss, introduce in the fryer and cook at 380 degrees F for 15 minutes. Divide between plates and serve.

Nutrition:
Calories 271, fat 12, fiber 4, carbs 6, protein 12

Buttery Haddock and Parsley

Prep time: 10 minutes **Cooking time:** 16 minutes **Servings:** 2

7 oz haddock fillet	2 tablespoons butter, melted
1 teaspoon minced garlic	½ teaspoon salt
1 teaspoon fresh parsley, chopped	½ teaspoon ground celery root

1. Cut the fish fillet on 2 servings. In the shallow bowl mix up butter and minced garlic. Then add salt, celery root, and fresh parsley. After this, carefully brush the fish fillets with the butter mixture. Then wrap every fillet in the foil. Preheat the air fryer to 385F. Put the wrapped haddock fillets in the air fryer and cook for 16 minutes.

Nutrition:
Calories 215, fat 12.5, fiber 0.1, carbs 0.5, protein 24.3

Italian Shrimp Bowls

Preparation time: 5 minutes **Cooking time:** 10 minutes
Servings: 4

pounds shrimp, peeled and deveined A drizzle of olive oil	¼ cup chicken stock
1 tablespoon Italian seasoning Salt and black pepper to the taste	1 teaspoon red pepper flakes, crushed 8 garlic cloves, crushed

1. Grease a pan that fits your air fryer with the oil, add the shrimp and the rest of the ingredients, toss, introduce the pan in the fryer and cook at 390 degrees F for 10 minutes. Divide into bowls and serve.

Nutrition:
Calories 261, fat 12, fiber 6, carbs 7, protein 12

Tarragon and Spring Onions Salmon

Prep time: 15 minutes **Cooking time:** 15 minutes **Servings:** 4

12 oz salmon fillet	2 spring onions, chopped
1 tablespoon ghee, melted	1 teaspoon peppercorns
½ teaspoon salt	½ teaspoon ground black pepper
1 teaspoon tarragon	½ teaspoon dried cilantro

1. Cut the salmon fillet on 4 servings. Then make the parchment pockets and place the fish fillets in the parchment pockets. Sprinkle the salmon with salt, ground black pepper, tarragon, and dried cilantro. After this, top the fish with spring onions, peppercorns, and ghee. Preheat the air fryer to 385F. Arrange the salmon pockets in the air fryer in one layer and cook them for 15 minutes.

Nutrition:
Calories 154, fat 8.5, fiber 0.8, carbs 3.2, protein 16.9

Shrimp and Scallions

Prep time: 3 minutes **Cooking time:** 10 minutes **Servings:** 4

1 pound shrimp, peeled and deveined	2 tablespoons olive oil
1 tablespoon scallions, chopped	1 cup chicken stock

1. In a pan that fits your air fryer, mix the shrimp with the oil, onion and the stock, introduce the pan in the fryer and cook at 380 degrees F for 10 minutes. Divide into bowls and serve.

Nutrition:
Calories 261, fat 6, fiber 8, carbs 16, protein 6

Lemon Octopus

Prep time: 10 minutes **Cooking time:** 26 minutes **Servings:** 4

11 oz octopus	1 teaspoon chili flakes
1 chili pepper, chopped	1 tablespoon coconut oil, melted
½ teaspoon salt	1 cup of water
1 tablespoon lemon juice	

1. Pour water in the pan and bring it to boil. Chop the octopus and put it in the boiling water. Close the lid and cook the seafood for 25 minutes. After this, remove the octopus from the water and sprinkle with chili flakes, chili pepper, coconut oil, salt, and lemon juice.
2. Transfer them in the air fryer and cook for 1 minute at 390F.

Nutrition:
Calories 159, fat 5.1, fiber 0.1, carbs 3.6, protein 23.3

Garlic Fish and Balsamic Salsa

Prep time: 5 minutes **Cooking time:** 15 minutes **Servings:** 4

4 sea bass fillets, boneless	1 tablespoon olive oil
3 tomatoes, roughly chopped	2 spring onions, chopped
¼ cup chicken stock	A pinch of salt and black pepper
3 garlic cloves, minced	1 tablespoon balsamic vinegar

1. In a blender, combine all the ingredients except the fish and pulse well. Put the mix in a pan that fits the air fryer, add the fish, toss gently, introduce the pan in the fryer and cook at 380 degrees F for 15 minutes. Divide between plates and serve.

Nutrition:
Calories 261, fat 11, fiber 4, carbs 7, protein 11

French Clams

Prep time: 5 minutes **Cooking time:** 3 minutes **Servings:** 5

2-pounds clams, raw, shells removed	1 tablespoon Herbs de Provence
1 tablespoon sesame oil	1 garlic clove, diced

1. Put the clams in the bowl and sprinkle with Herbs de Provence, sesame oil, and diced garlic. Shake the seafood well. Preheat the air fryer to 390F. Put the clams in the air fryer and cook them for 3 minutes. When the clams are cooked, shake them well and transfer in the serving plates.

Nutrition:
Calories 45, fat 3, fiber 0, carbs 0.9, protein 3.5

Butter Flounder Fillets

Preparation time: 5 minutes **Cooking time:** 20 minutes **Servings:** 4

4 flounder fillets, boneless	A pinch of salt and black pepper
1 cup parmesan, grated	4 tablespoons butter, melted
2 tablespoons olive oil	

1. In a bowl, mix the parmesan with salt, pepper, butter and the oil and stir well. Arrange the fish in a pan that fits the air fryer, spread the parmesan mix all over, introduce in the fryer and cook at 400 degrees F for 20 minutes. Divide between plates and serve with a side salad.

Nutrition:
Calories 251, fat 14, fiber 5, carbs 6, protein 12

Rosemary Sea bass

Prep time: 10 minutes **Cooking time:** 15 minutes **Servings:** 4

15 oz sea bass, trimmed, cleaned, washed	1 teaspoon salt
1 teaspoon dried rosemary	½ teaspoon lemon zest, grated
2 tablespoons sesame oil	1 tablespoon apple cider vinegar
2 oz Parmesan, grated	

1. In the shallow bowl mix up apple cider vinegar and sesame oil. Sprinkle the sea bass with salt, dried rosemary, and lemon zest. After this, brush the fish with sesame oil mixture. Preheat the air fryer to 400F. Put the fish in the air fryer basket and cook it for 14 minutes. Then flip the fish on another side and top with grated Parmesan. Cook it for 1 minute more.

Nutrition:
Calories 366, fat 16.6, fiber 0.2, carbs 7.5, protein 4.6

Shrimp and Balsamic Okra

Preparation time: 5 minutes **Cooking time:** 10 minutes **Servings:** 4

1 pound shrimp, peeled and deveined	2 tablespoons coconut aminos
1 and ½ cups okra	3 tablespoons balsamic vinegar
½ cup chicken stock	A pinch of salt and black pepper
1 tablespoon parsley, chopped	

1. In a pan that fits your air fryer, mix all the ingredients, toss, introduce in the fryer and cook at 380 degrees F for 10 minutes. Divide into bowls and serve.

Nutrition:
Calories 251, fat 10, fiber 3, carbs 4, protein 8

Almond Sea Bream

Prep time: 15 minutes **Cooking time:** 10 minutes **Servings:** 3

1-pound sea bream steaks (pieces)	1 egg, beaten
1 tablespoon coconut flour	1 teaspoon garlic powder
1 tablespoon almond butter, melted	½ teaspoon Erythritol
½ teaspoon chili powder	1 teaspoon apple cider vinegar

1. In the shallow bowl mix up garlic powder, coconut flour, chili powder, and Erythritol. Sprinkle the sea bream steaks with apple cider vinegar and dip in the beaten egg. After this, coat every fish steak in the coconut flour mixture. Preheat the air fryer to 390F. Place the fish steak in the air fryer in one layer and sprinkle with almond butter. Cook them for 5 minutes from each side.

Nutrition:
Calories 273, fat 9.9, fiber 1.6, carbs 3.4, protein 39.8

Coconut Flounder

Prep time: 5 minutes **Cooking time:** 12 minutes **Servings:** 2

2 flounder fillets, boneless	2 garlic cloves, minced
2 teaspoons coconut aminos	2 tablespoons lemon juice
A pinch of salt and black pepper	½ teaspoon stevia
2 tablespoons olive oil	

1. In a pan that fits your air fryer, mix all the ingredients, toss, introduce in the fryer and cook at 390 degrees F for 12 minutes. Divide into bowls and serve

Nutrition:
Calories 251, fat 13, fiber 3, carbs 5, protein 10

Paprika Prawns

Prep time: 15 minutes **Cooking time:** 5 minutes **Servings:** 5

3-pound prawns, peeled	1 tablespoon ground turmeric
1 teaspoon smoked paprika	1 tablespoon coconut milk
1 teaspoon avocado oil	½ teaspoon salt

1. Put the prawns in the bowl and sprinkle them with ground turmeric, smoked paprika, and salt. Then add coconut milk and leave them for 10 minutes to marinate. Meanwhile, preheat the air fryer to 400F. Put the marinated prawns in the air fryer basket and sprinkle with avocado oil. Cook the prawns for 3 minutes. Then shake them well and cook for 2 minutes more.

Nutrition:
Calories 338, fat 5.6, fiber 0.6, carbs 5.5, protein 62.2

Flounder with Ginger Mushrooms

Preparation time: 5 minutes **Cooking time:** 15 minutes **Servings:** 4

4 flounder fillets, boneless	2 tablespoons coconut aminos A pinch of salt and black pepper
and ½ teaspoons ginger, grated	2 teaspoons olive oil
green onions, chopped	2 cups mushrooms, sliced

1. Heat u a pan that fits your air fryer with the oil over medium-high heat, add the mushrooms and all the other ingredients except the fish, toss and sauté for 5 minutes. Add the fish, toss gently, introduce the pan in the fryer and cook at 390 degrees F for 10 minutes. Divide between plates and serve.

Nutrition:
Calories 271, fat 12, fiber 4, carbs 6, protein 11

Lemon and Thyme Sea bass

Prep time: 10 minutes **Cooking time:** 15 minutes **Servings:** 3

8 oz sea bass, trimmed, peeled	4 lemon slices
1 tablespoon thyme	2 teaspoons sesame oil
1 teaspoon salt	

1. Fill the sea bass with lemon slices and rub with thyme, salt, and sesame oil. Then preheat the air fryer to 385F and put the fish in the air fryer basket. Cook it for 12 minutes. Then flip the fish on another side and cook it for 3 minutes more.

Nutrition:
Calories 216, fat 7.9, fiber 0.6, carbs 6.3, protein 0.2

Buttery Chives Trout

Preparation time: 10 minutes **Cooking time:** 12 minutes **Servings:** 4

4 trout fillets, boneless	4 tablespoons butter, melted
Salt and black pepper to the taste Juice of 1 lime	tablespoon chives, chopped
1 tablespoon parsley, chopped	

1. Mix the fish fillets with the melted butter, salt and pepper, rub gently, put the fish in your air fryer's basket and cook at 390 degrees F for 6 minutes on each side. Divide between plates and serve with lime juice drizzled on top and with parsley and chives sprinkled at the end.

Nutrition:
Calories 221, fat 11, fiber 4, carbs 6, protein 9

Italian Halibut and Asparagus

Prep time: 10 minutes **Cooking time:** 7 minutes **Servings:** 2

2 halibut fillets	4 oz asparagus, trimmed
1 tablespoon avocado oil	½ teaspoon garlic powder
1 teaspoon Italian seasonings	1 teaspoon butter
1 teaspoon salt	1 tablespoon lemon juice

1. Chop the halibut fillet roughly and sprinkle with garlic powder and Italian seasonings. Preheat the air fryer to 400F. Put the asparagus in the air fryer basket and sprinkle it with salt. Then put the fish over the asparagus and sprinkle it with avocado oil and lemon juice. Cook the meal for 8 minutes. Then transfer it in the serving plates and top with butter.

Nutrition:
Calories 367, fat 10.3, fiber 1.6, carbs 3.5, protein 62.1

Parmesan and Garlic Trout

Preparation time: 5 minutes **Cooking time:** 15 minutes **Servings:** 4

tablespoons olive oil 2 garlic cloves, minced	½ cup chicken stock
Salt and black pepper to the taste 4 trout fillets, boneless	¾ cup parmesan, grated
¼ cup tarragon, chopped	

1. In a pan that fits your air fryer, mix all the ingredients except the fishand the parmesan and whisk. Add the fish and grease it well with this mix.
2. Sprinkle the parmesan on top, put the pan in the air fryer and cook at 380 degrees F for 15 minutes. Divide everything between plates and serve.

Nutrition:
Calories 271, fat 12, fiber 4, carbs 6, protein 11

Italian Mackerel

Prep time: 20 minutes **Cooking time:** 15 minutes **Servings:** 2

8 oz mackerel, trimmed	1 tablespoon Italian seasonings
1 teaspoon keto tomato sauce	2 tablespoons ghee, melted
½ teaspoon salt	

1. Rub the mackerel with Italian seasonings, and tomato sauce. After this, rub the fish with salt and leave for 15 minutes in the fridge to marinate. Meanwhile, preheat

the air fryer to 390F. When the time of marinating is finished, brush the fish with ghee and wrap in the baking paper. Place the wrapped fish in the air fryer and cook it for 15 minutes.

Nutrition:
Calories 433, fat 35, fiber 0.1, carbs 1.3, protein 27.2

Thyme Crab and Tomato Sauce

Preparation time: 5 minutes **Cooking time:** 20 minutes **Servings:** 4

2 tablespoons olive oil	1 cup green bell pepper, chopped 4 garlic cloves, chopped
8 tomatoes, chopped	½ teaspoon garlic powder 1 teaspoon thyme, dried
1 teaspoon sweet paprika	¼ cup chicken stock
1 and ½ pound crab meat	A pinch of salt and black pepper
1 tablespoon chives, chopped	

1. Heat up a pan that fist the air fryer with the oil over medium heat, add bell pepper and the garlic and sauté for 2 minutes. Add the rest of the ingredients except the crab meat, stir, bring to a boil and simmer for 6 minutes more. Add the crab meat, put the pan in the fryer and cook at 380 degrees F for 15 minutes. Divide into bowls and serve.

Nutrition:
Calories 261, fat 11, fiber 4, carbs 6, protein 10

Ginger Cod Mix

Prep time: 15 minutes **Cooking time:** 11 minutes **Servings:** 4

1-pound cod fillet	1 teaspoon minced ginger
½ teaspoon ground ginger	1 tablespoon avocado oil
½ teaspoon salt	½ teaspoon ground paprika
½ teaspoon dried thyme	

1. Rub the cod fillet with minced ginger and sprinkle with avocado oil. Leave the fish for 10 minutes to marinate. Meanwhile, mix up ground ginger, salt, ground paprika, and thyme in the shallow bowl. Rub the marinated cod with the spice mixture. Preheat the air fryer to 390F. Put the cod in the air fryer basket and cook it for 6 minutes. After this, flip the fish on another side and cook for 5 minutes more.

Nutrition:
Calories 98, fat 1.5, fiber 0.4, carbs 0.7, protein 20.4

Sea Bass and Broccoli

Preparation time: 5 minutes **Cooking time:** 20 minutes **Servings:** 4

4 black sea bass fillets, boneless	1 pound broccoli florets
4 tablespoons butter, melted	½ teaspoon red pepper flakes, crushed
1 teaspoon lemon zest, grated	A pinch of salt and black pepper

1. In a pan that fits your air fryer, mix the broccoli with the other ingredients except the fish and half of the butter, toss, put the pan in the fryer and cook at 380 degrees F for 8 minutes. Add the fish greased with the rest of the butter, cook at 380 degrees F for 12 minutes more,

divide between plates and serve.

Nutrition:
Calories 251, fat 15, fiber 4, carbs 6, protein 12

Ham Tilapia

Prep time: 15 minutes **Cooking time:** 10 minutes **Servings:** 4

16 oz tilapia fillet	4 ham slices
1 teaspoon sunflower oil	½ teaspoon salt
1 teaspoon dried rosemary	

1. Cut the tilapia on 4 servings. Sprinkle every fish serving with salt, dried rosemary, and sunflower oil. Then carefully wrap the fish fillets in the ham slices and secure with toothpicks. Preheat the air fryer to 400F. Put the wrapped tilapia in the air fryer basket in one layer and cook them for 10 minutes. Gently flip the fish on another side after 5 minutes of cooking.

Nutrition:
Calories 150, fat 4.7, fiber 0.5, carbs 1.3, protein 25.8

Paprika Snapper Mix

Preparation time: 5 minutes **Cooking time:** 14 minutes **Servings:** 4

4 snapper fillets, boneless and skin scored 2 tablespoons sweet paprika	tablespoons olive oil
A pinch of salt and black pepper 6 spring onions, chopped	Juice of ½ lemon

1. In a bowl, mix the paprika with the rest of the ingredients except the fish and whisk well. Rub the fish with this mix, place the fillets in your air fryer's basket and cook at 390 degrees F for 7 minutes on each side.
2. Divide between plates and serve with a side salad.

Nutrition:
Calories 241, fat 12, fiber 4, carbs 6, protein 13

Cheddar Trout

Prep time: 10 minutes **Cooking time:** 13 minutes **Servings:** 4

10 oz trout fillet	1 teaspoon chili flakes
½ teaspoon chili powder	½ teaspoon salt
1 teaspoon dried parsley	1 oz Cheddar cheese, shredded
1 tablespoon avocado oil	

1. Chop the trout and put in the air fryer baking pan. Then sprinkle the fish with chili flakes, chili powder, salt, and dried parsley. Sprinkle the trout with avocado oil and stir gently. Preheat the air fryer to 390F. Cover the baking pan with foil and put it in the air fryer. Cook the fish for 10 minutes. After this, remove the foil and top the trout with Cheddar cheese. Cook the meal for 3 minutes at 400F.

Nutrition:
Calories 169, fat 8.9, fiber 0.3, carbs 0.5, protein 20.7

Char and Fennel

Prep time: 5 minutes **Cooking time:** 18 minutes **Servings:** 4

char fillets, boneless	3 tablespoons olive oil
1 fennel bulb, sliced with a mandolin	A pinch of salt and black pepper
5 garlic cloves, minced	teaspoon caraway seeds
tablespoons balsamic vinegar	1 tablespoon lemon juice
1 tablespoon lemon peel, grated	½ cup dill, chopped

1. In a pan that fits your air fryer, mix the fish with all the other ingredients, toss, introduce in the air fryer and cook at 390 degrees F for 18 minutes. Divide the fish between plates and serve with a side salad.

Nutrition:
Calories 251, fat 16, fiber 4, carbs 6, protein 13

Sea Bream Mix

Prep time: 15 minutes **Cooking time:** 8 minutes **Servings:** 4

1 tablespoon keto tomato sauce	1 tablespoon avocado oil
1 teaspoon ground black pepper	½ teaspoon salt
12 oz sea bream fillet	

1. Cut the sea bream fillet on 4 servings. After this, in the mixing bowl mix up tomato sauce, avocado oil, salt, and ground black pepper. Rub the fish fillets with tomato mixture from both sides. Preheat the air fryer to 390F. Line the air fryer basket with foil. Put the sea bream fillets on the foil and cook them for 8 minutes.

Nutrition:
Calories 124, fat 3.3, fiber 0.5, carbs 1.3, protein 20.7

Halibut and Capers Mix

Prep time: 5 minutes **Cooking time:** 18 minutes **Servings:** 4

4 halibut fillets, boneless	A pinch of salt and black pepper 1 shallot, chopped
2 garlic cloves, minced 1 cup parsley, chopped	1 tablespoon chives, chopped
1 tablespoon lemon zest, grated	1 tablespoon capers, drained and chopped
1 tablespoon lemon juice tablespoon butter, melted	1 tablespoon olive oil

1. Heat up a pan that fits your air fryer with the oil and the butter over medium-high heat, add the shallot and the garlic and sauté for 2 minutes. Add the rest of the ingredients except the fish, toss and sauté for 3 minutes more. Add the fish, sear for 1 minute on each side, toss it gently with the herbed mix, place the pan in the air fryer and cook at 380 degrees F for 12 minutes. Divide everything between plates and serve.

Nutrition:
Calories 220, fat 12, fiber 2, carbs 6, protein 10

Paprika Duck

Prep time: 5 minutes **Cooking time:** 28 minutes **Servings:** 6

10 oz duck skin	1 teaspoon sunflower oil
½ teaspoon salt	½ teaspoon ground paprika

1. Preheat the air fryer to 375F. Then sprinkle the duck skin with sunflower oil, salt, and ground paprika. Put the duck skin in the air fryer and cook it for 18 minutes. Then flip it on another side and cook for 10 minutes more or until it is crunchy from both sides.

Nutrition:
Calories 265, fat 23.9, fiber 0.1, carbs 0.1, protein 11.6

Coriander Cod and Green Beans

Prep time: 15 minutes **Cooking time:** 15 minutes **Servings:** 4

12 oz cod fillet	½ cup green beans, trimmed and halved
1 tablespoon avocado oil	1 teaspoon salt
1 teaspoon ground coriander	

1. Cut the cod fillet on 4 servings and sprinkle every serving with salt and ground coriander. After this, place the fish on 4 foil squares. Top them with green beans and avocado oil and wrap them into parcels. Preheat the air fryer to 400F. Place the cod parcels in the air fryer and cook them for 15 minutes.

Nutrition:
Calories 88, fat 1.3, fiber 1.1, carbs 2.8, protein 16.2

Chili Red Snapper

Prep time: 5 minutes **Cooking time:** 15 minutes **Servings:** 4

4 red snapper fillets, boneless	A pinch of salt and black pepper
2 garlic cloves, minced	2 tablespoons coconut aminos
2 tablespoons lime juice	1 tablespoon hot chili paste
2 tablespoons olive oil	

1. In a bowl, mix all the ingredients except the fish and whisk well. Rub the fish with this mix, place it in your air fryer's basket and cook at 380 degrees F for 15 minutes. Serve with a side salad.

Nutrition:
Calories 220, fat 13, fiber 4, carbs 6, protein 11

Basil Paprika Calamari

Prep time: 20 minutes **Cooking time:** 4 minutes **Servings:** 2

8 oz calamari, peeled, trimmed	1 teaspoon ghee, melted
1 teaspoon fresh basil, chopped	½ teaspoon smoked paprika
½ teaspoon white pepper	1 tablespoon apple cider vinegar

1. In the shallow bowl mix up melted ghee, basil, smoked paprika, white pepper, and apple cider vinegar. After this, sprinkle the calamari with ghee mixture and leave for 15 minutes to marinate. After this, roughly slice the calamari. Preheat the air fryer to 400F. Put the sliced calamari in the air fryer and cook for 2 minutes. Shake the seafood well and cook for 2 minutes more.

Nutrition:
Calories 128, fat 3.8, fiber 0.4, carbs 4.2, protein 17.8

Hot Chicken Wings

Prep time: 5 minutes **Cooking time:** 30 minutes **Servings:** 4

tablespoon olive oil	pounds chicken wings 1 tablespoon lime juice
2 teaspoons smoked paprika	1 teaspoon red pepper flakes, crushed Salt and black pepper to the taste

1. In a bowl, mix the chicken wings with all the other ingredients and toss well. Put the chicken wings in your air fryer's basket and cook at 380 degrees F for 15 minutes on each side. Divide between plates and serve with a side salad.

Nutrition:
Calories 280, fat 13, fiber 3, carbs 6, protein 14

Almond Coconut Chicken Tenders

Prep time: 5 minutes **Cooking time:** 20 minutes **Servings:** 4

4 chicken breasts, skinless, boneless and cut into tenders

A pinch of salt and black pepper

1/3 cup almond flour 2 eggs, whisked

9 ounces coconut flakes

1. Season the chicken tenders with salt and pepper, dredge them in almond flour, then dip in eggs and roll in coconut flakes. Put the chicken tenders in your air fryer's basket and cook at 400 degrees F for 10 minutes on each side. Divide between plates and serve with a side salad.

Nutrition:
Calories 250, fat 12, fiber 4, carbs 6, protein 15

Chili Chicken Cutlets

Prep time: 20 minutes **Cooking time:** 16 minutes **Servings:** 4

15 oz chicken fillet

1 teaspoon white pepper

1 teaspoon ghee, melted

½ teaspoon onion powder

¼ teaspoon chili flakes

1. Chop the chicken fillet into the tiny pieces. Then sprinkle the chopped chicken with white pepper, onion powder, and chili flakes. Stir the mixture until homogenous. Make the medium-size cutlets from the mixture. Preheat the air fryer to 365F. Brush the air fryer basket with ghee and put the chicken cutlets inside. Cook them for 8 minutes and then flip on another side with the help of the spatula. Transfer the cooked chicken cutlets on the serving plate.

Nutrition:
Calories 214, fat 9, fiber 0.2, carbs 0.6, protein 30.9

Marinated Chicken

Preparation time: 10 minutes **Cooking time:** 30 minutes **Servings:** 4

½ cups Keto tomato sauce

1 teaspoon onion powder

A pinch of salt and black pepper

1 tablespoon coconut aminos

½ teaspoon chili powder

pounds chicken drumsticks

1. In bowl, mix the chicken drumsticks with all the other ingredients, toss and keep in the fridge for 10 minutes. Drain the drumsticks, put them in your air fryer's basket and cook at 380 degrees F for 15 minutes on each side. Divide everything between plates and serve.

Nutrition:
Calories 254, fat 14, fiber 4, carbs 6, protein 15

Swordfish with Capers and Tomatoes

Preparation time: 5 minutes **Cooking time:** 10 minutes **Servings:** 2

1-inch thick swordfish steaks A pinch of salt and black pepper 30 ounces tomatoes, chopped

2 tablespoons capers, drained

1 tablespoon red vinegar

2 tablespoons oregano, chopped

1. In a pan that fits the air fryer, combine all the ingredients, toss, put the pan in the fryer and cook at 390 degrees F for 10 minutes, flipping the fish halfway. Divide the mix between plates and serve.

Nutrition:
Calories 280, fat 12, fiber 4, carbs 6, protein 11

Crab Stuffed Flounder

Prep time: 10 minutes **Cooking time:** 12 minutes **Servings:** 3

9 oz flounder fillets

4 oz crab meat, chopped

1 tablespoon mascarpone

½ teaspoon ground nutmeg

2 spring onions, diced

½ teaspoon dried thyme

2 oz Parmesan, grated

1 egg, beaten

1. Line the air fryer baking pan with baking paper. After this, cut the flounder fillet on3 servings and transfer them in the baking pan in one layer. Sprinkle the fish fillets with ground nutmeg and dried thyme. Then top them with chopped crab meat, spring onions, and Parmesan. In the mixing bowl, mix up mascarpone and egg. Pour the liquid over the cheese. Preheat the air fryer to 385F. Place the baking pan with fish in the air fryer and cook the meal for 12 minutes.

Nutrition:
Calories 230, fat 8.3, fiber 0.3, carbs 2.8, protein 33.9

Butter Paprika Swordfish

Prep time: 5 minutes **Cooking time:** 12 minutes **Servings:** 4

4 swordfish fillets, boneless

1 tablespoon olive oil

¾ teaspoon sweet paprika

2 teaspoons basil, dried Juice of 1 lemon

2 tablespoons butter, melted

1. In a bowl, mix the oil with the other ingredients except the fish fillets and whisk. Brush the fish with this mix, place it in your air fryer's basket and cook for 6 minutes on each side. Divide between plates and serve with a side salad.

Nutrition:
Calories 216, fat 11, fiber 3, carbs 6, protein 12

Caribbean Ginger Sea bass

Prep time: 15 minutes **Cooking time:** 10 minutes **Servings:** 2

¼ habanero, chopped

1 teaspoon Caribbean spices

8 oz sea bass, trimmed

½ teaspoon Erythritol

1 teaspoon smoked paprika

¼ teaspoon minced ginger

1 tablespoon avocado oil

1. In the mixing bowl mix up Caribbean spices, Erythritol, and smoked paprika. Then rub the sea bass with the spice mixture well. In the shallow bowl, whisk together minced ginger and avocado oil. Brush the fish with the ginger mixture. Preheat the air fryer to 400F. Put the sea bass in the air fryer and cook it for 10 minutes.

Nutrition:
Calories 291, fat 8.3, fiber 1.1, carbs 9.4, protein 0.4

Lemon Branzino

Prep time: 10 minutes **Cooking time:** 8 minutes **Servings:** 4

1-pound branzino, trimmed, washed

1 teaspoon Cajun seasoning

1 tablespoon sesame oil

1 tablespoon lemon juice

1 teaspoon salt

1. Rub the branzino with salt and Cajun seasoning carefully. Then sprinkle the fish with the lemon juice and sesame oil. Preheat the air fryer to 380F. Place the fish in the air fryer and cook it for 8 minutes.

Nutrition:
Calories 141, fat 5.9, fiber 0, carbs 0.1, protein 21

Trout and Shallots

Prep time: 5 minutes **Cooking time:** 12 minutes **Servings:** 4

4 trout fillets, boneless

½ cup butter, melted

Juice of 1 lime

½ cup olive oil

garlic cloves, minced 6

shallots, chopped

A pinch of salt and black pepper

1. In a pan that fits the air fryer, combine the fish with the shallots and the rest of the ingredients, toss gently, put the pan in the machine and cook at 390 degrees F for 12 minutes, flipping the fish halfway. Divide between plates and serve with a side salad.

Nutrition:

Calories 270, fat 12, fiber 4, carbs 6, protein 12

Sea Bass with Vinaigrette

Prep time: 5 minutes **Cooking time:** 12 minutes **Servings:** 4

black sea bass fillets, boneless and skin scored

2 tablespoons olive oil

A pinch of salt and black pepper

3 tablespoons black olives, pitted and chopped

3 garlic cloves, minced

1 tablespoon rosemary, chopped Juice of 1 lime

1. In a bowl, mix the oil with the olives and the rest of the ingredients except the fish and whisk well. Place the fish in a pan that fits the air fryer, spread the rosemary vinaigrette all over, put the pan in the machine and cook at 380 degrees F for 12 minutes, flipping the fish halfway. Divide between plates and serve.

Nutrition:

Calories 220, fat 12, fiber 4, carbs 6, protein 10

Chili Squid Rings

Prep time: 15 minutes **Cooking time:** 10 minutes **Servings:** 2

8 oz squid tube, trimmed, washed

4 oz chorizo, chopped

1 teaspoon olive oil

1 teaspoon chili flakes

1 tablespoon keto mayonnaise

1. Preheat the air fryer to 400F and put the chopped chorizo in the air fryer basket. Sprinkle it with chili flakes and olive oil and cook for 6 minutes. Then shake chorizo well. Slice the squid tube into the rings and add in the air fryer. Cook the meal for 4 minutes at 400F. Shake the cooked meal well and transfer it in the plates. Sprinkle the meal with keto mayonnaise.

Nutrition:

Calories 338, fat 25.5, fiber 0, carbs 1.1, protein 25.7

Pesto Chicken

Prep time: 10 minutes **Cooking time:** 25 minutes **Servings:** 4

12 oz chicken legs

1 teaspoon sesame oil

½ teaspoon chili flakes

4 teaspoons pesto sauce

1. In the shallow bowl mix up pesto sauce, chili flakes, and sesame oil. Then rub the chicken legs with the pesto mixture. Preheat the air fryer to 390F. Put the chicken legs in the air fryer basket and cook them for 25 minutes.

Nutrition:

Calories 194, fat 9.6, fiber 0.1, carbs 0.3, protein 25.1

Trout and Tomato Zucchinis Mix

Preparation time: 5 minutes **Cooking time:** 15 minutes **Servings:** 4

3 zucchinis, cut in medium chunks

4 trout fillets, boneless

2 tablespoons olive oil

¼ cup keto tomato sauce

Salt and black pepper to the taste

1 garlic clove, minced

tablespoon lemon juice

½ cup cilantro, chopped

1. In a pan that fits your air fryer, mix the fish with the other ingredients, toss, introduce in the fryer and cook at 380 degrees F for 15 minutes. Divide everything between plates and serve right away.

Nutrition:

Calories 220, fat 12, fiber 4, carbs 6, protein 9

Poultry Recipes

Chicken and Rice Casserole

Preparation time: 5 minutes **Cooking time:** 35 minutes **Servings:** 4

cups cauliflower florets, chopped

A pinch of salt and black pepper

A drizzle of olive oil

6 ounces coconut cream

2 tablespoons butter, melted

2 teaspoons thyme, chopped

1 garlic clove, minced

1 tablespoon parsley, chopped

4 chicken thighs, boneless and skinless

1. Heat up a pan with the butter over medium heat, add the cream and the other ingredients except the cauliflower, oil and the chicken, whisk, bring to a simmer and cook for 5 minutes. Heat up a pan with the oil over medium-high heat, add the chicken and brown for 2 minutes on each side. In a baking dish that fits the air fryer, mix the chicken with the cauliflower, spread the coconut cream mix all over, put the pan in the machine and cook at 380 degrees F for 20 minutes. Divide between plates and serve hot.

Nutrition:

Calories 280, fat 14, fiber 4, carbs 6, protein 20

Hazelnut Crusted Chicken

Prep time: 10 minutes **Cooking time:** 10 minutes **Servings:** 4

1-pound chicken fillet

3 oz hazelnuts, grinded

2 egg whites, whisked

½ teaspoon ground black pepper

½ teaspoon salt

1 tablespoon coconut flour

1 teaspoon avocado oil

1. Cut the chicken on 4 tenders and sprinkle them with ground black pepper and salt. In the mixing bowl mix up grinded hazelnuts and coconut flour. Then dip the chicken tenders in the whisked egg and coat in the hazelnut mixture. Sprinkle every chicken tender with avocado oil. Preheat the air fryer to 365F. Place the prepared chicken tenders in the preheated air fryer and cook for 10 minutes.

Nutrition:

Calories 369, fat 21.8, fiber 2.9, carbs 5, protein 38.2

Oregano Chicken and Green Beans

Preparation time: 5 minutes **Cooking time:** 35 minutes
Servings: 4

4 chicken breasts, skinless, boneless and halved 10 ounces chicken stock	1 teaspoon oregano, dried
10 ounces green beans, trimmed and halved 2 tablespoons olive oil	A pinch of salt and black pepper 1 tablespoon parsley, chopped

1. Heat up a pan that fits the air fryer with the oil over medium-high heat, add the chicken and brown for 2 minutes on each side. Add the remaining ingredients, toss a bit, put the pan in the machine and cook at 380 degrees F for 30 minutes. Divide everything between plates and serve.

Nutrition:
Calories 241, fat 11, fiber 5, carbs 6, protein 14

Chicken with Tomatoes and Peppers

Preparation time: 5 minutes **Cooking time:** 25 minutes
Servings: 4

4 chicken breasts, skinless, boneless and halved 2 zucchinis, sliced	4 tomatoes, cut into wedges
2 yellow bell peppers, cut into wedges	2 tablespoons olive oil
1 teaspoon Italian seasoning	

1. In a baking dish that fits your air fryer, mix all the ingredients, toss, introduce in the fryer and cook at 380 degrees F for 25 minutes. Divide everything between plates and serve.

Nutrition:
Calories 280, fat 12, fiber 4, carbs 6, protein 14

Lemongrass Hens

Prep time: 20 minutes **Cooking time:** 65 minutes **Servings:** 4

14 oz hen (chicken)	1 teaspoon lemongrass
1 teaspoon ground coriander	1 oz celery stalk, chopped
1 teaspoon dried cilantro	3 spring onions, diced
2 tablespoons avocado oil	2 tablespoons lime juice
½ teaspoon lemon zest, grated	1 teaspoon salt
1 tablespoon apple cider vinegar	1 teaspoon chili powder
½ teaspoon ground black pepper	

1. In the mixing bowl mix up lemongrass, ground coriander, dried cilantro, lime juice, lemon zest, salt, apple cider vinegar, and ground black pepper. Then add spring onions and celery stalk. After this, rub the hen with the spice mixture and leave for 10 minutes to marinate. Meanwhile, preheat the air fryer to 375F. Put the hen in the air fryer and cook it for 55 minutes. Then flip it on another side and cook for 10 minutes more.

Nutrition:
Calories 177, fat 4.1, fiber 1.41, carbs 4.4, protein 29.3

Paprika Chicken Breasts

Preparation time: 5 minutes **Cooking time:** 20 minutes
Servings: 4

4 chicken breasts, skinless and boneless	1 teaspoon chili powder
A pinch of salt and black pepper A drizzle of olive oil	1 teaspoon smoked paprika
1 teaspoon garlic powder	1 tablespoon parsley, chopped

1. Season chicken with salt and pepper, and rub it with the oil and all the other ingredients except the parsley Put the chicken breasts in your air fryer's basket and cook at 350 degrees F for 10 minutes on each side. Divide between plates, sprinkle the parsley on top and serve.

Nutrition:
Calories 222, fat 11, fiber 4, carbs 6, protein 12

Provolone Meatballs

Prep time: 10 minutes **Cooking time:** 12 minutes **Servings:** 6

12 oz ground chicken	½ cup coconut flour
2 egg whites, whisked	1 teaspoon ground black pepper
1 egg yolk	1 teaspoon salt
4 oz Provolone cheese, grated	1 teaspoon ground oregano
½ teaspoon chili powder	1 tablespoon avocado oil

1. In the mixing bowl mix up ground chicken, ground black pepper, egg yolk, salt, Provolone cheese, ground oregano, and chili powder. Stir the mixture until homogenous and make the small meatballs. Dip the meatballs in the whisked egg whites and coat in the coconut flour. Preheat the air fryer to 370F. Put the chicken meatballs in the air fryer basket and cook them for 6 minutes from both sides.

Nutrition:
Calories 234, fat 11.7, fiber 3.7, carbs 6.6, protein 24.3

Thyme and Okra Chicken Thighs

Preparation time: 5 minutes **Cooking time:** 30 minutes
Servings: 4

4 chicken thighs, bone-in and skinless	A pinch of salt and black pepper
1 cup okra	½ cup butter, melted Zest of 1 lemon, grated 4 garlic cloves, minced
tablespoon thyme, chopped	1 tablespoon parsley, chopped

1. Heat up a pan that fits your air fryer with half of the butter over medium heat, add the chicken thighs and brown them for 2-3 minutes on each side. Add the rest of the butter, the okra and all the remaining ingredients, toss, put the pan in the air fryer and cook at 370 degrees F for 20 minutes.
2. Divide between plates and serve.

Nutrition:
Calories 270, fat 12, fiber 4, carbs 6, protein 14

Lemon and Chili Chicken Drumsticks

Prep time: 10 minutes **Cooking time:** 20 minutes **Servings:** 6

6 chicken drumsticks	1 teaspoon dried oregano
1 tablespoon lemon juice	½ teaspoon lemon zest, grated
1 teaspoon ground cumin	½ teaspoon chili flakes
1 teaspoon garlic powder	½ teaspoon ground coriander
1 tablespoon avocado oil	

1. Rub the chicken drumsticks with dried oregano, lemon juice, lemon zest, ground cumin, chili flakes, garlic powder, and ground coriander. Then sprinkle them with avocado oil and put in the air fryer. Cook the chicken drumsticks for 20 minutes at 375F.

Nutrition:
Calories 85, fat 3.1, fiber 0.3, carbs 0.9, protein 12.9

Garlic Chicken Wings

Prep time: 5 minutes **Cooking time:** 30 minutes **Servings:** 4

pounds chicken wings	¼ cup olive oil Juice of 2 lemons
Zest of 1 lemon, grated	A pinch of salt and black pepper
2 garlic cloves, minced	

1. In a bowl, mix the chicken wings with the rest of the ingredients and toss well. Put the chicken wings in your air fryer's basket and cook at 400 degrees F for 30 minutes, shaking halfway. Divide between plates and serve with a side salad.

Nutrition:
Calories 263, fat 14, fiber 4, carbs 6, protein 15

Ginger and Coconut Chicken

Preparation time: 5 minutes **Cooking time:** 20 minutes **Servings:** 4

chicken breasts, skinless, boneless and halved 4 tablespoons coconut aminos	1 teaspoon olive oil 2 tablespoons stevia
Salt and black pepper to the taste	¼ cup chicken stock
1 tablespoon ginger, grated	

1. In a pan that fits the air fryer, combine the chicken with the ginger and all the ingredients and toss.. Put the pan in your air fryer and cook at 4380 degrees F for 20, shaking the fryer halfway. Divide between plates and serve with a side salad.

Nutrition:
Calories 256, fat 12, fiber 4, carbs 6, protein 14

Pesto Chicken

Prep time: 10 minutes **Cooking time:** 25 minutes **Servings:** 4

cup basil pesto	tablespoons olive oil
A pinch of salt and black pepper 1 and ½ pounds chicken wings	

1. In a bowl, mix the chicken wings with all the ingredients and toss well. Put the meat in the air fryer's basket and cook at 380 degrees F for 25 minutes. Divide between plates and serve.

Nutrition:
Calories 244, fat 11, fiber 4, carbs 6, protein 17

Cream Cheese Chicken Mix

Prep time: 15 minutes **Cooking time:** 16 minutes **Servings:** 4

1-pound chicken wings	¼ cup cream cheese
1 tablespoon apple cider vinegar	1 teaspoon Truvia
½ teaspoon smoked paprika	½ teaspoon ground nutmeg
1 teaspoon avocado oil	

1. In the mixing bowl mix up cream cheese, Truvia, apple cider vinegar, smoked paprika, and ground nutmeg. Then add the chicken wings and coat them in the cream cheese mixture well. Leave the chicken winds in the cream cheese mixture for 10-15 minutes to marinate. Meanwhile, preheat the air fryer to 380F. Put the chicken wings in the air fryer and cook them for 8 minutes. Then flip the chicken wings on another and brush with cream cheese marinade. Cook the chicken wings for 8 minutes more.

Nutrition:
Calories 271, fat 13.7, fiber 0.2, carbs 1.2, protein 34

Buttery Chicken Wings

Prep time: 5 minutes **Cooking time:** 30 minutes **Servings:** 4

pounds chicken wings	Salt and black pepper to the taste 3 garlic cloves, minced
tablespoons butter, melted	½ cup heavy cream
½ teaspoon basil, dried	½ teaspoon oregano, dried
¼ cup parmesan, grated	

1. In a baking dish that fits your air fryer, mix the chicken wings with all the ingredients except the parmesan and toss. Put the dish to your air fryer and cook at 380 degrees F for 30 minutes. Sprinkle the cheese on top, leave the mix aside for 10 minutes, divide between plates and serve.

Nutrition:
Calories 270, fat 12, fiber 3, carbs 6, protein 17

Parmesan and Dill Chicken

Prep time: 15 minutes **Cooking time:** 20 minutes **Servings:** 6

18 oz chicken breast, skinless, boneless	5 oz pork rinds
3 oz Parmesan, grated	3 eggs, beaten
1 teaspoon chili flakes	1 teaspoon ground paprika
2 tablespoons avocado oil	1 teaspoon Erythritol
¼ teaspoon onion powder	1 teaspoon cayenne pepper
1 chili pepper, minced	½ teaspoon dried dill

1. In the shallow bowl mix up chili flakes, ground paprika, Erythritol. Onion powder, and cayenne pepper. Add dried dill and stir the mixture gently.
2. Then rub the chicken breast in the spice mixture. Then rub the chicken with minced chili pepper. Dip the chicken breast in the beaten eggs. After this, coat it in the Parmesan and dip in the eggs again. Then coat the chicken in the pork rinds and sprinkle with avocado oil. Preheat the air fryer to 380F. Put the chicken breast in the air fryer and cook it for 16 minutes. Then flip the chicken breast on another side and cook it for 4 minutes more.

Nutrition:
Calories 318, fat 16.5, fiber 0.5, carbs 1.5, protein 40.7

Tomato Chicken Mix

Prep time: 10 minutes **Cooking time:** 18 minutes **Servings:** 4

1-pound chicken breast, skinless, boneless	1 tablespoon keto tomato sauce
1 teaspoon avocado oil	½ teaspoon garlic powder

1. In the small bowl mix up tomato sauce, avocado oil, and garlic powder. Then brush the chicken breast with the tomato sauce mixture well. Preheat the air fryer to 385F. Place the chicken breast in the air fryer and cook it for 15 minutes. Then flip it on another side and cook for 3 minutes more. Slice the cooked chicken breast into servings.

Nutrition:

Calories 139, fat 3, fiber 0.2, carbs 2, protein 24.2

Chicken with Asparagus and Zucchini

Preparation time: 15 minutes **Cooking time:** 25 minutes **Servings:** 4

pound chicken thighs, boneless and skinless Juice of 1 lemon	tablespoons olive oil 3 garlic cloves, minced
1 teaspoon oregano, dried	½ pound asparagus, trimmed and halved A pinch of salt and black pepper
1 zucchinis, halved lengthwise and sliced into half-moons	

1. In a bowl, mix the chicken with all the ingredients except the asparagus and the zucchinis, toss and leave aside for 15 minutes. Add the zucchinis and the asparagus, toss, put everything into a pan that fits the air fryer, and cook at 380 degrees F for 25 minutes. Divide everything between plates and serve.

Nutrition:

Calories 280, fat 11, fiber 4, carbs 6, protein 17

Hoisin Chicken

Prep time: 25 minutes **Cooking time:** 22 minutes **Servings:** 4

½ teaspoon hoisin sauce	½ teaspoon salt
½ teaspoon chili powder	½ teaspoon ground black pepper
½ teaspoon ground cumin	¼ teaspoon xanthan gum
1 teaspoon apple cider vinegar	1 tablespoon sesame oil
3 tablespoons coconut cream	½ teaspoon minced garlic
½ teaspoon chili paste	1-pound chicken drumsticks
2 tablespoons almond flour	

1. Rub the chicken drumsticks with salt, chili powder, ground black pepper, ground cumin, and leave for 10 minutes to marinate. Meanwhile, in the mixing bowl mix up chili paste, minced garlic, coconut cream, apple cider vinegar, xanthan gum, and almond flour. Coat the chicken drumsticks in the coconut cream mixture well, and leave to marinate for 10 minutes more. Preheat the air fryer to 375F. Put the chicken drumsticks in the air fryer and cook them for 22 minutes.

Nutrition:

Calories 279, fat 14.5, fiber 1.7, carbs 3.4, protein 32.4

Coconut Chicken

Prep time: 15 minutes **Cooking time:** 12 minutes **Servings:** 4

12 oz chicken fillet (3 oz each fillet)	4 teaspoons coconut flakes
1 egg white, whisked	1 teaspoon salt
½ teaspoon ground black pepper	Cooking spray

1. Beat the chicken fillets with the kitchen hammer and sprinkle with salt and ground black pepper. Then dip every chicken chop in the whisked egg white and coat in the coconut flakes. Preheat the air fryer to 360F. Put the chicken chops in the air fryer and spray with cooking spray. Cook the chicken chop for 7 minutes. Then flip them on another side and cook for 5 minutes. The cooked chicken chops should have a golden brown color.

Nutrition:

Calories 172, fat 6.9, fiber 0.2, carbs 0.5, protein 25.6

Chicken and Olives Mix

Preparation time: 10 minutes **Cooking time:** 30 minutes **Servings:** 4

8 chicken thighs, boneless and skinless A pinch of salt and black pepper	2 tablespoons olive oil
1 teaspoon oregano, dried	½ teaspoon garlic powder
1 cup pepperoncini, drained and sliced	½ cup black olives, pitted and sliced
½ cup kalamata olives, pitted and sliced	¼ cup parmesan, grated

1. Heat up a pan that fits the air fryer with the oil over medium-high heat, add the chicken and brown for 2 minutes on each side. Add salt, pepper, and all the other ingredients except the parmesan and toss. Put the pan in the air fryer, sprinkle the parmesan on top and cook at 370 degrees F for 25 minutes. Divide the chicken mix between plates and serve.

Nutrition:

Calories 270, fat 14, fiber 4, carbs 6, protein 18

Chicken and Ghee Mix

Prep time: 15 minutes **Cooking time:** 30 minutes **Servings:** 4

12 oz chicken legs	1 teaspoon nutritional yeast
1 teaspoon chili flakes	½ teaspoon ground cumin
½ teaspoon garlic powder	1 teaspoon ground turmeric
½ teaspoon ground paprika	1 teaspoon Splenda
¼ cup coconut flour	1 tablespoon ghee, melted

1. In the mixing bowl mix up nutritional yeast, chili flakes, ground cumin, garlic powder, ground turmeric, ground paprika, Splenda, and coconut flour. Then brush every chicken leg with ghee and coat well in the coconut flour mixture. Preheat the air fryer to 380F. Place the chicken legs in the air fryer in one layer. Cook them for 15 minutes. Then flip the chicken legs on another side and cook them for 15 minutes more.

Nutrition:

Calories 238, fat 10.9, fiber 3.5, carbs 6.8, protein 26.7

Sun-dried Tomatoes and Chicken Mix

Prep time: 5 minutes **Cooking time:** 25 minutes **Servings:** 4

4 chicken thighs, skinless, boneless 1 tablespoon olive oil	A pinch of salt and black pepper 1 tablespoon thyme, chopped
1 cup chicken stock	3 garlic cloves, minced
½ cup coconut cream	cup sun-dried tomatoes, chopped 4 tablespoons parmesan, grated

1. Heat up a pan that fits the air fryer with the oil over medium-high heat, add the chicken, salt, pepper and the garlic, and brown for 2-3 minutes on each side. Add the rest of the ingredients except the parmesan, toss, put the pan in the air fryer and cook at 370 degrees F for 20 minutes. Sprinkle the parmesan on top, leave the mix aside for 5 minutes, divide everything between plates and serve.

Nutrition:
Calories 275, fat 12, fiber 4, carbs 6, protein 17

Cauliflower Stuffed Chicken

Prep time: 20 minutes **Cooking time:** 25 minutes **Servings:** 5

1 ½-pound chicken breast, skinless, boneless	½ cup cauliflower, shredded
1 jalapeno pepper, chopped	1 teaspoon ground nutmeg
1 teaspoon salt	¼ cup Cheddar cheese, shredded
½ teaspoon cayenne pepper	1 tablespoon cream cheese
1 tablespoon sesame oil	½ teaspoon dried thyme

1. Make the horizontal cut in the chicken breast. In the mixing bowl mix up shredded cauliflower, chopped jalapeno pepper, ground nutmeg, salt, and cayenne pepper. Fill the chicken cut with the shredded cauliflower and secure the cut with toothpicks. Then rub the chicken breast with cream cheese, dried thyme, and sesame oil. Preheat the air fryer to 380F. Put the chicken breast in the air fryer and cook it for 20 minutes. Then sprinkle it with Cheddar cheese and cook for 5 minutes more.

Nutrition:
Calories 266, fat 9.6, fiber 0.5, carbs 1.2, protein 41.3

Ginger Chicken and Lemon Sauce

Preparation time: 5 minutes **Cooking time:** 25 minutes **Servings:** 4

tablespoons spring onions, minced 1 tablespoon ginger, grated	4 garlic cloves, minced
2 tablespoons coconut aminos 8 chicken drumsticks	½ cup chicken stock
Salt and black pepper to the taste 1 teaspoon olive oil	¼ cup cilantro, chopped 1 tablespoon lemon juice

1. Heat up a pan with the oil over medium-high heat, add the chicken drumsticks, brown them for 2 minutes on each side and transfer to a pan that fits the fryer. Add all the other ingredients, toss everything, put the pan in the fryer and cook at 370 degrees F for 20 minutes. Divide the chicken and lemon sauce between plates and serve.

Nutrition:
Calories 267, fat 11, fiber 4, carbs 6, protein 16

Dill Chicken Quesadilla

Prep time: 15 minutes **Cooking time:** 10 minutes **Servings:** 2

2 low carb tortillas	7 oz chicken breast, skinless, boneless, boiled
1 tablespoon cream cheese	1 teaspoon butter, melted
1 teaspoon minced garlic	1 teaspoon fresh dill, chopped
½ teaspoon salt	2 oz Monterey Jack cheese, shredded
Cooking spray	

1. Shred the chicken breast with the help of the fork and put it in the bowl. Add cream cheese, butter, minced garlic, dill, and salt. Add shredded Monterey jack cheese and stir the shredded chicken. Then put 1 tortilla in the air fryer baking pan. Top it with the shredded chicken mixture and cover with the second corn tortilla. Cook the meal for 5 minutes at 400F.

Nutrition:
Calories 337, fat 16.7, fiber 7.1, carbs 13.1, Protein 31.6

Mozzarella Chicken and Spinach

Prep time: 5 minutes **Cooking time:** 24 minutes **Servings:** 6

6 chicken breasts, skinless, boneless and halved A pinch of salt and black pepper	2 tablespoons olive oil
1 pound mozzarella, sliced	1 teaspoon Italian seasoning
2 cups baby spinach	2 tomatoes, sliced
1 tablespoon basil, chopped	

1. Make slits in each chicken breast halves, season with salt, pepper and Italian seasoning and stuff with mozzarella, spinach and tomatoes. Drizzle the oil over stuffed chicken, put it in your air fryer's basket and cook at 370 degrees F for 12 minutes on each side. Divide between plates and serve with basil sprinkled on top.

Nutrition:
Calories 285, fat 12, fiber 4, carbs 7, protein 15

Cinnamon Chicken Thighs

Prep time: 5 minutes **Cooking time:** 30 minutes **Servings:** 4

2 pounds chicken thighs	A pinch of salt and black pepper
2 tablespoons olive oil	½ teaspoon cinnamon, ground

1. Season the chicken thighs with salt and pepper, and rub with the rest of the ingredients. Put the chicken thighs in air fryer's basket, cook at 360 degrees F for 15 minutes on each side, divide between plates and serve.

Nutrition:
Calories 271, fat 12, fiber 4, carbs 6, protein 13

Pepper Turkey Bacon

Prep time: 10 minutes **Cooking time:** 8 minutes **Servings:** 2

7 oz turkey bacon	1 teaspoon coconut oil, melted
½ teaspoon ground black pepper	

1. Slice the turkey bacon if needed and sprinkle it with ground black pepper and coconut oil. Preheat the air fryer to 400F. Arrange the turkey bacon in the air fryer in one layer and cook it for 4 minutes. Then flip the bacon on another side and cook for 4 minutes more.

Nutrition:
Calories 149, fat 5.5, fiber 0.1, carbs 0.3, protein 19.3

Vinegar Chicken

Prep time: 20 minutes **Cooking time:** 15 minutes **Servings:** 4

16 oz chicken thighs, skinless	1 teaspoon ground celery root
1 teaspoon dried celery leaves	1 teaspoon apple cider vinegar
½ teaspoon salt	1 tablespoon sunflower oil

1. Rub the chicken thighs with the celery root, dried celery leaves, and salt. Then sprinkle the chicken with apple cider vinegar and sunflower oil.
2. Leave it for 15 minutes to marinate. After this, preheat the air fryer to 385F. Put the chicken thighs in the air fryer and cook them for 12 minutes. Then flip the chicken on another side and cook for 3 minutes more.
3. Transfer the cooked chicken thighs on the plate.

Nutrition:
Calories 247, fat 11.9, fiber 0, carbs 0, protein 32.8

Chili and Paprika Chicken Wings

Prep time: 10 minutes **Cooking time:** 12 minutes **Servings:** 5

1-pound chicken wings	1 teaspoon ground paprika
1 teaspoon chili powder	½ teaspoon salt
1 tablespoon sunflower oil	

1. Pour the sunflower oil in the shallow bowl. Add chili powder and ground paprika. Gently stir the mixture. Sprinkle the chicken wings with red chili mixture and salt. Preheat the air fryer to 400F. Place the chicken wings in the preheated air fryer in one layer and cook for 6 minutes. Then flip the wings on another side and cook for 6 minutes more.

Nutrition:
Calories 200, fat 9.7, fiber 0.3, carbs 0.5, protein 26.4

Chives and Lemon Chicken

Prep time: 5 minutes **Cooking time:** 20 minutes **Servings:** 4

1 pound chicken tenders, boneless, skinless A pinch of salt and black pepper tablespoon chives, chopped A drizzle of olive oil	Juice of 1 lemon

1. In a bowl, mix the chicken tenders with all ingredients except the chives, toss, put the meat in your air fryer's basket and cook at 370 degrees F for 10 minutes on each side. Divide between plates and serve with chives sprinkled on top.

Nutrition:
Calories 230, fat 13, fiber 4, carbs 6, protein 16

Sweet Turmeric Chicken Wings

Prep time: 15 minutes **Cooking time:** 15 minutes **Servings:** 8

8 chicken wings	1 teaspoon Splenda
1 teaspoon ground turmeric	½ teaspoon cayenne pepper
1 tablespoon avocado oil	

1. Mix up Splenda and avocado oil and stir the mixture until Splenda is dissolved. Then rub the chicken wings with ground turmeric and cayenne pepper. Brush the chicken wings with sweet avocado oil from both sides. Preheat the air fryer to 390F. Place the chicken wings in the air fryer and cook them for 15 minutes.

Nutrition:
Calories 105, fat 6.9, fiber 0.2, carbs 0.8, protein 9.2

Red Vinegar and Chicken Mix

Preparation time: 5 minutes **Cooking time:** 30 minutes **Servings:** 4

pounds chicken wings, halved	¼ cup red vinegar
4 garlic cloves, minced	Salt and black pepper to the taste 4 tablespoons olive oil
tablespoon garlic powder 1 teaspoon turmeric powder	

1. In a bowl, mix the chicken with all the other ingredients and toss well. Put the chicken wings in your air fryer's basket and cook at 370 degrees F for 30 minutes, flipping the meat halfway. Divide everything between plates and serve with a side salad.

Nutrition:
Calories 250, fat 12, fiber 4, carbs 6, protein 15

Bacon Chicken Mix

Prep time: 15 minutes **Cooking time:** 25 minutes **Servings:** 2

2 chicken legs	4 oz bacon, sliced
½ teaspoon salt	½ teaspoon ground black pepper
1 teaspoon sesame oil	

1. Sprinkle the chicken legs with salt and ground black pepper and wrap in the sliced bacon. After this, preheat the air fryer to 385F. Put the chicken legs in the air fryer and sprinkle with sesame oil. Cook the bacon chicken legs for 25 minutes.

Nutrition:
Calories 437, fat 30.8, fiber 0.1, carbs 1.2, protein 36.5

Oregano and Lemon Chicken Drumsticks

Prep time: 15 minutes **Cooking time:** 21 minutes **Servings:** 4

4 chicken drumsticks, with skin, bone-in	1 teaspoon dried cilantro
½ teaspoon dried oregano	½ teaspoon salt
1 teaspoon lemon juice	1 teaspoon butter, softened
2 garlic cloves, diced	

1. In the mixing bowl mix up dried cilantro, oregano, and salt. Then fill the chicken drumstick's skin with a cilantro mixture. Add butter and diced garlic. Sprinkle the chicken with lemon juice. Preheat the air fryer to 375F. Put the chicken drumsticks in the air fryer and cook them for 21 minutes.

Nutrition:
Calories 89, fat 3.6, fiber 0.1, carbs 0.7, protein 12.8

Spicy Thyme Chicken Breast

Prep time: 10 minutes **Cooking time:** 17 minutes **Servings:** 3

1-pound chicken breast, skinless, boneless	1 teaspoon garlic powder
1 teaspoon dried thyme	1 teaspoon salt
½ teaspoon ground black pepper	½ teaspoon cayenne pepper
2 teaspoons sunflower oil	

1. Sprinkle the chicken breast with garlic powder, dried thyme, salt, ground black pepper, and cayenne pepper. Then gently brush the chicken with sunflower oil and put it in the air fryer. Cook the chicken breast for 17 minutes at 385F. Slice the cooked chicken into servings.

Nutrition:
Calories 206, fat 7, fiber 0.4, carbs 1.3, protein 32.3

Thyme and Sage Turkey Breasts

Preparation time: 10 minutes **Cooking time:** 25 minutes
Servings: 4

turkey breasts, skinless, boneless and halved 4 tablespoons butter, melted tablespoons rosemary, chopped 2 tablespoons parsley, chopped A pinch of salt and black pepper 2 cups chicken stock	2 tablespoons thyme, chopped 2 tablespoons sage, chopped celery stalks, chopped

1. Heat up a pan that fits your air fryer with the butter over medium-high heat, add the turkey and brown for 2-3 minutes on each side. Add the herbs, stock, celery, salt and pepper, toss, put the pan in your air fryer, cook at 390 degrees F for 20 minutes. Divide between plates and serve.

Nutrition:
Calories 284, fat 14, fiber 2, carbs 6, protein 20

Onion and Cayenne Chicken Tenders

Prep time: 15 minutes **Cooking time:** 10 minutes **Servings:** 2

8 oz chicken fillet	1 teaspoon minced onion
¼ teaspoon onion powder	¼ teaspoon salt
½ teaspoon cayenne pepper	Cooking spray

1. Cut the chicken fillet on 2 tenders and sprinkle with salt, onion powder, and cayenne pepper. Then preheat the air fryer to 365F. Spray the air fryer basket with cooking spray from inside and place the chicken tenders in it. Top the chicken with minced onion and cook for 10 minutes at 365F.

Nutrition:
Calories 219, fat 8.5, fiber 0.2, carbs 0.7, protein 32.9

Nutmeg Chicken Rolls

Prep time: 15 minutes **Cooking time:** 25 minutes **Servings:** 5

1-pound chicken fillet	2 oz celery stalk, chopped
¼ teaspoon ground paprika	¼ teaspoon ground nutmeg
½ teaspoon garlic powder	1 teaspoon ghee, melted
½ teaspoon salt	1 teaspoon dried oregano
1 teaspoon cream cheese	1 teaspoon avocado oil
1 cup spinach, chopped	

1. Cut the chicken fillet on 5 pieces and beat them gently with the help of the kitchen hammer. In the end, you should get 5 flat chicken fillets. Sprinkle the chicken fillets with ground paprika, nutmeg, garlic powder, salt, and dried oregano. Then put the ghee in the skillet and preheat it for 1-2 minutes over the medium heat. Add spinach and cream cheese. Add chopped celery stalk and cook the greens over the low heat for 10 minutes. Then express the fluid from the spinach. With the help of the spoon put the expressed greens on the chicken fillets. After this, roll the chicken into the rolls and secure with toothpicks or kitchen thread if needed. Preheat the air fryer to 375F. Put the chicken rolls in the air fryer and sprinkle with avocado oil. Cook the rolls for 12 minutes.

Nutrition:
Calories 189, fat 8, fiber 0.6, carbs 1.1, protein 26.7

Turkey and Butter Sauce

Preparation time: 5 minutes **Cooking time:** 24 minutes
Servings: 4

turkey breast, skinless, boneless and cut into 4 pieces A pinch of salt and black pepper tablespoons rosemary, chopped	Juice of 1 lemon 2 tablespoons butter, melted

1. In a bowl, mix the butter with the rosemary, lemon juice, salt and pepper and whisk really well. Brush the turkey pieces with the rosemary butter, put them your air fryer's basket, cook at 380 degrees F for 12 minutes on each side. Divide between plates and serve with a side salad.

Nutrition:
Calories 236, fat 12, fiber 4, carbs 6, protein 13

Spicy Chicken and Tomato Sauce

Prep time: 15 minutes + 8 hours for marinating
Cooking time: 18 minutes
Servings: 8

8 chicken drumsticks	½ teaspoon cayenne pepper
½ teaspoon chili powder	¼ teaspoon jalapeno pepper, minced
½ teaspoon ground cumin	1 teaspoon dried thyme
1 teaspoon keto tomato sauce	1 tablespoon nut oil
½ teaspoon salt	

1. In the mixing bowl mix up tomato sauce and nut oil. Then add minced jalapeno pepper and stir the mixture until homogenous. Rub the chicken drumsticks with chili powder, cayenne pepper, dried cumin, thyme, and sprinkle with salt. Then brush the chicken with tomato sauce mixture and leave to marinate for overnight or for at least 8 hours. Preheat the air fryer to 375F. Put the marinated chicken drumsticks in the air fryer and cook them for 18 minutes.

Nutrition:
Calories 95, fat 4.4, fiber 0.2, carbs 0.3, protein 12.7

Mustard and Garlic Turkey

Preparation time: 5 minutes **Cooking time:** 20 minutes
Servings: 4

1 big turkey breast, skinless, boneless and cubed 4 garlic cloves, minced 1 tablespoon mustard	Salt and black pepper to the taste 1 and ½ tablespoon olive oil

1. In a bowl, mix the chicken with the garlic and the other ingredients and toss. Put the turkey in your air fryer's basket, cook at 360 degrees F for 20 minutes, divide between plates and serve with a side salad.

Nutrition:
Calories 240, fat 12, fiber 4, carbs 6, protein 15

Garlic Chicken Sausages

Prep time: 20 minutes **Cooking time:** 10 minutes **Servings:** 4

1 garlic clove, diced	1 spring onion, chopped
1 cup ground chicken	½ teaspoon salt
½ teaspoon ground black pepper	4 sausage links
1 teaspoon olive oil	

1. In the mixing bowl, mix up a diced garlic clove, onion, ground chicken, salt, and ground black pepper. Then fill the sausage links with the ground chicken mixture. Cut every sausage into halves and secure the endings.
2. Preheat the air fryer to 365. Brush the sausages with olive oil and put it in the air fryer. Cook them for 10 minutes. Then flip the sausages on another side and cook for 5 minutes more. Increase the cooking time to 390F and cook for 8 minutes for faster results

Nutrition:
Calories 130, fat 8.3, fiber 0.1, carbs 1, protein 12.2

Oregano Duck Spread

Prep time: 15 minutes **Cooking time:** 10 minutes **Servings:** 6

½ cup butter, softened	12 oz duck liver
1 tablespoon sesame oil	1 teaspoon salt
1 tablespoon dried oregano	½ onion, peeled

1. Preheat the air fryer to 395F. Chop the onion. Put the duck liver in the air fryer, add onion, and cook the ingredients for 10 minutes. Then transfer the duck pate in the food processor and process it for 2-3 minutes or until the liver is smooth (it depends on the food processor power). Then add onion and blend the mixture for 2 minutes more. Transfer the liver mixture into the bowl. After this, add oregano, salt, sesame oil, and butter. Stir the duck liver with the help of the spoon and transfer it in the bowl.
2. Refrigerate the pate for 10-20 minutes before serving.

Nutrition:
Calories 227, fat 20.4, fiber 0.5, carbs 1.8, protein 9.9

Balsamic Garlic Turkey

Preparation time: 5 minutes **Cooking time:** 30 minutes **Servings:** 4

big turkey breast, skinless, boneless and cut into 4 slices 3 tablespoons balsamic vinegar	garlic cloves, minced
tablespoons butter, melted	A pinch of salt and black pepper 1 tablespoon chives, chopped

1. Heat up a pan that fits the air fryer with the butter over medium-high heat, add the garlic and sauté for 2 minutes. Add the turkey, brown for 2 minutes on each side and take off the heat. Add the rest of the ingredients, toss, put the pan in your air fryer and cook at 380 degrees F for 20 minutes. Divide everything between plates and serve.

Nutrition:
Calories 283, fat 12, fiber 3, carbs 5, protein 15

Ginger Turkey and Cherry Tomatoes

Preparation time: 5 minutes **Cooking time:** 25 minutes **Servings:** 4

pound turkey breast, skinless, boneless and cubed 1 cup heavy cream	A pinch of salt and black pepper 4 ounces cherry tomatoes, halved 1 tablespoon ginger, grated
tablespoons red chili powder 2 teaspoons olive oil	

1. Heat up a pan that fits the air fryer with the oil over medium heat, add the turkey and brown for 2 minutes on each side. Add the rest of the ingredients, toss, put the pan in the machine and cook at 380 degrees F for 20 minutes. Divide everything between plates and serve.

Nutrition.
Calories 267, fat 13, fiber 4, carbs 6, protein 16

Cayenne and Turmeric Chicken Strips

Prep time: 15 minutes **Cooking time:** 14 minutes **Servings:** 6

2-pound chicken breast, skinless, boneless	1 teaspoon salt
1 teaspoon ground turmeric	½ teaspoon cayenne pepper
1 egg, beaten	2 tablespoons coconut flour

1. Cut the chicken breast into the strips and sprinkle with salt, ground turmeric, and cayenne pepper. Then add beaten egg in the chicken strips and stir the mixture. After this, add coconut flour and stir it. Preheat the air fryer to 400F. Put ½ part of all chicken strips in the air fryer basket in one layer and cook them for 7 minutes. Repeat the same steps with the remaining chicken strips.

Nutrition:
Calories 195, fat 4.9, fiber 1, carbs 1.7, protein 33.4

Paprika Turkey and Shallot Sauce

Preparation time: 5 minutes **Cooking time:** 30 minutes **Servings:** 4

1 big turkey breast, skinless, boneless and cubed 1 tablespoon olive oil	¼ teaspoon sweet paprika
Salt and black pepper to the taste 1 cup chicken stock	3 tablespoons butter, melted 4 shallots, chopped

1. Heat up a pan that fits the air fryer with the olive oil and the butter over medium high heat, add the turkey cubes, and brown for 3 minutes on each side. Add the shallots, stir and sauté for 5 minutes more. Add the paprika, stock, salt and pepper, toss, put the pan in the air fryer and cook at 370 degrees F for 20 minutes. Divide into bowls and serve.

Nutrition:
Calories 236, fat 12, fiber 4, carbs 6, protein 15

Turkey and Lime Gravy

Preparation time: 5 minutes **Cooking time:** 25 minutes
Servings: 4

1 big turkey breast, skinless, boneless, cubed and browned Juice of 1 lime	Zest of 1 lime, grated 1 cup chicken stock
3 tablespoons parsley, chopped 4 tablespoons butter, melted	2 tablespoons thyme, chopped A pinch of salt and black pepper

1. Heat up a pan that fits the air fryer with the butter over medium heat, add all the ingredients except the turkey, whisk, bring to a simmer and cook for 5 minutes. Add the turkey cubes, put the pan in the air fryer and cook at 380 degrees F for 20 minutes. Divide the meat between plates, drizzle the gravy all over and serve.

Nutrition:
Calories 284, fat 13, fiber 3, carbs 5, protein 15

Turkey and Leeks

Preparation time: 5 minutes **Cooking time:** 30 minutes
Servings: 4

1 turkey breast, skinless, boneless and cut into strips A pinch of salt and black pepper	1 tablespoon olive oil 1 cup veggie stock
4 leeks, sliced	2 tablespoon chives, chopped

1. Heat up a pan that fits your air fryer with the oil over medium heat, add the meat and brown for 2 minutes on each side. Add the remaining ingredients, toss, put the pan in the machine and cook at 380 degrees F for 25 minutes. Divide everything between plates and serve with a side salad.

Nutrition:
Calories 257, fat 12, fiber 4, carbs 5, protein 14

Cumin Turkey and Celery

Preparation time: 5 minutes **Cooking time:** 30 minutes
Servings: 4

1 big turkey breast, skinless, boneless and sliced 4 garlic cloves, minced	tablespoons olive oil
celery stalks, roughly chopped 1 teaspoon turmeric powder 1 tablespoon smoked paprika 1 tablespoon garlic powder	1 teaspoon cumin, ground

1. In a pan that fits the air fryer, combine the turkey and the other ingredients, toss, put the pan in the machine and cook at 380 degrees F for 30 minutes. Divide everything between plates and serve.

Nutrition:
Calories 285, fat 12, fiber 3, carbs 6, protein 16

Thyme Chicken Meatballs

Prep time: 20 minutes **Cooking time:** 11 minutes **Servings:** 6

14 oz ground chicken	2 oz scallions, chopped
1 egg yolk	½ teaspoon dried thyme
½ teaspoon salt	1 tablespoon almond flour
1 teaspoon sesame oil	

1. Whisk the egg yolk and mix it up with ground chicken. Add dried thyme, salt, and almond flour. Stir the mixture until smooth and add scallions.
2. Mix up the mixture and make the medium-size meatballs. Use the scooper or make them with the help of the fingertips. Preheat the air fryer to 375F. Put the chicken meatballs in the air fryer and sprinkle with sesame oil.
3. Cook them for 7 minutes. Then flip the chicken meatballs on another side and cook for 4 minutes more. The time of cooking depends on the size of the meatballs.

Nutrition:
Calories 171, fat 8.8, fiber 0.8, carbs 1.8, protein 20.8

Almond Turkey and Shallots

Preparation time: 5 minutes **Cooking time:** 25 minutes
Servings: 2

1 big turkey breast, skinless, boneless and halved 1/3 cup almonds, chopped	Salt and black pepper to the taste
1 tablespoon sweet paprika	2 tablespoons olive oil
2 shallots, chopped	

1. In a pan that fits the air fryer, combine the turkey with all the other ingredients, toss, put the pan in the machine and cook at 370 degrees F for 25 minutes. Divide everything between plates and serve.

Nutrition:
Calories 274, fat 12, fiber 3, carbs 5, protein 14

Lemon Chicken Fillets

Prep time: 15 minutes **Cooking time:** 14 minutes **Servings:** 2

1 lemon pepper	¼ cup Cheddar cheese, shredded
8 oz chicken fillets	½ teaspoon dried cilantro
1 teaspoon coconut oil, melted	¼ teaspoon smoked paprika

1. Cut the lemon pepper into halves and remove the seeds. Then cut the chicken fillet into 2 fillets. Make the horizontal cuts in every chicken fillet. Then sprinkle the chicken fillets with smoked paprika and dried cilantro. After this, fill them with lemon pepper halves and Cheddar cheese. Preheat the air fryer to 385F. Put the chicken fillets in the air fryer and sprinkle with melted coconut oil. Cook the chicken for 14 minutes.
2. Carefully transfer the chicken fillets in the serving plates.

Nutrition:
Calories 293, fat 15.4, fiber 0.1, carbs 0.4, protein 36.4

Buttery Turkey and Mushroom Sauce

Prep time: 5 minutes **Cooking time:** 25 minutes **Servings:** 4

6 cups leftover turkey meat, skinless, boneless and shredded A pinch of salt and black pepper 3 tablespoons butter, melted 1 pound mushrooms, sliced 2 spring onions, chopped	1 tablespoon parsley, chopped 1 cup chicken stock

1. Heat up a pan that fits the air fryer with the butter over medium-high heat, add the mushrooms and sauté for 5 minutes. Add the rest of the ingredients, toss, put the pan in the machine and cook at 370 degrees F for 20 minutes. Divide everything between plates and serve.

Nutrition:
Calories 285, fat 11, fiber 3, carbs 5, protein 14

Ricotta and Thyme Chicken

Prep time: 15 minutes **Cooking time:** 18 minutes **Servings:** 3

3 chicken thighs, boneless 1 teaspoon ricotta cheese Cooking spray	2 teaspoons adobo sauce 1 teaspoon dried thyme

1. In the mixing bowl mix up adobo sauce and ricotta cheese, Add dried thyme and churn the mixture. Then brush the chicken thighs with adobo sauce mixture and leave for 10 minutes to marinate. Preheat the air fryer to 385F. Spray the air fryer basket with cooking spray and put the chicken thighs inside. Cook them for 18 minutes.

Nutrition:
Calories 138, fat 7.2, fiber 0.1, carbs 1.4, protein 19.2

Coconut Turkey and Spinach Mix

Prep time: 5 minutes **Cooking time:** 15 minutes **Servings:** 4

1 pound turkey meat, ground and browned 1 tablespoon garlic, minced tablespoons coconut aminos 4 cups spinach leaves	tablespoon ginger, grated A pinch of salt and black pepper

1. In a pan that fits your air fryer, combine all the ingredients and toss. Put the pan in the air fryer and cook at 380 degrees F for 15 minutes Divide everything into bowls and serve.

Nutrition:
Calories 240, fat 12, fiber 3, carbs 5, protein 13

Garlic Turkey and Lemon Asparagus

Prep time: 5 minutes **Cooking time:** 25 minutes **Servings:** 4

1 pound turkey breast tenderloins, cut into strips	1 pound asparagus, trimmed and cut into medium pieces A pinch of salt and black pepper
1 tablespoon lemon juice	teaspoon coconut aminos 2 tablespoons olive oil
garlic cloves, minced	¼ cup chicken stock

1. Heat up a pan that fits the air fryer with the oil over medium-high heat, add the meat and brown for 2 minutes on each side. Add the rest of the ingredients, toss, put the pan in the machine and cook at 380 degrees F for 20 minutes. Divide everything between plates and serve

Nutrition:
Calories 264, fat 14, fiber 4, carbs 6, protein 16

Coriander Chicken Breast

Prep time: 25 minutes **Cooking time:** 20 minutes **Servings:** 5

15 oz chicken breast, skinless, boneless	1 teaspoon lemongrass
1 teaspoon ground black pepper	1 teaspoon salt
1 teaspoon chili powder	1 teaspoon smoked paprika
2 teaspoons apple cider vinegar	1 teaspoon lemon juice
1 tablespoon sunflower oil	1 teaspoon dried basil
½ teaspoon ground coriander	2 tablespoons water
1 tablespoon heavy cream	

1. Make the marinade: In the bowl mix up lemongrass, ground black pepper, salt, chili powder, smoked paprika, apple cider vinegar, lemon juice, sunflower oil, dried basil, ground coriander, water, and heavy cream. Then chop the chicken breast roughly and put it in the marinade. Stir it well and leave for 20 minutes in the fridge. Then preheat the air fryer to 375F. Put the marinated chicken breast pieces in the air fryer and cook them for 20 minutes. Shake the chicken pieces after 10 minutes of cooking to avoid burning. The cooked chicken breast pieces should have a light brown color.

Nutrition:
Calories 137, fat 6.2, fiber 0.5, carbs 1, protein 18.3z

Chicken Pockets

Prep time: 15 minutes **Cooking time:** 4 minutes **Servings:** 4

2 low carb tortillas	2 oz Cheddar cheese, grated
1 tomato, chopped	1 teaspoon fresh cilantro, chopped
½ teaspoon dried basil	2 teaspoons butter
6 oz chicken fillet, boiled	1 teaspoon sunflower oil
½ teaspoon salt	

1. Cut the tortillas into halves. Shred the chicken fillet with the help of the fork and put it in the bowl. Add chopped tomato, grated cheese, basil, cilantro, and alt. Then grease the tortilla halves with butter from one side. Put the shredded chicken mixture on half of every tortilla piece and fold them into the pockets. Preheat the air fryer to 400F. Brush every tortilla pocket with sunflower oil and put it in the air fryer. Cook the meal for 4 minutes.

Nutrition:
Calories 208, fat 12, fiber 3.7, carbs 6.8, protein 17.5

Ground Turkey Mix

Prep time: 5 minutes **Cooking time:** 25 minutes **Servings:** 4

pound turkey meat, ground	A pinch of salt and black pepper
2 tablespoons olive oil	teaspoons parsley flakes
1 pound green beans, trimmed and halved	2 teaspoons garlic powder

1. Heat up a pan that fits the air fryer with the oil over medium-high heat, add the meat and brown it for 5 minutes. Add the remaining ingredients, toss, put the pan in the machine and cook at 370 degrees F for 20 minutes. Divide between plates and serve.

Nutrition:
Calories 274, fat 12, fiber 3, carbs 6, protein 15

Basil Mascarpone Chicken Fillets

Prep time: 15 minutes **Cooking time:** 12 minutes **Servings:** 4

1 tablespoon fresh basil, chopped	4 oz Mozzarella, sliced
12 oz chicken fillet	1 tablespoon nut oil
1 teaspoon chili flakes	1 teaspoon mascarpone

1. Brush the air fryer pan with nut oil. Then cut the chicken fillet on 4 servings and beat them gently with a kitchen hammer. After this, sprinkle the chicken fillets with chili flakes and put in the air fryer pan in one layer. Top the fillets with fresh basil and sprinkle with mascarpone. After this, top the chicken fillets with sliced Mozzarella. Preheat the air fryer to 375F. Put the pan with Caprese chicken fillets in the air fryer and cook them for 12 minutes.

Nutrition:
Calories 274, fat 14.9, fiber 0, carbs 1.1, protein 32.8

Turkey with Cabbage

Prep time: 5 minutes **Cooking time:** 25 minutes **Servings:** 4

1 pound turkey meat, ground	A pinch of salt and black pepper
2 tablespoons butter, melted	1 ounce chicken stock
1 small red cabbage head, shredded	1 tablespoon sweet paprika, chopped
1 tablespoon parsley, chopped	

1. Heat up a pan that fits the air fryer with the butter, add the meat and brown for 5 minutes. Add all the other ingredients, toss, put the pan in the air fryer and cook at 380 degrees F for 20 minutes. Divide everything between plates and serve.

Nutrition:
Calories 284, fat 13, fiber 4, carbs 5, protein 14

Fried Chicken Halves

Prep time: 20 minutes **Cooking time:** 75 minutes **Servings:** 4

16 oz whole chicken	1 tablespoon dried thyme
1 teaspoon ground cumin	1 teaspoon salt
1 tablespoon avocado oil	

1. Cut the chicken into halves and sprinkle it with dried thyme, cumin, and salt. Then brush the chicken halves with avocado oil. Preheat the air fryer to 365F. Put the chicken halves in the air fryer and cook them for 60 minutes. Then flip the chicken halves on another side and cook them for 15 minutes more.

Nutrition:
Calories 224, fat 9, fiber 0.5, carbs 0.9, protein 33

Cheddar Garlic Turkey

Prep time: 5 minutes **Cooking time:** 20 minutes **Servings:** 4

1 big turkey breast, skinless, boneless and cubed Salt and black pepper to the taste	¼ cup cheddar cheese, grated
¼ teaspoon garlic powder	
1 tablespoon olive oil	

1. Rub the turkey cubes with the oil, season with salt, pepper and garlic powder and dredge in cheddar cheese. Put the turkey bits in your air fryer's basket and cook at 380 degrees F for 20 minutes. Divide between plates and serve with a side salad.

Nutrition:
Calories 240, fat 11, fiber 2, carbs 5, protein 12

Chicken Bites and Chili Sauce

Prep time: 15 minutes **Cooking time:** 10 minutes **Servings:** 5

15 oz chicken fillet	1 tablespoon peanut oil
1 teaspoon chili sauce	1 teaspoon lemon zest, grated
½ teaspoon onion powder	1 egg, beaten
½ teaspoon salt	

1. Cut the chicken fillet on 5 pieces and sprinkle with chili sauce, lemon zest, onion powder, and salt. Then dip every chicken piece in the beaten egg.
2. Preheat the air fryer to 400F. Sprinkle the air fryer basket with peanut oil. Put the chicken bites in the air fryer in one layer and cook them for 5 minutes from each side.

Nutrition:
Calories 199, fat 9.9, fiber 0, carbs 0.4, protein 25.7

Fennel Duck Legs

Prep time: 5 minutes **Cooking time:** 30 minutes **Servings:** 4

4 duck legs	A pinch of salt and black pepper
3 teaspoons fennel seeds, crushed	4 teaspoons thyme, dried
2 tablespoons olive oil	

1. In a bowl, mix the duck legs with all the other ingredients and toss well. Put the duck legs in your air fryer's basket and cook at 380 degrees F for 15 minutes on each side. Divide between plates and serve

Nutrition:
Calories 274, fat 11, fiber 4, carbs 6, protein 14

Turkey and Coconut Broccoli

Prep time: 5 minutes **Cooking time:** 25 minutes **Servings:** 4

1 pound turkey meat, ground	teaspoon ginger, grated
2 garlic cloves, minced	
teaspoons coconut aminos	2 broccoli heads, florets
3 tablespoons olive oil	separated and then halved A pinch of salt and black pepper
1 teaspoon chili paste	

1. Heat up a pan that fits the air fryer with the oil over medium heat, add the meat and brown for 5 minutes. Add the rest of the ingredients, toss, put the pan in the fryer and cook at 380 degrees F for 20 minutes. Divide everything between plates and serve.

Nutrition:
Calories 274, fat 11, fiber 3, carbs 6, protein 12

Dill Chicken Fritters

Prep time: 20 minutes **Cooking time:** 16 minutes **Servings:** 8

1-pound chicken breast, skinless, boneless	3 oz coconut flakes
1 tablespoon ricotta cheese	1 teaspoon mascarpone
1 teaspoon dried dill	½ teaspoon salt
1 egg yolk	1 teaspoon avocado oil

1. Cut the chicken breast into the tiny pieces and put them in the bowl. Add coconut flakes, ricotta cheese, mascarpone, dried dill, salt, and egg yolk. Then make the chicken fritters with the help of the fingertips. Preheat the air fryer to 360F. Line the air fryer basket with baking paper and put the chicken cakes in the air fryer. Sprinkle the chicken fritters with avocado oil and cook for 8 minutes. Then flip the chicken fritters on another side and cook them for 8 minutes more.

Nutrition:
Calories 114, fat 5.9, fiber 1, carbs 1.9, protein 13.1

Turkey and Chili Kale

Preparation time: 5 minutes **Cooking time:** 25 minutes
Servings: 4

1 pound turkey meat, ground	A pinch of salt and black pepper 2 tablespoons olive oil
1 teaspoon coconut aminos 2 spring onions, minced	4 cups kale, chopped
1 tablespoon garlic, chopped 1 red chili pepper, chopped	½ cup chicken stock

1. Heat up a pan that fits your air fryer with the oil over medium heat, add the meat, salt, pepper, spring onions and the garlic, stir and sauté for 5 minutes. Add the rest of the ingredients, toss, put the pan in the fryer and cook at 380 degrees F for 20 minutes. Divide between plates and serve

Nutrition:
Calories 261, fat 12, fiber 2, carbs 5, protein 13

Chili Pepper Duck Bites

Prep time: 15 minutes **Cooking time:** 15 minutes **Servings:** 4

8 oz duck breast, skinless, boneless	1 teaspoon Erythritol
½ teaspoon salt	1 teaspoon chili pepper
1 tablespoon butter, softened	½ teaspoon minced garlic
½ teaspoon dried dill	

1. Cut the duck breast into small pieces (bites). Then sprinkle them with salt, chili pepper, Erythritol, dried dill, and minced garlic. Leave the duck pieces for 10-15 minutes to marinate. Meanwhile, preheat the air fryer to 365F. Sprinkle the duck bites with butter and put in the air fryer. Cook the duck bites for 10 minutes. Then shake them well and cook for 5 minutes more at 400F.

Nutrition:
Calories 100, fat 5.2, fiber 0.1, carbs 0.3, protein 12.6

Cumin Turkey and Tomato Mix

Preparation time: 5 minutes **Cooking time:** 25 minutes
Servings: 4

1 pound turkey meat, cubed and browned A pinch of salt and black pepper	1 green bell pepper, chopped 3 garlic cloves, chopped
1 and ½ teaspoons cumin, ground 12 ounces veggies stock	1 cup tomatoes, chopped

1. In a pan that fits your air fryer, mix the turkey with the rest of the ingredients, toss, put the pan in the machine and cook at 380 degrees F for 25 minutes. Divide into bowls and serve.

Nutrition:
Calories 274, fat 12, fiber 4, carbs 6, protein 15

Creamy Duck Strips

Prep time: 15 minutes **Cooking time:** 17 minutes **Servings:** 5

12 oz duck breast, skinless, boneless	½ cup coconut flour
1/3 cup heavy cream	1 teaspoon salt
1 teaspoon white pepper	

1. Cut the duck breast on the small strips (fingers) and sprinkle with salt and white pepper. Then dip the duck fingers in the heavy cream and coat in the coconut flour. Preheat the air fryer to 375F. Put the duck fingers in the air fryer basket in one layer and cook them for 10 minutes. Then flip the duck fingers on another side and cook them for 7 minutes more

Nutrition:
Calories 172, fat 7.7, fiber 4.9, carbs 7.7, protein 17.6

Oregano Turkey and Spinach Bowls

Preparation time: 5 minutes **Cooking time:** 25 minutes
Servings: 4

- 1 pound turkey meat, ground Salt and black pepper to the taste 2 tablespoons olive oil
- 10 ounces keto tomato sauce
- tablespoon oregano, chopped 2 cups spinach

1. Heat up a pan that fits your air fryer with the oil over medium heat, add the turkey, oregano, salt and pepper, stir and brown for 5 minutes. Add the tomato sauce, toss, put the pan in the machine and cook at 370 degrees F for 15 minutes. Add spinach, toss, cook for 5 minutes more, divide everything into bowls and serve.

Nutrition:
Calories 263, fat 12, fiber 3, carbs 6, protein 16

Chili Spring Onions and Turkey Pie

Prep time: 15 minutes **Cooking time:** 30 minutes **Servings:** 6

10 oz ground turkey	3 tablespoons coconut oil, softened
½ teaspoon baking powder	1 egg, beaten
1 cup coconut flour	1 teaspoon xanthan gum
¼ teaspoon salt	1 teaspoon chili flakes
2 spring onions, chopped	1 teaspoon smoked paprika
1 teaspoon dried parsley	1 teaspoon sesame oil

1. Make the pie dough: in the mixing bowl mix up coconut oil, baking powder, egg, coconut flour, and xanthan gum. Add salt and knead the non-sticky soft dough. Line the air fryer baking pan with parchment. Cut the dough into halves and roll up with the help of the rolling pin. Put the first put of dough in the baking pan and flatten it gently with the help of the fingertips. Then in the mixing bowl, mix up ground turkey, chili flakes, diced onion, smoked paprika, and dried parsley. Put the ground turkey mixture over the flattened dough. Cover the ground turkey with remaining dough. Secure the edges of the pie and brush it with the sesame oil. Preheat the air fryer to 380F. Put the pie in the air fryer and cook it for 30 minutes. Cool the cooked pie to the room temperature and then remove it from the baking pan. Cut the pie into the servings.

Nutrition:
Calories 184, fat 13.9, fiber 1.6, carbs 2.8, protein 14.3

Duck and Walnut Rice

Preparation time: 5 minutes **Cooking time:** 20 minutes
Servings: 4

ounces mushrooms, sliced	2 cups cauliflower florets, riced
2 tablespoons olive oil	
½ cup walnuts, toasted and chopped 2 cups chicken stock	A pinch of salt and black pepper
½ cup parsley, chopped	2 pounds duck breasts, boneless and skin scored

1. Heat up a pan that fits the air fryer with the oil over medium-high heat, add the duck breasts skin side down and brown for 4 minutes. Add the mushrooms, cauliflower, salt and pepper, and cook for 1 minute more. Add the stock, introduce the pan in the air fryer and cook at 380 degrees F for 15 minutes. Divide the mix between plates, sprinkle the parsley and walnuts on top and serve.

Nutrition:
Calories 268, fat 12, fiber 4, carbs 6, protein 17

Duck Legs and Scallions Mix

Prep time: 10 minutes **Cooking time:** 16 minutes **Servings:** 2

2 duck legs	1 teaspoon olive oil
½ teaspoon ground cumin	1 teaspoon salt
1 tablespoon scallions, chopped	

1. In the shallow bowl mix up ground cumin and salt. Then rub the duck legs with the spice mixture. After this, mix up the scallions and olive oil.
2. Sprinkle the duck legs with the scallions mix. Preheat the air fryer to 385F. Put the duck legs in the air fryer and cook them for 8 minutes. Then flip the duck legs on another side and cook for 8 minutes.

Nutrition:
Calories 157, fat 6.9, fiber 0.2, carbs 0.7, protein 22

Duck and Blackberry Mix

Preparation time: 5 minutes **Cooking time:** 25 minutes
Servings: 4

4 duck breasts, boneless and skin scored A pinch of salt and black pepper	2 tablespoons olive oil
1 and ½ cups chicken stock 2 spring onions, chopped	4 garlic cloves, minced
1 and ½ cups blackberries, pureed 2 tablespoons butter, melted	

1. Heat up a pan that fits the air fryer with the oil and the butter over medium-high heat, add the duck breasts skin side down and sear for 5 minutes. Add the remaining ingredients, toss, put the pan in the air fryer and cook at 370 degrees F for 20 minutes. Divide the duck and sauce between plates and serve.

Nutrition:
Calories 265, fat 14, fiber 3, carbs 5, protein 14

Balsamic Ginger Duck

Prep time: 10 minutes **Cooking time:** 30 minutes **Servings:** 4

12 oz duck legs	1 tablespoon balsamic vinegar
1 teaspoon Splenda	½ teaspoon minced ginger
½ teaspoon harissa	1 tablespoon avocado oil

1. Rub the duck legs with minced ginger, harissa, Splenda, and avocado oil. Then sprinkle the duck legs with ½ tablespoon of balsamic vinegar.
2. Preheat the air fryer to 385F. Place the duck legs in the air fryer and cook them for 30 minutes. Sprinkle the cooked duck legs with the balsamic vinegar and place it in the serving plates.

Nutrition:
Calories 165, fat 5.6, fiber 0.2, carbs 1.6, protein 24.9

Five Spice Duck Legs

Prep time: 5 minutes **Cooking time:** 25 minutes **Servings:** 4

4 duck legs	2 garlic cloves, minced
1 teaspoon five spice	A pinch of salt and black pepper
2 tablespoons olive oil	1 teaspoon hot chili powder

1. In a bowl, mix the duck legs with all the other ingredients and rub them well. Put the duck legs in your air fryer's basket and cook at 380 degrees F for 25 minutes, flipping them halfway. Divide between plates and serve.

Nutrition:
Calories 287, fat 12, fiber 4, carbs 6, protein 17

Lime and Thyme Duck

Prep time: 15 minutes **Cooking time:** 17 minutes **Servings:** 4

1-pound duck breast, skinless, boneless	2 oz preserved lime, sliced
1 teaspoon apple cider vinegar	1 tablespoon olive oil
½ teaspoon salt	½ teaspoon dried thyme

1. Cut the duck breast on 4 pieces and sprinkle with salt, dried thyme, apple cider vinegar, and oil. Mix up the duck pieces well and put on the foil.
2. Then pot the reserved lime over the duck and wrap the foil. Preheat the air fryer to 375F and put the wrapped duck breast in the air fryer basket.
3. Cook it for 17 minutes.

Nutrition:
Calories 184, fat 8.4, fiber 0.1, carbs 1.1, protein 25

Chicken Wonton Rolls

Prep time: 15 minutes **Cooking time:** 10 minutes **Servings:** 4

4 wonton wraps	8 oz chicken fillet
1 garlic clove, diced	1 teaspoon keto tomato sauce
1 teaspoon butter, melted	¼ teaspoon chili flakes
½ teaspoon ground turmeric	

1. Slice the chicken on the small strips and sprinkle with chili flakes, ground turmeric, and butter. Preheat the air fryer to 365F. Put the sliced chicken in the air fryer and cook it for 10 minutes. Then transfer the chicken in the bowl. Add tomato sauce and diced garlic. Mix up the chicken and place it on the wonton wraps. Roll them.

Nutrition:
Calories 132, fat 5.2, fiber 0.2, carbs 3.1, protein 17.1

Cinnamon Balsamic Duck

Preparation time: 5 minutes **Cooking time:** 20 minutes
Servings: 2

duck breasts, boneless and skin scored	A pinch of salt and black pepper
¼ teaspoon cinnamon powder	4 tablespoons stevia
tablespoons balsamic vinegar	

1. In a bowl, mix the duck breasts with the rest of the ingredients and rub well. Put the duck breasts in your air fryer's basket and cook at 380 degrees F for 10 minutes on each side. Divide everything between plates and serve.

Nutrition:
Calories 294, fat 12, fiber 4, carbs 6, protein 15

Chinese Chili Chicken

Prep time: 15 minutes **Cooking time:** 20 minutes **Servings:** 6

6 chicken wings	1 tablespoon coconut aminos
1 teaspoon ground ginger	1 teaspoon salt
1 teaspoon minced garlic	2 tablespoons apple cider vinegar
1 tablespoon olive oil	1 chili pepper, chopped

1. Put the chicken wings in the bowl and sprinkle with coconut aminos and ground ginger. Add salt, minced garlic, apple cider vinegar, olive oil, and chopped chili. Mix up the chicken wings and leave them for 15 minutes to marinate. Meanwhile, preheat the air fryer to 380F. Place the marinated chicken wings in the air fryer and cook them for 20 minutes. Flip the chicken wings from time to time to avoid the burning.

Nutrition:
Calories 303, fat 13.2, fiber 0.1, carbs 1, protein 42.3

Duck with Olives

Preparation time: 5 minutes **Cooking time:** 25 minutes
Servings: 2

2 duck legs	1 teaspoon cinnamon powder 1 tablespoon olive oil
garlic clove, minced	A pinch of salt and black pepper
ounces black olives, pitted and sliced Juice of ½ lime	1 tablespoon parsley, chopped

1. In a bowl, mix the duck legs with cinnamon, oil, garlic, salt and pepper, and rub well. Heat up a pan that fits the air fryer over medium-high heat, add duck legs and brown for 2-3 minutes on each side. Add the remaining ingredients to the pan, put the pan in the air fryer and cook at 400 degrees F for 10 minutes on each side. Divide between plates and serve.

Nutrition:
Calories 276, fat 12, fiber 4, carbs 6, protein 14

Cardamom and Almond Duck

Preparation time: 5 minutes **Cooking time:** 30 minutes
Servings: 4

duck legs	Juice of ½ lemon
Zest of ½ lemon, grated	tablespoon cardamom, crushed
¼ teaspoon allspice	tablespoons almonds, toasted and chopped
2 tablespoons olive oil	

1. In a bowl, mix the duck legs with the remaining ingredients except the almonds and toss. Put the duck legs in your air fryer's basket and cook at 380 degrees F for 15 minutes on each side. Divide the duck legs between plates, sprinkle the almonds on top and serve with a side salad.

Nutrition:
Calories 284, fat 12, fiber 4, carbs 6, protein 18

Duck and Strawberry Sauce

Prep time: 15 minutes **Cooking time:** 15 minutes **Servings:** 4

1-pound duck breast, skinless, boneless	1 tablespoon Erythritol
2 tablespoons water	1 oz strawberry
½ teaspoon salt	½ teaspoon ground paprika
¼ teaspoon ground cinnamon	1 teaspoon chili powder
1 teaspoon sesame oil	

1. Rub the duck breast with salt and chili powder. Then brush it with sesame oil. Preheat the air fryer to 380F. Put the duck breast in the air fryer and cook it for 12 minutes. Meanwhile, make the sweet sauce: in the small bowl mix up Erythritol, water, ground paprika, and ground cinnamon.
2. Mash the strawberry and add it in the Erythritol mixture. Stir it well and microwave it for 10 seconds. Then stir the sauce and microwave it for 10 seconds more. Repeat the same steps 2 times more. Then rush the duck breast with ½ part of sweet sauce and cook for 3 minutes more. Slice the cooked duck breast and sprinkle it with remaining sauce.

Nutrition:
Calories 162, fat 5.8, fiber 0.5, carbs 1.2, protein 25.1

Spring Chicken Mix

Preparation time: 10 minutes **Cooking time:** 20 minutes
Servings: 4

pounds duck breast, skinless, boneless and cubed	½ cup spring onions, chopped Salt and black pepper to the taste
1 tablespoon olive oil	2 garlic cloves, minced
¼ teaspoon red pepper flakes, crushed	1 tablespoons sesame seeds, toasted

1. Heat up a pan that fits your air fryer with the oil over medium heat, add the meat, toss and brown for 5 minutes. Add the rest of the ingredients except the sesame seeds, toss, introduce in the fryer and cook at 380 degrees F for 15 minutes. Add sesame seeds, toss, divide between plates and serve.

Nutrition:
Calories 264, fat 12, fiber 4, carbs 6, protein 17

Chicken Satay

Prep time: 10 minutes **Cooking time:** 14 minutes **Servings:** 4

4 chicken wings	1 teaspoon olive oil
1 teaspoon keto tomato sauce	1 teaspoon dried cilantro
½ teaspoon salt	

1. String the chicken wings on the wooden skewers. Then in the shallow bowl mix up olive oil, tomato sauce, dried cilantro, and salt. Spread the chicken skewers with the tomato mixture. Preheat the air fryer to 390F. Arrange the chicken satay in the air fryer and cook the meal for 10 minutes. Then flip the chicken satay on another side and cook it for 4 minutes more.

Nutrition:
Calories 170, fat 11.9, fiber 0.2, carbs 5.7, protein 9.8

Simple Paprika Duck

Prep time: 5 minutes **Cooking time:** 25 minutes **Servings:** 4

1 pound duck breasts, skinless, boneless and cubed Salt and black pepper to the taste	1 tablespoon olive oil
½ teaspoon sweet paprika	¼ cup chicken stock
1 teaspoon thyme, chopped	

1. Heat up a pan that fits your air fryer with the oil over medium heat, add the duck pieces, and brown them for 5 minutes. Add the rest of the ingredients, toss, put the pan in the machine and cook at 380 degrees F for 20 minutes. Divide between plates and serve.

Nutrition:
Calories 264, fat 14, fiber 4, carbs 6, protein 18

Celery Chicken Mix

Prep time: 15 minutes **Cooking time:** 9 minutes **Servings:** 4

1 teaspoon fennel seeds	½ teaspoon ground celery
½ teaspoon salt	1 tablespoon olive oil
12 oz chicken fillet	

1. Cut the chicken fillets on 4 chicken chops. In the shallow bowl mix up fennel seeds and olive oil. Rub the chicken chops with salt and ground celery. Preheat the air fryer to 365F. Brush the chicken chops with the fennel oil and place it in the air fryer basket. Cook them for 9 minutes.

Nutrition:
Calories 193, fat 9.9, fiber 0.2, carbs 0.3, protein 24.7

Vanilla and Peppercorn Duck

Preparation time: 5 minutes **Cooking time:** 30 minutes **Servings:** 4

4 duck legs, skin on Juice of ½ lemon	1 teaspoon cinnamon powder
1 teaspoon vanilla extract	10 peppercorns, crushed
1 tablespoon balsamic vinegar	1 tablespoon olive oil
A pinch of salt and black pepper	

1. Heat up a pan with the oil over medium-high heat, add the duck legs and sear them for 3 minutes on each side. Transfer to a pan that fits the air fryer, add the remaining ingredients, toss, put the pan in the air fryer and cook at 380 degrees F for 22 minutes. Divide duck legs and cooking juices between plates and serve.

Nutrition:
Calories 271, fat 13, fiber 4, carbs 6, protein 15

Nutmeg Duck Meatballs

Prep time: 20 minutes **Cooking time:** 10 minutes **Servings:** 6

1-pound ground duck	½ teaspoon ground cloves
½ teaspoon ground nutmeg	½ teaspoon salt
1 teaspoon dried cilantro	2 tablespoons almond flour
Cooking spray	

1. In the mixing bowl mix up ground duck, ground cloves, ground nutmeg, salt, dried cilantro, and almond flour. With the help of the fingertips make the duck meatballs and sprinkle them with cooking spray. Preheat the air fryer to 385F. Put the duck meatballs in the air fryer basket in one layer and cook them for 5 minutes. Then flip the meatballs on another side and cook them for 5 minutes more.

Nutrition:
Calories 244, fat 16.3, fiber 1.7, carbs 3.4, protein 22.8

Duck with Mushrooms and Coriander

Preparation time: 5 minutes **Cooking time:** 25 minutes **Servings:** 6

6 duck breasts, boneless, skin on and scored 1 tablespoon balsamic vinegar	1 tablespoon coconut aminos
A pinch of salt and black pepper 2 courgettes, sliced	¼ pound oyster mushrooms, sliced
½ bunch coriander, chopped 2 tablespoons olive oil	garlic cloves, minced

1. Heat up a pan that fits your air fryer with the oil over medium heat, add the duck breasts skin side down and sear for 5 minutes. Add the rest of the ingredients, cook for 2 minutes more, transfer the pan to the air fryer and cook at 380 degrees F for 20 minutes. Divide everything between plates and serve.

Nutrition:
Calories 2764, fat 12, fiber 4, carbs 6, protein 14

Hot Chicken Skin

Prep time: 10 minutes **Cooking time:** 30 minutes **Servings:** 4

½ teaspoon chili paste	8 oz chicken skin
1 teaspoon sesame oil	½ teaspoon chili powder
½ teaspoon salt	

1. In the shallow bowl mix up chili paste, sesame oil, chili powder, and salt. Then brush the chicken skin with chili mixture well and leave for 10 minutes to marinate. Meanwhile, preheat the air fryer to 365F. Put the marinated chicken skin in the air fryer and cook it for 20 minutes. When the time is finished, flip the chicken skin on another side and cook it for 10 minutes more or until the chicken skin is crunchy.

Nutrition:
Calories 298, fat 25.4, fiber 0.1, carbs 5.7, protein 10.9

Chicken Wings and Vinegar Sauce

Prep time: 10 minutes **Cooking time:** 12 minutes **Servings:** 4

4 chicken wings	1 teaspoon Erythritol
1 teaspoon water	1 teaspoon apple cider vinegar
1 teaspoon salt	¼ teaspoon ground paprika
½ teaspoon dried oregano	Cooking spray

1. Sprinkle the chicken wings with salt and dried oregano. Then preheat the air fryer to 400F. Place the chicken wings in the air fryer basket and cook them for 8 minutes. Flip the chicken wings on another side after 4 minutes of cooking. Meanwhile, mix up Erythritol, water, apple cider vinegar, and ground paprika in the saucepan and bring the liquid to boil. Stir the liquid well and cook it until Erythritol is dissolved. After this, generously brush the chicken wings with sweet Erythritol liquid and cook them in the air fryer at 400F for 4 minutes more.

Nutrition:
Calories 100, fat 6.7, fiber 0.2, carbs 0.3, protein 9.2
Meat Recipes

Duck with Peppers and Pine Nuts Sauce

Preparation time: 5 minutes **Cooking time:** 25 minutes **Servings:** 4

duck breast fillets, skin-on	1 tablespoon balsamic vinegar 4 tablespoons olive oil
1 red bell pepper, roasted, peeled and chopped 1/3 cup basil, chopped	1 tablespoon pine nuts 1 teaspoon tarragon
1 garlic clove, minced	1 tablespoon lemon juice

1. Heat up a pan that fist your air fryer with half of the oil over medium heat, add the duck fillets skin side up and cook for 2-3 minutes. Add the vinegar, toss and cook for 2 minutes more. In a blender, combine the rest of the oil with the remaining ingredients and pulse well. Pour this over the duck, put the pan in the fryer and cook at 370 degrees F for 16 minutes.
2. Divide everything between plates and serve.

Nutrition:
Calories 270, fat 14, fiber 3, carbs 6, protein 16

Coconut Crusted Chicken

Prep time: 15 minutes **Cooking time:** 9 minutes **Servings:** 5

15 oz chicken fillet	5 eggs, beaten
1 teaspoon salt	½ cup coconut flour
1 teaspoon dried oregano	Cooking spray

1. Cut the chicken fillet on 5 chops and beat them gently with the help of the kitchen hammer. After this, sprinkle the chicken chops with dried oregano and salt. Dip every chicken chop in the beaten eggs and coat in the coconut flour. Preheat the air fryer to 360F. Place the chicken in the air fryer in one layer and cook for 5 minutes. Then flip them on another side and cook for 4 minutes more or until the schnitzels are light brown.

Nutrition:
Calories 287, fat 12.7, fiber 4.9, carbs 7.7, protein 32.6

Paprika Duck and Eggplant Mix

Prep time: 5 minutes **Cooking time:** 25 minutes **Servings:** 4

1 pound duck breasts, skinless, boneless and cubed 2 eggplants, cubed	A pinch of salt and black pepper
2 tablespoons olive oil	1 tablespoon sweet paprika
½ cup keto tomato sauce	

1. Heat up a pan that fits your air fryer with the oil over medium heat, add the duck pieces and brown for 5 minutes. Add the rest of the ingredients, toss, introduce the pan in the fryer and cook at 370 degrees F for 20 minutes. Divide between plates and serve.

Nutrition:
Calories 285, fat 14, fiber 4, carbs 6, protein 16

Za'atar Chives Chicken

Prep time: 10 minutes **Cooking time:** 18 minutes **Servings:** 4

1-pound chicken drumsticks, bone-in	1 tablespoon zaatar
1 teaspoon garlic powder	½ teaspoon lemon zest, grated
1 teaspoon chives, chopped	1 tablespoon avocado oil

1. In the mixing bowl mix up zaatar, garlic powder, lemon zest, chives, and avocado oil. Then rub the chicken drumsticks with the zaatar mixture.
2. Preheat the air fryer to 375F. Put the chicken drumsticks in the air fryer basket and cook for 15 minutes. Then flip the drumsticks on another side and cook them for 3 minutes more.

Nutrition:
Calories 201, fat 7.1, fiber 0.3, carbs 0.8, protein 31.4

Curry Duck Mix

Prep time: 5 minutes **Cooking time:** 25 minutes **Servings:** 4

15 ounces duck breasts, skinless, boneless and cubed 1 tablespoon olive oil	2 shallots, chopped
Salt and black pepper to the taste 5 ounces heavy cream	teaspoon curry powder
½ bunch coriander, chopped	

1. Heat up a pan that fits your air fryer with the oil over medium heat, add the duck, toss and brown for 5 minutes. Add the rest of the ingredients, toss, introduce the pan in the air fryer and cook at 370 degrees F for 20 minutes. Divide the mix into bowls and serve.

Nutrition:
Calories 274, fat 14, fiber 4, carbs 7, protein 16

Rosemary Partridge

Prep time: 15 minutes **Cooking time:** 14 minutes **Servings:** 4

10 oz partridges	1 teaspoon dried rosemary
1 tablespoon butter, melted	1 teaspoon salt

1. Cut the partridges into the halves and sprinkle with dried rosemary and salt. Then brush them with melted butter. Preheat the air fryer to 385F. Put the partridge halves in the air fryer and cook them for 8 minutes. Then flip the poultry on another side and cook for 6 minutes more.

Nutrition:
Calories 175, fat 7.8, fiber 0.1, carbs 0.2, protein 25.2

Yogurt Chicken Thighs

Prep time: 25 minutes **Cooking time:** 20 minutes **Servings:** 4

4 chicken thighs, skinless, boneless	2 tablespoons plain yogurt
1 teaspoon cayenne pepper	1 teaspoon dried cilantro
½ teaspoon ground cloves	1 tablespoon apple cider vinegar
1 teaspoon olive oil	

1. Make the marinade: in the mixing bowl mix up plain yogurt, cayenne pepper, dried cilantro, ground cloves, and apple cider vinegar. Then put the chicken thighs in the marinade and mix up well. Marinate the chicken for 20 minutes in the fridge. Then preheat the air fryer to 380F. Sprinkle the chicken thighs with olive oil and place in the air fryer. Cook them for 20 minutes.

Nutrition:
Calories 296, fat 12.2, fiber 0.2, carbs 1, protein 42.8

Duck and Asparagus Mix

Prep time: 5 minutes **Cooking time:** 25 minutes **Servings:** 4

duck breast fillets, boneless	½ cup keto tomato sauce
Salt and black pepper to the taste 1 cup red bell pepper, chopped	A drizzle of olive oil
	½ pound asparagus, trimmed and halved
½ cup cheddar cheese, grated	

1. Heat up a pan that fits your air fryer with the oil over medium heat, add the duck fillets and brown for 5 minutes. Add the rest of the ingredients except the cheese, toss, put the pan in the air fryer and cook at 370 degrees F for 20 minutes. Sprinkle the cheese on top, divide the mix between plates and serve.

Nutrition:
Calories 263, fat 12, fiber 4, carbs 6, protein 14

Duck and Lettuce Salad

Preparation time: 5 minutes **Cooking time:** 20 minutes **Servings:** 4

2 duck breasts, boneless and skin on 1 teaspoon coconut oil, melted	A pinch of salt and black pepper 2 shallots, sliced
12 cherry tomatoes, halved	1 tablespoon balsamic vinegar 3 cups lettuce leaves, torn
12 mint leaves, torn	

For the dressing:

1 tablespoon lemon juice	½ tablespoon balsamic vinegar 2 and ½ tablespoons olive oil
½ teaspoon mustard	

1. Heat up a pan that fits your air fryer with the coconut oil over medium heat, add the duck breasts skin side down and cook for 3 minutes. Add salt, pepper, shallots, tomatoes and 1 tablespoon balsamic vinegar, toss, put the pan in the fryer and cook at 370 degrees F for 17 minutes. Cool this mix down, thinly slice the duck breast and put it along with the tomatoes and shallots in a bowl. Add mint and salad leaves and toss. In a separate bowl, mix ½ tablespoon vinegar with lemon juice, oil and mustard and whisk well. Pour this over the duck salad, toss and serve.

Nutrition:
Calories 241, fat 10, fiber 2, carbs 5, protein 15

Ginger Partridges

Prep time: 15 minutes **Cooking time:** 20 minutes **Servings:** 6

18 oz partridges, trimmed	3 oz bacon, sliced
1 teaspoon minced ginger	1 tablespoon avocado oil
½ teaspoon garlic powder	1 teaspoon salt
½ teaspoon smoked paprika	

1. Rub the partridges with minced ginger and sprinkle with garlic powder, salt, and smoked paprika. Then wrap the poultry in the sliced bacon and sprinkle with avocado oil. Preheat the air fryer to 375F. Place the wrapped partridges in the air fryer basket and cook them for 20 minutes. Flip them on another side after 10 minutes of cooking.

Nutrition:
Calories 260, fat 12.1, fiber 0.2, carbs 0.8, protein 35.6

Balsamic Duck and Cranberry Sauce

Prep time: 5 minutes **Cooking time:** 25 minutes **Servings:** 4

4 duck breasts, boneless, skin-on and scored A pinch of salt and black pepper	1 tablespoon olive oil
¼ cup balsamic vinegar	½ cup dried cranberries

1. Heat up a pan that fits your air fryer with the oil over medium-high heat, add the duck breasts skin side down and cook for 5 minutes. Add the rest of the ingredients, toss, put the pan in the fryer and cook at 380 degrees F for 20 minutes. Divide between plates and serve.

Nutrition:
Calories 287, fat 12, fiber 4, carbs 6, protein 16

Stuffed Chicken

Prep time: 15 minutes **Cooking time:** 11 minutes **Servings:** 2

8 oz chicken fillet	3 oz Blue cheese
½ teaspoon salt	½ teaspoon thyme
1 teaspoon sesame oil	

1. Cut the fillet into halves and beat them gently with the help of the kitchen hammer. After this, make the horizontal cut in every fillet. Sprinkle the chicken with salt and thyme. Then fill it with Blue cheese and secure the cut with the help of the toothpick. Sprinkle the stuffed chicken fillets with sesame oil. Preheat the air fryer to 385F. Put the chicken fillets in the air fryer and cook them for 7 minutes. Then carefully flip the chicken fillets on another side and cook for 4 minutes more.

Nutrition:
Calories 386, fat 22.9, fiber 0.1, carbs 1.2, protein 41.9

Parsley Duck

Preparation time: 10 minutes **Cooking time:** 25 minutes **Servings:** 4

4 duck breast fillets, boneless, skin-on and scored	2 tablespoons olive oil
2 tablespoons parsley, chopped Salt and black pepper to the taste 1 cup chicken stock	1 teaspoon balsamic vinegar

1. Heat up a pan that fits your air fryer with the oil over medium heat, add the duck breasts skin side down and sear for 5 minutes. Add the rest of the ingredients, toss, put the pan in the fryer and cook at 380 degrees F for 20 minutes. Divide everything between plates and serve

Nutrition:
Calories 274, fat 14, fiber 4, carbs 6, protein 16

Fried Herbed Chicken Wings

Prep time: 10 minutes **Cooking time:** 11 minutes **Servings:** 4

1 tablespoon Emperor herbs chicken spices	8 chicken wings
Cooking spray	

1. Generously sprinkle the chicken wings with Emperor Herbs chicken spices and place in the preheated to 400F air fryer. Cook the chicken wings for 6 minutes from each side.

Nutrition:
Calories 220, fat 14.3, fiber 0.6, carbs 3.9, protein 17.7

Duck and Coconut Milk Mix

Preparation time: 5 minutes **Cooking time:** 25 minutes **Servings:** 4

garlic cloves, minced	duck breasts, boneless, skin-on and scored 2 tablespoons olive oil
¼ teaspoon coriander, ground 14 ounces coconut milk	Salt and black pepper to the taste 1 cup basil, chopped

1. Heat up a pan that fits your air fryer with the oil over medium heat, add the duck breasts, skin side down and sear for 5 minutes. Add the rest of the ingredients, toss, put the pan in the fryer and cook at 380 degrees F for 20 minutes. Divide between plates and serve.

Nutrition:
Calories 274, fat 13, fiber 3, carbs 5, protein 16

Chicken, Mushrooms and Peppers Pan

Prep time: 10 minutes **Cooking time:** 22 minutes **Servings:** 5

1-pound chicken breast, skinless, boneless	1 teaspoon minced ginger
½ teaspoon minced garlic	1 tablespoon coconut aminos
1 teaspoon lemon juice	5 oz cremini mushrooms, sliced
¼ cup bell pepper, sliced	5 oz cauliflower, chopped
1 teaspoon ground paprika	½ teaspoon cayenne pepper
1 tablespoon avocado oil	1 teaspoon salt

1. Preheat the air fryer to 375F. In the mixing bowl mix up sliced mushrooms, cauliflower, and bell pepper. Sprinkle the ingredients with salt, ½ tablespoon avocado oil, cayenne pepper, and ground paprika. Mix up the vegetables and place them in the air fryer basket. Cook the ingredients for 5 minutes. Then shake them well and cook for 3 minutes more. Transfer the cooked vegetables into the bowl. Then preheat the air fryer to 380F. Slice the chicken breast into the strips. Sprinkle the sliced chicken breast with minced ginger, minced garlic, and sprinkle with coconut aminos and lemon juice. Place the chicken breast in the air fryer and cook it for 13 minutes. Then add cooked vegetables and mix up the meal. Cook it for 1 minute more.

Nutrition:
Calories 130, fat 2.8, fiber 1.4, carbs 4.6, protein 20.7

Creamy Duck and Lemon Sauce

Preparation time: 5 minutes **Cooking time:** 25 minutes **Servings:** 4

2 spring onions, chopped	2 tablespoons butter, melted 4 garlic cloves, minced
1 and ½ teaspoons coriander, ground Salt and black pepper to the taste	15 ounces tomatoes, crushed
¼ cup lemon juice	and ½ pounds duck breast, skinless, boneless and cubed
½ cup cilantro, chopped	½ cup chicken stock
½ cup heavy cream	

1. Heat up a pan that fits your air fryer with the butter over medium heat, add the duck pieces and cook for 5 minutes. Add the rest of the ingredients except the cilantro, toss, introduce the pan in the fryer and cook at 370 degrees F for 20 minutes. Divide between plates and serve.

Nutrition:
Calorie 284, fat 12, fiber 4, carbs 6, protein 17

Paprika Liver Spread

Prep time: 10 minutes **Cooking time:** 8 minutes **Servings:** 6

1-pound chicken liver	2 tablespoons ghee
1 teaspoon salt	1 teaspoon smoked paprika
¼ cup hot water	

1. Preheat the air fryer to 400F. Wash and trim the chicken liver and arrange it in the air fryer basket. Cook the ingredients for 5 minutes. Then flip them on another side and cook for 3 minutes more. When the chicken liver is cooked, transfer it in the blender. Add ghee, salt, and smoked paprika. Add hot water and blend the mixture until smooth. Then transfer the cooked chicken pâté in the bowl and store it in the fridge for up to 3 days.

Nutrition:
Calories 167, fat 9.2, fiber 0.3, carbs 1.4, protein 18.6

Pork and Peppers Mix

Preparation time: 5 minutes **Cooking time:** 25 minutes **Servings:** 4

1 pound pork tenderloin, sliced	¼ cup cilantro, chopped
½ teaspoon garlic powder	1 green bell pepper, julienned
1 tablespoon olive oil	
½ teaspoon chili powder	½ teaspoon cumin, ground

1. Heat up a pan that fits the air fryer with the oil over medium heat, add the pork and brown for 5 minutes. Add the rest of the ingredients, toss, put the pan in the air fryer and cook at 400 degrees F for 20 minutes. Divide between plates and serve.

Nutrition:
Calories 284, fat 13, fiber 4, carbs 6, protein 17

Cardamom Lamb Mix

Prep time: 30 minutes **Cooking time:** 20 minutes **Servings:** 2

10 oz lamb sirloin	1 oz fresh ginger, sliced
2 oz spring onions, chopped	¼ teaspoon ground cinnamon
½ teaspoon ground cardamom	½ teaspoon fennel seeds
½ teaspoon chili flakes	¼ teaspoon salt
1 tablespoon avocado oil	

1. Put the fresh ginger in the blender. Add onion, ground cardamom, cinnamon, fennel seeds, chili flakes, salt, and avocado oil. Blend the mixture until you get the smooth mass. After this, make the small cuts in the lamb sirloin. Rub the meat with the blended spice mixture and leave it for 20 minutes to marinate. Meanwhile, preheat the air fryer to 350F. Put the marinated lamb sirloin in the air fryer and cook it for 20 minutes. Flip the meat on another side in halfway. Slice the cooked meat.

Nutrition:
Calories 355, fat 18.8, fiber 1.1, carbs 7, protein 36.6

Bacon Stuffing

Prep time: 25 minutes **Cooking time:** 10 minutes **Servings:** 6

10 oz uncured bacon, chopped, cooked	3 oz hazelnuts, chopped
1 teaspoon dried sage	½ teaspoon salt
½ teaspoon ground black pepper	1 egg yolk
2 oz celery stalk, chopped	1/3 cup coconut flour
¼ teaspoon baking powder	3 tablespoons coconut oil, softened
1 egg, beaten	1 teaspoon sesame oil

1. Make the cornbread: in the mixing bowl mix up coconut flour, baking powder, coconut oil, and beaten egg. Stir the mixture until it is smooth and homogenous. After this, brush the air fryer pan with sesame oil. Put the cornbread mixture in the air fryer pan and flatten it well. Preheat the air fryer to 385F. Put the pan with cornbread in the air fryer and cook it for 5 minutes or until it is light brown. Then remove the cornbread from the air fryer and let it cool well. Meanwhile, in the mixing bowl mix up chopped bacon, hazelnuts, dried sage, salt, and ground black pepper. Add celery stalk and egg yolk, then crumble the cooked cornbread and add it in the bacon mixture. Stir it well and transfer in the pan. Flatten the mixture well. Cook it in the air fryer at 400F for 5 minutes.

Nutrition:
Calories 208, fat 18.9, fiber 4.3, carbs 7.1, protein 5

Italian Pork

Prep time: 10 minutes **Cooking time:** 50 minutes **Servings:** 2

8 oz pork loin	1 tablespoon sesame oil
½ teaspoon salt	1 teaspoon Italian herbs

1. In the shallow bowl mix up Italian herbs, salt, and sesame oil. Then brush the pork loin with the Italian herbs mixture and wrap in the foil. Preheat the air fryer to 350F. Put the wrapped pork loin in the air fryer and cook it for 50 minutes. When the time is over, remove the meat from the air fryer and discard the foil. Slice the pork loin into the servings.

Nutrition:
Calories 335, fat 22.6, fiber 0, carbs 0, protein 31

Creamy Pork Mix

Prep time: 5 minutes **Cooking time:** 25 minutes **Servings:** 4

1 pound pork stew meat, cubed	4 teaspoons sweet paprika
A pinch of salt and black pepper	1 cup coconut cream
1 tablespoon butter, melted	1 tablespoon parsley, chopped

1. Heat up a pan that fits the air fryer with the butter over medium heat, add the meat and brown for 5 minutes. Add the remaining ingredients, toss, put the pan in the air fryer, cook at 390 degrees F for 20 minutes more, divide into bowls and serve.

Nutrition:
Calories 273, fat 12, fiber 4, carbs 6, protein 20

Smoked Pork

Prep time: 20 minutes **Cooking time:** 20 minutes **Servings:** 5

1-pound pork shoulder	1 tablespoon liquid smoke
1 tablespoon olive oil	1 teaspoon salt

1. Mix up liquid smoke, salt, and olive oil in the shallow bowl. Then carefully brush the pork shoulder with the liquid smoke mixture from each side. Make the small cuts in the meat. Preheat the air fryer to 390F. Put the pork shoulder in the air fryer basket and cook the meat for 10 minutes. After this, flip the meat on another side and cook it for 10 minutes more.
2. Let the cooked pork shoulder rest for 10-15 minutes. Shred it with the help of 2 forks.

Nutrition:
Calories 289, fat 22.2, fiber 0, carbs 0, protein 21.1

Balsamic Pork Chops

Prep time: 5 minutes **Cooking time:** 25 minutes **Servings:** 4

4 pork chops	tablespoon smoked paprika 1 tablespoon olive oil
tablespoons balsamic vinegar	½ cup chicken stock
A pinch of salt and black pepper	

1. In a bowl, mix the pork chops with the rest of the ingredients and toss. Put the pork chops in your air fryer's basket and cook at 390 degrees F for 25 minutes. Divide between plates and serve.

Nutrition:
Calories 276, fat 12, fiber 4, carbs 6, protein 22

Oregano Pork Chops

Prep time: 5 minutes **Cooking time:** 25 minutes **Servings:** 4

4 pork chops	A pinch of salt and black pepper 2/3 cup cream cheese, soft
¼ teaspoon garlic powder	¼ teaspoon oregano, dried
10 ounces beef stock	1 tablespoon mustard
¼ teaspoon thyme, dried 1 tablespoon olive oil	tablespoon parsley, chopped

1. In a baking dish that fits your air fryer, mix all the ingredients, introduce the pan in the fryer and cook at 400 degrees F for 25 minutes. Divide everything between plates and serve.

Nutrition:
Calories 284, fat 14, fiber 4, carbs 6, protein 22

Cilantro Steak

Prep time: 25 minutes **Cooking time:** 25 minutes **Servings:** 4

1-pound flank steak	1 oz fresh cilantro, chopped
1 garlic clove, diced	1 oz fresh parsley, chopped
1 egg, hard-boiled, peeled	½ green bell pepper, chopped
1 tablespoon avocado oil	½ teaspoon salt
½ teaspoon ground black pepper	1 teaspoon peanut oil

1. In the mixing bowl, mix up fresh cilantro, diced garlic, parsley, and avocado oil. Then slice the flank steak in one big fillet (square) and brush it with a cilantro mixture. Then chop the egg roughly and put it on the steak. Add chopped bell pepper. After this, roll the meat and secure it with the kitchen thread. Carefully rub the meat roll with salt and ground black pepper. Then sprinkle the meat roll with peanut oil. Preheat the air fryer to 400F. Put the meat in the air fryer basket and cook it for 25 minutes.

Nutrition:
Calories 261, fat 12.2, fiber 0.9, carbs 2.5, protein 33.6

Garlic Pork Chops

Prep time: 5 minutes **Cooking time:** 25 minutes **Servings:** 4

tablespoons olive oil 4 pork chops	A pinch of salt and black pepper
4 garlic cloves, minced	tablespoons cider vinegar

1. Heat up a pan that fits the air fryer with the oil over medium-high heat, add the pork chops and brown for 5 minutes. Add the rest of the ingredients, toss, put the pan in your air fryer and cook at 400 degrees F for 20 minutes. Divide between plates and serve.

Nutrition:
Calories 273, fat 13, fiber 4, carbs 6, protein 22

Tamales

Prep time: 25 minutes **Cooking time:** 20 minutes **Servings:** 6

10 oz pork stew meat	1 teaspoon almond butter
½ teaspoon dried parsley	1 teaspoon salsa Verde
¼ teaspoon garlic powder	1 cup cauliflower, shredded
1 egg, beaten	1 tablespoon almond flour
1 tablespoon flax meal	½ teaspoon cayenne pepper
3 oz Cheddar cheese, shredded	Cooking spray

1. Grind the pork stew meat and put it in the skillet. Add almond butter and dried parsley and cook the meat on medium heat for 10 minutes. Stir it from time to time. After this, add salsa Verde, and garlic powder and stir the ingredients well. Remove the skillet from the heat. Make the tamale dough: in the mixing bowl, mix up shredded cauliflower, egg, almond flour, flax meal, and cayenne pepper. When the mixture is homogenous, add Cheddar cheese. Mix up the mixture well. After this, cut the foil into medium size squares and spray it with cooking spray. Put the tamale dough in the prepared foil squares. Then top the dough with cooked meat. Roll the foil in the shape of tamales. Preheat the air fryer to 395F. Put the tamales in foil in the air fryer in one layer. Cook the meal for 8 minutes.

Nutrition:
Calories 217, fat 14.1, fiber 1.7, carbs 3.4, protein 19.8

Garlic Pork and Bok Choy

Prep time: 5 minutes **Cooking time:** 35 minutes **Servings:** 4

4 pork chops, boneless 1 bok choy head, torn 2 cups chicken stock	2 tablespoons coconut aminos 2 garlic cloves, minced
A pinch of salt and black pepper	2 tablespoons coconut oil, melted

1. Heat up a pan that fits the air fryer with the oil over medium-high heat, add the pork chops and brown for 5 minutes. Add the garlic, salt and pepper and cook for another minute. Add the rest of the ingredients except the bok choy and cook at 380 degrees F for 25 minutes. Add the bok choy, cook for 5 minutes more, divide everything between plates and serve.

Nutrition:
Calories 284, fat 14, fiber 4, carbs 6, protein 17

Creamy Cheesy Bacon Dip

Prep time: 15 minutes **Cooking time:** 12 minutes **Servings:** 6

6 teaspoon cream cheese	½ cup heavy cream
1 teaspoon dried sage	1 cup Monterey Jack cheese, shredded
½ teaspoon chili flakes	1 tablespoon chives, chopped
1 teaspoon avocado oil	½ teaspoon salt
6 oz bacon, chopped	

1. Preheat the air fryer to 400F. Put the chopped bacon in the air fryer and cook it for 6 minutes. Stir it after 3 minutes of cooking. After this, transfer the cooked bacon in the baking pan. Add cream cheese, heavy cream, Monterey Jack cheese, chili flakes, chives, avocado oil, sage, and salt.
2. Mix up the mixture. Clean the air fryer basket and insert the baking pan with bacon dip inside. Cook it at 385F for 6 minutes.

Nutrition:
Calories 271, fat 22.5, fiber 0, carbs 1, protein 15.6

Cream Cheese Pork

Prep time: 15 minutes **Cooking time:** 20 minutes **Servings:** 4

16 oz pork tenderloin	1 teaspoon liquid smoke
1 teaspoon mustard	1 teaspoon cream cheese
½ teaspoon ground paprika	1 teaspoon avocado oil

1. In the mixing bowl mix up liquid smoked, mustard, cream cheese, and ground paprika. Add avocado oil and. Stir the mixture. Then rub the pork tenderloin with the smoky mixture and wrap in the foil. Preheat the air fryer to 375F. Put the wrapped tenderloin in the air fryer basket and cook it for 20 minutes. Then discard the foil and slice the tenderloin into the servings.

Nutrition:
Calories 171, fat 4.7, fiber 0.3, carbs 0.5, protein 30

Basil Pork

Prep time: 5 minutes **Cooking time:** 25 minutes **Servings:** 4

pork chops	A pinch of salt and black pepper 2 teaspoons basil, dried
2 tablespoons olive oil	½ teaspoon chili powder

1. In a pan that fits your air fryer, mix all the ingredients, toss, introduce in the fryer and cook at 400 degrees F for 25 minutes. Divide everything between plates and serve.

Nutrition:
Calories 274, fat 13, fiber 4, carbs 6, protein 18

Cajun Pork and Peppers Mix

Prep time: 5 minutes **Cooking time:** 35 minutes **Servings:** 2

pound pork stew meat, cut into strips 1 tablespoon Cajun seasoning	red bell peppers, sliced
pound tomatoes, chopped	tablespoons coconut oil, melted A pinch of salt and black pepper
4 garlic cloves, minced	

1. Heat up a pan that fits the air fryer with the oil over medium-high heat, add the pork meat, seasoning, garlic, salt and pepper, toss and brown for 5 minutes. Add the remaining ingredients, toss, put the pan in the fryer and cook at 390 degrees F for 30 minutes. Divide everything between plates and serve.

Nutrition:
Calories 284, fat 13, fiber 4, carbs 6, protein 19

Parmesan Meatballs

Prep time: 15 minutes **Cooking time:** 8 minutes **Servings:** 6

10 oz ground beef	4 oz ground pork
1 tablespoon taco seasoning	1 oz Parmesan, grated
1 teaspoon dried cilantro	1 teaspoon sesame oil

1. In the mixing bowl mix up ground beef, ground pork, taco seasonings, and dried cilantro. When the mixture is homogenous, add Parmesan cheese and stir it well. With the help of the scooper make the medium-size meatballs. Preheat the air fryer to 385F. Brush the air fryer basket with sesame oil from inside and put the meatballs. Arrange them in one layer.
2. Cook the meatballs for 8 minutes. Flip them on another side after 4 minutes of cooking.

Nutrition:
Calories 142, fat 5.4, fiber 0, carbs 1.2, protein 20.8

Pork and Garlic Sauce

Preparation time: 5 minutes **Cooking time:** 25 minutes **Servings:** 4

pound pork tenderloin, sliced A pinch of salt and black pepper 4 tablespoons butter, melted	teaspoons garlic, minced 1 teaspoon sweet paprika

1. Heat up a pan that fits the air fryer with the butter over medium heat, add all the ingredients except the pork medallions, whisk well and simmer for 4-5 minutes. Add the pork, toss, put the pan in your air fryer and cook at 380 degrees F for 20 minutes. Divide between plates and serve with a side salad.

Nutrition:
Calories 284, fat 12, fiber 4, carbs 6, protein 19

Mustard Pork

Prep time: 5 minutes **Cooking time:** 30 minutes **Servings:** 4

1 pound pork tenderloin, trimmed A pinch of salt and black pepper 2 tablespoons olive oil	3 tablespoons mustard
2 tablespoons balsamic vinegar	

1. In a bowl, mix the pork tenderloin with the rest of the ingredients and rub well. Put the roast in your air fryer's basket and cook at 380 degrees F for 30 minutes. Slice the roast, divide between plates and serve.

Nutrition:
Calories 274, fat 13, fiber 4, carbs 7, protein 22

Chili Pork

Preparation time: 5 minutes **Cooking time:** 25 minutes **Servings:** 4

2 teaspoons chili paste 2 garlic cloves, minced 4 pork chops	1 shallot, chopped
1 and ½ cups coconut milk 2 tablespoons olive oil	tablespoons coconut aminos Salt and black pepper to the taste

1. In a pan that fits your air fryer, mix the pork the rest of the ingredients, toss, introduce the pan in the fryer and cook at 400 degrees F for 25 minutes, shaking the fryer halfway. Divide everything into bowls and serve.

Nutrition:
Calories 267, fat 12, fiber 4, carbs 6, protein 18

Cilantro Beef Meatballs

Prep time: 20 minutes **Cooking time:** 7 minutes **Servings:** 4

1 cup ground beef	3 oz Cheddar cheese, shredded
1 tablespoons flax meal	1 teaspoon fresh cilantro, chopped
1 garlic clove, diced	1 chili pepper, chopped
1 egg, beaten	1 teaspoon ground coriander
¼ cup scallions, diced	½ teaspoon ground black pepper
1 teaspoon avocado oil	

1. Put the ground beef in the bowl and mix it up with flax meal, cilantro, garlic clove, chili pepper, egg, ground coriander, diced onion, and ground black pepper. When the mixture is homogenous, add shredded Cheddar cheese and stir the mixture with the help of the spoon. Make the small meatballs from the ground beef mixture. Then preheat the air fryer to 380F. Brush the air fryer basket with avocado oil from inside and arrange the prepared meatballs in one layer. Cook them for 7 minutes or until the meatballs are light brown.

Nutrition:
Calories 180, fat 13, fiber 0.8, carbs 2.1, protein 13.8

Pork with Peppercorn Tomato Sauce

Preparation time: 5 minutes **Cooking time:** 25 minutes **Servings:** 4

tablespoon mustard	¼ cup keto tomato sauce 4 pork chops
A pinch of salt and black pepper 1 teaspoon garlic powder	teaspoons smoked paprika
1 and ½ teaspoons peppercorns, crushed A pinch of cayenne pepper	A drizzle of olive oil

1. Heat up a pan that fits your air fryer with the oil over medium heat, add the pork chops and brown for 5 minutes. Add the rest of the ingredients, toss, put the pan in the fryer and cook at 400 degrees F for 20 minutes. Divide everything between plates and serve.

Nutrition:
Calories 280, fat 13, fiber 4, carbs 6, protein 18

Spiced Chops

Prep time: 10 minutes **Cooking time:** 12 minutes **Servings:** 3

10 oz pork chops, bone-in (3 pork chops)	1 teaspoon Erythritol
1 teaspoon ground black pepper	1 teaspoon ground paprika
½ teaspoon onion powder	¼ teaspoon garlic powder
2 teaspoons olive oil	

1. In the mixing bowl mix up Erythritol, ground black pepper, ground paprika, onion powder, and garlic powder. Then rub the pork chops with the spice mixture from both sides. After this, sprinkle the meat with olive oil. Leave the meat for 5-10 minutes to marinate. Preheat the air fryer to 400F. Put the pork chops in the air fryer and cook them for 6 minutes.
2. Then flip the meat on another side and cook it for 6 minutes more.

Nutrition:

Calorie 335, fat 26.7, fiber 0.5, carbs 1.3, protein 21.5

Lemon Pork

Prep time: 15 minutes **Cooking time:** 25 minutes **Servings:** 4

4 pork chops	2 tablespoons olive oil
A pinch of salt and black pepper 2 garlic cloves, minced	4 teaspoons mustard
2 teaspoons lemon zest, grated Juice of 1 lemon	

1. In a bowl, mix the pork chops with the other ingredients, toss and keep in the fridge for 15 minutes Put the pork chops in your air fryer's basket and cook at 390 degrees F for 25 minutes. Divide between plates and serve with a side salad.

Nutrition:

Calories 287, fat 13, fiber 4, carbs 6, protein 20

Thyme and Turmeric Pork

Prep time: 10 minutes **Cooking time:** 15 minutes **Servings:** 4

1-pound pork tenderloin	½ teaspoon salt
½ teaspoon ground turmeric	1 tablespoon dried thyme
1 tablespoon avocado oil	

1. Rub the pork tenderloin with salt, ground turmeric, and dried thyme. Then brush it with avocado oil. Preheat the air fryer to 370F. Place the pork tenderloin in the air fryer basket and cook it for 15 minutes. You can flip the meat on another side during cooking if desired.

Nutrition:

Calories 170, fat 4.5, fiber 0.5, carbs 0.8, protein 29.8

Wrapped Pork

Prep time: 20 minutes **Cooking time:** 16 minutes **Servings:** 2

8 oz pork tenderloin	4 bacon slices
½ teaspoon salt	1 teaspoon olive oil
½ teaspoon chili powder	

1. Sprinkle the pork tenderloin with salt and chili powder. Then wrap it in the bacon slices and sprinkle with olive oil. Secure the bacon with toothpicks if needed. After this, preheat the air fryer to 375F. Put the wrapped pork tenderloin in the air fryer and cook it for 7 minutes. After this, carefully flip the meat on another side and cook it for 9 minutes more. When the meat is cooked, remove the toothpicks from it (if the toothpicks were used) and slice the meat.

Nutrition:

Calories 390, fat 22.3, fiber 0.2, carbs 0.9, protein 43.8

Garlic Pork Medallions

Prep time: 30 minutes **Cooking time:** 50 minutes **Servings:** 4

1-pound pork loin	2 tablespoons apple cider vinegar
2 tablespoons lemon juice	¼ cup heavy cream
1 teaspoon salt	1 teaspoon white pepper
1 garlic clove, diced	3 spring onions, diced
1 teaspoon lemon zest, grated	2 tablespoons avocado oil

1. Make the marinade: in the mixing bowl mix up apple cider vinegar, lemon juice, heavy cream, salt, white pepper, diced garlic, onion, and lemon zest. Then add avocado oil and whisk the marinade carefully. Chop the pork loin roughly and put in the marinade. Coat the meat in the marinade carefully (use the spoon for this) and leave it for 20 minutes in the fridge. Meanwhile, preheat the air fryer to 365F. Put the marinated meat in the air fryer and cook it for 50 minutes. Stir the meat during cooking to avoid burning.

Nutrition:

Calories 319, fat 19.6, fiber 0.7, carbs 2.2, protein 31.5

Coconut Pork and Green Beans

Preparation time: 5 minutes **Cooking time:** 25 minutes **Servings:** 4

4 pork chops	2 tablespoons coconut oil, melted 2 garlic cloves, minced
A pinch of salt and black pepper	½ pound green beans, trimmed and halved 2 tablespoons keto tomato sauce

1. Heat up a pan that fits the air fryer with the oil over medium heat, add the pork chops and brown for 5 minutes. Add the rest of the ingredients, put the pan in the machine and cook at 390 degrees F for 20 minutes. Divide everything between plates and serve

Nutrition:

Calories 284, fat 13, fiber 4, carbs 6, protein 22

Greek Pork and Spinach

Preparation time: 5 minutes **Cooking time:** 25 minutes **Servings:** 4

2 pounds pork tenderloin, cut into strips 2 tablespoons coconut oil, melted cup cherry tomatoes, halved 1 cup feta cheese, crumbled	A pinch of salt and black pepper 6 ounces baby spinach

1. Heat up a pan that fits your air fryer with the oil over medium high heat, add the pork and brown for 5 minutes. Add the rest of the ingredients except the spinach and the cheese, put the pan to your air fryer, cook at 390 degrees F for 15 minutes. Add the spinach, toss, and cook for 5 minutes more. Divide between plates and serve with feta cheese sprinkled on top.

Nutrition:

Calories 284, fat 12, fiber 4, carbs 7, protein 22

Chili Tomato Pork

Prep time: 15 minutes **Cooking time:** 15 minutes **Servings:** 3

12 oz pork tenderloin	1 tablespoon grain mustard
1 tablespoon swerve	1 tablespoon keto tomato sauce
1 teaspoon chili pepper, grinded	¼ teaspoon garlic powder
1 tablespoon olive oil	

1. In the mixing bowl mix up grain mustard, swerve, tomato sauce, chili pepper, garlic powder, and olive oil. Rub the pork tenderloin with mustard mixture generously and leave for 5-10 minutes to marinate. Meanwhile, preheat the air fryer to 370F. Put the marinated pork tenderloin in the air fryer baking pan. Then insert the baking pan in the preheated air fryer and cook the meat for 15 minutes. Cool the cooked meat to the room temperature and slice it into the servings.

Nutrition:
Calories 212, fat 9, fiber 0.2, carbs 6.4, protein 29.8

Pork and Asparagus

Preparation time: 5 minutes **Cooking time:** 35 minutes **Servings:** 4

pounds pork loin, boneless and cubed	¾ cup beef stock
tablespoons olive oil	tablespoons keto tomato sauce
1 pound asparagus, trimmed and halved	½ tablespoon oregano, chopped Salt and black pepper to the taste

1. Heat up a pan that fits your air fryer with the oil over medium heat, add the pork, toss and brown for 5 minutes. Add the rest of the ingredients, toss a bit, put the pan in the fryer and cook at 380 degrees F for 30 minutes. Divide everything between plates and serve.

Nutrition:
Calories 287, fat 13, fiber 4, carbs 6, protein 18

Cinnamon Ghee Pork Chops

Preparation time: 5 minutes **Cooking time:** 35 minutes **Servings:** 4

4 pork chops, bone-in	A pinch of salt and black pepper 2 and ½ tablespoons ghee, melted
½ teaspoon chipotle chili powder	½ teaspoon cinnamon powder
½ teaspoon garlic powder	½ teaspoon allspice
1 teaspoon coconut sugar	

1. Rub the pork chops with all the other ingredients, put them in your air fryer's basket and cook at 380 degrees F for 35 minutes. Divide the chops between plates and serve with a side salad.

Nutrition:
Calories 287, fat 14, fiber 4, carbs 7, protein 18

Creamy Pork Chops

Prep time: 15 minutes **Cooking time:** 10 minutes **Servings:** 4

2 pork chops	¼ cup coconut flakes
3 tablespoons almond flour	½ teaspoon salt
½ teaspoon dried parsley	1 egg, beaten
1 tablespoon heavy cream	1 teaspoon butter, melted

1. Cut every pork chops into 2 chops. Then sprinkle them with salt and dried parsley. After this, in the mixing bowl mix up coconut flakes and almond flour. In the separated bowl mix up egg, heavy cream, and melted butter. Coat the pork chops in the almond flour mixture and them dip in the egg mixture. Repeat the same steps one more time. Then coat the pork chops in the remaining almond flour mixture. Place the meat in the air fryer basket. Cook the pork chops for 10 minutes at 400F. Flip them on another side after 5 minutes of cooking.

Nutrition:
Calories 303, fat 25.6, fiber 2.7, carbs 5.5, protein 15.1

Shoulder

Prep time: 20 minutes **Cooking time:** 20 minutes **Servings:** 4

1-pound pork shoulder, boneless	3 spring onions, chopped
1 teaspoon dried dill	1 teaspoon keto tomato sauce
1 tablespoon water	1 teaspoon salt
2 tablespoons sesame oil	1 teaspoon ground black pepper
½ teaspoon garlic powder	

1. In the shallow bowl mix up salt, ground black pepper, and garlic powder. Then add dried dill. Sprinkle the pork shoulder with a spice mixture from each side. Then in the separated bowl, mix up tomato sauce, water, and sesame oil. Brush the meat with the tomato mixture. Then place it on the foil. Add spring onions. Wrap the pork shoulder. Preheat the air fryer to 395F. Put the wrapped pork shoulder in the air fryer basket and cook it for 20 minutes. Let the cooked meat rest for 5-10 minutes and then discard the foil.

Nutrition:
Calories 401, fat 31.1, fiber 0.5, carbs 2.3, protein 26.8

Cocoa Ribs

Preparation time: 5 minutes **Cooking time:** 45 minutes **Servings:** 4

2 tablespoons cocoa powder	½ teaspoon cinnamon powder
½ teaspoon chili powder	1 tablespoon coriander, chopped
½ teaspoon cumin, ground	A pinch of salt and black pepper Cooking spray
2 racks of ribs	

1. Grease the ribs with the cooking spray, mix with the other ingredients and rub very well. Put the ribs in your air fryer's basket and cook at 390 degrees F for 45 minutes. Divide between plates and serve with a side salad.

Nutrition:
Calories 284, fat 14, fiber 5, carbs 7, protein 20

Beef and Thyme Cabbage Mix

Preparation time: 5 minutes **Cooking time:** 25 minutes
Servings: 4

pounds beef, cubed	½ pound bacon, chopped
	2 shallots, chopped
1 napa cabbage, shredded	A pinch of salt and black
2 garlic cloves, minced	pepper 2 tablespoons olive oil
1 teaspoon thyme, dried 1 cup beef stock	

1. Heat up a pan that fits the air fryer with the oil over medium-high heat, add the beef and brown for 3 minutes. Add the bacon, shallots and garlic and cook for 2 minutes more. Add the rest of the ingredients, toss, put the pan in the air fryer and cook at 390 degrees F for 20 minutes. Divide between plates and serve.

Nutrition:
Calories 284, fat 14, fiber 2, carbs 6, protein 19

Butter Beef

Prep time: 10 minutes **Cooking time:** 10 minutes **Servings:** 4

4 beef steaks (3 oz each steak)	4 tablespoons butter, softened
1 teaspoon ground black pepper	½ teaspoon salt

1. In the shallow bowl mix up softened butter, ground black pepper, and salt. Then brush the beef steaks with the butter mixture from each side. Preheat the air fryer to 400F. Put the butter steaks in the air fryer and cook them for 5 minutes from each side.

Nutrition:
Calories 261, fat 16.8, fiber 0.1 carbs 0.4, protein 26

Spicy Pork

Prep time: 8 hours **Cooking time:** 20 minutes **Servings:** 6

2-pound pork shoulder, boneless	1 teaspoon salt
1 teaspoon chili powder	1 teaspoon five spices powder
1 tablespoon apple cider vinegar	1 teaspoon Erythritol
¼ teaspoon keto tomato sauce	1 teaspoon ground black pepper
2 tablespoons water	1 tablespoon avocado oil

1. Pierce the pork shoulder with the help of the knife. Then make the sauce: in the mixing bowl mix up salt, chili powder, five spices powder, apple cider vinegar, Erythritol, tomato sauce, ground black pepper, and water. Whisk the mixture until it is smooth. Then put the pork shoulder in the sauce and coat well. Leave the meat in the sauce for 8 hours. When the time is finished, preheat the air fryer to 390F. Brush the marinated meat with avocado oil and put it in the preheated air fryer. Cook the meat for 15 minutes. Then flip it on another side and cook for 5 minutes more. Let the cooked pork shoulder rest for 10 minutes before serving.

Nutrition:
Calories 448, fat 32.7, fiber 0.4, carbs 0.7, protein 35.3

Almond Meatloaf

Preparation time: 5 minutes **Cooking time:** 25 minutes
Servings: 4

1 pound beef meat, ground	1 egg, whisked
3 tablespoons almond meal Cooking spray	
Salt and black pepper to the taste 1 tablespoon parsley, chopped	1 tablespoon oregano, chopped 2 spring onions, chopped

1. In a bowl, mix all the ingredients except the cooking spray, stir well and put in a loaf pan that fits the air fryer. Put the pan in the fryer and cook at 390 degrees F for 25 minutes. Slice and serve hot.

Nutrition:
Calories 284, fat 14, fiber 3, carbs 6, protein 18

Nutmeg Pork Cutlets

Prep time: 10 minutes **Cooking time:** 11 minutes **Servings:** 3

3 pork cutlets (3 oz each cutlet)	2 oz Parmesan, grated
1 tablespoon almond flour	½ teaspoon chili powder
¼ teaspoon ground nutmeg	1 teaspoon sesame oil
1 teaspoon lemon juice	1 egg, beaten

1. In the mixing bowl mix up Parmesan, almond flour, chili powder, and ground nutmeg. In the separated bowl mix up lemon juice and egg. After this, dip the pork cutlets in the egg mixture and then coat in the Parmesan mixture. Sprinkle every coated cutlet with sesame oil. Preheat the air fryer to 400F. Place the pork cutlets in the air fryer basket and cook them for 6 minutes. Then carefully flip them on another side and cook for 5 minutes more.

Nutrition:
Calories 423, fat 33, fiber 1.2, carbs 3.2, protein 29.1

Cashew Ginger Pork

Preparation time: 5 minutes **Cooking time:** 20 minutes
Servings: 4

1 pound pork tenderloin, thinly cut into strips 1 egg, whisked	1 green onion, chopped 1 red bell pepper, sliced 1/3 cup cashews
1 tablespoon ginger, grated 3 garlic cloves, minced tablespoons coconut aminos A pinch of salt and black pepper	tablespoon olive oil

1. Heat up a pan that fits your air fryer with the oil over medium-high heat, add the pork and brown for 3 minutes. Add the rest of the ingredients except the egg, toss and cook for 1 minute more. Add the egg, toss, put the pan in the fryer and cook at 380 degrees F for 15 minutes, shaking the fryer halfway. Divide everything into bowls and serve.

Nutrition:
Calories 274, fat 12, fiber 4, carbs 6, protein 19

Garlic Pork and Ginger Sauce

Preparation time: 5 minutes **Cooking time:** 35 minutes **Servings:** 4

1 pound pork tenderloin, cut into strips 1 garlic clove, minced	A pinch of salt and black pepper 1 tablespoon ginger, grated
3 tablespoons coconut aminos	2 tablespoons coconut oil, melted

1. Heat up a pan that fits the air fryer with the oil over medium-high heat, add the meat and brown for 3 minutes. Add the rest of the ingredients, cook for 2 minutes more, put the pan in the fryer and cook at 380 degrees F for 30 minutes Divide between plates and serve with a side salad.

Nutrition:

Calories 284, fat 13, fiber 4, carbs 6, protein 18

Spiced Hot Ribs

Prep time: 25 minutes **Cooking time:** 35 minutes **Servings:** 4

1-pound pork baby back ribs	½ teaspoon fennel seeds
½ teaspoon ground cumin	½ teaspoon ground coriander
½ teaspoon smoked paprika	½ teaspoon garlic powder
½ teaspoon onion powder	¼ teaspoon ground nutmeg
1 teaspoon cayenne pepper	1 teaspoon dried oregano
1 tablespoon coconut oil, melted	4 tablespoons apple cider vinegar

1. In the mixing bowl mix up fennel seeds, cumin, coriander, smoked paprika, garlic powder, onion powder, ground nutmeg, cayenne pepper, and dried oregano. Then rub the pork baby back ribs with spice mixture well and sprinkle with apple cider vinegar. Then brush the ribs with coconut oil and leave for 15 minutes to marinate. Then preheat the air fryer to 355F. Put the pork baby back ribs in the air fryer and cook them for 35 minutes. Flip the ribs on another side after 15 minutes of cooking.

Nutrition:

Calories 455, fat 37.5, fiber 0.6, carbs 1.6, protein 26

Paprika Beef and Spinach

Preparation time: 5 minutes **Cooking time:** 25 minutes **Servings:** 4

1 and ½ pounds beef meat, cubed Salt and black pepper to the taste 2 cup baby spinach	3 tablespoons olive oil
1 tablespoon sweet paprika	¼ cup beef stock

1. In a pan that fits your air fryer mix all the ingredients except the spinach, toss, introduce the pan the fryer and cook at 390 degrees F for 20 minutes. Add the spinach, cook for 5 minutes more, divide everything between plates and serve.

Nutrition:

Calories 294, fat 13, fiber 3, carbs 6, protein 19

Creamy Pork Schnitzel

Prep time: 15 minutes **Cooking time:** 10 minutes **Servings:** 2

8 oz pork cutlets (4 oz each cutlet)	1 teaspoon sunflower oil
1 egg, beaten	1 tablespoon heavy cream
½ cup coconut flour	½ teaspoon ground black pepper
½ teaspoon salt	

1. Beat the pork cutlets with the help of the kitchen hammer and sprinkle them with ground black pepper and salt. After this, mix up egg and heavy cream. Dip the pork cutlets in the egg mixture and then coat in the coconut flour. Repeat the same steps one more time. Then preheat the air fryer to 400F. Sprinkle the pork cutlets with sunflower oil and put them in the air fryer. Cook the schnitzels for 5 minutes from each side.

Nutrition:

Calories 261, fat 15.3, fiber 12.1, carbs 18.7, protein 12.6

Beef and Zucchini Sauté

Prep time: 5 minutes **Cooking time:** 25 minutes **Servings:** 4

pound beef meat, cut into thin strips 1 zucchini, roughly cubed	tablespoons coconut aminos
2 garlic cloves, minced	¼ cup cilantro, chopped 2 tablespoons avocado oil

1. Heat up a pan that fits your air fryer with the oil over medium heat, add the meat and brown for 5 minutes. Add the rest of the ingredients, toss, put the pan in the fryer and cook at 380 degrees F for 20 minutes. Divide everything into bowls and serve.

Nutrition:

Calories 284, fat 13, fiber 4, carbs 6, protein 16

Beef and Broccoli

Prep time: 5 minutes **Cooking time:** 25 minutes **Servings:** 4

1 pound beef, cubed	1 broccoli head, florets separated
2 tablespoons olive oil	1 teaspoon coconut aminos
1 teaspoon stevia	1/3 cup balsamic vinegar 2 garlic cloves, minced

1. In a pan that fits your air fryer, mix the beef with the rest of the ingredients, toss, put the pan in the fryer and cook at 390 degrees F for 225 minutes. Divide into bowls and serve hot.

Nutrition:

Calories 274, fat 12, fiber 4, carbs 6, protein 16

Strawberry Pork Ribs

Prep time: 10 minutes **Cooking time:** 35 minutes **Servings:** 4

1-pound pork ribs, chopped	1 teaspoon Erythritol
1 tablespoon strawberries, pureed	½ teaspoon chili powder
1 teaspoon olive oil	

1. In the shallow mix up Erythritol, strawberries, and chili powder. Sprinkle the pork ribs with the sweet mixture well. Then brush the meat with olive oil. Preheat the air fryer to 350F. Place the pork ribs in the air fryer and cook them for 35 minutes. Transfer the cooked ribs on the serving plate.

Nutrition:

Calories 322, fat 21.3, fiber 0.1, carbs 0.6, protein 30.1

Beef, Lettuce and Cabbage Salad

Preparation time: 5 minutes **Cooking time:** 25 minutes
Servings: 4

1 pound beef, cubed tablespoon coconut oil, melted 6 ounces iceberg lettuce, shredded 2 tablespoons cilantro, chopped	¼ cup coconut aminos tablespoons chives, chopped 1 zucchini, shredded
½ green cabbage head, shredded 2 tablespoons almonds, sliced	1 tablespoon sesame seeds
½ tablespoon white vinegar	A pinch of salt and black pepper

1. Heat up a pan that fits the air fryer with the oil over medium-high heat, add the meat and brown for 5 minutes. Add the aminos, zucchini, cabbage, salt and pepper, toss, put the pan in the fryer and cook at 370 degrees F for 20 minutes. Cool the mix down, transfer to a salad bowl, add the rest of the ingredients, toss well and serve.

Nutrition:

Calories 270, fat 12, fiber 4, carbs 6, protein 16

Hot Pork Belly

Prep time: 15 minutes **Cooking time:** 40 minutes **Servings:** 6

1-pound pork belly	1 teaspoon ground black pepper
1 teaspoon salt	1 garlic clove, peeled, chopped
1 teaspoon chili pepper	1 teaspoon chili flakes
1 teaspoon dried rosemary	1 tablespoon coconut oil, melted

1. Pierce the pork belly with the help of the knife to get many small cuts. Then rub it with ground black pepper, salt, chili pepper, chili flakes, and dried rosemary. After this, fill the cuts in the pork belly with chopped garlic. Then brush the pork belly with coconut oil. Preheat the air fryer to 365F. Put the prepared pork belly in the air fryer and cook it for 40 minutes.

Nutrition:

Calories 371, fat 22.7, fiber 0.2, carbs 0.6, protein 35

Adobo Pork Chops

Prep time: 15 minutes **Cooking time:** 20 minutes **Servings:** 5

5 pork chops	1 tablespoon lemon juice
1 tablespoon sesame oil	½ teaspoon garlic powder
1 teaspoon adobo seasonings	1/3 cup coconut flour
3 eggs, beaten	

1. Sprinkle the pork chops with lemon juice, garlic powder, and adobo seasonings. Then dip the meat in the beaten eggs and coat in the coconut flour. Repeat the same steps with remaining beaten eggs and coconut flour. After this, sprinkle the pork chops with sesame oil and put in the air fryer in one layer. Cook 3 pork chops per one time. Cook the pork chops for 10 minutes at 350F. Then flip them on another side and cook for 10 minutes more.

Nutrition:

Calories 357, fat 26.6, fiber 3.2, carbs 5.3, protein 23

Creamy Beef and Mushrooms

Preparation time: 5 minutes **Cooking time:** 25 minutes
Servings: 2

pound beef, cut into strips	tablespoons coconut oil, melted A pinch of salt and black pepper 1 shallot, chopped
2 garlic cloves, minced	10 white mushrooms, sliced 1 tablespoon coconut aminos 1 tablespoon mustard
cup beef stock	¼ cup coconut cream
¼ cup parsley, chopped	

1. Heat up a pan that fits your air fryer with the oil over medium-high heat, add the meat and brown for 2 minutes. Add the garlic, shallots, mushrooms, salt and pepper, and cook for 3 minutes more. Add the remaining ingredients except the parsley, toss, put the pan in the fryer and cook at 390 degrees F for 20 minutes. Divide the mix into bowls and serve with parsley sprinkled on top.

Nutrition:

Calories 280, fat 134, fiber 5, carbs 7, protein 17

Ranch Ribs

Prep time: 20 minutes **Cooking time:** 40 minutes **Servings:** 4

12 oz pork ribs, boneless	1 tablespoon ranch dressing
1 teaspoon keto tomato sauce	1 teaspoon apple cider vinegar
1 teaspoon Splenda	1 teaspoon avocado oil
½ teaspoon ground black pepper	½ teaspoon salt

1. In the mixing bowl mix up ranch dressing, tomato sauce, apple cider vinegar Splenda, avocado oil, ground black pepper, and salt. Then brush the pork ribs with the ranch dressing mix well and leave for 15 minutes to marinate. Meanwhile, preheat the air fryer to 350F. Arrange the pork ribs in the air fryer basket and cook them for 40 minutes. Flip the ribs on another side during cooking to avoid burning.

Nutrition:

Calories 241, fat 15.2, fiber 0.2, carbs 1.5, protein 22.6

Beef and Spring Onions

Preparation time: 5 minutes **Cooking time:** 15 minutes
Servings: 2

cups corned beef, cooked and shredded	2 garlic cloves, minced
pound radishes, quartered A pinch of salt and black pepper	2 spring onions, chopped

1. In a pan that fits your air fryer, mix the beef with the rest of the ingredients, toss, put the pan in the fryer and cook at 390 degrees F for 15 minutes. Divide everything into bowls and serve.

Nutrition:

Calories 267, fat 13, fiber 2, carbs 5, protein 15

Cumin Pork Steak

Prep time: 10 minutes **Cooking time:** 25 minutes **Servings:** 4

16 oz pork steak (4 oz every steak)	1 tablespoon sesame oil
½ teaspoon ground paprika	½ teaspoon ground cumin
½ teaspoon salt	½ teaspoon dried garlic

1. Sprinkle every pork steak with ground paprika, ground cumin, salt, and dried garlic. Then sprinkle the meat with sesame oil. Preheat the air fryer to 400F. Put the pork steak in the air fryer in one layer and cook them for 15 minutes. Then flip the steaks on another side and cook them for 10 minutes more.

Nutrition:
Calories 326, fat 22.3, fiber 0.4, carbs 0.1, protein 29.

Beef with Tomato Sauce and Fennel

Prep time: 5 minutes **Cooking time:** 20 minutes **Servings:** 4

tablespoons olive oil	pound beef, cut into strips
	1 fennel bulb, sliced
Salt and black pepper to the taste 1 teaspoon sweet paprika	¼ cup keto tomato sauce

1. Heat up a pan that fits the air fryer with the oil over medium-high heat, add the beef and brown for 5 minutes. Add the rest of the ingredients, toss, put the pan in the machine and cook at 380 degrees F for 15 minutes. Divide the mix between plates and serve.

Nutrition:
Calories 284, fat 13, fiber 4, carbs 6, protein 15

Beef and Tomato Sauce

Prep time: 15 minutes **Cooking time:** 15 minutes **Servings:** 4

1-pound beef loin tri-tip	1 tablespoon keto tomato sauce
1 teaspoon avocado oil	

1. Pierce the beef loin tri-tip with a fork to get many small cuts. In the shallow bowl mix up tomato sauce and avocado oil. Brush the beef loin with the BBQ sauce mixture from each side and transfer in the air fryer. Cook the meat at 400F for 15 minutes. When the beef loin is cooked, remove it from the air fryer and let it rest for 5 minutes. Slice the meat into the servings.

Nutrition:
Calories 214, fat 9.6, fiber 0.1, carbs 1.5, protein 30.3
Ground Beef Mix

Prep time: 5 minutes **Cooking time:** 20 minutes **Servings:** 4

pound beef, ground	A pinch of salt and black pepper A drizzle of olive oil
spring onions, chopped 3 red chilies, chopped	1 cup beef stock
6 garlic cloves, minced	1 green bell pepper, chopped 8 ounces tomatoes, chopped 2 tablespoons chili powder

1. Heat up a pan that fits your air fryer with the oil over medium-high heat, add the beef and brown for 3 minutes. Add the rest of the ingredients, toss, put the pan in the fryer and cook at 380 degrees F for 16 minutes.
2. Divide into bowls and serve.

Nutrition:
Calories 276, fat 12, fiber 3, carbs 6, protein 17

Chives Beef

Prep time: 25 minutes **Cooking time:** 10 minutes **Servings:** 2

10 oz flank steak	2 tablespoons coconut flour
1 teaspoon sunflower oil	½ teaspoon garlic powder
2 tablespoons apple cider vinegar	1 teaspoon coconut aminos
4 tablespoons water	1 tablespoon Erythritol
1 teaspoon chives, chopped	

1. Slice the flank steak into the long thin strips and sprinkle with coconut flour Shake the meat gently. Preheat the air fryer to 395F. Put the sliced flank steak in the air fryer and cook it for 5 minutes from each side.
2. Meanwhile, pour sunflower oil in the saucepan. Add garlic powder, apple cider vinegar, soy sauce, water, and Erythritol. Bring the liquid to boil and remove from the heat. When the meat is cooked, put it in the hot sauce and mix up well. Leave the meat to soak in the sauce for 5-10 minutes.

Nutrition:
Calories 338, fat 15.4, fiber 3.1, carbs 5.4, protein 41.2

Corned Beef

Prep time: 10 minutes **Cooking time:** 4 minutes **Servings:** 5

5 wonton wraps	8 oz corned beef, cooked
1 egg, beaten	3 oz Swiss cheese, shredded
1 teaspoon sunflower oil	

1. Shred the corned beef with the help of the fork and mix it up with Swiss cheese. Then put the corned beef mixture on the wonton wraps and roll them into rolls. Dip every corned beef roll in the beaten egg. Preheat the air fryer to 400F. Put the wonton rolls in the air fryer in one layer and sprinkle with sunflower oil. Cook the meal for 2 minutes from each side or until the rolls are golden brown.

Nutrition:
Calories 172, fat 12.2, fiber 0, carbs 3, protein 12.3

Garlic Fillets

Prep time: 20 minutes **Cooking time:** 15 minutes **Servings:** 4

1-pound beef filet mignon	1 teaspoon minced garlic
1 tablespoon peanut oil	½ teaspoon salt
1 teaspoon dried oregano	

1. Chop the beef into the medium size pieces and sprinkle with salt and dried oregano. Then add minced garlic and peanut oil and mix up the meat well. Place the bowl with meat in the fridge for 10 minutes to marinate.
2. Meanwhile, preheat the air fryer to 400F. Put the marinated beef pieces in the air fryer and cook them for 10 minutes Then flip the beef on another side and cook for 5 minutes more.

Nutrition:
Calories 213, fat 11.5, fiber 0.2, carbs 0.5, protein 25.2

Hot Paprika Beef

Prep time: 5 minutes **Cooking time:** 20 minutes **Servings:** 4

1 tablespoon hot paprika 4 beef steaks	Salt and black pepper to the taste 1 tablespoon butter, melted

1. In a bowl, mix the beef with the rest of the ingredients, rub well, transfer the steaks to your air fryer's basket and cook at 390 degrees F for 10 minutes on each side. Divide the steaks between plates and serve with a side salad.

Nutrition:

Calories 280, fat 12, fiber 4, carbs 6, protein 17

Lamb Meatballs

Prep time: 5 minutes **Cooking time:** 30 minutes **Servings:** 8

spring onions, chopped tablespoons cilantro, chopped 2 tablespoons mint, chopped	tablespoon garlic, minced A pinch of salt and black pepper Zest of 1 lemon
Juice of 1 lemon	½ cup almond meal 3 eggs, whisked
2 and ½ pounds lamb meat, ground Cooking spray	

1. In a bowl, mix all the ingredients except the cooking spray, stir well and shape medium meatballs out of this mix. Put the cakes in your air fryer, grease them with cooking spray and cook at 390 degrees F for 15 minutes on each side. Divide between plates and serve with a side salad.

Nutrition:

Calories 283, fat 13, fiber 4, carbs 6, protein 15

Roasted Cilantro Lamb Chops

Preparation time: 5 minutes **Cooking time:** 24 minutes **Servings:** 6

12 lamb chops	A pinch of salt and black pepper
½ cup cilantro, chopped	1 green chili pepper, chopped 1 garlic clove, minced
Juice of 1 lime	3 tablespoons olive oil

1. In a bowl, mix the lamb chops with the rest of the ingredients and rub well. Put the chops in your air fryer's basket and cook at 400 degrees F for 12 minutes on each side. Divide between plates and serve.

Nutrition:

Calories 284, fat 10, fiber 3, carbs 6, protein 16

Rosemary Steaks

Preparation time: 5 minutes **Cooking time:** 24 minutes **Servings:** 4

4 rib eye steaks	A pinch of salt and black pepper 1 tablespoon olive oil
1 teaspoon sweet paprika 1 teaspoon cumin, ground	1 teaspoon resemary, chopped

1. In a bowl, mix the steaks with the rest of the ingredients, toss and put them in your air fryer's basket. Cook at 380 degrees F for 12 minutes on each side, divide between plates and serve.

Nutrition:

Calories 283, fat 12, fiber 3, carbs 6, protein 17

Stuffed Beef

Prep time: 20 minutes **Cooking time:** 25 minutes **Servings:** 4

1-pound beef tenderloin	1 oz dried tomatoes, chopped
1 teaspoon salt	2 spring onions, chopped
1 garlic clove, diced	½ teaspoon chili powder
1 tablespoon sunflower oil	½ teaspoon dried rosemary

1. Make the cuts in the beef tenderloin to get the shape of the square fillet. Then sprinkle the meat with salt, chili powder, and dried rosemary.
2. Massage the meat gently with the help of the fingertips. Then sprinkle the meat with dried tomatoes, diced garlic, and onion. Roll the heat into the roll and then secure it with the kitchen thread. Sprinkle the beef roll with sunflower oil. Preheat the air fryer to 375F. Put the beef roll in the air fryer and cook it for 15 minutes. Then flip the meat on another side and cook it for 10 minutes more. Then cool the meat to the room temperature and discard the kitchen tread. Slice the stuffed beef roll into the servings.

Nutrition:

Calories 271, fat 14, fiber 0.4, carbs 1.5, protein 33.1

Beef with Ghee Mushroom Mix

Preparation time: 5 minutes **Cooking time:** 25 minutes **Servings:** 4

4 beef steaks	tablespoon olive oil
A pinch of salt and black pepper 2 tablespoons ghee, melted	garlic cloves, minced
5 cups wild mushrooms, sliced 1 tablespoon parsley, chopped	

1. Heat up a pan that fits the air fryer with the oil over medium-high heat, add the steaks and sear them for 2 minutes on each side. Add the rest of the ingredients, toss, transfer the pan to your air fryer and cook at 380 degrees F for 20 minutes. Divide between plates and serve.

Nutrition:

Calories 283, fat 14, fiber 4, carbs 6, protein 17

Sesame Lamb Chops

Prep time: 10 minutes **Cooking time:** 11 minutes **Servings:** 6

6 lamb chops (3 oz each lamb chop)	1 tablespoon sesame oil
1 tablespoon za'atar seasonings	

1. Rub the lamb chops with za'atar seasonings and sprinkle with sesame oil. Preheat the air fryer to 400F. Then arrange the lamb chops in the air fryer in one layer and cook them for 5 minutes. Then flip the pork chops on another side and cook them for 6 minutes more.

Nutrition:

Calories 183, fat 8.8, fiber 0.3, carbs 0.3, protein 24.2

Mustard Beef Mix

Prep time: 15 minutes **Cooking time:** 30 minutes **Servings:** 7

2-pound beef ribs, boneless	1 tablespoon Dijon mustard
1 tablespoon sunflower oil	1 teaspoon ground paprika
1 teaspoon cayenne pepper	

1. In the shallow bowl mix up Dijon mustard and sunflower oil. Then sprinkle the beef ribs with ground paprika and cayenne pepper. After this, brush the meat with Dijon mustard mixture and leave for 10 minutes to marinate. Meanwhile, preheat the air fryer to 400F. Put the beef ribs in the air fryer to and cook them for 10 minutes. Then flip the ribs on another side and reduce the air fryer heat to 325F. Cook the ribs for 20 minutes more.

Nutrition:
Calories 262, fat 10.3, fiber 0.3, carbs 0.4, protein 39.5

Adobo Oregano Beef

Preparation time: 5 minutes **Cooking time:** 30 minutes **Servings:** 4

pound beef roast, trimmed	½ teaspoon oregano, dried
¼ teaspoon garlic powder	A pinch of salt and black pepper
½ teaspoon turmeric powder	1 tablespoon olive oil

1. In a bowl, mix the roast with the rest of the ingredients, and rub well. Put the roast in the air fryer's basket and cook at 390 degrees F for 30 minutes. Slice the roast, divide it between plates and serve with a side salad.

Nutrition:
Calories 294, fat 12, fiber 3, carbs 6, protein 19

Chili Loin Medallions

Prep time: 20 minutes **Cooking time:** 15 minutes **Servings:** 4

1-pound pork loin	4 oz bacon, sliced
1 teaspoon ground cumin	1 teaspoon coconut oil, melted
½ teaspoon salt	½ teaspoon chili flakes

1. Slice the pork loin on the meat medallions and sprinkle them with ground cumin, salt, and chili flakes. Then wrap every meat medallion in the sliced bacon and sprinkle with coconut oil. Place the wrapped medallions in the air fryer basket in one layer and cook them for 10 minutes at 375F. Then carefully flip the meat medallions on another side and cook them for 5 minutes more.

Nutrition:
calorie 440, fat 28.9, fiber 0.1, carbs 0.7, protein 41.6

Marinated Beef

Preparation time: 5 minutes **Cooking time:** 35 minutes **Servings:** 4

2 tablespoons olive oil 3 garlic cloves, minced	Salt and black pepper to the taste 4 medium beef steaks
cup balsamic vinegar	

1. In a bowl, mix steaks with the rest of the ingredients, and toss. Transfer the steaks to your air fryer's basket and cook at 390 degrees F for 35 minutes, flipping them halfway. Divide between plates and serve with a side salad.

Nutrition:
Calories 273, fat 14, fiber 4, carbs 6, protein 19

Meatballs and Sauce

Preparation time: 5 minutes **Cooking time:** 25 minutes **Servings:** 4

tablespoons olive oil	2 spring onions, chopped
	1 egg, whisked
2 tablespoons rosemary, chopped 2 pounds beef, ground	1 garlic clove, minced
A pinch of salt and black pepper 24 ounces tomatoes, crushed	

1. In a bowl, mix the beef with all the ingredients except the oil and the tomatoes, stir well and shape medium meatballs out of this mix. Heat up a pan that fits the air fryer with the oil over medium-high heat, add the meatballs and cook for 2 minutes on each side. Add the tomatoes, toss, put the pan in the fryer and cook at 370 degrees F for 20 minutes. Divide into bowls and serve.

Nutrition:
Calories 273, fat 10, fiber 3, carbs 6, protein 15

Steak Rolls

Prep time: 25 minutes **Cooking time:** 18 minutes **Servings:** 4

12 oz pork steaks (3 oz each steak)	1 green bell pepper
2 oz asparagus, trimmed	1 teaspoon ground black pepper
¼ teaspoon salt	1 teaspoon sunflower oil
1 teaspoon chili flakes	1 teaspoon avocado oil

1. Beat every pork steak with the kitchen hammer gently. Then sprinkle the meat with chili flakes and avocado oil and place it in the air fryer in one layer. Cook the meat for 8 minutes at 375F. Then remove the meat from the air fryer and cool to the room temperature. Meanwhile, cut the bell pepper on the thin wedges. Mix up together pepper wedges and asparagus. Add ground black pepper, salt, and sunflower oil. Mix up the vegetables. After this, place the vegetables on the pork steaks and roll them. Secure the meat with toothpicks if needed. Then transfer the steak bundles in the air fryer in one layer and cook them for 10 minutes at 365F.

Nutrition:
Calories 231, fat 13.3, fiber 0.9, carbs 3.2, protein 23.9

Basil Beef and Avocado

Prep time: 5 minutes **Cooking time:** 25 minutes **Servings:** 4

4 flank steaks	garlic clove, minced 1/3 cup beef stock
avocados, peeled, pitted and sliced 1 teaspoon chili flakes	½ cup basil, chopped
2 spring onions, chopped 2 teaspoons olive oil	A pinch of salt and black pepper

1. Heat up a pan that fits the air fryer with the oil over medium-high heat, add the steaks and cook for 2 minutes on each side. Add the rest of the ingredients except the avocados, put the pan in the air fryer and cook at 380 degrees F for 15 minutes. Add the avocado slices, cook for 5 minutes more, divide everything between plates and serve.

Nutrition:
Calories 273, fat 12, fiber 3, carbs 6, protein 18

Nutmeg Baby Back Ribs

Prep time: 15 minutes **Cooking time:** 40 minutes **Servings:** 3

10 oz baby back ribs, roughly chopped	1 teaspoon ground cumin
½ teaspoon ground nutmeg	½ teaspoon salt
1 teaspoon cayenne pepper	1 tablespoon sunflower oil
1 teaspoon keto tomato sauce	1 tablespoon lemon juice

1. In the mixing bowl mix up ground cumin, ground nutmeg, salt, cayenne pepper, sunflower oil, tomato sauce, lemon juice. Then rub the ribs with the spice mixture and leave for 10 minutes to marinate. Meanwhile, preheat the air fryer to 355F. Wrap the ribs in the foil and place it in the preheated air fryer. Cook the ribs for 40 minutes.

Nutrition:

Calories 262, fat 16.7, fiber 0.3, carbs 1.6, protein 25.1

Beef Casserole

Preparation time: 5 minutes **Cooking time:** 30 minutes **Servings:** 4

1 tablespoon olive oil	1 and ½ cups coconut cream
½ cup parmesan, grated 1 pound beef, ground	1 bunch spring onions, chopped 1 tablespoon keto tomato sauce A pinch of salt and black pepper 2 cups cheddar cheese, ground
1 pound cherry tomatoes, chopped	

1. Heat up a pan with the oil over medium-high heat, add the beef and brown for 5 minutes. Add spring onions, tomatoes, salt and pepper and cook for 3-4 minutes more. Transfer this to a pan that fits the air fryer, pour the cream, sprinkle the parmesan and cheddar on top, put the pan in the fryer and cook at 380 degrees F for 20 minutes. Divide between plates and serve.

Nutrition:

Calories 273, fat 13, fiber 4, carbs 6, protein 18

Garlic Burgers

Prep time: 15 minutes **Cooking time:** 15 minutes **Servings:** 4

1-pound ground beef	2 spring onions, diced
¼ teaspoon garlic powder	1 teaspoon ground black pepper
1 teaspoon salt	1 tablespoon flax meal
1 egg yolk	1 teaspoon nut oil

1. In the mixing bowl mix up ground beef, spring onion, garlic powder, ground black pepper, salt, flax meal, and egg yolk. Stir the mixture to get the homogenous texture. After this, make 4 burgers with the help of the fingertips. Put the prepared burgers in the freezer for 5 minutes.
2. Meanwhile, preheat the air fryer to 370F. Then put the burgers in the hot air fryer and sprinkle them with nut oil. Cook the burgers for 8 minutes. Then flip them on another side and cook for 7 minutes more.

Nutrition:

Calories 255, fat 10, fiber 1.3, carbs 3.7, protein 35.8

Dill Beef and Artichokes

Prep time: 5 minutes **Cooking time:** 30 minutes **Servings:** 4

½ pounds beef stew meat, cubed A pinch of salt and black pepper	tablespoons olive oil 2 shallots, chopped
cup beef stock	garlic cloves, minced
½ teaspoon dill, chopped	12 ounces artichoke hearts, drained and chopped

1. Heat up a pan that fits the air fryer with the oil over medium-high heat, add the meat and brown for 5 minutes. Add the rest of the ingredients except the dill, transfer the pan to your air fryer and cook at 380 degrees F for 25 minutes shaking the air fryer halfway. Divide everything into bowls and serve with the dill sprinkled on top.

Nutrition:

Calories 273, fat 13, fiber 4, carbs 6, protein 18

Beef and Garlic Onions Sauce

Prep time: 15 minutes **Cooking time:** 20 minutes **Servings:** 6

2-pound beef shank	1 teaspoon ground black pepper
1 teaspoon salt	1 oz crushed tomatoes
1 teaspoon sesame oil	3 tablespoons apple cider vinegar
1 garlic clove, diced	3 tablespoons water
3 spring onions, chopped	

1. Sprinkle the beef shank with ground black pepper and salt and put in the air fryer. Sprinkle the meat with sesame oil. Cook it for 20 minutes at 390F. Flip the meat on another side after 10 minutes of cooking.
2. Meanwhile, make the sauce: put crushed tomatoes in the saucepan. Add apple cider vinegar, garlic clove, water, and spring onions. Bring the liquid to boil and remove it from the heat. When the meat is cooked, chop it into the servings and sprinkle with hot sauce.

Nutrition:

Calories 293, fat 10.2, fiber 0.3, carbs 1, protein 46.1

Mustard Beef and Garlic Spinach

Prep time: 5 minutes **Cooking time:** 20 minutes **Servings:** 4

3 garlic cloves, minced	½ pound beef, cut into strips 2 tablespoons coconut oil, melted 2 cups baby spinach
tablespoons chives, chopped 4 tablespoons mustard	Salt and black pepper to the taste

1. In a pan that fits the air fryer, combine all the ingredients, put the pan in the air fryer and cook at 390 degrees F for 20 minutes. Divide between plates and serve.

Nutrition:

Calories 283, fat 14, fiber 2, carbs 6, protein 19

Garlic Dill Leg of Lamb

Prep time: 15 minutes **Cooking time:** 21 minutes **Servings:** 2

9 oz leg of lamb, boneless	1 teaspoon minced garlic
2 tablespoons butter, softened	½ teaspoon dried dill
½ teaspoon salt	

1. In the shallow bowl mix up minced garlic, butter, dried dill, and salt. Then rub the leg of lamb with butter mixture and place it in the air fryer. Cook it at 380F for 21 minutes.

Nutrition:

Calories 105, fat 11.5, fiber 0.1, carbs 0.6, protein 0.3

Lemon Osso Bucco

Prep time: 15 minutes **Cooking time:** 40 minutes **Servings:** 4

3 spring onions, chopped	1 garlic clove, diced
1 oz celery, chopped	1-pound veal shank, boneless, chopped
½ teaspoon salt	½ teaspoon ground black pepper
1 tablespoon ghee	1 tablespoon keto tomato sauce
2 tablespoons water	½ teaspoon dried thyme
1 teaspoon lemon juice	1 teaspoon sunflower oil

1. Preheat the air fryer to 370F. In the mixing bowl mix up spring onions, garlic, celery, salt, ground black pepper, ghee, tomato sauce, water, dried thyme, lemon juice, and sunflower oil. Add the veal shank and mix up the ingredients carefully. Then cover the mixture with foil and transfer in the air fryer. Cook Osso Bucco for 40 minutes. Cool the cooked meal to the room temperature.

Nutrition:
Calories 268, fat 11.4, fiber 0.8, carbs 3, protein 36.2

Rosemary Lamb Steak

Prep time: 10 minutes **Cooking time:** 12 minutes **Servings:** 2

12 oz lamb steak (6 oz each lamb steak)	1 teaspoon dried rosemary
1 teaspoon minced onion	1 tablespoon avocado oil
½ teaspoon salt	

2. Rub the lamb steaks with minced onion and salt. In the shallow bowl mix up dried rosemary and avocado oil. Sprinkle the meat with rosemary mixture. After this, preheat the air fryer to 400F. Put the lamb steaks in the air fryer in one layer and cook them for 6 minutes. Then flip the meat on another side and cook it for 6 minutes more.

Nutrition:
Calories 328, fat 13.5, fiber 0.6, carbs 0.9, protein 47.9

Pork Roulade

Prep time: 15 minutes **Cooking time:** 17 minutes **Servings:** 2

2 pork chops	1 teaspoon German mustard
1 teaspoon scallions, diced	1 pickled cucumber, diced
1 teaspoon almond butter	½ teaspoon ground black pepper
1 teaspoon olive oil	

1. Beat the pork chops gently with the help of the kitchen hammer and place them o the chopping board overlap. Then rub the meat with ground black pepper and German mustard. Top it with scallions, diced pickled cucumber, and almond butter. Roll the meat into the roulade and secure it with the kitchen thread. Then sprinkle the roulade with olive oil. Preheat the air fryer to 390F. Put the roulade in the air fryer and cook it for 17 minutes. Slice the cooked roulade.

Nutrition:
Calories 354, fat 27.2, fiber 1.9, carbs 7.7, protein 21

Minty Lamb Mix

Prep time: 5 minutes **Cooking time:** 24 minutes **Servings:** 4

8 lamb chops	A pinch of salt and black pepper 1 cup mint, chopped
garlic clove, minced Juice of 1 lemon	tablespoons olive oil

1. In a blender, combine all the ingredients except the lamb and pulse well. Rub lamb chops with the mint sauce, put them in your air fryer's basket and cook at 400 degrees F for 12 minutes on each side. Divide everything between plates and serve.

Nutrition:
Calories 284, fat 14, fiber 3, carbs 6, protein 16

Herbed Lamb Chops

Prep time: 15 minutes **Cooking time:** 12 minutes **Servings:** 4

4 lamb chops (3 oz each lamb chop)	½ teaspoon dried thyme
1 teaspoon dried rosemary	2 tablespoons avocado oil
1 teaspoon keto tomato sauce	½ teaspoon salt

1. In the shallow bowl mix up dried thyme, salt, and dried rosemary. Then in the separated bowl mix up tomato sauce and avocado oil. Sprinkle the lamb chops with the spice mixture and then brush with the tomato sauce mixture. Preheat the air fryer to 390F. Put the lamb chops in the air fryer and cook them for 6 minutes from each side.

Nutrition:
Calories 170, fat 7.2, fiber 0.5, carbs 0.9, protein 24

Smoked Chili Lamb Chops

Prep time: 5 minutes **Cooking time:** 20 minutes **Servings:** 4

4 lamb chops	4 garlic cloves, minced
½ teaspoon chili powder	¼ teaspoon smoked paprika
	2 tablespoons olive oil
A pinch of salt and black pepper	

1. In a bowl, mix the lamb with the rest of the ingredients and toss well. Transfer the chops to your air fryer's basket and cook at 390 degrees F for 10 minutes on each side. Serve with a side salad.

Nutrition:
Calories 274, fat 12, fiber 4, carbs 6, protein 17

Tomato Riblets

Prep time: 30 minutes **Cooking time:** 40 minutes **Servings:** 4

1-pound pork riblets	2 tablespoons Erythritol
½ teaspoon ground paprika	½ teaspoon chili powder
1 teaspoon yellow mustard	2 tablespoons apple cider vinegar
1 teaspoon keto tomato sauce	¼ cup of water
1 teaspoon salt	

1. In the mixing bowl mix up Erythritol, ground paprika, chili powder, yellow mustard, apple cider vinegar, tomato sauce, and water. Add salt. Whisk the mixture until homogenous. Then put the pork riblets in the homogenous mixture and mix up well. Leave the meat for 20 minutes in this sauce. After this, preheat the air fryer to 355F. Put the pork riblets in the air fryer and cook them for 40 minutes. Flip the pork ribs on another side after 20 minutes of cooking.

Nutrition:
Calories 265, fat 17.2, fiber 1.3, carbs 6.5, protein 21.5

Marjoram Lamb

Preparation time: 5 minutes **Cooking time:** 25 minutes
Servings: 4

4 lamb chops	2 tablespoons olive oil
Salt and black pepper to the taste 1 tablespoon marjoram, chopped 3 garlic cloves, minced	1 teaspoon thyme, dried
½ cup keto tomato sauce	

1. Heat up a pan that fits the air fryer with the oil over medium-high heat, add the lamb chops and brown for 5 minutes. Add the rest of the ingredients, toss, put the pan in the fryer and cook at 390 degrees F for 20 minutes more. Divide into bowls and serve right away.

Nutrition:

Calories 274, fat 14, fiber 3, carbs 6, protein 14

Italian Fennel Lamb

Prep time: 10 minutes **Cooking time:** 22 minutes **Servings:** 6

18 oz rack of lamb	1 teaspoon Italian seasonings
½ teaspoon cayenne pepper	½ teaspoon dried thyme
½ teaspoon dried cumin	1 teaspoon fennel seeds
½ teaspoon lemon zest, grated	1 tablespoon coconut oil, melted
½ teaspoon onion powder	

1. Sprinkle the rack of lamb with Italian seasonings, cayenne pepper, dried thyme, cumin, fennel seeds, and onion powder. Then sprinkle the meat with lemon zest and coconut oil. Preheat the air fryer to 385F. Put the rack off the lamb in the air fryer basket and cook it for 22 minutes.

Nutrition:

Calories 168, fat 10.2, fiber 0.2, carbs 0.7, protein 17.4

American Garlic Ribs

Prep time: 25 minutes **Cooking time:** 30 minutes **Servings:** 4

11-pound pork spare ribs	¼ cup keto tomato sauce
1 tablespoon lemon juice	1 tablespoon avocado oil
1 teaspoon Splenda	1 tablespoon American style yellow mustard
½ teaspoon minced garlic	1 teaspoon chili pepper
½ teaspoon ground black pepper	

1. In the mixing bowl mix up tomato sauce, lemon juice, avocado oil, Splenda, yellow mustard, minced garlic, chili pepper, and ground black pepper. Stir the mixture until homogenous. Then rub the spare ribs with the mustard mixture and leave for 20 minutes to marinate. Preheat the air fryer to 355F and place the marinated spare ribs in the air fryer basket.
2. Cook the meal for 30 minutes.

Nutrition:

Calories 237, fat 18.5, fiber 0.5, carbs 3.3, protein 13.1

Lamb with Olives

Preparation time: 5 minutes **Cooking time:** 35 minutes
Servings: 4

and ½ pounds lamb meat, cubed 2 tablespoons olive oil	A pinch of salt and black pepper
¼ cup kalamata olives, pitted and sliced 4 garlic cloves, minced rosemary springs, chopped 6 tomatoes, cubed	Zest of 1 lemon, grated

1. Heat up a pan that fits your air fryer with the oil over medium heat, add the meat and brown for 5 minutes. Add the rest of the ingredients, toss, put the pan in the air fryer and cook at 380 degrees F for 30 minutes.
2. Divide everything into bowls and serve.

Nutrition:

Calories 274, fat 10, fiber 4, carbs 6, protein 15

Cayenne Ghee Oxtails

Prep time: 15 minutes **Cooking time:** 65 minutes **Servings:** 6

2-pound beef oxtail	1 teaspoon salt
1 teaspoon cayenne pepper	1 tablespoon sesame oil
½ teaspoon ground coriander	2 tablespoons apple cider vinegar
½ teaspoon dried thyme	1 tablespoon ghee

1. Chop the oxtail roughly and sprinkle with salt, cayenne pepper, sesame oil, ground coriander, and apple cider vinegar. Add dried thyme and shake the oxtail well. Then put the meat in the air fryer baking pan and add ghee. Preheat the air fryer to 360F. Put the pan with the oxtail in the air fryer and cook it for 65 minutes.

Nutrition:

Calories 414, fat 24.5, fiber 0.1, carbs 0.3, protein 46.7

Oregano and Rosemary Lamb Skewers

Preparation time: 10 minutes **Cooking time:** 20 minutes
Servings: 4

2 pounds lamb meat, cubed	¼ cup olive oil
tablespoon garlic, minced 1 tablespoon oregano, dried	½ teaspoon rosemary, dried 2 tablespoons lemon juice
A pinch of salt and black pepper 1 tablespoon red vinegar	red bell peppers, cut into medium pieces

1. In a bowl, mix all the ingredients and toss them well. Thread the lamb and bell peppers on skewers, place them in your air fryer's basket and cook at 380 degrees F for 10 minutes on each side. Divide between plates and serve with a side salad.

Nutrition:

Calories 274, fat 12, fiber 3, carbs 6, protein 16

Hot Pepper Lamb Mix

Preparation time: 5 minutes **Cooking time:** 35 minutes
Servings: 4

1 pound lamb leg, boneless and sliced 2 tablespoons olive oil	A pinch of salt and black pepper 2 garlic cloves, minced
1 tablespoon rosemary, chopped	½ cup walnuts, chopped
¼ teaspoon red pepper flakes	½ teaspoon mustard seeds
½ teaspoon Italian seasoning 1 tablespoon parsley, chopped	

1. In a bowl, mix the lamb with all the ingredients except the walnuts and parsley, rub well, put the slices your air fryer's basket and cook at 370 degrees F for 35 minutes, flipping the meat halfway. Divide between plates, sprinkle the parsley and walnuts on top and serve with a side salad.

Nutrition:
Calories 283, fat 13, fiber 4, carbs 6, protein 15

Garlic Chili Steak

Prep time: 20 minutes **Cooking time:** 35 minutes **Servings:** 4

1-pound lamb sirloin	1 teaspoon chili paste
1 tablespoon avocado oil	½ teaspoon dried thyme
¼ teaspoon minced ginger	¼ teaspoon chili powder
½ teaspoon salt	

1. In the shallow bowl mix up chili paste, avocado oil, dried thyme, minced ginger, and chili powder. Then sprinkle the lamb sirloin with salt and rub with chili paste mixture. Use the gloves for this step. Leave the meat for at least 15 minutes to marinate. Preheat the air fryer to 355F. Put the meat in the air fryer basket and cook it for 20 minutes. Then flip the meat on another side and cook it for 15 minutes more.

Nutrition:
Calories 241, fat 11.1, fiber 0.3, carbs 1, protein 32.3

Lamb and Salsa

Preparation time: 5 minutes **Cooking time:** 35 minutes
Servings: 4

1 tablespoon chipotle powder	A pinch of salt and black pepper 1 and ½ pounds lamb loin, cubed 2 tablespoons red vinegar
4 tablespoons olive oil 2 tomatoes, cubed	2 cucumbers, sliced
2 spring onions, chopped Juice of ½ lemon	¼ cup mint, chopped

1. Heat up a pan that fits your air fryer with half of the oil over medium-high heat, add the lamb, stir and brown for 5 minutes. Add the chipotle powder, salt pepper and the vinegar, toss, put the pan in the air fryer and cook at 380 degrees F for 30 minutes. In a bowl, mix tomatoes with cucumbers, onions, lemon juice, mint and the rest of the oil and toss. Divide the lamb between plates, top each serving with the cucumber salsa and serve.

Nutrition:
Calories 284, fat 13, fiber 3, carbs 6, protein 14

Lamb Burgers

Prep time: 15 minutes **Cooking time:** 16 minutes **Servings:** 2

8 oz lamb, minced	½ teaspoon salt
½ teaspoon ground black pepper	½ teaspoon dried cilantro
1 tablespoon water	Cooking spray

1. In the mixing bowl mix up minced lamb, salt, ground black pepper, dried cilantro, and water.
2. Stir the meat mixture carefully with the help of the spoon and make 2 burgers.
3. Preheat the air fryer to 375F.
4. Spray the air fryer basket with cooking spray and put the burgers inside. Cook them for 8 minutes from each side.

Nutrition:
Calories 219, fat 8.3, fiber 0.5, carbs 1.8, protein 32

Lime Lamb Curry

Preparation time: 5 minutes **Cooking time:** 35 minutes
Servings: 4

2 tablespoons olive oil	1 and ½ pounds lamb meat, cubed A pinch of salt and black pepper 15 ounces tomatoes, chopped Juice of 2 limes
teaspoon sweet paprika 1 cup beef stock	1-inch ginger, grated 2 hot chilies, chopped
red bell peppers, chopped	2 teaspoons turmeric powder 1 tablespoon green curry paste
4 garlic cloves, minced	

1. Heat up a pan that fits your air fryer with the oil over medium heat, add the meat and brown for 5 minutes. Add the rest of the ingredients, toss, put the pan in the fryer and cook at 380 degrees F for 30 minutes. Divide everything into bowls and serve.

Nutrition:
Calories 284, fat 12, fiber 3, carbs 5, protein 16

Lamb Sausages

Prep time: 25 minutes **Cooking time:** 10 minutes **Servings:** 4

4 sausage links	12 oz ground lamb
1 teaspoon minced garlic	½ teaspoon onion powder
1 teaspoon dried parsley	½ teaspoon salt
1 teaspoon ghee	½ teaspoon ground ginger
1 tablespoon sesame oil	

1. In the mixing bowl mix up ground lamb, minced garlic, onion powder, dried parsley, salt, and ground ginger. Then fill the sausage links with the ground lamb mixture. Secure the ends of the sausages. Brush the air fryer basket with sesame oil from inside and put the sausages. Then sprinkle the sausages with ghee. Cook the lamb sausages for 10 minutes at 400F. Flip them on another side after 5 minutes of cooking.

Nutrition:
Calories 201, fat 10.7, fiber 0.1, carbs 0.7, protein 24

Lamb and Vinaigrette

Preparation time: 10 minutes **Cooking time:** 30 minutes
Servings: 4

4 lamb loin slices	A pinch of salt and black pepper 3 garlic cloves, minced
2 teaspoons thyme, chopped 2 tablespoons olive oil	1/3 cup parsley, chopped
1/3 cup sun-dried tomatoes, chopped 2 tablespoons balsamic vinegar	2 tablespoons water

1. In a blender, combine all the ingredients except the lamb slices and pulse well. In a bowl, mix the lamb with the tomato vinaigrette and toss well.
2. Put the lamb in your air fryer's basket and cook at 380 degrees F for 15 minutes on each side. Divide everything between plates and serve.

Nutrition:
Calories 273, fat 13, fiber 4, carbs 6, protein 17

Ginger and Turmeric Lamb

Prep time: 15 minutes **Cooking time:** 25 minutes **Servings:** 4

16 oz rack of lamb	1 teaspoon ginger paste
½ teaspoon ground ginger	½ teaspoon salt
½ teaspoon ground paprika	¼ teaspoon ground turmeric
1 tablespoon butter, melted	1 teaspoon olive oil

1. In the mixing bowl mix up ground ginger, ginger paste, salt, ground paprika, turmeric, butter, and olive oil. Then brush the rack of lamb with the butter mixture and put it in the air fryer. Cook the rack of lamb for 25 minutes at 380F.

Nutrition:
Calories 229, fat 14.2, fiber 0.2, carbs 0.6, protein 23.2

Parmesan Lamb Cutlets

Preparation time: 5 minutes **Cooking time:** 30 minutes
Servings: 4

8 lamb cutlets	A pinch of salt and black pepper 3 tablespoons mustard
3 tablespoons olive oil	½ cup coconut flakes
¼ cup parmesan, grated	2 tablespoons parsley, chopped 2 tablespoons chives, chopped
1 tablespoon rosemary, chopped	

1. In a bowl, mix the lamb cutlets with all the ingredients except the parmesan and the coconut flakes and toss well. Dredge the cutlets in parmesan and coconut flakes, put them in your air fryer's basket and cook at 390 degrees F for 15 minutes on each side. Divide between plates and serve.

Nutrition:
Calories 284, fat 13, fiber 3, carbs 6, protein 17

Mint and Rosemary Lamb

Prep time: 2 hours **Cooking time:** 35 minutes **Servings:** 2

12 oz leg of lamb, boneless	1 teaspoon dried rosemary
½ teaspoon dried mint	1 garlic clove, diced
½ teaspoon salt	¼ teaspoon ground black pepper
1 teaspoon apple cider vinegar	1 tablespoon olive oil

1. In the mixing bowl mix up dried rosemary, mint, diced garlic, salt, ground black pepper, apple cider vinegar, and olive oil. Then rub the leg of lamb with the spice mixture and leave for 2 hours to marinate. After this, preheat the air fryer to 400F. Put the leg of lamb in the air fryer and sprinkle with all remaining spice mixture. Cook the meal for 25 minutes. Then flip the meat on another side and cook it for 10 minutes more.

Nutrition:
Calories 382, fat 19.6, fiber 0.4, carbs 1.1, protein 47.9

Lamb and Scallion Balls

Preparation time: 5 minutes **Cooking time:** 30 minutes
Servings: 4

½ pounds lamb, ground 1 scallion, chopped	A pinch of salt and black pepper
½ cup pine nuts, toasted and chopped 1 tablespoon thyme, chopped	garlic cloves, minced 1 tablespoon olive oil 1 egg, whisked

1. In a bowl, mix the lamb with the rest of the ingredients except the oil, stir well and shape medium meatballs out of this mix. Grease the meatballs with the oil, put them in your air fryer's basket and cook at 380 degrees F for 15 minutes on each side. Divide between plates and serve with a side salad.

Nutrition:
Calories 287, fat 12, fiber 3, carbs 6, protein 17

Spicy Buttered Steaks

Prep time: 15 minutes **Cooking time:** 17 minutes **Servings:** 4

1-pound beef rib eye steak, bone-in (4 steaks)	1 tablespoon butter
1 teaspoon garlic, diced	½ teaspoon lime zest, grated
½ teaspoon ground paprika	½ teaspoon ground ginger
½ teaspoon chipotle powder	1 teaspoon salt
½ teaspoon chili flakes	

1. Rub the meat steaks with garlic, lime zest, ground paprika, ground ginger, chipotle powder, salt, and chili flakes, Then melt the butter and brush the meat with it. Put the steaks in the air fryer and cook them for 17 minutes at 400F. Flip the meat on another side after 10 minutes of cooking.

Nutrition:
Calories 287, fat 22.9, fiber 1.1, carbs 3, protein 15.7

Moroccan Lamb and Garlic

Preparation time: 5 minutes **Cooking time:** 30 minutes
Servings: 4

8 lamb cutlets	A pinch of salt and black pepper 4 tablespoons olive oil
½ cup mint leaves 6 garlic cloves	1 tablespoon cumin, ground 1 tablespoon coriander seeds Zest of 2 lemons, grated
3 tablespoons lemon juice	

1. In a blender, combine all the ingredients except the lamb and pulse well. Rub the lamb cutlets with this mix, place them in your air fryer's basket and cook at 380 degrees F for 15 minutes on each side. Serve with a side salad.

Nutrition:
Calories 284, fat 13, fiber 3, carbs 5, protein 15

Ribs and Chimichuri Mix

Prep time: 10 minutes **Cooking time:** 35 minutes **Servings:** 4

1-pound pork baby back ribs, boneless	2 tablespoons chimichuri sauce
½ teaspoon salt	

1. Sprinkle the ribs with salt and brush with chimichuri sauce. Then preheat the air fryer to 365F. Put the pork ribs in the air fryer and cook for 35 minutes.

Nutrition:
Calories 504, fat 43.3, fiber 1, carbs 1, protein 25.9

Roasted Lamb

Preparation time: 5 minutes **Cooking time:** 30 minutes
Servings: 4

8 lamb cutlets	2 tablespoons olive oil
A pinch of salt and black pepper 2 tablespoons rosemary, chopped 2 garlic cloves, minced	A pinch of cayenne pepper

1. In a bowl, mix the lamb with the rest of the ingredients and rub well. Put the lamb in the fryer's basket and cook at 380 degrees F for 30 minutes, flipping them halfway. Divide the cutlets between plates and serve.

Nutrition:
Calories 274, fat 12, fiber 3, carbs 5, protein 15

Peppermint Lamb

Prep time: 15 minutes **Cooking time:** 12 minutes **Servings:** 4

1-pound lamb chops	2 oz celery ribs, chopped
½ teaspoon lemon zest, grated	½ teaspoon garlic, minced
½ teaspoon peppermint	1 tablespoon ghee
½ teaspoon ground black pepper	1 teaspoon olive oil

1. Put the celery ribs in the blender. Add lemon zest, garlic, peppermint, ghee, ground black pepper, and olive oil. Pulse the mixture for 1-2 minutes. Then carefully rub the lamb chops with blended mixture and put the meat in the air fryer. Cook the lamb chops for 6 minutes from each side 400F.

Nutrition:
Calories 314, fat 17.5, fiber 0.9, carbs 3.4, protein 34.7

Mustard Chives and Basil Lamb

Preparation time: 10 minutes **Cooking time:** 30 minutes
Servings: 4

8 lamb cutlets	A pinch of salt and black pepper A drizzle of olive oil
2 garlic cloves, minced 1 tablespoon chives, chopped 1 tablespoon basil, chopped	¼ cup mustard 1 tablespoon oregano, chopped 1 tablespoon mint chopped

1. In a bowl, mix the lamb with the rest of the ingredients and rub well. Put the cutlets in your air fryer's basket and cook at 380 degrees F for 15 minutes on each side. Divide between plates and serve with a side salad.

Nutrition:
Calories 284, fat 13, fiber 3, carbs 6, protein 14

Lamb with Paprika Cilantro Sauce

Preparation time: 5 minutes **Cooking time:** 30 minutes
Servings: 4

1 pound lamb, cubed 1 cup coconut cream	3 tablespoons sweet paprika 2 tablespoons olive oil
2 tablespoons cilantro, chopped Salt and black pepper to the taste	

1. Heat up a pan that fits your air fryer with the oil over medium-high heat, add the meat and brown for 5 minutes. Add the rest of the ingredients, toss, put the pan in the air fryer and cook at 380 degrees F for 25 minutes. Divide everything into bowls and serve.

Nutrition:
Calories 287, fat 13, fiber 2, carbs 6, protein 12

Sweet Pork Belly

Prep time: 15 minutes **Cooking time:** 55 minutes **Servings:** 6

1-pound pork belly	1 teaspoon Splenda
1 teaspoon salt	1 teaspoon white pepper
1 teaspoon butter, softened	½ teaspoon onion powder

1. Sprinkle the pork belly with salt, white pepper, and onion powder. Then preheat the air fryer to 385F. Put the pork belly in the air fryer and cook it for 45 minutes. Then turn the pork belly on another side and spread it with butter. After this, top the pork belly with Splenda and cook it at 400f for 10 minutes.

Nutrition:
Calories 359, fat 21, fiber 0.1, carbs 1.1, protein 35

Lamb Chops and Lemon Yogurt Sauce

Preparation time: 5 minutes **Cooking time:** 30 minutes
Servings: 4

4 lamb chops	A pinch of salt and black pepper 1 cup Greek yogurt
2 tablespoons coconut oil, melted 1 teaspoon lemon zest, grated	½ teaspoon turmeric powder

1. In a bowl, mix the lamb chops with the rest of the ingredients and toss well. Put the chops in your air fryer's basket and cook at 380 degrees F for 15 minutes on each side. Divide between plates and serve.

Nutrition:
Calories 283, fat 13, fiber 3, carbs 6, protein 15

Lime Meatballs

Prep time: 15 minutes **Cooking time:** 7 minutes **Servings:** 4

½ teaspoon lime zest, grated	1 tablespoon lime juice
10 oz ground lamb	1 teaspoon ground black pepper
1 garlic clove, minced	½ teaspoon minced ginger
1 teaspoon avocado oil	

1. In the mixing bowl mix up lime zest, lime juice, ground lamb, minced garlic, and ginger. With the help of the scooper make the meatballs and put them in the freezer for 5-10 minutes. Meanwhile, preheat the air fryer to 380F. Brush the air fryer basket with avocado oil from inside and put the meatballs. Cook them for 7 minutes.

Nutrition:

Calories 138, fat 5.4, fiber 0.3, carbs 1.1, protein 20.1

Cinnamon Lamb Meatloaf

Prep time: 5 minutes **Cooking time:** 35 minutes **Servings:** 4

pounds lamb, ground	A pinch of salt and black pepper
½ teaspoon hot paprika A drizzle of olive oil	2 tablespoons parsley, chopped 2 tablespoons cilantro, chopped 1 teaspoon cumin, ground
¼ teaspoon cinnamon powder 1 teaspoon coriander, ground 1 egg 1 teaspoon lemon juice	2 tablespoons keto tomato sauce 4 scallions, chopped

1. In a bowl, combine the lamb with the rest of the ingredients except the oil and stir really well. Grease a loaf pan that fits the air fryer with the oil, add the lamb mix and shape the meatloaf. Put the pan in the air fryer and cook at 380 degrees F for 35 minutes. Slice and serve.

Nutrition:

Calories 263, fat 12, fiber 3, carbs 6, protein 15

Salty Lamb Chops

Prep time: 15 minutes **Cooking time:** 8 minutes **Servings:** 4

1-pound lamb chops	1 egg, beaten
½ teaspoon salt	½ cup coconut flour
Cooking spray	

1. Chop the lamb chops into small pieces (popcorn) and sprinkle with salt. Then add a beaten egg and stir the meat well. After this, add coconut flour and shake the lamb popcorn until all meat pieces are coated. Preheat the air fryer to 380F. Put the lamb popcorn in the air fryer and spray it with cooking spray. Cook the lamb popcorn for 4 minutes. Then shake the meat well and cook it for 4 minutes more.

Nutrition:

Calories 297, fat 11.9, fiber 6, carbs 9.1, protein 36.2

Peppercorn Lamb with Rhubarb

Preparation time: 5 minutes **Cooking time:** 30 minutes **Servings:** 4

1 and ½ pound lamb ribs	A pinch of salt and black pepper
1 tablespoon black peppercorns, ground 1 tablespoon white peppercorns, ground 1 tablespoon fennel seeds, ground	tablespoon coriander seeds, ground 4 rhubarb stalks, chopped
¼ cup balsamic vinegar 2 tablespoons olive oil	

1. Heat up a pan that fits your air fryer with the oil over medium heat, add the lamb and brown for 2 minutes. Add the rest of the ingredients, toss, bring to a simmer for 2 minutes and take off the heat. Put the pan in the fryer and cook at 380 degrees for 25 minutes. Divide everything into bowls and serve.

Nutrition:

Calories 283, fat 13, fiber 2, carbs 6, protein 17

Orange Carne Asada

Prep time: 15 minutes **Cooking time:** 14 minutes **Servings:** 4

¼ lime	2 tablespoons orange juice
1 teaspoon dried cilantro	1 chili pepper, chopped
1 tablespoon sesame oil	1 tablespoon apple cider vinegar
½ teaspoon chili paste	½ teaspoon ground cumin
½ teaspoon salt	1-pound beef skirt steak

1. Chop the lime roughly and put it in the blender. Add orange juice, dried cilantro, chili pepper, sesame oil, apple cider vinegar, chili paste, ground cumin, and salt. Blend the mixture until smooth. Cut the skirt steak on 4 servings. Then brush every steak with blended lime mixture and leave for 10 minutes to marinate. Meanwhile, preheat the air fryer to 400F. Put the steaks in the air fryer in one layer and cook them for 7 minutes. Flip the meat on another side and cook it for 7 minutes more.

Nutrition:

Calories 272, fat 15, fiber 0.2, carbs 1.7, protein 30.4

Vegetable Recipes

Turmeric Zucchini Patties

Prep time: 15 minutes **Cooking time:** 10 minutes **Servings:** 4

2 zucchinis, trimmed, grated	1 egg yolk
½ teaspoon salt	1 teaspoon ground turmeric
½ teaspoon ground paprika	1 teaspoon cream cheese
3 tablespoons flax meal	1 teaspoon sesame oil

1. Squeeze the juice from the zucchinis and put them in the big bowl. Add egg yolk, salt, ground turmeric, ground paprika, flax meal, and cream cheese. Stir the mixture well with the help of the spoon. Then make medium size patties from the zucchini mixture. Preheat the air fryer to 385F. Brush the air fryer basket with sesame oil and put the patties inside. Cook them for 5 minutes from each side.

Nutrition:

Calories 67, fat 4.7 fiber 2.8, carbs 5.5, protein 3.1

Herbed Asparagus and Sauce

Preparation time: 4 minutes **Cooking time:** 10 minutes **Servings:** 4

1 pound asparagus, trimmed 2 tablespoons olive oil	A pinch of salt and black pepper 1 teaspoon garlic powder
1 teaspoon oregano, dried	cup basil, chopped
1 cup Greek yogurt	
½ cup parsley, chopped	¼ cup chives, chopped
¼ cup lemon juice	garlic cloves, minced

1. In a bowl, mix the asparagus with the oil, salt, pepper, oregano and garlic powder, and toss. Put the asparagus in the air fryer's basket and cook at 400 degrees F for 10 minutes. Meanwhile, in a blender, mix the yogurt with basil, chives, parsley, lemon juice and garlic cloves and pulse well. Divide the asparagus between plates, drizzle the sauce all over and serve.

Nutrition:

Calories 194, fat 6, fiber 2, carbs 4, protein 8

Cheesy Green Patties

Prep time: 20 minutes **Cooking time:** 6 minutes **Servings:** 2

1 ½ cup fresh spinach, chopped	3 oz provolone cheese, shredded
1 egg, beaten	¼ cup almond flour
½ teaspoon salt	Cooking spray

1. Put the chopped spinach in the blender and blend it until you get a smooth mixture. After this, transfer the grinded spinach in the big bowl. Add shredded provolone cheese, beaten egg, almond flour, and salt. Stir the spinach mixture with the help of the spoon until it is homogenous. Then make the patties from the spinach mixture. Preheat the air fryer to 400F. Spray the air fryer basket with cooking spray from inside and put the spinach patties. Cook them for 3 minutes and then flip on another side.
2. Cook the patties for 3 minutes more or until they are light brown.

Nutrition:

Calories 206, fat 15.4, fiber 0.9, carbs 2.7, protein 15

Balsamic Asparagus and Tomatoes

Preparation time: 5 minutes **Cooking time:** 10 minutes **Servings:** 4

pound asparagus, trimmed	cups cherry tomatoes, halved
¼ cup parmesan, grated	½ cup balsamic vinegar 2 tablespoons olive oil
A pinch of salt and black pepper	

1. In a bowl, mix the asparagus with the rest of the ingredients except the parmesan, and toss. Put the asparagus and tomatoes in your air fryer's basket and cook at 400 degrees F for 10 minutes Divide between plates and serve with the parmesan sprinkled on top.

Nutrition:

Calories 173, fat 4, fiber 2, carbs 4, protein 8

Mozzarella Green Beans

Prep time: 10 minutes **Cooking time:** 6 minutes **Servings:** 4

1 cup green beans, trimmed	2 oz Mozzarella, shredded
1 teaspoon butter	½ teaspoon chili flakes
¼ cup beef broth	

1. Sprinkle the green beans with chili flakes and put in the air fryer baking pan. Add beef broth and butter. Then top the vegetables with shredded Mozzarella. Preheat the air fryer to 400F. Put the pan with green beans in the air fryer and cook the meal for 6 minutes.

Nutrition:

Calories 80, fat 3.7, fiber 1.9, carbs 5.8, protein 6.3

Cheddar Asparagus

Preparation time: 5 minutes **Cooking time:** 10 minutes **Servings:** 4

2 pounds asparagus, trimmed	2 tablespoons olive oil
1 cup cheddar cheese, shredded 4 garlic cloves, minced	4 bacon slices, cooked and crumbled

1. In a bowl, mix the asparagus with the other ingredients except the bacon, toss and put in your air fryer's basket. Cook at 400 degrees F for 10 minutes, divide between plates, sprinkle the bacon on top and serve.

Nutrition:

Calories 172, fat 6, fiber 2, carbs 5, protein 8

Sesame Fennel

Prep time: 10 minutes **Cooking time:** 15 minutes **Servings:** 2

8 oz fennel bulb	1 teaspoon sesame oil
½ teaspoon salt	1 teaspoon white pepper

1. Trim the fennel bulb and cut it into halves. Then sprinkle the fennel bulb with salt, white pepper, and sesame oil. Preheat the air fryer to 370F. Put the fennel bulb halves in the air fryer and cook them for 15 minutes.

Nutrition:

Calories 58, fat 2.5, fiber 3.8, carbs 9, protein 1.5

Mustard Garlic Asparagus

Preparation time: 5 minutes **Cooking time:** 12 minutes
Servings: 4

1 pound asparagus, trimmed	2 tablespoons olive oil
¼ cup mustard	3 garlic cloves, minced
½ cup parmesan, grated	

1. In a bowl, mix the asparagus with the oil, garlic and mustard and toss really well. Put the asparagus spears in your air fryer's basket and cook at 400 degrees F for 12 minutes. Divide between plates, sprinkle the parmesan on top and serve.

Nutrition:
Calories 162, fat 4, fiber 4, carbs 6, protein 9

Mozzarella Asparagus Mix

Preparation time: 5 minutes **Cooking time:** 10 minutes
Servings: 4

pound asparagus, trimmed	A pinch of salt and black pepper 2 cups mozzarella, shredded
2 tablespoons olive oil	
½ cup balsamic vinegar	cups cherry tomatoes, halved

1. In a pan that fits your air fryer, mix the asparagus with the rest of the ingredients except the mozzarella and toss. Put the pan in the air fryer and cook at 400 degrees F for 10 minutes. Divide between plates and serve.

Nutrition:
Calories 200, fat 6, fiber 2, carbs 3, protein 6

Thyme Radish Mix

Prep time: 10 minutes **Cooking time:** 5 minutes **Servings:** 3

2 cups radish, trimmed	½ teaspoon onion powder
½ teaspoon salt	½ teaspoon thyme
½ teaspoon ground black pepper	½ teaspoon ground paprika
1 teaspoon ghee	

1. Chop the radish roughly and mix it up with onion powder, salt, thyme, ground black pepper, ad paprika. After this, preheat the air fryer to 375F. Put the roughly chopped radish in the air fryer and cook it for 2 minutes. Then add ghee, shake well and cook the vegetables for 3 minutes more.

Nutrition:
Calories 29, fat 1.6, fiber 1.5, carbs 3.5, protein 0.7

Paprika Asparagus

Preparation time: 5 minutes **Cooking time:** 10 minutes
Servings: 4

1 pound asparagus, trimmed 3 tablespoons olive oil	A pinch of salt and black pepper 1 tablespoon sweet paprika

1. In a bowl, mix the asparagus with the rest of the ingredients and toss. Put the asparagus in your air fryer's basket and cook at 400 degrees F for 10 minutes. Divide between plates and serve.

Nutrition:
Calories 200, fat 5, fiber 2, carbs 4, protein 6

Nutmeg Okra

Prep time: 10 minutes **Cooking time:** 10 minutes **Servings:** 4

1-pound okra, trimmed	3 oz pancetta, sliced
½ teaspoon ground nutmeg	½ teaspoon salt
1 teaspoon sunflower oil	

1. Sprinkle okra with ground nutmeg and salt. Then put the vegetables in the air fryer and sprinkle with sunflower. Chop pancetta roughly. Top the okra with pancetta and cook the meal for 10 minutes at 360F.

Nutrition:
Calories 172, fat 10.4, fiber 3.7, carbs 8.9, protein 10.1

Lemon Asparagus

Preparation time: 5 minutes **Cooking time:** 12 minutes
Servings: 4

1 pound asparagus, trimmed	A pinch of salt and black pepper 2 tablespoons olive oil
3 garlic cloves, minced	3 tablespoons parmesan, grated Juice of 1 lemon

1. In a bowl, mix the asparagus with the rest of the ingredients and toss. Put the asparagus in your air fryer's basket and cook at 390 degrees F for 12 minutes. Divide between plates and serve.

Nutrition:
Calories 175, fat 5, fiber 2, carbs 4, protein 8

Feta Peppers

Prep time: 15 minutes **Cooking time:** 10 minutes **Servings:** 4

5 oz Feta, crumbled	8 oz banana pepper, trimmed
1 teaspoon sesame oil	1 garlic clove, minced
½ teaspoon fresh dill, chopped	1 teaspoon lemon juice
½ teaspoon lime zest, grated	

1. Clean the seeds from the peppers and cut them into halves. Then sprinkle the peppers with sesame oil and put in the air fryer. Cook them for 10 minutes at 385F. Flip the peppers on another side after 5 minutes of cooking. Meanwhile, mix up minced garlic, fresh dill, lemon juice, and lime zest. Put the cooked banana peppers on the plate and sprinkle with lemon juice mixture. Then top the vegetables with crumbled feta.

Nutrition:
Calories 107, fat 8.7, fiber 0.2, carbs 2.2, protein 5.2

Spicy Kale

Preparation time: 5 minutes **Cooking time:** 10 minutes
Servings: 4

1 pound kale, torn	1 tablespoon olive oil 1 teaspoon hot paprika
A pinch of salt and black pepper 2 tablespoons oregano, chopped	

1. In a pan that fits the air fryer, combine all the ingredients and toss. Put the pan in the air fryer and cook at 380 degrees F for 10 minutes. Divide between plates and serve.

Nutrition:
Calories 140, fat 3, fiber 2, carbs 3, protein 5

Buffalo Broccoli

Prep time: 15 minutes **Cooking time:** 6 minutes **Servings:** 4

2 cups broccoli florets	¼ cup of coconut milk
½ teaspoon salt	½ teaspoon chili flakes
1/3 cup coconut flour	1 tablespoon Buffalo sauce
Cooking spray	

1. Sprinkle the broccoli florets with salt and chili flakes. Then dip them in the coconut milk and coat in the coconut flour. Preheat the air fryer to 400F. Put the broccoli florets in the air fryer, spray with cooking spray, and cook them for 6 minutes. When the broccoli is cooked, transfer in the bowl and sprinkle with Buffalo sauce.

Nutrition:
Calories 98, fat 5.4, fiber 5.6, carbs 10.1, protein 3.6

Kale and Sprouts

Prep time: 5 minutes **Cooking time:** 15 minutes **Servings:** 8

1 pound Brussels sprouts, trimmed 2 cups kale, torn	tablespoon olive oil
Salt and black pepper to the taste 3 ounces mozzarella, shredded	

1. In a pan that fits the air fryer, combine all the ingredients except the mozzarella and toss. Put the pan in the air fryer and cook at 380 degrees F for 15 minutes. Divide between plates, sprinkle the cheese on top and serve.

Nutrition:
Calories 170, fat 5, fiber 3, carbs 4, protein 7

Paprika Leeks

Prep time: 15 minutes **Cooking time:** 8 minutes **Servings:** 3

2 big leeks, roughly sliced	1 egg, beaten
½ teaspoon ground paprika	½ teaspoon salt
½ teaspoon ground turmeric	2 tablespoons almond flour
Cooking spray	

1. Sprinkle the leek slices with ground paprika, salt, and ground turmeric. After this, dip every leek slice in the egg and coat in the almond flour. Preheat the air fryer to 400f and put the leek bites inside. Spray them with the cooking spray and cook for 8 minutes. Shake after 4 minutes of cooking.

Nutrition:
Calories 150, fat 10.9, fiber 3.3, carbs 9.2, protein 6.5

Coconut Broccoli

Prep time: 5 minutes **Cooking time:** 30 minutes **Servings:** 4

3 tablespoons ghee, melted	2 cups cheddar, grated 1
15 ounces coconut cream	cup parmesan, grated 1
2 eggs, whisked	tablespoon mustard
1 pound broccoli florets	A pinch of salt and black pepper 1 tablespoon parsley, chopped

1. Grease a baking pan that fits the air fryer with the ghee and arrange the broccoli on the bottom. Add the cream, mustard, salt, pepper and the eggs and toss. Sprinkle the cheese on top, put the pan in the air fryer and cook at 380 degrees F for 30 minutes. Divide between plates and serve.

Nutrition:
Calories 244, fat 12, fiber 3, carbs 5, protein 12

Zucchini and Squash Mix

Prep time: 15 minutes **Cooking time:** 12 minutes **Servings:** 4

10 oz Kabocha squash	½ zucchini, chopped
3 spring onions, chopped	1 teaspoon dried thyme
2 teaspoons ghee	1 teaspoon salt
1 teaspoon ground turmeric	

1. Chop the squash into small cubes and sprinkle with salt and ground turmeric. Put the squash in the bowl, add zucchini, spring onions, dried thyme, and ghee. Shake the vegetables gently. Preheat the air fryer to 400F. Put the vegetable mixture in the air fryer and cook for 12 minutes. Shake the vegetables after 6 minutes of cooking to avoid burning.

Nutrition:
Calories 45, fat 1.8, fiber 1.3, carbs 6.8, protein 1.1

Broccoli and Cranberries Mix

Preparation time: 5 minutes **Cooking time:** 25 minutes **Servings:** 4

1 broccoli head, florets separated 2 shallots, chopped	A pinch of salt and black pepper
½ cup cranberries	½ cup almonds, chopped
6 bacon slices, cooked and crumbled 3 tablespoons balsamic vinegar	

1. In a pan that fits the air fryer, combine the broccoli with the rest of the ingredients and toss. Put the pan in the air fryer and cook at 380 degrees F for 25 minutes. Divide between plates and serve.

Nutrition:
Calories 173, fat 7, fiber 2, carbs 4, protein 8

Coconut Kohlrabi Mash

Prep time: 10 minutes **Cooking time:** 20 minute **Servings:** 6

12 oz kohlrabi, chopped	2 tablespoons coconut cream
1 teaspoon salt	½ cup Monterey Jack cheese, shredded
¼ cup chicken broth	½ teaspoon chili flakes

1. In the air fryer pan mix up kohlrabi, coconut cream, salt, Monterey jack cheese, chicken broth, and chili flakes. Then preheat the air fryer to 255F. Cook the meal for 20 minutes.

Nutrition:
Calories 64, fat 4.2, fiber 2.2, carbs 3.9, protein 3.6

Broccoli and Scallions Sauce

Preparation time: 5 minutes **Cooking time:** 15 minutes **Servings:** 4

1 broccoli head, florets separated Salt and black pepper to the taste	½ cup keto tomato sauce
1 tablespoon sweet paprika	¼ cup scallions, chopped 1 tablespoon olive oil

1. In a pan that fits the air fryer, combine the broccoli with the rest of the ingredients, toss, put the pan in the fryer and cook at 380 degrees F for 15 minutes. Divide between plates and serve.

Nutrition:
Calories 163, fat 5, fiber 2, carbs 4, protein 8

Cheesy Rutabaga

Prep time: 15 minutes **Cooking time:** 8 minutes **Servings:** 2

6 oz rutabaga, chopped	2 oz Jarlsberg cheese, grated
1 tablespoon butter	½ teaspoon dried parsley
½ teaspoon salt	½ teaspoon minced garlic
3 tablespoons heavy cream	

1. In the mixing bowl mix up a rutabaga, dried parsley, salt, and minced garlic. Then add heavy cream and mix up the vegetables well. After this, preheat the air fryer to 375F. Put the rutabaga mixture in the air fryer and cook it for 6 minutes. Then stir it well and top with grated cheese. Cook the meal for 2 minutes more. Transfer the cooked rutabaga in the plates and top with butter.

Nutrition:

Calories 262, fat 22.4, fiber 2.2, carbs 7.8, protein 8.7

Chili Lime Broccoli

Preparation time: 5 minutes **Cooking time:** 15 minutes **Servings:** 4

pound broccoli florets 2 tablespoons olive oil	tablespoons chili sauce Juice of 1 lime
A pinch of salt and black pepper	

1. In a bowl, mix the broccoli with the other ingredients and toss well. Put the broccoli in your air fryer's basket and cook at 400 degrees F for 15 minutes. Divide between plates and serve.

Nutrition:

Calories 173, fat 6, fiber 2, carbs 6, protein 8

Paprika Jicama

Prep time: 15 minutes **Cooking time:** 7 minutes **Servings:** 5

15 oz jicama, peeled	½ teaspoon salt
½ teaspoon ground paprika	½ teaspoon chili flakes
1 teaspoon sesame oil	

1. Preheat the air fryer to 400F. Cut Jicama into the small sticks and sprinkle with salt, ground paprika, and chili flakes. Then put the Jicama stick in the air fryer and sprinkle with sesame oil. Cook the vegetables for 4 minutes. Then shake them well and cook for 3 minutes.

Nutrition:

Calories 34, fat 0.8, fiber 3.5, carbs 6.4, protein 0.5

Parmesan Veggie Mix

Preparation time: 5 minutes **Cooking time:** 15 minutes **Servings:** 4

1 broccoli head, florets separated	½ pound asparagus, trimmed Juice of 1 lime
Salt and black pepper to the taste 2 tablespoons olive oil	3 tablespoons parmesan, grated

1. In a bowl, mix the asparagus with the broccoli and all the other ingredients except the parmesan, toss, transfer to your air fryer's basket and cook at 400 degrees F for 15 minutes. Divide between plates, sprinkle the parmesan on top and serve.

Nutrition:

Calories 172, fat 5, fiber 2, carbs 4, protein 9

Squash Noodles

Prep time: 20 minutes **Cooking time:** 5 minutes **Servings:** 4

12 oz scallop squash	1 teaspoon butter, softened
1 oz Parmesan, grated	1 teaspoon sesame oil
¼ teaspoon cayenne pepper	

1. Make the noodles from the scallop squash. Use the spiralizer for this step. Then place the vegetable noodles in the air fryer and sprinkle with sesame oil. Cook them for 5 minutes at 385F. Transfer the cooked noodles in the serving plates and sprinkle with butter and cayenne pepper. Then top the vegetables with Parmesan,

Nutrition:

Calories 57, fat 3.8, fiber 0, carbs 3.6, protein 3.3

Almond Broccoli and Chives

Preparation time: 5 minutes **Cooking time:** 12 minutes **Servings:** 4

1 pound broccoli florets 3 garlic cloves, minced	A pinch of salt and black pepper 3 tablespoons coconut oil, melted
½ cup almonds, chopped	1 tablespoon chives, chopped 2 tablespoons red vinegar

1. In a bowl, mix the broccoli with the garlic, salt, pepper, vinegar and the oil and toss. Put the broccoli in your air fryer's basket and cook at 380 degrees F for 12 minutes. Divide between plates and serve with almonds and chives sprinkled on top.

Nutrition:

Calories 180, fat 4, fiber 2, carbs 4, protein 6

Cayenne Eggplant Puree

Prep time: 15 minutes **Cooking time:** 15 minutes **Servings:** 2

1 large eggplant, trimmed, peeled	1 teaspoon cayenne pepper
¼ cup chicken broth	1 garlic clove, peeled
½ teaspoon salt	1 teaspoon dried parsley
½ teaspoon avocado oil	

1. Sprinkle the eggplant with salt and avocado oil. Put it in the air fryer and cook for 15 minutes at 390F. Then cool the cooked eggplant gently and chop roughly. Transfer it in the blender. Add chicken broth, cayenne pepper, garlic, and dried parsley. Grind the mixture until it smooth.
2. Transfer the cooked meal in the bowl.

Nutrition:

Calories 69, fat 0.9, fiber 8.4, carbs 14.7, protein 3.1

Butter Broccoli

Preparation time: 5 minutes **Cooking time:** 15 minutes **Servings:** 4

pound broccoli florets	A pinch of salt and black pepper
1 teaspoons sweet paprika	½ tablespoon butter, melted

1. In a bowl, mix the broccoli with the rest of the ingredients, and toss. Put the broccoli in your air fryer's basket, cook at 350 degrees F for 15 minutes, divide between plates and serve.

Nutrition:

Calories 130, fat 3, fiber 3, carbs 4, protein 8

Swiss Asparagus

Prep time: 10 minutes **Cooking time:** 6 minutes **Servings:** 4

12 oz asparagus, trimmed	2 eggs, beaten
¼ cup Swiss cheese, shredded	½ cup coconut flour
1 teaspoon olive oil	1 teaspoon salt

1. In the mixing bowl mix up Swiss cheese, coconut flour, and salt. Then dip the asparagus in the beaten eggs and coat in the coconut flour mixture.
2. Repeat the same steps one more time and transfer the coated asparagus in the air fryer basket. Cook the vegetables for 6 minutes at 395F.

Nutrition:
Calories 154, fat 7.8, fiber 7.8, carbs 12.8, protein 9.5

Halloumi Skewers

Prep time: 15 minutes **Cooking time:** 14 minutes **Servings:** 4

10 oz halloumi cheese	1 eggplant
1 green bell pepper	1 teaspoon dried cilantro
1 tablespoon avocado oil	½ teaspoon salt
1 teaspoon chili flakes	

1. Chop eggplant, pepper, and eggplant roughly. Then chop halloumi. Put all ingredients from the list above in the big bowl and shake well. Then string the ingredients on the wooden skewers and place in the air fryer. Cook the kebabs for 14 minutes at 400F. Flip the kebabs on another side after 6 minutes of cooking.

Nutrition:
Calories 301, fat 21.9, fiber 4.6, carbs 11, protein 16.8

Coconut Parmesan Kale

Preparation time: 5 minutes **Cooking time:** 15 minutes **Servings:** 4

2 pounds kale, torn	A pinch of salt and black pepper 2 tablespoons olive oil
2 garlic cloves, minced	1 and ½ cups coconut cream
½ teaspoon nutmeg, ground	½ cup parmesan, grated

1. In a pan that fits your air fryer, mix the kale with the rest of the ingredients, toss, introduce the pan in the fryer and cook at 400 degrees F for 15 minutes. Divide between plates and serve.

Nutrition:
Calories 135, fat 3, fiber 2, carbs 4, protein 6

Garlic Balsamic Tomatoes

Preparation time: 5 minutes **Cooking time:** 15 minutes **Servings:** 4

1 tablespoon olive oil	1 pound cherry tomatoes, halved 1 tablespoon dill, chopped
6 garlic cloves, minced	1 tablespoon balsamic vinegar Salt and black pepper to the taste

1. In a pan that fits the air fryer, combine all the ingredients, toss gently, put the pan in the air fryer and cook at 380 degrees F for 15 minutes. Divide between plates and serve.

Nutrition:
Calories 121, fat 3, fiber 2, carbs 4, protein 6

Lime Kale and Bell Peppers Bowls

Prep time: 5 minutes **Cooking time:** 10 minutes **Servings:** 4

cups kale, torn	A pinch of salt and black pepper
1 and ½ cups avocado, peeled, pitted and cubed 1 cup red bell pepper, sliced	¼ cup olive oil
tablespoon mustard	tablespoons lime juice
tablespoon white vinegar	

1. In a pan that fits the air fryer, combine the kale with salt, pepper, avocado and half of the oil, toss, put in your air fryer and cook at 360 degrees F for 10 minutes. In a bowl, combine the kale mix with the rest of the ingredients, toss and serve.

Nutrition:
Calories 131, fat 3, fiber 2, carbs 4, protein 5

Okra Salad

Prep time: 10 minutes **Cooking time:** 6 minutes **Servings:** 2

6 oz okra, sliced	3 oz green beans, chopped
1 cup arugula, chopped	1 teaspoon lemon juice
1 teaspoon olive oil	½ teaspoon salt
2 eggs, beaten	1 tablespoon coconut flakes
Cooking spray	

1. In the mixing bowl mix up sliced okra and green beans. Add cooking spray and salt and mix up the mixture well. Then add beaten eggs and shake it. After this, sprinkle the vegetables with coconut flakes and shake okra and green beans to coat them in the coconut flakes. Preheat the air fryer to 400F. Put the vegetable mixture in the air fryer and cook it for 6 minutes. Shake the mixture after 3 minutes of cooking. After this, mix up cooked vegetables with arugula, lemon juice, and sprinkle with olive oil. Shake the salad.

Nutrition:
Calories 142, fat 7.8, fiber 4.6, carbs 10.5, protein 8.3

Balsamic Garlic Kale

Preparation time: 2 minutes **Cooking time:** 12 minutes **Servings:** 6

tablespoons olive oil 3 garlic cloves, minced	2 and ½ pounds kale leaves
Salt and black pepper to the taste 2 tablespoons balsamic vinegar	

1. In a pan that fits the air fryer, combine all the ingredients and toss. Put the pan in your air fryer and cook at 300 degrees F for 12 minutes. Divide between plates and serve.

Nutrition:
Calories 122, fat 4, fiber 3, carbs 4, protein 5

Paprika Kale and Olives

Prep time: 5 minutes **Cooking time:** 15 minutes **Servings:** 4

an ½ pounds kale, torn 2 tablespoons olive oil tablespoons black olives, pitted and sliced	Salt and black pepper to the taste 1 tablespoon hot paprika

1. In a pan that fits the air fryer, combine all the ingredients and toss. Put the pan in your air fryer, cook at 370 degrees F for 15 minutes, divide between plates and serve.

Nutrition:
Calories 154, fat 3, fiber 2, carbs 4, protein 6

Creamy Cauliflower

Prep time: 10 minutes **Cooking time:** 12 minutes **Servings:** 4

1-pound cauliflower	1 teaspoon taco seasonings
1 tablespoon heavy cream	1 teaspoon olive oil

1. Chop the cauliflower roughly and sprinkle it with taco seasonings and heavy cream. Then sprinkle the cauliflower with olive oil. Preheat the air fryer to 400F. Cook it for 12 minutes. Shake the vegetables every 3 minutes.

Nutrition:

Calories 56, fat 2.7, fiber 2.8, carbs 7.1, protein 2.3

Roasted Cauliflower

Prep time: 15 minutes **Cooking time:** 25 minutes **Servings:** 4

12 oz cauliflower head	2 tablespoons butter, melted
1 teaspoon ground turmeric	½ teaspoon salt
¼ teaspoon cayenne pepper	1 bacon slice, chopped

1. In the mixing bowl mix up butter, ground turmeric, salt, and cayenne pepper Then fill the cauliflower head with chopped bacon. After this, brush the vegetable with melted butter mixture generously. Preheat the air fryer to 365F. Put the cauliflower head in the air fryer basket and cook it for 25 minutes.

Nutrition:

Calories 100, fat 7.9, fiber 2.3, carbs 5, protein 3.6

Coconut Mushrooms Mix

Preparation time: 5 minutes **Cooking time:** 15 minutes **Servings:** 4

1 pound brown mushrooms, sliced 1 pound kale, torn	Salt and black pepper to the taste 2 tablespoons olive oil
14 ounces coconut milk	

1. In a pan that fits your air fryer, mix the kale with the rest of the ingredients and toss. Put the pan in the fryer, cook at 380 degrees F for 15 minutes, divide between plates and serve.

Nutrition:

Calories 162, fat 4, fiber 1, carbs 3, protein 5

Cilantro Broccoli Mix

Preparation time: 5 minutes **Cooking time:** 15 minutes **Servings:** 4

1 broccoli head, florets separated 2 cups cherry tomatoes, quartered A pinch of salt and black pepper 1 tablespoon cilantro, chopped Juice of 1 lime	A drizzle of olive oil

1. In a pan that fits the air fryer, combine the broccoli with tomatoes and the rest of the ingredients except the cilantro, toss, put the pan in the air fryer and cook at 380 degrees F for 15 minutes. Divide between plates and serve with cilantro sprinkled on top.

Nutrition:

Calories 141, fat 3, fiber 2, carbs 4, protein 5

Cumin Garlic

Prep time: 5 minutes **Cooking time:** 10 minutes **Servings:** 4

2 garlic bulbs	½ teaspoon cumin seeds
1 teaspoon olive oil	

1. In the shallow bowl mix up cumin seeds and olive oil. Then brush the garlic bulbs with oil mixture and put them in the air fryer. Cook the garlic for 10 minutes at 375F.

Nutrition:

Calories 18, fat 1.2, fiber 0, carbs 1.6, protein 0.1

Rosemary Olives Mix

Preparation time: 5 minutes **Cooking time:** 15 minutes **Servings:** 4

cups black olives, pitted and halved A handful basil, chopped	2 rosemary springs, chopped 2 red bell peppers, sliced
12 ounces tomatoes, chopped 4 garlic cloves, minced	2 tablespoons olive oil

1. In a pan that fits the air fryer, combine the olives with the rest of the ingredients, toss, put the pan in the fryer and cook at 380 degrees F for 15 minutes. Divide between plates and serve.

Nutrition:

Calories 173, fat 6, fiber 2, carbs 4, protein 5

Almond Eggplant Meatballs

Prep time: 15 minutes **Cooking time:** 8 minutes **Servings:** 7

3 eggplants, peeled, boiled	1 egg, beaten
1 teaspoon minced garlic	3 spring onions, chopped
½ cup almond flour	1 teaspoon chives
½ teaspoon chili flakes	½ teaspoon salt
1 teaspoon sesame oil	

1. Chop the boiled eggplants and squeeze the juice from them. After this, transfer the eggplants in the blender. Add egg, minced garlic, spring onions, almond flour, chives, chili flakes, and salt. Grind the mixture until it is homogenous and smooth. After this, make the eggplant meatballs from the mixture with the help of the scooper. Preheat the air fryer to 380F. Put the eggplant meatballs in the air fryer and sprinkle them with sesame oil. Cook the meatballs for 8 minutes.

Nutrition:

Calories 87, fat 2.7, fiber 8.6, carbs 14.8, protein 3.6

Mustard Cabbage

Prep time: 10 minutes **Cooking time:** 40 minutes **Servings:** 4

1-pound white cabbage	1 teaspoon mustard
1 teaspoon ground black pepper	½ teaspoon salt
3 tablespoons butter, melted	½ teaspoon ground paprika
½ teaspoon chili flakes	1 teaspoon dried thyme

1. In the mixing bowl mix up mustard, ground black pepper, salt, butter, ground paprika, chili flakes, and dried thyme. Brush the cabbage with the mustard mixture generously and place it in the air fryer. Cook the cabbage for 40 minutes at 365F. Then cool the cooked vegetable to the room temperature and slice into servings.

Nutrition:

Calories 111, fat 9.1, fiber 3.3, carbs 7.5, protein 1.9

Dill Green
Cajun Zucchini and Broccoli

Prep time: 10 minutes **Cooking time:** 15 minutes **Servings:** 2

½ zucchini, chopped	2 spring onions, chopped
¼ cup broccoli, chopped	1 teaspoon Cajun seasonings
1 teaspoon nut oil	2 oz fennel bulb, chopped

1. In the mixing bowl mix up all ingredients. Then preheat the air fryer to 385F. Put the mixture in the air fryer and cook it for 15 minutes. Shake the vegetables every 5 minutes.

Nutrition:
Calories 46, fat 2.5, fiber 2, carbs 5.8, protein 1.4

Lime Olives and Zucchini

Preparation time: 5 minutes **Cooking time:** 12 minutes **Servings:** 4

4 zucchinis, sliced	cup kalamata olives, pitted Salt and black pepper to the taste 2 tablespoons lime juice
tablespoons olive oil	2 teaspoons balsamic vinegar

1. In a pan that fits your air fryer, mix the olives with all the other ingredients, toss, introduce in the fryer and cook at 390 degrees F for 12 minutes. Divide the mix between plates and serve.

Nutrition:
Calories 150, fat 4, fiber 2, carbs 4, protein 5

Cream Cheese Green Beans

Prep time: 15 minutes **Cooking time:** 5 minutes **Servings:** 2

8 oz green beans	1 egg, beaten
1 teaspoon cream cheese	¼ cup almond flour
¼ cup coconut flakes	½ teaspoon ground black pepper
½ teaspoon salt	1 teaspoon sesame oil

1. In the mixing bowl mix up cream cheese, egg, and ground black pepper. Add salt. In the separated bowl mix up coconut flakes and almond flour. Preheat the air fryer to 400F. Dip the green beans in the egg mixture and then coat in the coconut flakes mixture. Repeat the step one more time and transfer the vegetables in the air fryer. Sprinkle them with sesame oil and cook for 5 minutes. Shake the vegetables after 2 minutes of cooking if you don't put green beans in one layer.

Nutrition:
Calories 149, fat 10.3, fiber 5.3, carbs 10.9, protein 6.1

Tomato Artichokes Mix

Preparation time: 5 minutes **Cooking time:** 15 minutes **Servings:** 4

14 ounces artichoke hearts, drained 1 tablespoon olive oil	2 cups black olives, pitted
	3 garlic cloves, minced
½ cup keto tomato sauce 1 teaspoon garlic powder	

1. In a pan that fits your air fryer, mix the olives with the artichokes and the other ingredients, toss, put the pan in the fryer and cook at 350 degrees F for 15 minutes. Divide the mix between plates and serve.

Nutrition:
Calories 180, fat 4, fiber 3, carbs 5, protein 6

Taco Okra

Prep time: 10 minutes **Cooking time:** 10 minutes **Servings:** 3

9 oz okra, chopped	1 teaspoon taco seasoning
1 teaspoon sunflower oil	

1. In the mixing bowl mix up chopped okra, taco seasoning, and sunflower oil. Then preheat the air fryer to 385F. Put the okra mixture in the air fryer and cook it for 5 minutes. Then shake the vegetables well and cook them for 5 minutes more.

Nutrition:
Calories 51, fat 1.7, fiber 2.7, carbs 7, protein 1.6

Spicy Olives and Tomato Mix

Preparation time: 5 minutes **Cooking time:** 15 minutes **Servings:** 4

2 cups kalamata olives, pitted	2 small avocados, pitted, peeled and sliced
¼ cup cherry tomatoes, halved Juice of 1 lime	1 tablespoon coconut oil, melted

1. In a pan that fits the air fryer, combine the olives with the other ingredients, toss, put the pan in your air fryer and cook at 370 degrees F for 15 minutes. Divide the mix between plates and serve.

Nutrition:
Calories 153, fat 3, fiber 3, carbs 4, protein 6

Chili Fried Brussels Sprouts

Prep time: 10 minutes **Cooking time:** 15 minutes **Servings:** 5

1-pound Brussels sprouts	1 teaspoon chili flakes
3 eggs, beaten	3 tablespoons coconut flakes
1 teaspoon salt	1 teaspoon sesame oil

1. Cut Brussels sprouts into halves and put them in the bowl. Add chili flakes, eggs, and salt. Shake the vegetables well and then sprinkle them with coconut flakes. Shake the vegetables well. Preheat the air fryer to 385F. Put Brussels sprouts in the air fryer and cook them for 10 minutes. Then shake the vegetables well and cook for 5 minutes more.

Nutrition:
Calories 96, fat 4.8, fiber 3.7, carbs 8.9, protein 6.5

Green Beans and Tomato Sauce

Preparation time: 5 minutes **Cooking time:** 15 minutes **Servings:** 4

½ pound green beans, trimmed and halved 1 cup black olives, pitted and halved	¼ cup bacon, cooked and crumbled 1 tablespoon olive oil
¼ cup keto tomato sauce	

1. In a pan that fits the air fryer, combine all the ingredients, toss, put the pan in the air fryer and cook at 380 degrees F for 15 minutes. Divide between plates and serve.

Nutrition:
Calories 160, fat 4, fiber 3, carbs 5, protein 4

Cauliflower Falafel

Prep time: 15 minutes **Cooking time:** 12 minutes **Servings:** 4

1 cup cauliflower, shredded	1 teaspoon almond flour
½ teaspoon ground cumin	¼ teaspoon ground coriander
½ teaspoon garlic powder	½ teaspoon salt
¼ teaspoon cayenne pepper	1 egg, beaten
1 teaspoon tahini paste	2 tablespoons flax meal
½ teaspoon sesame oil	

1. In the mixing bowl mix up shredded cauliflower, almond flour, ground cumin, coriander, garlic powder, salt, and cayenne pepper. Add egg and flax meal and stir the mixture until homogenous with the help of the spoon. After this, make the medium size balls (falafel) and press them gently. Preheat the air fryer to 375F. Put the falafel in the air fryer and sprinkle with sesame oil. Cook the falafel for 6 minutes from each side. Sprinkle the cooked falafel with tahini paste.

Nutrition:
Calories 92, fat 7.2, fiber 2.6, carbs 4.6, protein 4.5

Parmesan Cauliflower Gnocchi

Prep time: 15 minutes **Cooking time:** 4 minutes **Servings:** 4

2 cups cauliflower, boiled	2 oz parmesan, grated
1 egg yolk	1 teaspoon ground black pepper
1 teaspoon cream cheese	3 tablespoons coconut flour
1 tablespoon butter	1 teaspoon dried cilantro

1. Put the boiled cauliflower in the blender and grind it until you get the smooth mixture. Then squeeze the cauliflower to get rid of the water and transfer in the bowl. Add grated Parmesan, egg yolk, ground black pepper, cream cheese, and coconut flour. Knead the dough. Then make the log and cut it into pieces (gnocchi). Preheat the air fryer to 390F. Put the gnocchi in the air fryer in one layer and cook them for 4 minutes. Meanwhile, in the mixing bowl mix up butter and dried cilantro. Microwave the mixture until it is melted. When the gnocchi is cooked, place them in the plate and top with the melted butter mixture.

Nutrition:
Calories 128, fat 8.4, fiber 3.6, carbs 7.1, protein 7.5

Lemon Parsley Peppers

Preparation time: 5 minutes **Cooking time:** 15 minutes **Servings:** 4

and ½ pounds mixed bell peppers, halved and deseeded 2 teaspoons lemon zest, grated A handful parsley, chopped A drizzle of olive oil	tablespoons balsamic vinegar 2 tablespoons lemon juice

1. Put the peppers in your air fryer's basket and cook at 350 degrees F for 15 minutes. Peel the bell peppers, mix them with the rest of the ingredients, toss and serve.

Nutrition:
Calories 151, fat 2, fiber 3, carbs 5, protein 5

Coconut Celery and Sprouts

Preparation time: 5 minutes **Cooking time:** 12 minutes **Servings:** 4

1 celery stalks, roughly chopped 1 cup coconut cream	Salt and black pepper to the taste 1 tablespoon parsley, chopped
1 tablespoon coconut oil, melted	½ pound Brussels sprouts, halved

1. Heat up a pan that fits the air fryer with the oil over medium heat, add the sprouts and celery, stir and cook for 2 minutes. Add the cream and the remaining ingredients, toss, put the pan in the air fryer and cook at 380 degrees F for 10 minutes. Transfer to bowls and serve.

Nutrition:
Calories 140, fat 3, fiber 2, carbs 5, protein 6

Cajun Peppers

Preparation time: 4 minutes **Cooking time:** 12 minutes **Servings:** 4

- tablespoon olive oil
- ½ pound mixed bell peppers, sliced 1 cup black olives, pitted and halved
- ½ tablespoon Cajun seasoning

1. In a pan that fits the air fryer, combine all the ingredients. Put the pan it in your air fryer and cook at 390 degrees F for 12 minutes. Divide the mix between plates and serve.

Nutrition:
Calories 151, fat 3, fiber 2, carbs 4, protein 5

Broccoli Patties

Prep time: 15 minutes **Cooking time:** 8 minutes **Servings:** 4

½ teaspoon onion powder	1 cup broccoli, shredded
½ teaspoon salt	½ teaspoon chili flakes
1 teaspoon ground paprika	1 egg, beaten
¼ cup coconut flour	1 teaspoon chives, chopped

1. In the mixing bowl mix up onion powder, shredded broccoli, salt, chili flakes, ground paprika, and chives. After this, add egg and stir the mixture with the help of the spoon. Add coconut flour and stir it well again. Make the patties with the help of the fingertips. Then preheat the air fryer to 385F and put the patties in the air fryer basket. Cook them for 4 minutes from each side.

Nutrition:
Calories 67, fat 2.5, fiber 4.2, carbs 8.2, protein 3.8

Olives, Spinach and Vinaigrette

Preparation time: 5 minutes **Cooking time:** 12 minutes **Servings:** 4

tablespoons balsamic vinegar A bunch of cilantro, chopped Salt and black pepper to the taste 1 tablespoon olive oil	2 cups black olives, pitted 1 cup baby spinach

1. In a pan that fits the air fryer, combine all the ingredients and toss. Put the pan in the air fryer and cook at 370 degrees F for 12 minutes. Transfer to bowls and serve.

Nutrition:
Calories 132, fat 4, fiber 2, carbs 4, protein 4

Cauliflower Balls

Prep time: 15 minutes **Cooking time:** 5 minute **Servings:** 2

1 cup cauliflower, shredded	3 oz Mozzarella, shredded
1 egg yolk	1 tablespoon coconut flour
½ teaspoon salt	½ teaspoon ground black pepper
1 teaspoon cream cheese	1 teaspoon sesame oil

1. In the mixing bowl mix up shredded cauliflower, shredded Mozzarella, egg yolk, coconut flour, salt, ground black pepper, and cream cheese. Stir the mixture until it is smooth. With the help of 2 spoons make the balls.
2. Preheat the air fryer to 400F. Put the balls in the air fryer and sprinkle them with sesame oil. Cook the cauliflower rice balls for 5 minutes.

Nutrition:

Calories 204, fat 13.3, fiber 2.9, carbs 7.1, protein 15.3

Garlic Mushrooms

Prep time: 10 minutes **Cooking time:** 5 minutes **Servings:** 4

4 Portobello mushroom caps	4 teaspoons olive oil
1 teaspoon garlic, diced	

1. Trim the mushrooms if needed. Preheat the air fryer to 400F. In the mixing bowl mix up oil and garlic. Sprinkle the mushrooms with garlic mixture and put in the how air fryer. Cook the mushroom steaks for 5 minutes.

Nutrition:

Calories 61, fat 4.7, fiber 1, carbs 3.2, protein 3

Avocado and Green Beans

Preparation time: 5 minutes **Cooking time:** 15 minutes **Servings:** 4

- 1 pint mixed cherry tomatoes, halved 1 avocado, peeled, pitted and cubed
- ¼ pound green beans, trimmed and halved 2 tablespoons olive oil
1. In a pan that fits your air fryer, mix the tomatoes with the rest of the ingredients, toss, put the pan in the machine and cook at 360 degrees F for 15 minutes. Transfer to bowls and serve.

Nutrition:

Calories 151, fat 3, fiber 2, carbs 4, protein 4

Lemongrass Rice Mix

Prep time: 10 minutes **Cooking time:** 10 minutes **Servings:** 4

½ cup broccoli, shredded	½ cup cauliflower, shredded
¼ teaspoon lemongrass	1 teaspoon ground turmeric
¼ cup beef broth	1 teaspoon butter
½ teaspoon salt	3 oz Cheddar cheese, shredded

1. In the mixing bowl mix up shredded broccoli and cauliflower. Add lemongrass, turmeric, and salt. Then transfer the mixture in the air fryer baking pan and add beef broth. Add butter and top the keto rice with Cheddar cheese. Preheat the air fryer to 365F. Put the pan with "rice" in the air fryer and cook it for 10 minutes.

Nutrition:

Calories 106, fat 8.2, fiber 0.7, carbs 2.1, protein 6.2

Jalapeno Asparagus and Green Onions

Prep time: 5 minutes **Cooking time:** 15 minutes **Servings:** 4

1 pound asparagus, trimmed 2 green onions, chopped	jalapeno pepper, chopped 1 tablespoon olive oil
teaspoons chili powder	A pinch of salt and black pepper 10 cherry tomatoes, halved

1. In a pan that fits your air fryer, mix the asparagus with tomatoes and the rest of the ingredients, toss, put the pan in the fryer and cook at 390 degrees F for 15 minutes. Divide the mix between plates and serve.

Nutrition:

Calories 173, fat 4, fiber 2, carbs 4, protein 6

Dill Tomato

Prep time: 10 minutes **Cooking time:** 8 minutes **Servings:** 2

1 oz Parmesan, sliced	1 tomato
1 teaspoon fresh dill, chopped	1 teaspoon olive oil
¼ teaspoon dried thyme	

1. Trim the tomato and slice it on 2 pieces. Then preheat the air fryer to 350F. Top the tomato slices with sliced Parmesan, chopped fresh dill, and thyme. Sprinkle the tomatoes with olive oil and put in the air fryer. Cook the meal for 8 minutes. Remove cooked tomato parm from the air fryer with the help of the spatula.

Nutrition:

Calories 73, fat 5.5, fiber 0.5, carbs 2.1, protein 4.9

Tomato Salad

Preparation time: 5 minutes **Cooking time:** 15 minutes **Servings:** 4

10 cherry tomatoes, halved	½ pound kale leaves, torn
Salt and black pepper to the taste	¼ cup veggie stock
2 tablespoons keto tomato sauce	

1. In a pan that fits your air fryer, mix tomatoes with the remaining ingredients, toss, put the pan in the fryer and cook at 360 degrees F for 15 minutes. Divide between plates and serve right away.

Nutrition:

Calories 161, fat 2, fiber 2, carbs 4, protein 6

Tamari Eggplant

Prep time: 10 minutes **Cooking time:** 30 minutes **Servings:** 6

3 eggplants, trimmed	1 teaspoon tamari sauce
1 tablespoon olive oil	1 teaspoon liquid stevia
½ teaspoon liquid smoke	½ teaspoon smoked paprika
¼ teaspoon cayenne pepper	¼ teaspoon salt

1. Slice the eggplants on the long pieces. In the mixing bowl mix up tamari sauce, olive oil, liquid stevia, liquid smoke, smoked paprika, cayenne pepper, and salt. Then brush every eggplant piece with tamari sauce mixture. Preheat the air fryer to 400F. Put the eggplant bacon (pieces) in the air fryer in one layer and cook them for 4 minutes from each side or until the eggplant slices are light crunchy. Cook the remaining eggplant bacon.

Nutrition:

Calories 90, fat 2.9, fiber 9.8, carbs 16.3, protein 2.8

Beans

Prep time: 5 minutes **Cooking time:** 15 minutes **Servings:** 4

1 pound green beans, trimmed	1 tablespoon coconut oil, melted 2 garlic cloves, minced
Salt and black pepper to the taste	½ cup bacon, cooked and chopped 2 tablespoons dill, chopped

1. In a pan that fits the air fryer, combine the green beans with the rest of the ingredients, toss, put the pan in the machine and cook at 390 degrees F for 15 minutes. Divide everything between plates and serve.

Nutrition:

Calories 180, fat 3, fiber 2, carbs 4, protein 6

Mint Fennel and Berry Mix

Prep time: 5 minutes **Cooking time:** 12 minutes **Servings:** 4

2 fennel bulbs, trimmed and sliced 1 cup blueberries	2 ounces mozzarella, shredded 2 tablespoons mint, chopped
A pinch of salt and black pepper 2 tablespoons olive oil	and ½ teaspoons mustard 1 teaspoon coconut aminos 1 teaspoon balsamic vinegar

tablespoons shallots, chopped

1. Heat up a pan that fits the air fryer with the oil over medium heat, add the shallots, stir and cook for 2 minutes. Add the fennel and the blueberries, toss gently and take the pan off the heat. In a bowl, combine the mint with mustard, coconut aminos and vinegar and whisk well. Add this over the fennel mix, toss, put the pan in the air fryer and cook at 350 degrees F for 10 minutes. Divide between plates and serve with the mozzarella sprinkled on top.

Nutrition:

Calories 162, fat 5, fiber 3, carbs 4, protein 6

Spinach and Mushroom Wellington

Prep time: 15 minutes **Cooking time:** 45 minutes **Servings:** 4

1 cup mushrooms, chopped	¼ cup spring onions, diced
1 teaspoon apple cider vinegar	½ teaspoon salt
½ teaspoon ground black pepper	1 teaspoon olive oil
¼ cup fresh spinach, chopped	½ cup coconut flour
1 egg, beaten	3 tablespoons coconut oil

1. Preheat the skillet over the medium pan and pour the coconut oil in it. Add mushrooms and spring onions and cook the vegetables for 10 minutes. Stir them from time to time. Add spinach. Then sprinkle the vegetables with salt, ground black pepper, and apple cider vinegar. Stir well. Make the dough: in the mixing bowl mix up coconut oil, egg, and coconut flour.
2. Knead the soft dough and roll it up in the shape of the square. Then put the spinach-mushroom mixture on the dough square and roll it. Secure the edges in the shape of the Wellington. Preheat the air fryer to 365F. Put mushroom Wellington in the air fryer and cook it for 35 minutes.

Nutrition:

Calories 192, fat 15, fiber 6.4, carbs 10.6, protein 5.1

Chives Lemon Endives Mix

Prep time: 5 minutes **Cooking time:** 10 minutes **Servings:** 4

4 endives, trimmed and halved Salt and black pepper to the taste 1 tablespoon coconut oil, melted 1 tablespoon lemon juice	½ teaspoon nutmeg, ground 1 tablespoon chives, chopped

1. In a bowl, mix the endives with the rest of the ingredients except the chives and toss well. Put the endives in your air fryer's basket and cook at 360 degrees F for 10 minutes. Divide the endives between plates, sprinkle the chives on top and serve.

Nutrition:

Calories 162, fat 4, fiber 3, carbs 5, protein 7

Kabocha Fries

Prep time: 15 minutes **Cooking time:** 11 minutes **Servings:** 2

6 oz Kabocha squash, peeled	½ teaspoon olive oil
½ teaspoon salt	

1. Cut the Kabocha squash into the shape of the French fries and sprinkle with olive oil. Preheat the air fryer to 390F. Put the Kabocha squash fries in the air fryer basket and cook them for 5 minutes. Then shake them well and cook for 6 minutes more. Sprinkle the cooked Kabocha fries with salt and mix up well.

Nutrition:

Calories 40, fat 1.2, fiber 1, carbs 7, protein 1

Smoked Tempeh

Prep time: 10 minutes **Cooking time:** 6 minutes **Servings:** 2

1 cup tempeh	1 teaspoon apple cider vinegar
1 teaspoon sesame oil	½ teaspoon garlic powder
1 teaspoon liquid smoke	1 teaspoon butter, melted

1. In the shallow bowl mix up melted butter, liquid smoke, garlic powder, sesame oil, and apple cider vinegar. Cut the tempeh into halves and brush with apple cider vinegar mixture from both sides. After this, preheat the air fryer to 400F. Put the tempeh in the air fryer and cook it for 3 minutes from each side or until it is light brown. Transfer the cooked tempeh to the serving plate. Vegan Reuben is cooked.

Nutrition:

Calories 200, fat 13.2, fiber 0.1, carbs 8.3, protein 15.5

Basil Tomato and Eggplant Mix

Prep time: 20 minutes **Cooking time:** 15 minutes **Servings:** 2

1 large eggplant	1 tablespoon keto tomatoes sauce
2 oz Mozzarella, sliced	1 tablespoon fresh basil
½ tomato, sliced	1 teaspoon olive oil
½ teaspoon ground black pepper	

1. Trim the eggplant from one side and cut it in the shape of Hasselback. Then sprinkle it with ground black pepper and olive oil. After this, fill the eggplant Hasselback with sliced Mozzarella, basil, and tomato one-by-one. Preheat the air fryer to 400F. Brush the eggplant with marinara sauce and place it in the air fryer. Cook the vegetable for 15 minutes. Cool the cooked eggplant to the room temperature and transfer in the serving plates.

Nutrition:

Calories 168, fat 8, fiber 8.6, carbs 16.5, protein 10.6

Lime Green Beans and Sauce

Prep time: 5 minutes **Cooking time:** 8 minutes **Servings:** 4

1 pound green beans, trimmed 1 tablespoon lime juice	A pinch of salt and black pepper 2 tablespoons ghee, melted
1 teaspoon chili powder	

1. In a bowl, mix the ghee with the rest of the ingredients except the green beans and whisk really well. Mix the green beans with the lime sauce, toss, put them in your air fryer's basket and cook at 400 degrees F for 8 minutes. Serve right away.

Nutrition:
Calories 151, fat 4, fiber 2, carbs 4, protein 6

Cheddar Zucchini Mix

Prep time: 15 minutes **Cooking time:** 20 minutes **Servings:** 4

1 zucchini, sliced	½ teaspoon ground nutmeg
½ teaspoon sesame oil	½ teaspoon cayenne pepper
½ teaspoon smoked paprika	½ cup Cheddar cheese, shredded
7 oz chicken, boiled, shredded	1 tablespoon marinara sauce

1. Preheat the air fryer to 400F. Then line the air fryer basket with baking paper. Put the zucchini in the air fryer basket in one layer and sprinkle them with ground nutmeg, sesame oil, cayenne pepper, and smoked paprika. Cook the zucchini for 10 minutes. After this, sprinkle the zucchini with marinara sauce and top with shredded chicken and Cheddar cheese. Cook the nachos for 10 minutes more.

Nutrition:
Calories 151, fat 7.1, fiber 0.9, carbs 2.8, protein 18.7

Mustard Endives

Prep time: 5 minutes **Cooking time:** 15 minutes **Servings:** 4

endives, trimmed	3 tablespoons olive oil
A pinch of salt and black pepper 1 teaspoon mustard	2 tablespoons white vinegar
½ cup walnuts, chopped	

1. In a bowl, mix the oil with salt, pepper, mustard and vinegar and whisk really well. Add the endives, toss and transfer them to your air fryer's basket. Cook at 350 degrees F for 15 minutes, divide between plates and serve with walnuts sprinkled on top.

Nutrition:
Calories 154, fat 4, fiber 3, carbs 6, protein 7

Parsley Savoy Cabbage Mix

Preparation time: 5 minutes **Cooking time:** 15 minutes **Servings:** 4

Savoy cabbage, shredded 2 spring onions, chopped	tablespoons keto tomato sauce Salt and black pepper to the taste 1 tablespoon parsley, chopped

1. In a pan that fits your air fryer, mix the cabbage the rest of the ingredients except the parsley, toss, put the pan in the fryer and cook at 360 degrees F for 15 minutes. Divide between plates and serve with parsley sprinkled on top.

Nutrition:
Calories 163, fat 4, fiber 3, carbs 6, protein 7

Spinach Tortillas

Prep time: 15 minutes **Cooking time:** 10 minutes **Servings:** 2

1 cup spinach, chopped	½ cup coconut flour
½ teaspoon salt	1 egg, beaten
1 cup water, boiled, hot	1 teaspoon butter, softened

1. Put spinach in the bowl and add hot water. Leave the greens in hot water for 5 minutes. Then remove the spinach from the water and transfer in the blender. Blend it until you get a smooth texture. Put the blended spinach in the bowl and add coconut flour, salt, egg, and butter. Knead the soft dough and cut it into small pieces. Roll up every dough piece in the tortilla shape. Preheat the air fryer to 400F. Put the spinach tortilla in the air fryer and cook it for 2 minutes from each side. Repeat the same steps with all remaining tortillas.

Nutrition:
Calories 192, fat 9.2, fiber 12.3, carbs 18.7, protein 9.2

Ghee Savoy Cabbage

Preparation time: 5 minutes **Cooking time:** 15 minutes **Servings:** 4

1 Savoy cabbage head, shredded Salt and black pepper to the taste 1 and ½ tablespoons ghee, melted	¼ cup coconut cream
1 tablespoon dill, chopped	

1. In a pan that fits the air fryer, combine all the ingredients except the coconut cream, toss, put the pan in the air fryer and cook at 390 degrees F for 10 minutes. Add the cream, toss, cook for 5 minutes more, divide between plates and serve.

Nutrition:
Calories 173, fat 5, fiber 3, carbs 5, protein 8

Parmesan Cauliflower Tortillas

Prep time: 15 minutes **Cooking time:** 8 minutes **Servings:** 2

½ cup cauliflower, boiled, shredded	1 tablespoon almond flour
1 egg yolk	1 teaspoon dried dill
1 oz Parmesan, grated	¼ teaspoon ground turmeric
½ teaspoon sesame oil	

1. In the mixing bowl mix up shredded cauliflower and Parmesan. Then microwave the mixture for 15 seconds. Stir it until smooth and add almond flour, egg yolk, dried dill, and ground turmeric. Knead the soft and non-sticky dough. Then cut it on 2 pieces and roll up with the help of the rolling pin in the shape of the tortillas. Sprinkle every tortilla with the sesame oil. Preheat the air fryer to 395F. Put the first tortilla in the air fryer and cook it for 2 minutes from each side. Cook the second tortilla.

Nutrition:
Calories 114, fat 8.4, fiber 1.1, carbs 3.2, protein 6.5

Coconut Fried Mushrooms

Prep time: 10 minutes **Cooking time:** 5 minutes **Servings:** 2

6 oz white mushrooms	2 tablespoons almond flour
1 teaspoon coconut flour	½ teaspoon sesame oil
½ teaspoon salt	1 tablespoon cream cheese
½ teaspoon ground nutmeg	

1. Trim the mushrooms and sprinkle with salt and ground nutmeg. Then mix up mushrooms and cream cheese. In the bowl mix up almond flour and coconut flour. Coat the mushrooms in the coconut flour mixture. Preheat the air fryer to 400F. Put the mushrooms in the air fryer and sprinkle with sesame oil. Cook the mushrooms for 5 minutes.

Nutrition:
Calories 214, fat 17.5, fiber 4.5, carbs 9.9, protein 9.3

Turmeric Dill Cabbage

Prep time: 5 minutes **Cooking time:** 15 minutes **Servings:** 4

green cabbage head, shredded	¼ cup ghee, melted
teaspoons turmeric powder	
1 tablespoon dill, chopped	

1. In a pan that fits your air fryer, mix the cabbage with the rest of the ingredients except the dill, toss, put the pan in the fryer and cook at 370 degrees F for 15 minutes. Divide everything between plates and serve with dill sprinkled on top.

Nutrition:
Calories 173, fat 5, fiber 3, carbs 6, protein 7

Ghee Lemony Endives

Preparation time: 5 minutes **Cooking time:** 15 minutes **Servings:** 4

tablespoons ghee, melted	A pinch of salt and black pepper 1 tablespoon lemon juice
12 endives, trimmed	

1. In a bowl, mix the endives with the ghee, salt, pepper and lemon juice and toss. Put the endives in the fryer's basket and cook at 350 degrees F for 15 minutes. Divide between plates and serve.

Nutrition:
Calories 163, fat 4, fiber 3, carbs 5, protein 6

Stuffed Peppers

Prep time: 10 minutes **Cooking time:** 15 minutes **Servings:** 4

2 green bell peppers	2 teaspoons cream cheese
½ teaspoon minced garlic	1 teaspoon fresh parsley, chopped
½ teaspoon cayenne pepper	4 oz Monterey jack cheese, shredded
2 teaspoons almond butter	

1. Cut the peppers into halves and remove the seeds. In the mixing bowl mix up cream cheese, minced garlic, parsley, cayenne pepper, shredded cheese, and almond butter. Stir the mixture carefully with the help of the spoon. Then fill the bell pepper halves with the cheese mixture and put in the air fryer in one layer. Cook the meal for 15 minutes at 385F.

Nutrition:
Calories 181, fat 13.9, fiber 1.7, carbs 6.5, protein 9.4

Balsamic Oregano Endives

Preparation time: 5 minutes **Cooking time:** 15 minutes **Servings:** 4

endives, halved	1 tablespoon olive oil
A pinch of salt and black pepper 2 tablespoons balsamic vinegar 3 tablespoons ghee, melted	tablespoons oregano, chopped

1. Heat up a pan that fits your air fryer with the oil and the ghee over medium heat, add the rest of the ingredients except the endives, whisk and cook for 3 minutes. Add the endives, toss and take off the heat. Put the endives in your air fryer's basket and cook at 350 degrees F for 12 minutes. Divide between plates and serve with the ghee mix drizzled on top.

Nutrition:
Calories 143, fat 4, fiber 3, carbs 6, protein 7

Harissa Broccoli Spread

Prep time: 15 minutes **Cooking time:** 6 minutes **Servings:** 4

2 cups broccoli, chopped	1 teaspoon tahini
2 tablespoons sesame oil	1 teaspoon salt
1 garlic clove	1 teaspoon coconut oil, melted
1 teaspoon harissa	

1. Preheat the air fryer to 400F. Put the broccoli and garlic clove in the air fryer basket and sprinkle with 1 teaspoon of sesame oil. Cook the vegetables for 6 minutes. Then transfer the cooked broccoli and garlic in the blender and grind the ingredients until you get the smooth texture.

2. Add salt, all remaining sesame oil, coconut oil, and harissa. After this, add tahini and blend the mixture for 30 seconds more. Transfer the cooked hummus in the bowl.

Nutrition:
Calories 98, fat 9, fiber 1.3 carbs 4, protein 1.6

Chives Endives

Preparation time: 5 minutes **Cooking time:** 15 minutes **Servings:** 4

4 endives, trimmed	A pinch of salt and black pepper
¼ cup goat cheese, crumbled 1 teaspoon lemon zest, grated 1 tablespoon lemon juice	2 tablespoons chives, chopped 2 tablespoons olive oil

1. In a bowl, mix the endives with the other ingredients except the cheese and chives and toss well. Put the endives in your air fryer's basket and cook at 380 degrees F for 15 minutes. Divide the corn between plates and serve with cheese and chives sprinkled on top.

Nutrition:
Calories 140, fat 4, fiber 3, carbs 5, protein 7

Cheese Zucchini Rolls

Prep time: 20 minutes **Cooking time:** 10 minutes **Servings:** 2

1 large zucchini, trimmed	1 teaspoon keto tomato sauce
3 oz Mozzarella, sliced	1 teaspoon olive oil

1. Slice the zucchini on the long thin slices. Then sprinkle every zucchini slice with marinara sauce and top with sliced Mozzarella. Roll the zucchini and secure it with toothpicks. Preheat the air fryer to 385F. Put the zucchini rolls in the air fryer and sprinkle them with olive oil. Cook the zucchini rolls for 10 minutes.

Nutrition:

Calories 168, fat 10.2, fiber 1.9, carbs 7.3, protein 14

Endives Sauté

Prep time: 5 minutes **Cooking time:** 15 minutes **Servings:** 4

4 endives, trimmed and sliced	A pinch of salt and black pepper 1 tablespoon olive oil
2 shallots, chopped	1 cup white mushrooms, sliced
½ cup parmesan, grated	1 tablespoon parsley, chopped Juice of ½ lemon

1. Heat up a pan that fits the air fryer with the oil over medium-high heat, add the shallots and sauté for 2 minutes. Add the mushrooms, stir and cook for 1-2 minutes more. Add the rest of the ingredients except the parmesan and the parsley, toss, put the pan in the air fryer and cook at 380 degrees F for 10 minutes. Divide everything between plates and serve.

Nutrition:

Calories 170, fat 4, fiber 3, carbs 5, protein 8

Thyme Mushroom Pan

Prep time: 10 minutes **Cooking time:** 8 minutes **Servings:** 2

1/2 pound cremini mushrooms, sliced	1 cup coconut cream
1 teaspoon avocado oil	¼ teaspoon minced garlic
½ teaspoon dried thyme	

1. In the air fryer's pan, mix the mushrooms with the cream and the other ingredients, toss and cook at 380 degrees F for 8 minutes. Divide into bowls and serve.

Nutrition:

Calories 128, fat 5.5, fiber 5, carbs 4.5, protein 12.8

Parsley Asparagus

Preparation time: 5 minutes **Cooking time:** 15 minutes **Servings:** 4

pound asparagus, trimmed	A pinch of salt and black pepper 2 cherry tomatoes, chopped
1 fennel bulb, quartered	
chili peppers, chopped	2 tablespoons cilantro, chopped 2 tablespoons parsley, chopped 2 tablespoons olive oil
2 tablespoons lemon juice	

1. Heat up a pan that fits the air fryer with the oil over medium-high heat, add chili peppers and the fennel and sauté for 2 minutes. Add the rest of the ingredients, toss, put the pan in the air fryer and cook at 380 degrees F for 12 minutes. Divide everything between plates and serve.

Nutrition:

Calories 163, fat 4, fiber 2, carbs 4, protein 7

Parmesan Spinach Balls

Prep time: 15 minutes **Cooking time:** 5 minutes **Servings:** 4

2 cups spinach, chopped	4 oz Parmesan, grated
½ teaspoon ground nutmeg	½ teaspoon ground black pepper
1 egg, beaten	½ cup coconut flour
1 teaspoon avocado oil	

1. Put the spinach in the blender and grind it. Then transfer the grinded spinach in the bowl and mix it up with grated Parmesan, ground nutmeg, ground black pepper, and egg. Stir the mixture carefully and add coconut flour. Mix it up with the help of the spoon. Then make the spinach balls with the help of the fingertips. Preheat the air fryer to 400F. Put the spinach balls in the air fryer and sprinkle with avocado oil. Cook the spinach balls bites for 5 minutes.

Nutrition:

Calories 184, fat 10, fiber 6.5, carbs 11, protein 14

Collard Greens Sauté

Preparation time: 5 minutes **Cooking time:** 12 minutes **Servings:** 4

pound collard greens, trimmed	fennel bulbs, trimmed and quartered 2 tablespoons olive oil
Salt and black pepper to the taste	½ cup keto tomato sauce

1. In a pan that fits your air fryer, mix the collard greens with the fennel and the rest of the ingredients, toss, put the pan in the fryer and cook at 350 degrees F for 12 minutes. Divide everything between plates and serve.

Nutrition:

Calories 163, fat 4, fiber 3, carbs 5, protein 6

Lemon Roasted Peppers

Prep time: 10 minutes **Cooking time:** 8 minutes **Servings:** 4

4 shishito peppers	1 teaspoon lemon juice
½ teaspoon sesame oil	

1. Pierce the shishito peppers to make many small cuts and sprinkle them with lemon juice and sesame oil. Preheat the air fryer to 400F. Put the peppers in the air fryer basket and cook them for 4 minutes from each side.

Nutrition:

Calories 20, fat 0.6, fiber 2, carbs 3, protein 1

Mustard Greens, Green Beans and Sauce

Preparation time: 10 minutes **Cooking time:** 12 minutes **Servings:** 4

bunch mustard greens, trimmed 1 pound green beans, halved	tablespoons olive oil
¼ cup keto tomato sauce	Salt and black pepper to the taste 1 tablespoon balsamic vinegar
3 garlic cloves, minced	

1. In a pan that fits your air fryer, mix the mustard greens with the rest of the ingredients, toss, put the pan in the fryer and cook at 350 degrees F for 12 minutes. Divide everything between plates and serve.

Nutrition:

Calories 163, fat 4, fiber 3, carbs 4, protein 7

Cauliflower Pizza Crust

Prep time: 10 minutes **Cooking time:** 6 minutes **Servings:** 6

1 cup cauliflower, shredded	1 egg
½ cup Cheddar cheese, shredded	1 teaspoon salt
1 teaspoon keto tomato sauce	1 tablespoon coconut flakes
1 teaspoon avocado oil	

1. Crack the egg in the bowl and whisk it gently. Add shredded cauliflower, cheese, salt, tomato sauce, and coconut flakes. Stir the mixture well. Then put on the baking paper and roll up in the shape of the pizza crust.
2. Sprinkle it with avocado oil. Preheat the air fryer to 400F. Put the baking paper with pizza crust in the air fryer and cook it for 6 minutes.

Nutrition:

Calories 57, fat 4.3, fiber 0.5, carbs 1.4, protein 3.7

Dessert Recipes

Lemon Zucchini Bread

Prep time: 10 minutes **Cooking time:** 40 minutes **Servings:** 12

cups almond flour	2 teaspoons baking powder
¾ cup swerve	½ cup coconut oil, melted
	1 teaspoon lemon juice
1 teaspoon vanilla extract	cup zucchini, shredded 1
3 eggs, whisked	tablespoon lemon zest
	Cooking spray

1. In a bowl, mix all the ingredients except the cooking spray and stir well. Grease a loaf pan that fits the air fryer with the cooking spray, line with parchment paper and pour the loaf mix inside. Put the pan in the air fryer and cook at 330 degrees F for 40 minutes. Cool down, slice and serve.

Nutrition:

Calories 143, fat 11, fiber 1, carbs 3, protein 3

Orange Muffins

Prep time: 10 minutes **Cooking time:** 10 minutes **Servings:** 5

5 eggs, beaten	1 tablespoon poppy seeds
1 teaspoon vanilla extract	¼ teaspoon ground nutmeg
½ teaspoon baking powder	1 teaspoon orange juice
1 teaspoon orange zest, grated	5 tablespoons coconut flour
1 tablespoon Monk fruit	2 tablespoons coconut flakes
Cooking spray	

1. In the mixing bowl mix up eggs, poppy seeds, vanilla extract, ground nutmeg, baking powder, orange juice, orange zest, coconut flour, and Monk fruit. Add coconut flakes and mix up the mixture until it is homogenous and without any clumps. Preheat the air fryer to 360F. Spray the muffin molds with cooking spray from inside. Pour the muffin batter in the molds and transfer them in the air fryer. Cook the muffins for 10 minutes.

Nutrition:

Calories 119, fat 7.1, fiber 3.4, carbs 6.2, protein 7.5

Lemon Pie

Preparation time: 10 minutes **Cooking time:** 35 minutes **Servings:** 8

eggs, whisked	¾ cup swerve
¼ cup coconut flour	2 tablespoons butter, melted 1 teaspoon lemon zest, grated 1 teaspoon baking powder
1 teaspoon vanilla extract	½ teaspoon lemon extract
ounces coconut, shredded	
Cooking spray	

1. In a bowl, combine all the ingredients except the cooking spray and stir well. Grease a pie pan that fits the air fryer with the cooking spray, pour the mixture inside, put the pan in the air fryer and cook at 360 degrees F for 35 minutes. Slice and serve warm.

Nutrition:

Calories 212, fat 15, fiber 2, carbs 6, protein 4

Cocoa Cupcakes

Preparation time: 5 minutes **Cooking time:** 25 minutes **Servings:** 4

1/3 cup coconut flour	½ cup cocoa powder 3 tablespoons stevia
½ teaspoon baking soda	1 teaspoon baking powder
	4 eggs, whisked
1 teaspoon vanilla extract	4 tablespoons coconut oil, melted
¼ cup almond milk	
Cooking spray	

1. In a bowl, mix all the ingredients except the cooking spray and whisk well. Grease a cupcake tin that fits the air fryer with the cooking spray, pour the cupcake mix, put the pan in your air fryer, cook at 350 degrees F for 25 minutes, cool down and serve.

Nutrition:

Calories 103, fat 4, fiber 2, carbs 6, protein 3

Lemon Coffee Muffins

Prep time: 15 minutes **Cooking time:** 11 minutes **Servings:** 6

1 cup almond flour	3 tablespoons Erythritol
1 scoop protein powder	1 teaspoon vanilla extract
3 tablespoons coconut oil, melted	1 egg, beaten
½ teaspoon baking powder	½ teaspoon instant coffee
1 teaspoon lemon juice	2 tablespoons heavy cream
Cooking spray	

1. In the mixing bowl mix up almond flour, Erythritol, protein powder, vanilla extract, coconut oil, egg, baking powder, instant coffee, lemon juice, and heavy cream. With the help of the immersion blender, whisk the mixture until you get a smooth batter. After this, preheat the air fryer to 360F. Spray the muffin molds with cooking spray. Then fill ½ part of every muffin mold with muffin batter and transfer them in the air fryer basket. Cook the muffins for 11 minutes.

Nutrition:

Calories 136, fat 12, fiber 0.5, carbs 2.1, protein 5.7

Almond Cookies

Preparation time: 5 minutes **Cooking time:** 15 minutes **Servings:** 8

1 and ½ cups almonds, crushed 2 tablespoons erythritol	½ teaspoon baking powder
¼ teaspoon almond extract 2 eggs, whisked	

1. In a bowl, mix all the ingredients and whisk well. Scoop 8 servings of this mix on a baking sheet that fits the air fryer which you've lined with parchment paper. Put the baking sheet in your air fryer and cook at 350 degrees F for 15 minutes. Serve cold.

Nutrition:

Calories 125, fat 7, fiber 1, carbs 5, protein 4

Berry Cookies

Prep time: 15 minutes **Cooking time:** 9 minutes **Servings:** 4

2 teaspoons butter, softened	1 tablespoon Splenda
1 egg yolk	½ cup almond flour
1 oz strawberry, chopped, mashed	

1. In the mixing bowl mix up butter, Splenda, egg yolk, and almond flour. Knead the non-sticky dough. Then make the small balls from the dough. Use your finger to make small holes in every ball. Then fill the balls with mashed strawberries. Preheat the air fryer to 360F. Line the air fryer basket with baking paper and put the cookies inside. Cook them for 9 minutes.

Nutrition:

Calories 68, fat 4.8, fiber 0.5, carbs 4.4, protein 1.5

Coconut Walnuts

Preparation time: 5 minutes **Cooking time:** 40 minutes **Servings:** 12

1 and ¼ cups almond flour 1 cup swerve	1 cup butter, melted
½ cup coconut cream	1 and ½ cups coconut, flaked 1 egg yolk
¾ cup walnuts, chopped	½ teaspoon vanilla extract

1. In a bowl, mix the flour with half of the swerve and half of the butter, stir well and press this on the bottom of a baking pan that fits the air fryer.
2. Introduce this in the air fryer and cook at 350 degrees F for 15 minutes. Meanwhile, heat up a pan with the rest of the butter over medium heat, add the remaining swerve and the rest of the ingredients, whisk, cook for 1-2 minutes, take off the heat and cool down. Spread this well over the crust, put the pan in the air fryer again and cook at 350 degrees F for 25 minutes. Cool down, cut into bars and serve.

Nutrition:

Calories 182, fat 12, fiber 2, carbs 4, protein 4

Buttery Muffins

Prep time: 15 minutes **Cooking time:** 10 minutes **Servings:** 2

1 teaspoon of cocoa powder	2 tablespoons coconut flour
2 teaspoons swerve	½ teaspoon vanilla extract
2 teaspoons almond butter, melted	¼ teaspoon baking powder
1 teaspoon apple cider vinegar	¼ teaspoon ground cinnamon

1. In the mixing bowl mix up cocoa powder, coconut flour, swerve, vanilla extract, almond butter, baking powder, and apple cider vinegar. Then add ground cinnamon and stir the mixture with the help of the spoon until it is smooth. Pour the brownie mixture in the muffin molds and leave for 10 minutes to rest. Meanwhile, preheat the air fryer to 365F. Put the muffins in the air fryer basket and cook them for 10 minutes. Then remove the cooked brownie muffins from the air fryer and cool them completely.

Nutrition:

Calories 145, fat 10.4, fiber 5, carbs 10.7, protein 5.1

Lemon Butter Bars

Preparation time: 10 minutes **Cooking time:** 35 minutes **Servings:** 8

½ cup butter, melted 1 cup erythritol	and ¾ cups almond flour 3 eggs, whisked
Zest of 1 lemon, grated	
Juice of 3 lemons	

1. In a bowl, mix 1 cup flour with half of the erythritol and the butter, stir well and press into a baking dish that fits the air fryer lined with parchment paper. Put the dish in your air fryer and cook at 350 degrees F for 10 minutes. Meanwhile, in a bowl, mix the rest of the flour with the remaining erythritol and the other ingredients and whisk well. Spread this over the crust, put the dish in the air fryer once more and cook at 350 degrees F for 25 minutes. Cool down, cut into bars and serve.

Nutrition:

Calories 210, fat 12, fiber 1, carbs 4, protein 8

Nut Bars

Prep time: 15 minutes **Cooking time:** 30 minutes **Servings:** 10

½ cup coconut oil, softened	1 teaspoon baking powder
1 teaspoon lemon juice	1 cup almond flour
½ cup coconut flour	3 tablespoons Erythritol
1 teaspoon vanilla extract	2 eggs, beaten
2 oz hazelnuts, chopped	1 oz macadamia nuts, chopped
Cooking spray	

1. In the mixing bowl mix up coconut oil and baking powder. Add lemon juice, almond flour, coconut flour, Erythritol, vanilla extract, and eggs. Stir the mixture until it is smooth or use the immersion blender for this step. Then add hazelnuts and macadamia nuts. Stir the mixture until homogenous. After this, preheat the air fryer to 325F. Line the air fryer basket with baking paper. Then pour the nut mixture in the air fryer basket and flatten it well with the help of the spatula. Cook the mixture for 30 minutes. Then cool the mixture well and cut it into the serving bars.

Nutrition:

Calories 208, fat 19.8, fiber 3.5, carbs 9.5, protein 4

Berry Pie

Preparation time: 5 minutes **Cooking time:** 20 minutes **Servings:** 8

egg whites 1/3 cup swerve	1 and ½ cups almond flour Zest of 1 lemon, grated
teaspoon baking powder 1	cups strawberries, sliced
teaspoon vanilla extract	Cooking spray
1/3 cup butter, melted	

1. In a bowl, whisk egg whites well. Add the rest of the ingredients except the cooking spray gradually and whisk everything. Grease a tart pan with the cooking spray, and pour the strawberries mix. Put the pan in the air fryer and cook at 370 degrees F for 20 minutes. Cool down, slice and serve.

Nutrition:

Calories 182, fat 12, fiber 1, carbs 6, protein 5

Cream Cheese Scones

Prep time: 20 minutes **Cooking time:** 10 minutes **Servings:** 4

4 oz almond flour	½ teaspoon baking powder
1 teaspoon lemon juice	¼ teaspoon salt
2 teaspoons cream cheese	¼ cup coconut cream
1 teaspoon vanilla extract	1 tablespoon Erythritol
1 tablespoon heavy cream	Cooking spray

1. In the mixing bowl mix up almond flour, baking powder, lemon juice, and salt. Add cream cheese and stir the mixture gently. Mix up vanilla extract and coconut cream in the separated bowl. Add the coconut cream mixture in the almond flour mixture. Stir it gently and then knead the dough. Roll up the dough and cut it on squares (scones). Preheat the air fryer to 360F. Spray the air fryer basket with cooking spray and put the scones inside air fryer in one layer. Cook the scones for 10 minutes or until they are light brown. Then cool the scones to the room temperature. Meanwhile, mix up heavy cream and Erythritol. Then brush every scone with a sweet cream mixture.

Nutrition:
Calories 217, fat 19.6, fiber 3.4, carbs 7.4, protein 6.6

Creamy Nutmeg Cake

Prep time: 20 minutes **Cooking time:** 40 minutes **Servings:** 8

½ cup heavy cream	3 eggs, beaten
3 tablespoons cocoa powder	1 teaspoon vanilla extract
1 teaspoon baking powder	3 tablespoons Erythritol
1 cup almond flour	¼ teaspoon ground nutmeg
1 tablespoon avocado oil	1 teaspoon Splenda

1. Mix up heavy cream and eggs in the bowl. Add cocoa powder and stir the liquid until it is smooth. After this, add vanilla extract, baking powder, Erythritol, almond flour, ground nutmeg, and avocado oil. Whisk the mixture gently and pour it in the cake mold. Then cover the cake with foil. Secure the edges of the foil. Then pierce the foil with the help of the toothpick. Preheat the air fryer to 360F. Put the cake mold in the air fryer and cook it for 40 minutes. When the cake is cooked, remove it from the air fryer and cool completely. Remove the cake from the mold and them sprinkle with Splenda.

Nutrition:
Calories 81, fat 6.7, fiber 1.1, carbs 3.2, protein 3.4

Butter Donuts

Preparation time: 5 minutes **Cooking time:** 15 minutes **Servings:** 4

8 ounces coconut flour 2 tablespoons stevia	egg, whisked
and ½ tablespoons butter, melted 4 ounces coconut milk	teaspoon baking powder

1. In a bowl, mix all the ingredients and whisk well. Shape donuts from this mix, place them in your air fryer's basket and cook at 370 degrees F for 15 minutes. Serve warm.

Nutrition:
Calories 190, fat 12, fiber 1, carbs 4, protein 6

Cinnamon Donuts

Prep time: 20 minutes **Cooking time:** 6 minutes **Servings:** 4

1 teaspoon ground cardamom	½ teaspoon ground cinnamon
½ teaspoon baking powder	½ cup coconut flour
1 tablespoon Erythritol	1 egg, beaten
1 tablespoon butter, softened	¼ teaspoon salt
Cooking spray	

1. Preheat the air fryer to 355F. In the shallow bowl mix up ground cinnamon, ground cardamom, and Erythritol. After this, in the separated bowl mix up coconut flour, baking powder, egg, salt, and butter. Knead the non-sticky dough. Add more coconut flour if needed. Then roll up the dough and make 4 donuts with the help of the donut cutter. After this, coat every donut in the cardamom mixture. Let the donuts rest for 10 minutes in a warm place. Then spray the air fryer with cooking spray. Place the donuts in the air fryer basket in one layer and cook them for 6 minutes or until they are golden brown. Sprinkle the hot cooked donuts with the remaining cardamom mixture.

Nutrition:
Calories 114, fat 6.5, fiber 6.3, carbs 10, protein 4.5

Vanilla Cookies

Prep time: 10 minutes **Cooking time:** 20 minutes **Servings:** 12

eggs, whisked	tablespoon heavy cream
½ cup butter, melted	teaspoons vanilla extract 2 and ¾ cup almond flour
	Cooking spray
¼ cup swerve	

1. In a bowl, mix all the ingredients except the cooking spray and stir well. Shape 12 balls out of this mix, put them on a baking sheet that fits the air fryer greased with cooking spray and flatten them. Put the baking sheet in the air fryer and cook at 350 degrees F for 20 minutes. Serve the cookies cold.

Nutrition:
Calories 234, fat 13, fiber 2, carbs 4, protein 7

Mint Cake

Prep time: 15 minutes **Cooking time:** 9 minutes **Servings:** 2

1 tablespoon cocoa powder	2 tablespoons coconut oil, softened
2 tablespoons Erythritol	1 teaspoon peppermint
3 eggs, beaten	1 teaspoon spearmint, dried
4 teaspoons almond flour	Cooking spray

1. Preheat the air fryer to 375F. Melt the coconut oil in the microwave oven for 10 seconds. Then add cocoa powder and almond flour in the melted coconut oil. After this, add Erythritol, peppermint, and spearmint. Add eggs and whisk the mixture until smooth. Spray the ramekins with cooking spray and pour the chocolate mixture inside. Then put the ramekins with lava cakes in the preheated air fryer and cook them for 9 minutes. Then remove the cooked lava cakes from the air fryer and let them rest for 5 minutes before serving.

Nutrition:
Calories 538, fat 48.5, fiber 6.9, carbs 14.1, protein 20.8

Zucchinis Bars

Prep time: 10 minutes **Cooking time:** 15 minutes **Servings:** 12

3 tablespoons coconut oil, melted 6 eggs	3 ounces zucchini, shredded 2 teaspoons vanilla extract
½ teaspoon baking powder 4 ounces cream cheese	2 tablespoons erythritol

1. In a bowl, combine all the ingredients and whisk well. pour this into a baking dish that fits your air fryer lined with parchment paper, introduce in the fryer and cook at 320 degrees F, bake for 15 minutes. Slice and serve cold.

Nutrition:
Calories 178, fat 8, fiber 3, carbs 4, protein 5

Sesame Bars

Prep time: 15 minutes **Cooking time:** 10 minutes **Servings:** 6

1 cup coconut flour	2 tablespoons coconut flakes
2 eggs, beaten	1 teaspoon baking powder
¼ cup Erythritol	1 teaspoon vanilla extract
1 tablespoon butter, softened	1 teaspoon sesame seeds
Cooking spray	

1. Put coconut flour in the bowl. Add coconut flakes, eggs, baking powder, Erythritol, vanilla extract, and sesame seeds. Add butter. Stir the mixture with the help of the spoon until it is homogenous. Then roll up the dough into the square and cut into the bars. Preheat the air fryer to 325F, Line the air fryer with baking paper and put the coconut bars inside. Cook the coconut bars for 10 minutes.

Nutrition:
Calories 143, fat 7.5, fiber 8.2, carbs 13, protein 6

Walnut Bars

Preparation time: 5 minutes **Cooking time:** 16 minutes **Servings:** 4

1 egg	1/3 cup cocoa powder 3 tablespoons swerve
7 tablespoons ghee, melted	¼ cup almond flour
1 teaspoon vanilla extract	
¼ cup walnuts, chopped	½ teaspoon baking soda

1. In a bowl, mix all the ingredients and stir well. Spread this on a baking sheet that fits your air fryer lined with parchment paper, put it in the fryer and cook at 330 degrees F and bake for 16 minutes. Leave the bars to cool down, cut and serve.

Nutrition:
Calories 182, fat 12, fiber 1, carbs 3, protein 6

Aromatic Cup

Prep time: 10 minutes **Cooking time:** 15 minutes **Servings:** 1

1 egg, beaten	1 tablespoon peanut butter
½ teaspoon baking powder	1 teaspoon lemon juice
½ teaspoon vanilla extract	1 teaspoon Erythritol
2 tablespoons coconut flour	

1. Mix up all ingredients in the cup until homogenous. Then preheat the air fryer to 350F. Put the cup with blondies in the air fryer and cook it for 15 minutes.

Nutrition:
Calories 237, fat 15, fiber 7, carbs 14, protein 12.6

Chocolate Ramekins

Prep time: 5 minutes **Cooking time:** 15 minutes **Servings:** 6

cup blackberries	eggs
½ cup heavy cream	½ cup ghee, melted
¼ cup chocolate, melted 1 tablespoons stevia	2 teaspoons baking powder

1. In a bowl, mix the blackberries with the rest of the ingredients, whisk well, divide into ramekins, put them in the fryer and cook at 340 degrees F for 15 minutes. Serve cold.

Nutrition:
Calories 150, fat 2, fiber 2, carbs 4, protein 7

Cocoa Spread

Prep time: 10 minutes **Cooking time:** 5 minutes **Servings:** 4

2 oz walnuts, chopped	5 teaspoons coconut oil
½ teaspoon vanilla extract	1 tablespoon Erythritol
1 teaspoon of cocoa powder	

1. Preheat the air fryer to 350F. Put the walnuts in the mason jar. Add coconut oil, vanilla extract, Erythritol, and cocoa powder. Stir the mixture until smooth with the help of the spoon. Then place the mason jar with Nutella in the preheated air fryer and cook it for 5 minutes. Stir Nutella before serving.

Ginger Vanilla Cookies

Prep time: 10 minutes **Cooking time:** 15 minutes **Servings:** 12

2 cups almond flour 1 cup swerve	¼ cup butter, melted 1 egg
2 teaspoons ginger, grated	¼ teaspoon nutmeg, ground
1 teaspoon vanilla extract	
¼ teaspoon cinnamon powder	

1. In a bowl, mix all the ingredients and whisk well. Spoon small balls out of this mix on a lined baking sheet that fits the air fryer lined with parchment paper and flatten them. Put the sheet in the fryer and cook at 360 degrees F for 15 minutes. Cool the cookies down and serve.

Nutrition:
Calories 220, fat 13, fiber 2, carbs 4, protein 3

Vanilla Mozzarella Balls

Prep time: 20 minutes **Cooking time:** 4 minutes **Servings:** 8

2 eggs, beaten	1 teaspoon almond butter, melted
7 oz coconut flour	2 oz almond flour
5 oz Mozzarella, shredded	1 tablespoon butter
2 tablespoons swerve	1 teaspoon baking powder
½ teaspoon vanilla extract	Cooking spray

1. In the mixing bowl mix up butter and Mozzarella. Microwave the mixture for 10-15 minutes or until it is melted. Then add almond flour and coconut flour. Add swerve and baking powder. After this, add vanilla extract and stir the mixture. Knead the soft dough. Microwave the mixture for 2-5 seconds more if it is not melted enough. In the bowl mix up almond butter and eggs. Make 8 balls from the almond flour mixture and coat them in the egg mixture. Preheat the air fryer to 400F. Spray the air fryer basket with cooking spray from inside and place the bread rolls in one layer.
2. Cook the dessert for 4 minutes or until the bread roll is golden brown. Cool the cooked dessert completely and sprinkle with Splenda if desired.

Nutrition:
Calories 249, fat 14.4, fiber 10.9, carbs 8.3, protein 13.3

Cinnamon Raspberry Cupcakes

Preparation time: 10 minutes **Cooking time:** 20 minutes
Servings: 8

¾ cup raspberries	¼ cup ghee, melted 1 egg
½ cup swerve	¼ cup coconut flour
2 tablespoons almond meal	1 teaspoon cinnamon powder 3 tablespoons cream cheese
½ teaspoon baking soda	½ teaspoon baking powder Cooking spray

1. In a bowl, mix all the ingredients except the cooking spray and whisk well. Grease a cupcake pan that fits the air fryer with the cooking spray, pour the raspberry mix, put the pan in the machine and cook at 350 degrees F for 20 minutes. Serve the cupcakes cold.

Nutrition:
Calories 223, fat 7, fiber 2, carbs 4, protein 5

Raspberry Pop-Tarts

Prep time: 25 minutes **Cooking time:** 10 minutes **Servings:** 5

2 oz raspberries	½ cup almond flour
1 egg, beaten	1 tablespoon butter, softened
1 tablespoon Erythritol	½ teaspoon baking powder
1 egg white, whisked	Cooking spray

1. In the mixing bowl mix up almond flour, egg, butter, and baking powder Knead the soft non-sticky dough. Then mash the raspberries and mix them up with Erythritol. Cut the dough into halves. Then roll up every dough half into the big squares. After this, cut every square into 5 small squares. Put the mashed raspberry mixture on 5 mini squares. Then cover them with remaining dough squares. Secure the edges with the help of the fork. Then brush the pop-tarts with whisked egg white. Preheat the air fryer to 350F. Spray the air fryer basket with cooking spray, Then place the pop tarts in the air fryer basket in one layer. Cook them at 350F for 10 minutes. Cool the cooked pop-tarts totally and transfer in the serving plates.

Nutrition:
Calories 59, fat 4.7, fiber 1.1, carbs 2.3, protein 2.6

Lemon Berry Jam

Preparation time: 10 minutes **Cooking time:** 20 minutes
Servings: 12

¼ cup swerve	8 ounces strawberries, sliced 1 tablespoon lemon juice
¼ cup water	

1. In a pan that fits the air fryer, combine all the ingredients, put the pan in the machine and cook at 380 degrees F for 20 minutes. Divide the mix into cups, cool down and serve.

Nutrition:
Calories 100, fat 1, fiber 0, carbs 1, protein 1

Creamy Raspberry Cake

Prep time: 20 minutes **Cooking time:** 30 minutes **Servings:** 4

3 eggs, beaten	½ cup coconut flour
½ teaspoon baking powder	2 teaspoons Erythritol
1 teaspoon vanilla extract	1 tablespoon Truvia
½ cup heavy cream	1 oz raspberries, sliced
Cooking spray	

1. Make the cake batter: in the mixing bowl mix up beaten egg, coconut flour, baking powder, and Erythritol. Add vanilla extract and stir the mixture until smooth. Then preheat the air fryer to 330F. Spray the air fryer baking pan with cooking spray and pour the cake batter inside. Put the pan with batter in the preheated air fryer and cook it for 30 minutes. Meanwhile, make the cake frosting: whip the heavy cream. Then add Truvia and stir it well. When the cake is cooked, cool it well and remove it from the air fryer pan. Slice the cake into 2 cakes. Then spread one piece of cake with ½ part of whipped cream and top with sliced raspberries.
2. After this, cover it with the second piece of cakes. Top the cake with the remaining whipped cream.

Nutrition:
Calories 166, fat 10.9, fiber 5.5, carbs 11.1, protein 6.6

Blackberry Cream

Preparation time: 4 minutes **Cooking time:** 20 minutes
Servings: 6

2 cups blackberries Juice of ½ lemon	2 tablespoons water
teaspoon vanilla extract 2 tablespoons swerve	

1. In a bowl, mix all the ingredients and whisk well. Divide this into 6 ramekins, put them in the air fryer and cook at 340 degrees F for 20 minutes Cool down and serve.

Nutrition:
Calories 123, fat 2, fiber 2, carbs 4, protein 3

Coconut Almond Pies

Prep time: 25 minutes **Cooking time:** 26 minutes **Servings:** 6

8 oz almond flour	1 teaspoon vanilla extract
¼ teaspoon salt	2 tablespoons Erythritol
2 eggs, beaten	1 tablespoon coconut butter, melted
1 tablespoon xanthan gum	1 teaspoon flax meal
2 oz blueberries	Cooking spray

1. In the mixing bowl mix up vanilla extract, eggs, and coconut butter. Then add almond flour, salt, xanthan gum, and flax meal. Knead the non-sticky dough and roll it up. Then cut the dough on 6 pieces. Put the blueberries on every dough piece. Sprinkle the berries with Erythritol. Fold the dough pieces to make the pockets and secure the edges of them with the help of the fork. Preheat the air fryer to 350F. Place the hand pies in the air fryer in one layer (4 pies) and cook them for 13 minutes. Then remove the cooked pies from the air fryer and cool them to the room temperature.
2. Repeat the same steps with remaining uncooked pies.

Nutrition:
Calories 270, fat 21.8, fiber 7.7, carbs 13, protein 10

Coconut Cake

Preparation time: 5 minutes **Cooking time:** 20 minutes
Servings: 8

egg	tablespoons swerve
tablespoons coconut oil, melted	¼ cup coconut milk
tablespoons almond flour	½ teaspoon baking powder
1 tablespoon cocoa powder	

1. In a bowl, mix all the ingredients and stir well. Pour this into a cake pan that fits the air fryer, put the pan in the machine and cook at 340 degrees F for 20 minutes. Slice and serve.

Nutrition:
Calories 191, fat 12, fiber 2, carbs 4, protein 6

Coconut Chocolate

Prep time: 10 minutes **Cooking time:** 7 minutes **Servings:** 2

¼ teaspoon vanilla extract	1/3 cup coconut milk
1 teaspoon butter	1 tablespoon cocoa powder
½ oz dark chocolate	1 teaspoon Monk fruit

1. In the big cup whisk together coconut milk and cocoa powder. When the liquid is smooth, add vanilla extract and Monk fruit. Stir it gently. Then add dark chocolate and butter. Put the cup with chocolate mixture in the air fryer and cook it at 375F for 3 minutes. Then stir the liquid and cook it for 4 minutes more. Carefully remove the cups with hot chocolate from the air fryer. Stir the hot chocolate gently with the help of the teaspoon.

Nutrition:
Calories 156, fat 14.3, fiber 2.2, carbs 7.8, protein 1.7

Pumpkin Coconut Muffins

Prep time: 15 minutes **Cooking time:** 10 minutes **Servings:** 6

½ cup coconut flour	1 tablespoon almond flour
1 teaspoon pumpkin puree	½ teaspoon baking powder
½ teaspoon pumpkin spices	1 egg, beaten
3 teaspoons Erythritol	2 tablespoons butter, melted
Cooking spray	

1. In the mixing bowl mix up coconut flour, almond flour, baking powder, pumpkin spices, and Erythritol. Then add pumpkin puree, egg, and butter. Stir the mixture until you get the smooth batter. After this, spray the muffin molds with cooking spray. Pour the batter in the muffin molds.
2. Preheat the air fryer to 325F. Transfer the muffin molds in the air fryer and cook them for 10 minutes. Cool the muffins completely and remove them from muffin molds.

Nutrition:
Calories 119, fat 8.9, fiber 4.6, carbs 7.4, protein 4

Coconut and Berries Cream

Preparation time: 5 minutes **Cooking time:** 30 minutes
Servings: 6

12 ounces blackberries	6 ounces raspberries
12 ounces blueberries	¾ cup swerve
2 ounces coconut cream	

1. In a bowl, mix all the ingredients and whisk well. Divide this into 6 ramekins, put them in your air fryer and cook at 320 degrees F for 30 minutes. Cool down and serve it.

Nutrition:
Calories 100, fat 1, fiber 1, carbs 2, protein 2

Peanut Cookies

Prep time: 15 minutes **Cooking time:** 5 minutes **Servings:** 4

4 tablespoons peanut butter	4 teaspoons Erythritol
1 egg, beaten	¼ teaspoon vanilla extract

1. In the mixing bowl mix up peanut butter, Erythritol, egg, and vanilla extract. Stir the mixture with the help of the fork. Then make 4 cookies. Preheat the air fryer to 355F. Place the cookies in the air fryer and cook them for 5 minutes.

Nutrition:
Calories 110, fat 10.1, fiber 1, carbs 3.3, protein 5.4

Brownies

Preparation time: 10 minutes **Cooking time:** 25 minutes
Servings: 6

6 tablespoons cream cheese, soft 3 eggs, whisked	tablespoons cocoa powder
tablespoons coconut oil, melted	¼ cup almond flour
¼ cup coconut flour	¼ teaspoon baking soda 1 teaspoon vanilla extract
½ cup almond milk	3 tablespoons swerve Cooking spray

1. Grease a cake pan that fits the air fryer with the cooking spray. In a bowl, mix rest of the ingredients, whisk well and pour into the pan. Put the pan in your air fryer, cook at 370 degrees F for 25 minutes, cool the brownies down, slice and serve.

Nutrition:
Calories 182, fat 12, fiber 2, carbs 4, protein 6

Keto Butter Balls

Prep time: 15 minutes **Cooking time:** 10 minutes **Servings:** 4

1 tablespoon butter, softened1 tablespoon Erythritol	½ teaspoon ground cinnamon
1 tablespoon coconut flour	1 teaspoon coconut flakes
Cooking spray	

1. Put the butter, Erythritol, ground cinnamon, coconut flour, and coconut flakes. Then stir the mixture with the help of the fork until homogenous. Make 4 balls. Preheat the air fryer to 375F. Spray the air fryer basket with cooking spray and place the balls inside. Cook the dessert for 10 minutes.

Nutrition:
Calories 43, fat 3.3, fiber 1.3, carbs 2.9, protein 0.6

Avocado Chocolate Brownies

Prep time: 10 minutes **Cooking time:** 30 minutes **Servings:** 12

1 cup avocado, peeled and mashed	½ teaspoon vanilla extract
4 tablespoons cocoa powder	3 tablespoons coconut oil, melted 2 eggs, whisked
½ cup dark chocolate, unsweetened and melted	¾ cup almond flour
teaspoon baking powder	¼ teaspoon baking soda 1 teaspoon stevia

1. In a bowl, mix the flour with stevia, baking powder and soda and stir. Add the rest of the ingredients gradually, whisk and pour into a cake pan that fits the air fryer after you lined it with parchment paper. Put the pan in your air fryer and cook at 350 degrees F for 30 minutes. Cut into squares and serve cold.

Nutrition:
Calories 155, fat 6, fiber 2, carbs 6, protein 4

Cardamom Bombs

Prep time: 10 minutes **Cooking time:** 5 minutes **Servings:** 2

2 oz avocado, peeled	1 egg, beaten
½ teaspoon ground cardamom	1 tablespoon Erythritol
2 tablespoons coconut flour	1 teaspoon butter, softened

1. Put the avocado in the bowl and mash it with the help of the fork. Add egg and stir the mixture until it is smooth. Then add ground cardamom, Erythritol, and coconut flour. After this, add butter and stir the mixture well. Make the balls from the avocado mixture and press them gently.
2. Then preheat the air fryer to 400F. Put the avocado bombs in the air fryer and cook them for 5 minutes.

Nutrition:
Calories 143, fat 10.9, fiber 5, carbs 7.5, protein 4.9

Cream Cups

Preparation time: 5 minutes **Cooking time:** 10 minutes **Servings:** 6

tablespoons butter, melted	tablespoons coconut, shredded and unsweetened
8 ounces cream cheese, soft	3 eggs
tablespoons swerve	

1. In a bowl, mix all the ingredients and whisk really well. Divide into small ramekins, put them in the fryer and cook at 320 degrees F and bake for 10 minutes. Serve cold.

Nutrition:
Calories 164, fat 4, fiber 2, carbs 5, protein 5

Chia Jam

Preparation time: 10 minutes **Cooking time:** 30 minutes **Servings:** 12

cups blackberries	¼ cup swerve
tablespoons lemon juice	4 tablespoons chia seeds

1. In a pan that fits the air fryer, combine all the ingredients and toss. Put the pan in the machine and cook at 300 degrees F for 30 minutes. Divide into cups and serve cold.

Nutrition:
Calories 100, fat 2, fiber 1, carbs 3, protein 1

Butter Custard

Prep time: 15 minutes **Cooking time:** 35 minutes **Servings:** 2

¼ cup heavy cream	1 tablespoon Erythritol
1 teaspoon coconut flour	3 egg yolks
1 teaspoon butter	

1. Whip the heavy cream and them mix it up with Erythritol and coconut flour. Whisk the egg yolks and add them in the whipped cream mixture. Then grease 2 ramekins with butter and transfer the whipped cream mixture in the ramekins. Preheat the air fryer to 300F. Put the ramekins with custard in the air fryer and cook them for 35 minutes.

Nutrition:
Calories 155, fat 14.4, fiber 0.5, carbs 2.1, protein 4.6

Lemon Peppermint Bars

Prep time: 15 minutes **Cooking time:** 16 minutes **Servings:** 8

1 teaspoon peppermint	1 cup almond flour
1/3 cup peanut butter	½ teaspoon baking powder
1 teaspoon lemon juice	½ teaspoon orange zest, grated

1. In the bowl, mix up almond flour, peppermint, baking powder, and orange zest. Then add peanut butter and lemon juice. Knead the non-sticky dough. Cut the dough on 8 pieces and roll the balls. Press them gently to get the shape of the bars. Preheat the air fryer to 365F. Line the air fryer basket with baking paper. Put 4 cookies in the air fryer in one layer. Cook them for 8 minutes. Remove the cooked bars from the air fryer. Repeat the same steps with uncooked bars.

Nutrition:
Calories 84, fat 7.2, fiber 1.1, carbs 3.1, protein 3.5

Avocado Cream Pudding

Prep time: m5inutes **Cooking time:** 25 minutes **Serving:** 6

4 small avocados, peeled, pitted and mashed 2 eggs, whisked	1 cup coconut milk
¾ cup swerve	teaspoon cinnamon powder
½ teaspoon ginger powder	

1. In a bowl, mix all the ingredients and whisk well. Pour into a pudding mould, put it in the air fryer and cook at 350 degrees F for 25 minutes. Serve warm.

Nutrition:
Calories 192, fat 8, fiber 2, carbs 5, protein 4

Chocolate Candies

Prep time: 15 minutes **Cooking time:** 2 minutes **Servings:** 4

1 oz almonds, crushed	1 oz dark chocolate
2 tablespoons peanut butter	2 tablespoons heavy cream

1. Preheat the air fryer to 390F. Chop the dark chocolate and put it in the air fryer mold. Add peanut butter and heavy cream. Stir the mixture and transfer in the air fryer. Cook it for 2 minutes or until it starts to be melt. Then line the air tray with parchment. Put the crushed almonds on the tray in one layer. Then pour the cooked chocolate mixture over the almonds.
2. Flatten gently if needed and let it cool. Crack the cooked chocolate layer into the candies.

Nutrition:
Calories 154, fat 12.9, fiber 1.9, carbs 7.4, protein 3.9

Berry Pudding

Prep time: 5 minutes **Cooking time:** 15 minutes **Servings:** 6

cups coconut cream 1/3 tablespoons swerve Zest cup blackberries 1/3 cup of 1 lime, grated blueberries

1. In a blender, combine all the ingredients and pulse well. Divide this into 6 small ramekins, put them in your air fryer and cook at 340 degrees F for 15 minutes. Serve cold.

Nutrition:

Calories 173, fat 3, fiber 1, carbs 4, protein 4

Almond Bars

Prep time: 5 minutes **Cooking time:** 12 minutes **Servings:** 12

teaspoon vanilla extract 1 tablespoons erythritol cup almond butter, soft 1 egg

1. In a bowl, mix all the ingredients and whisk really well. Spread this on a baking sheet that fits the air fryer lined with parchment paper, introduce in the fryer and cook at 350 degrees F and bake for 12 minutes. Cool down, cut into bars and serve.

Nutrition:

Calories 130, fat 12, fiber 1, carbs 3, protein 5

Ginger Lemon Pie

Prep time: 15 minutes **Cooking time:** 30 minutes **Servings:** 6

2 eggs	6 tablespoons coconut flour
½ teaspoon vanilla extract	6 tablespoons ricotta cheese
½ teaspoon baking powder	1 teaspoon lemon juice
½ teaspoon ground ginger	3 tablespoons Erythritol
1 tablespoon butter, melted	

1. Crack the eggs and separate them on the egg whites and egg yolks. Then whisk the egg yolks with Erythritol until you get the lemon color mixture. Then whisk the egg whites to the soft peaks. Add egg whites in the egg yolk mixture. Then add ricotta cheese, baking powder, lemon juice, ground ginger, vanilla extract, Erythritol. Then add butter and coconut flour and stir the pie butter until smooth. Line the air fryer baking pan with the baking paper. Pour the pie batter inside. Preheat the air fryer to 330F. Put the baking pan with pie in the air fryer and cook it for 30 minutes.

Nutrition:

Calories 97, fat 5.9, fiber 3, carbs 5.8, protein 5.2

Vanilla Yogurt Cake

Preparation time: 5 minutes **Cooking time:** 30 minutes **Servings:** 12

6 eggs, whisked	1 teaspoon vanilla extract
	1 teaspoon baking powder
	9 ounces coconut flour
4 tablespoons stevia	8 ounces Greek yogurt

1. In a bowl, mix all the ingredients and whisk well. Pour this into a cake pan that fits the air fryer lined with parchment paper, put the pan in the air fryer and cook at 330 degrees F for 30 minutes.

Nutrition:

Calories 181, fat 13, fiber 2, carbs 4, protein 5

Cobbler

Prep time: 15 minutes **Cooking time:** 30 minutes **Servings:** 4

¼ cup heavy cream	1 egg, beaten
½ cup almond flour	1 teaspoon vanilla extract
2 tablespoons butter, softened	¼ cup hazelnuts, chopped

1. Mix up heavy cream, egg, almond flour, vanilla extract, and butter. Then whisk the mixture gently. Preheat the air fryer to 325F. Line the air fryer pan with baking paper. Pour ½ part of the batter in the baking pan, flatten it gently and top with hazelnuts. Then pour the remaining batter over the hazelnuts and place the pan in the air fryer. Cook the cobbler for 30 minutes.

Nutrition:

Calories 145, fat 14.2, fiber 0.8, carbs 2, protein 3

Almond Pudding

Preparation time: 10 minutes **Cooking time:** 20 minutes **Servings:** 6

24 ounces cream cheese, soft 2 tablespoons almond meal	¼ cup erythritol 3 eggs, whisked
1 tablespoon vanilla extract	½ cup heavy cream
12 ounces dark chocolate, melted	

1. In a bowl mix all the ingredients and whisk well. Divide this into 6 ramekins, put them in your air fryer and cook at 320 degrees F for 20 minutes. Keep in the fridge for 1 hour before serving.

Nutrition:

Calories 200, fat 7, fiber 2, carbs 4, protein 6

Vinegar Cake

Prep time: 25 minutes **Cooking time:** 30 minutes **Servings:** 4

2 teaspoons cream cheese	1 teaspoon Truvia
1 teaspoon vanilla extract	½ cup heavy cream
1 egg, beaten	1 teaspoon baking powder
1 teaspoon apple cider vinegar	1 ½ cup coconut flour
2 tablespoons butter, softened	Cooking spray

1. Pour heavy cream in the bowl. Add vanilla extract, egg, baking powder, apple cider vinegar, and butter. Stir the liquid until homogenous. Then add coconut flour. Whisk the liquid until smooth. Spray the pound cake mold with cooking spray. Pour the pound cake batter in the mold. Flatten its surface with the help of the spatula. Preheat the air fryer to 365F. Put the mold with the pound cake in the air fryer and cook it for 30 minutes.
2. When the cake is cooked, cool it to the room temperature. Meanwhile, in the shallow bowl whisk together cream cheese and Truvia. Then spread the surface of the pound cake with sweet cream cheese. Slice the dessert on the servings.

Nutrition:

Calories 339, fat 20.5, fiber 18, carbs 28.7, protein 10.9

Lemon Almond Biscotti

Prep time: 15 minutes **Cooking time:** 40 minutes **Servings:** 6

¼ cup almond, crushed	¼ cup butter, softened
2 eggs, beaten	1 teaspoon of cocoa powder
1 teaspoon vanilla extract	1 cup almond flour
1 teaspoon lemon zest, grated	½ teaspoon baking powder
1 teaspoon lemon juice	¼ cup heavy cream
1 teaspoon avocado oil	3 tablespoons Erythritol

1. In the mixing bowl mix up butter, eggs, cocoa powder, vanilla extract, almond flour, lemon zest, baking powder, lemon juice, heavy cream, and Erythritol. Then add almonds and knead the smooth dough, Brush the air fryer baking pan with avocado oil and put the dough inside. Flatten it well. Preheat the air fryer to 365F. Put the pan with dough inside and cook it for 25 minutes. Then slice the cooked dough on the pieces (biscotti). Place the biscotti in the air fryer basket and cook them for 15 minutes at 350F or until they are light brown.

Nutrition:
Calories 160, fat 15.4, fiber 1.2, carbs 2.7, protein 4

Plum Almond Cake

Preparation time: 10 minutes **Cooking time:** 30 minutes **Servings:** 8

½ cup butter, soft 3 eggs	½ cup swerve
¼ teaspoon almond extract 1 tablespoon vanilla extract 1 and ½ cups almond flour	½ cup coconut flour
2 teaspoons baking powder	¾ cup almond milk
4 plums, pitted and chopped	

1. In a bowl, mix all the ingredients and whisk well. Pour this into a cake pan that fits the air fryer after you've lined it with parchment paper, put the pan in the machine and cook at 370 degrees F for 30 minutes. Cool the cake down, slice and serve.

Nutrition:
Calories 183, fat 4, fiber 3, carbs 4, protein 7

Cream Cheese Muffins

Prep time: 15 minutes **Cooking time:** 11 minutes **Servings:** 4

4 teaspoons cream cheese	1 egg, beaten
½ teaspoon baking powder	1 teaspoon vanilla extract
4 teaspoons almond flour	4 teaspoons coconut flour
2 tablespoons heavy cream	2 teaspoons Erythritol
Cooking spray	

1. Make the muffin batter: mix up cream cheese, egg, baking powder, vanilla extract, almond flour, coconut flour, heavy cream, and Erythritol. Then spray the air fryer muffin molds with cooking spray. Pour the batter in the muffin molds (fill ½ part of every mold). Preheat the air fryer to 365F. Insert the muffin molds in the air fryer and cook the dessert for 11 minutes. Cool the cooked muffins and remove them from the molds.

Nutrition:
Calories 229, fat 19.5, fiber 4, carbs 8.3, protein 8.3

Cinnamon Fried Plums

Preparation time: 5 minutes **Cooking time:** 20 minutes **Servings:** 6

6 plums, cut into wedges 1 teaspoon ginger, ground	½ teaspoon cinnamon powder Zest of 1 lemon, grated
2 tablespoons water	10 drops stevia

1. In a pan that fits the air fryer, combine the plums with the rest of the ingredients, toss gently, put the pan in the air fryer and cook at 360 degrees F for 20 minutes. Serve cold.

Nutrition:
Calories 170, fat 5, fiber 1, carbs 3, protein 5

Creamy Crumble

Prep time: 15 minutes **Cooking time:** 20 minutes **Servings:** 4

4 oz rhubarb, chopped	¼ cup heavy cream
1 teaspoon ground cinnamon	¼ cup Erythritol
1 cup almond flour	1 egg, beaten
1 teaspoon avocado oil	4 teaspoons butter, softened

1. In the bowl mix up heavy cream, ground cinnamon, almond flour, egg, and butter, Stir the mixture until you get the crumbly texture. Then mix up rhubarb and Erythritol. Brush the air fryer mold with avocado oil.
2. Separate the crumbled dough on 4 parts. Put 1 part of the dough in the air fryer mold. Then sprinkle it with a small amount rhubarb. Repeat the same steps till you use all ingredients. Put the crumble in the air fryer. Cook it at 375F for 20 minutes.

Nutrition:
Calories 124, fat 11.4, fiber 1.9, carbs 4.1, protein 3.4

Baked Plum Cream

Prep time: 5 minutes **Cooking time:** 20 minutes **Servings:** 4

1 pound plums, pitted and chopped	¼ cup swerve
tablespoon lemon juice 1 and ½ cups heavy cream	

1. In a bowl, mix all the ingredients and whisk really well. Divide this into 4 ramekins, put them in the air fryer and cook at 340 degrees F for 20 minutes. Serve cold.

Nutrition:
Calories 171, fat 4, fiber 2, carbs 4, protein 4

Blackberries Cake

Prep time: 10 minutes **Cooking time:** 25 minutes **Servings:** 4

eggs, whisked	4 tablespoons swerve
2 tablespoons ghee, melted	¼ cup almond milk
1 and ½ cups almond flour	½ teaspoon baking powder
1 cup blackberries, chopped	
teaspoon lemon zest, grated	
1 teaspoon lemon juice	

1. In a bowl, mix all the ingredients and whisk well. Pour this into a cake pan that fits the air fryer lined with parchment paper, put the pan in your air fryer and cook at 340 degrees F for 25 minutes. Cool the cake down, slice and serve.

Nutrition:
Calories 193, fat 5, fiber 1, carbs 4, protein 4

Cardamom Coconut Cookies

Prep time: 15 minutes **Cooking time:** 10 minutes **Servings:** 6

3 tablespoons coconut oil, softened	4 tablespoons coconut flour
2 tablespoons flax meal	2 tablespoons Monk fruit
1 teaspoon poppy seeds	½ teaspoon baking powder
½ teaspoon lemon juice	¼ teaspoon ground cardamom
Cooking spray	

1. In the mixing bowl put coconut oil, coconut flour, flax meal, ad Monk fruit. Then add poppy seeds, baking powder, lemon juice, and cardamom. With the help of the fingertips knead the soft but non-sticky dough. Then make the cookies from the dough. Preheat the air fryer to 375F. Spray the air fryer basket with cooking spray. Place the cookies in the air fryer and cook them for 10 minutes.

Nutrition:
Calories 95, fat 8.7, fiber 2.8, carbs 4, protein 1.6

Butter Plums

Preparation time: 5 minutes **Cooking time:** 20 minutes **Servings:** 4

teaspoons cinnamon powder 4 plums, halved	4 tablespoons butter, melted 3 tablespoons swerve

1. In a pan that fits your air fryer, mix the plums with the rest of the ingredients, toss, put the pan in the air fryer and cook at 300 degrees F for 20 minutes. Divide into cups and serve cold.

Nutrition:
Calories 162, fat 3, fiber 2, carbs 4, protein 5

Nuts Cookies

Prep time: 15 minutes **Cooking time:** 10 minutes **Servings:** 6

½ cup butter, softened	1 cup coconut flour
3 oz macadamia nuts, grinded	½ teaspoon baking powder
3 tablespoons Erythritol	Cooking spray

1. In the mixing bowl mix up butter, coconut flour, grinded coconut nuts, baking powder, and Erythritol. Knead the non-sticky dough. Cut the dough into small pieces and roll them into balls. Press every cookie ball gently to get the shape of cookies. Preheat the air fryer to 365F. Spray the air fryer basket with cooking spray. Put the uncooked cookies in the air fryer and cook them for 8 minutes. Then cook for extra 2 minutes at 390F to get the light brown crust.

Nutrition:
Calories 331, fat 29.4, fiber 9.2, carbs 14.2, protein 5.3

Lemon Berries Stew

Preparation time: 10 minutes **Cooking time:** 20 minutes **Servings:** 4

1 pound strawberries, halved 4 tablespoons stevia	tablespoon lemon juice 1 and ½ cups water

1. In a pan that fits your air fryer, mix all the ingredients, toss, put it in the fryer and cook at 340 degrees F for 20 minutes. Divide the stew into cups and serve cold.

Nutrition:
Calories 176, fat 2, fiber 1, carbs 3, protein 5

Whipped Cream Cake

Prep time: 15 minutes **Cooking time:** 25 minutes **Servings:** 12

1 cup almond flour	½ cup coconut flour
¼ cup coconut oil, melted	3 eggs, beaten
1 teaspoon baking powder	1 teaspoon vanilla extract
1 teaspoon cream cheese	2 tablespoons Splenda
½ cup whipped cream	

1. In the mixing bowl mix up almond flour, coconut flour, coconut oil, eggs, baking powder, vanilla extract, and cream cheese. Whisk the mixture well with the help of the immersion blender. Then line the air fryer baking pan with baking paper. Pour the cake batter in the baking pan. Preheat the air fryer to 355F. Put the baking pan in the air fryer and cook it for 25 minutes. Then cool the cake well. Meanwhile, mix up Splenda and whipped cream cheese. Spread the cake with whipped cream mixture.

Nutrition:
Calories 119, fat 9.3, fiber 2.3, carbs 6, protein 3

Chocolate and Avocado Cream

Preparation time: 5 minutes **Cooking time:** 20 minutes **Servings:** 4

avocados, peeled, pitted and mashed 3 tablespoons chocolate, melted	4 tablespoons erythritol
3 tablespoons cream cheese, soft	

1. In a pan that fits the air fryer, combine all the ingredients, whisk, put the pan in the fryer and cook at 340 degrees F for 20 minutes. Divide into bowls and serve cold.

Nutrition:
Calories 200, fat 6, fiber 2, carbs 4, protein 5

Sweet Coconut Cream Pie

Prep time: 15 minutes **Cooking time:** 25 minutes **Servings:** 4

4 tablespoons coconut cream	1 teaspoon baking powder
1 teaspoon apple cider vinegar	1 egg, beaten
¼ cup coconut flakes	1 teaspoon vanilla extract
½ cup coconut flour	4 teaspoons Splenda
1 teaspoon xanthan gum	Cooking spray

1. Put all liquid ingredients in the bowl: coconut cream, apple cider vinegar, egg, and vanilla extract. Stir the liquid until homogenous and add baking powder, coconut flakes, coconut flour, Splenda, and xanthan gum. Stir the ingredients until you get the smooth texture of the batter. Spray the air fryer cake mold with cooking spray. Pour the batter in the cake mold.
2. Preheat the air fryer to 330F. Put the cake mold in the air fryer basket and cook it for 25 minutes. Then cool the cooked pie completely and remove it from the cake mold. Cut the cooked pie into servings.

Nutrition:
Calories 110, fat 6.6, fiber 3.9, carbs 9.9, protein 2.1

Cocoa Bombs

Prep time: 5 minutes **Cooking time:** 8 minutes **Servings:** 12

2 cups macadamia nuts, chopped 4 tablespoons coconut oil, melted 1 teaspoon vanilla extract

¼ cup cocoa powder 1/3 cup swerve

1. In a bowl, mix all the ingredients and whisk well. Shape medium balls out of this mix, place them in your air fryer and cook at 300 degrees F for 8 minutes. Serve cold.

Nutrition:

Calories 120, fat 12, fiber 1, carbs 2, protein 1

Cinnamon Squash Pie

Prep time: 15 minutes **Cooking time:** 35 minutes **Servings:** 6

2 tablespoons Splenda

5 eggs, beaten

¼ cup heavy cream

1 teaspoon butter

4 oz Kabocha squash, peeled

1 tablespoon Erythritol

4 tablespoons coconut flakes

1 teaspoon vanilla extract

¼ teaspoon ground cinnamon

1. Grate the Kabocha squash. Then grease the baking mold with butter and put the grated Kabocha squash inside. In the mixing bowl mix up Splenda, Erythritol, coconut flakes, heavy cream, vanilla extract, and ground cinnamon. Then pour the liquid over the Kabocha squash. Stir the mixture gently with the help of the fork. Then preheat the air fryer to 365F. Put the mold with pie in the air fryer and cook it for 35 minutes. Cool the cooked pie to the room temperature and cut into the servings.

Nutrition:

Calories 116, fat 7.2, fiber 0.6, carbs 6.7, protein 5.1

Avocado Cake

Prep time: 10 minutes **Cooking time:** 30 minutes **Servings:** 4

4 ounces raspberries

teaspoons baking powder

1 cup swerve

avocados, peeled, pitted and mashed 1 cup almonds flour

tablespoons butter, melted

4 eggs, whisked

1. In a bowl, mix all the ingredients, toss, pour this into a cake pan that fits the air fryer after you've lined it with parchment paper, put the pan in the fryer and cook at 340 degrees F for 30 minutes. Leave the cake to cool down, slice and serve.

Nutrition:

Calories 193, fat 4, fiber 2, carbs 5, protein 5

Blueberry Cookies

Prep time: 10 minutes **Cooking time:** 30 minutes **Servings:** 2

3 oz blueberries

½ teaspoon avocado oil

1. Put the blueberries in the blender and grind them until smooth. Then line the air fryer basket with baking paper. Brush it with the avocado oil. After this, pour the blended blueberries on the prepared baking paper and flatten it in one layer with the help of the spatula. Cook the blueberry leather for 30 minutes at 300F. Cut into cookies and serve.

Nutrition:

Calories 26, fat 0.3, fiber 1.1, carbs 6.2, protein 0.3

Cinnamon and Butter Pancakes

Prep time: 10 minutes **Cooking time:** 12 minutes **Servings:** 2

1 teaspoon ground cinnamon

1 teaspoon baking powder

½ teaspoon vanilla extract

4 tablespoons almond flour

2 teaspoons butter, softened

½ teaspoon lemon juice

¼ cup heavy cream

2 teaspoons Erythritol

1. Preheat the air fryer to 325F. Take 2 small cake mold and line them with baking paper. After this, in the mixing bowl mix up ground cinnamon, butter, baking powder, lemon juice, vanilla extract, heavy cream, almond flour, and Erythritol. Stir the mixture until it is smooth. Then pour the mixture in the prepared cake molds. Put the first cake mold in the air fryer and cook the pancake for 6 minutes. Then check if the pancake is cooked (it should have light brown color) and remove it from the air fryer. Repeat the same steps with the second pancake. It is recommended to serve the pancakes warm or hot.

Nutrition:

Calories 414, fat 37.4, fiber 6.7, carbs 14.7, protein 12.4

Strawberry Cups

Preparation time: 5 minutes **Cooking time:** 10 minutes **Servings:** 8

16 strawberries, halved

2 cups chocolate chips, melted

2 tablespoons coconut oil

1. In a pan that fits your air fryer, mix the strawberries with the oil and the melted chocolate chips, toss gently, put the pan in the air fryer and cook at 340 degrees F for 10 minutes. Divide into cups and serve cold.

Nutrition:

Calories 162, fat 5, fiber 3, carbs 5, protein 6

Cardamom Squares

Prep time: 15 minutes **Cooking time:** 20 minutes **Servings:** 4

4 tablespoons peanut butter

1 teaspoon vanilla extract

1 tablespoon Erythritol

1 tablespoon peanut, chopped

½ cup coconut flour

½ teaspoon ground cardamom

1. Put the peanut butter and peanut in the bowl. Add vanilla extract, coconut flour, and ground cardamom. Then add Erythritol and stir the mixture until homogenous. Preheat the air fryer to 330F. Line the air fryer basket with baking paper and pour the peanut butter mixture over it. Flatten it gently and cook for 20 minutes. Then remove the cooked mixture from the air fryer and cool it completely. Cut the dessert into the squares.

Nutrition:

Calories 181, fat 11.7, fiber 7.2, carbs 12.8, protein 7.6

144

Strawberry Cake

Prep time: 10 minutes **Cooking time:** 35 minutes **Servings:** 6

1 pound strawberries, chopped 1 cup cream cheese, soft	¼ cup swerve
1 tablespoon lime juice 1 egg, whisked	1 teaspoon vanilla extract
3 tablespoons coconut oil, melted 1 cup almond flour	2 teaspoons baking powder

1. In a bowl, mix all the ingredients, stir well and pour this into a cake pan lined with parchment paper. Put the pan in the air fryer, cook at 350 degrees F for 35 minutes, cool down, slice and serve.

Nutrition:

Calories 200, fat 6, fiber 2, carbs 4, protein 6

Butter Crumble

Prep time: 20 minutes **Cooking time:** 25 minutes **Servings:** 4

½ cup coconut flour	2 tablespoons butter, softened
2 tablespoon Erythritol	3 oz peanuts, crushed
1 tablespoon cream cheese	1 teaspoon baking powder
½ teaspoon lemon juice	

1. In the mixing bowl mix up coconut flour, butter, Erythritol, baking powder, and lemon juice. Stir the mixture until homogenous. Then place it in the freezer for 10 minutes. Meanwhile, mix up peanuts and cream cheese. Grate the frozen dough. Line the air fryer mold with baking paper. Then put ½ of grated dough in the mold and flatten it. Top it with cream cheese mixture. Then put remaining grated dough over the cream cheese mixture. Place the mold with the crumble in the air fryer and cook it for 25 minutes at 330F.

Nutrition:

Calories 252, fat 19.6, fiber 7.8, carbs 13.1, protein 8.8

Stevia Cake

Prep time: 5 minutes **Cooking time:** 40 minutes **Servings:** 6

2 tablespoons ghee, melted	1 cup mashed avocado 3
1 cup coconut, shredded	tablespoons stevia
teaspoon cinamon powder	2 teaspoons cinnamon powder

1. In a bowl, mix all the ingredients and stir well. Pour this into a cake pan lined with parchment paper, place the pan in the fryer and cook at 340 degrees F for 40 minutes. Cool the cake down, slice and serve.

Nutrition:

Calories 192, fat 4, fiber 2, carbs 5, protein 7

Cauliflower Rice Pudding

Preparation time: 5 minutes **Cooking time:** 25 minutes **Servings:** 4

1 and ½ cups cauliflower rice 2 cups coconut milk	3 tablespoons stevia
2 tablespoons ghee, melted	4 plums, pitted and roughly chopped

1. In a bowl, mix all the ingredients, toss, divide into ramekins, put them in the air fryer, and cook at 340 degrees F for 25 minutes. Cool down and serve.

Nutrition:

Calories 221, fat 4, fiber 1, carbs 3, protein 3

Sweet Balls

Prep time: 2 hours **Cooking time:** 5 minutes **Servings:** 4

1 tablespoon cream cheese	3 oz goat cheese
2 tablespoons almond flour	1 tablespoon coconut flour
1 egg, beaten Cooking spray	1 tablespoon Splenda

1. Mash the goat cheese and mix it up with cream cheese. Then add egg, Splenda, and almond flour. Stir the mixture until homogenous. Then make 4 balls and coat them in the coconut flour. Freeze the cheese balls for 2 hours. Preheat the air fryer to 390F. Then place the frozen balls in the air fryer, spray them with cooking spray and cook for 5 minutes or until the cheese balls are light brown.

Nutrition:

Calories 224, fat 16.8, fiber 2.3, carbs 7.7, protein 11.4

Chia Cinnamon Pudding

Preparation time: 10 minutes **Cooking time:** 25 minutes **Servings:** 6

cups coconut cream 6 egg yolks, whisked 2 tablespoons stevia 2 teaspoons cinnamon powder 1 tablespoon ghee, melted	¼ cup chia seeds

1. In a bowl, mix all the ingredients, whisk, divide into 6 ramekins, place them all in your air fryer and cook at 340 degrees F for 25 minutes. Cool the puddings down and serve.

Nutrition:

Calories 180, fat 4, fiber 2 carbs 5, protein 7

Seeds and Almond Cookies

Prep time: 15 minutes **Cooking time:** 9 minutes **Servings:** 6

1 teaspoon chia seeds	1 teaspoon sesame seeds
1 tablespoon pumpkin seeds, crushed	1 egg, beaten
2 tablespoons Splenda	1 teaspoon vanilla extract
1 tablespoon butter	4 tablespoons almond flour
¼ teaspoon ground cloves	1 teaspoon avocado oil

1. Put the chia seeds, sesame seeds, and pumpkin seeds in the bowl. Add egg, Splenda, vanilla extract, butter, avocado oil, and ground cloves. Then add almond flour and mix up the mixture until homogenous. Preheat the air fryer to 375F. Line the air fryer basket with baking paper. With the help of the scooper make the cookies and flatten them gently. Place the cookies in the air fryer. Arrange them in one layer. Cook the seeds cookies for 9 minutes.

Nutrition:

Calories 180, fat 13.7, fiber 3, carbs 9.6, protein 5.8

Peanuts Almond Biscuits

Prep time: 20 minutes **Cooking time:** 35 minutes **Servings:** 6

4 oz peanuts, chopped	2 tablespoons peanut butter
½ teaspoon apple cider vinegar	1 egg, beaten
6 oz almond flour	¼ cup of coconut milk
2 teaspoons Erythritol	1 teaspoon vanilla extract
Cooking spray	

1. In the bowl mix up peanut butter, apple cider vinegar, egg, almond flour, coconut milk, Erythritol, and vanilla extract. When the mixture is homogenous, add peanuts and knead the smooth dough. Then spray the cooking mold with cooking spray and place the dough inside. Preheat the air fryer to 350F. Put the mold with biscuits in the air fryer and cook it for 25 minutes. Then slice the cooked biscuits into pieces and return back in the air fryer. Cook them for 10 minutes more. Cool the cooked biscuits completely.

Nutrition:
Calories 334, fat 29.1, fiber 5.2, carbs 10.8, protein 13.4

Walnuts and Almonds Granola

Prep time: 4 minutes **Cooking time:** 8 minutes **Servings:** 6

cup avocado peeled, pitted and cubed	½ cup coconut flakes
tablespoons ghee, melted	¼ cup walnuts, chopped
¼ cup almonds, chopped 2 tablespoons stevia	

1. In a pan that fits your air fryer, mix all the ingredients, toss, put the pan in the fryer and cook at 320 degrees F for 8 minutes. Divide into bowls and serve right away.

Nutrition:
Calories 170, fat 3, fiber 2, carbs 4, protein 3

Hazelnut Vinegar Cookies

Prep time: 25 minutes **Cooking time:** 11 minutes **Servings:** 6

1 tablespoon flaxseeds	¼ cup flax meal
½ cup coconut flour	½ teaspoon baking powder
1 oz hazelnuts, chopped	1 teaspoon apple cider vinegar
3 tablespoons coconut cream	1 tablespoon butter, softened
3 teaspoons Splenda	Cooking spray

1. Put the flax meal in the bowl. Add flax seeds, coconut flour, baking powder, apple cider vinegar, and Splenda. Stir the mixture gently with the help of the fork and add butter, coconut cream, hazelnuts, and knead the non-sticky dough. If the dough is not sticky enough, add more coconut cream. Make the big ball from the dough and put it in the freezer for 10- 15 minutes. After this, preheat the air fryer to 365F. Make the small balls (cookies) from the flax meal dough and press them gently. Spray the air fryer basket with cooking spray from inside. Arrange the cookies in the air fryer basket in one layer (cook 3-4 cookies per one time) and cook them for 11 minutes. Then transfer the cooked cookies on the plate and cool them completely. Repeat the same steps with remaining uncooked cookies. Store the cookies in the glass jar with the closed lid.

Nutrition:
Calories 147, fat 10.3, fiber 6.3, carbs 11.1, protein 4.1

Sage Cream

Preparation time: 5 minutes **Cooking time:** 30 minutes **Servings:** 4

7 cups red currants 1 cup swerve	1 cup water
6 sage leaves	

1. In a pan that fits your air fryer, mix all the ingredients, toss, put the pan in the fryer and cook at 330 degrees F for 30 minutes. Discard sage leaves, divide into cups and serve cold.

Nutrition:
Calories 171, fat 4, fiber 2, carbs 3, protein 6

Peanut Butter Cookies

Prep time: 30 minutes **Cooking time:** 20 minutes **Servings:** 4

½ cup almond flour	2 tablespoons butter, softened
1 tablespoon Splenda	¼ teaspoon vanilla extract
4 teaspoons peanut butter	1 teaspoon Erythritol
Cooking spray	

1. Make the cookies: put the almond flour and butter in the bowl. Add Splenda and vanilla extract and knead the non-sticky dough. Then cut dough on 8 pieces. Make the balls and press them to get the flat cookies. Preheat the air fryer to 365F. Spray the air fryer basket with cooking spray and put the cookies in the air fryer in one layer – make 4 flat cookies per one time). Cook them for 10 minutes. Repeat the same steps with remaining cookies. Cool the cooked flat cookies completely. Meanwhile, mix up Erythritol and peanut butter. Then spread 4 flat cookies with peanut butter mixture and cover them with remaining cookies.

Nutrition:
Calories 118, fat 10.2, fiber 0.7, carbs 4.8, protein 2.1

Clove Crackers

Prep time: 20 minutes **Cooking time:** 33 minutes **Servings:** 8

1 cup almond flour	1 teaspoon xanthan gum
1 teaspoon flax meal	½ teaspoon salt
1 teaspoon baking powder	1 teaspoon lemon juice
½ teaspoon ground clove	2 tablespoons Erythritol
1 egg, beaten	3 tablespoons coconut oil, softened

1. In the mixing bowl mix up almond flour, xanthan gum, flax meal, salt, baking powder, and ground clove. Add Erythritol, lemon juice, egg, and coconut oil. Stir the mixture gently with the help of the fork. Then knead the mixture till you get a soft dough. Line the chopping board with parchment. Put the dough on the parchment and roll it up in a thin layer. Cut the thin dough into squares (crackers). Preheat the air fryer to 360F. Line the air fryer basket with baking paper. Put the prepared crackers in the air fryer basket in one layer and cook them for 11 minutes or until the crackers are dry and light brown. Repeat the same steps with remaining uncooked crackers.

Nutrition:
Calories 79, fat 7.5, fiber 1.8, carbs 2.5, protein 1.5

Currant Vanilla Cookies

Preparation time: 5 minutes **Cooking time:** 30 minutes
Servings: 6

cups almond flour	2 teaspoons baking soda
½ cup ghee, melted	½ cup swerve
1 teaspoon vanilla extract	½ cup currants

1. In a bowl, mix all the ingredients and whisk well. Spread this on a baking sheet lined with parchment paper, put the pan in the air fryer and cook at 350 degrees F for 30 minutes. Cool down, cut into rectangles and serve.

Nutrition:

Calories 172, fat 5, fiber 2, carbs 3, protein 5

Chocolate Fudge

Prep time: 15 minutes **Cooking time:** 30 minutes **Servings:** 8

½ cup butter, melted	1 oz dark chocolate, chopped, melted
2 tablespoons cocoa powder	3 tablespoons coconut flour
1 teaspoon vanilla extract	2 eggs, beaten
3 tablespoons Splenda	Cooking spray

1. In the bowl mix up melted butter and dark chocolate. Then add vanilla extract, eggs, and cocoa powder. Stir the mixture until smooth and add Splenda, and coconut flour. Stir it again until smooth. Then preheat the air fryer to 325F. Line the air fryer basket with baking paper and spray it with cooking spray. Pour the fudge mixture in the air fryer basket, flatten it gently with the help of the spatula. Cook the fudge for 30 minutes. Then cut it on the serving squares and cool the fudge completely.

Nutrition:

Calories 177, fat 14.8, fiber 1.6, carbs 8.3, protein 2.6

Cranberries Pudding

Preparation time: 5 minutes **Cooking time:** 20 minutes
Servings: 6

1 cup cauliflower rice 2 cups almond milk	½ cup cranberries
1 teaspoon vanilla extract	

1. In a pan that fits your air fryer, mix all the ingredients, whisk a bit, put the pan in the fryer and cook at 360 degrees F for 20 minutes. Stir the pudding, divide into bowls and serve cold.

Nutrition:

Calories 211, fat 5, fiber 2, carbs 4, protein 7

Merengues

Prep time: 15 minutes **Cooking time:** 65 minutes **Servings:** 6

2 egg whites	1 teaspoon lime zest, grated
1 teaspoon lime juice	4 tablespoons Erythritol

1. Whisk the egg whites until soft peaks. Then add Erythritol and lime juice and whisk the egg whites until you get strong peaks. After this, add lime zest and carefully stir the egg white mixture. Preheat the air fryer to 275F. Line the air fryer basket with baking paper. With the help of the spoon make the small merengues and put them in the air fryer in one layer. Cook the dessert for 65 minutes.

Nutrition:

Calories 6, fat 0, fiber 0, carbs 0.2, protein 1.2

Lemon Coconut Bars

Preparation time: 10 minutes **Cooking time:** 20 minutes
Servings: 12

1 cup coconut cream	¼ cup cashew butter, soft
¾ cup swerve 1 egg, whisked	Juice of 1 lemon
1 teaspoon lemon peel, grated 1 teaspoon baking powder	

1. In a bowl, combine all the ingredients gradually and stir well. Spoon balls this on a baking sheet lined with parchment paper and flatten them. Put the sheet in the fryer and cook at 350 degrees F for 20 minutes. Cut into bars and serve cold.

Nutrition:

Calories 121, fat 5, fiber 1, carbs 4, protein 2

Orange Cinnamon Cookies

Prep time: 15 minutes **Cooking time:** 24 minutes **Servings:** 10

3 tablespoons cream cheese	3 tablespoons Erythritol
1 teaspoon vanilla extract	½ teaspoon ground cinnamon
1 egg, beaten	1 cup almond flour
½ teaspoon baking powder	1 teaspoon butter, softened
½ teaspoon orange zest, grated	

1. Put the cream cheese and Erythritol in the bowl. Add vanilla extract, ground cinnamon, and almond flour. Stir the mixture with the help of the spoon until homogenous. Then add egg, almond flour, baking powder, and butter. Add orange zest and stir the mass until homogenous. Then knead it with the help of the fingertips. Roll up the dough with the help of the rolling pin. Then make the cookies with the help of the cookies cutter.
2. Preheat the air fryer to 365F. Line the air fryer basket with baking paper. Put the cookies on the baking paper and cook them for 8 minutes. The time of cooking depends on the cooking size.

Nutrition:

Calories 38, fat 3.3, fiber 0.4, carbs 1, protein 1.4

Mini Almond Cakes

Preparation time: 10 minutes **Cooking time:** 20 minutes
Servings: 4

3 ounces dark chocolate, melted	¼ cup coconut oil, melted
2 eggs, whisked	2 tablespoons swerve
	¼ teaspoon vanilla extract
	1 tablespoon almond flour
	Cooking spray

1. In bowl, combine all the ingredients except the cooking spray and whisk really well. Divide this into 4 ramekins greased with cooking spray, put them in the fryer and cook at 360 degrees F for 20 minutes. Serve warm.

Nutrition:

Calories 161, fat 12, fiber 1, carbs 4, protein 7

Currant Cream Ramekins

Preparation time: 5 minutes **Cooking time:** 20 minutes
Servings: 6

1 cup red currants, blended	1 cup black currants, blended 3 tablespoons stevia
cup coconut cream	

1. In a bowl, combine all the ingredients and stir well. Divide into ramekins, put them in the fryer and cook at 340 degrees F for 20 minutes. Serve the pudding cold.

Nutrition:

Calories 200, fat 4, fiber 2, carbs 4, protein 6

Chia Bites

Prep time: 15 minutes **Cooking time:** 8 minutes **Servings:** 2

½ scoop of protein powder	1 egg, beaten
3 tablespoons almond flour	1 oz hazelnuts, grinded
1 tablespoon flax meal	1 teaspoon Splenda
1 teaspoon butter, softened	1 teaspoon chia seeds, dried
¼ teaspoon ground clove	

1. In the mixing bowl mix up protein powder, almond flour, grinded hazelnuts, flax meal, chia seeds, ground clove, and Splenda. Then add egg and butter and stir it with the help of the spoon until you get a homogenous mixture. Cut the mixture into pieces and make 2 bites of any shape with the help of the fingertips. Preheat the air fryer to 365F. Line the air fryer basket with baking paper and put the protein bites inside.
2. Cook them for 8 minutes.

Nutrition:

Calories 433, fat 35.5, fiber 7, carbs 15.6, protein 20.2

Espresso Cinnamon Cookies

Preparation time: 5 minutes **Cooking time:** 15 minutes
Servings: 12

8 tablespoons ghee, melted	¼ cup brewed espresso
1 cup almond flour	
¼ cup swerve	½ tablespoon cinnamon powder 2 teaspoons baking powder
2 eggs, whisked	

1. In a bowl, mix all the ingredients and whisk well. Spread medium balls on a cookie sheet lined parchment paper, flatten them, put the cookie sheet in your air fryer and cook at 350 degrees F for 15 minutes. Serve the cookies cold.

Nutrition:

Calories 134, fat 12, fiber 2, carbs 4, protein 2

Turmeric Almond Pie

Prep time: 20 minutes **Cooking time:** 35 minutes **Servings:** 4

4 eggs, beaten	1 tablespoon poppy seeds
1 teaspoon ground turmeric	1 teaspoon vanilla extract
1 teaspoon baking powder	1 teaspoon lemon juice
1 cup almond flour	2 tablespoons heavy cream
¼ cup Erythritol	1 teaspoon avocado oil

1. Put the eggs in the bowl. Add vanilla extract, baking powder, lemon juice, almond flour, heavy cream, and Erythritol. Then add avocado oil and poppy seeds. Add turmeric. With the help of the immersion blender, blend the pie batter until it is smooth. Line the air fryer cake mold with baking paper. Pour the pie batter in the cake mold. Flatten the pie surface with the help of the spatula if needed. Then preheat the air fryer to 365F. Put the cake mold in the air fryer and cook the pie for 35 minutes. When the pie is cooked, cool it completely and remove it from the cake mold. Cut the cooked pie into the servings.

Nutrition:

Calories 149, fat 11.9, fiber 1.2, carbs 3.8, protein 7.7

Sponge Cake

Preparation time: 5 minutes **Cooking time:** 30 minutes
Servings: 8

1 cup ricotta, soft 1/3 swerve	3 eggs, whisked
1 cup almond flour	7 tablespoons ghee, melted 1 teaspoon baking powder Cooking spray

1. In a bowl, combine all the ingredients except the cooking spray and stir them very well. Grease a cake pan that fits the air fryer with the cooking spray and pour the cake mix inside. Put the pan in the fryer and cook at 350 degrees F for 30 minutes. Cool the cake down, slice and serve.

Nutrition:

Calories 210, fat 12, fiber 3, carbs 6, protein 9

Appendix 1 Measurement Conversion Chart

VOLUME EQUIVALENTS(DRY)

US STANDARD	METRIC (APPROXIMATE)
1/8 teaspoon	0.5 mL
1/4 teaspoon	1 mL
1/2 teaspoon	2 mL
3/4 teaspoon	4 mL
1 teaspoon	5 mL
1 tablespoon	15 mL
1/4 cup	59 mL
1/2 cup	118 mL
3/4 cup	177 mL
1 cup	235 mL
2 cups	475 mL
3 cups	700 mL
4 cups	1 L

VOLUME EQUIVALENTS(LIQUID)

US STANDARD	US STANDARD (OUNCES)	METRIC (APPROXIMATE)
2 tablespoons	1 fl.oz.	30 mL
1/4 cup	2 fl.oz.	60 mL
1/2 cup	4 fl.oz.	120 mL
1 cup	8 fl.oz.	240 mL
1 1/2 cup	12 fl.oz.	355 mL
2 cups or 1 pint	16 fl.oz.	475 mL
4 cups or 1 quart	32 fl.oz.	1 L
1 gallon	128 fl.oz.	4 L

TEMPERATURES EQUIVALENTS

FAHRENHEIT(F)	CELSIUS(C) (APPROXIMATE)
225 °F	107 °C
250 °F	120 °C
275 °F	135 °C
300 °F	150 °C
325 °F	160 °C
350 °F	180 °C
375 °F	190 °C
400 °F	205 °C
425 °F	220 °C
450 °F	235 °C
475 °F	245 °C
500 °F	260 °C

WEIGHT EQUIVALENTS

US STANDARD	METRIC (APPROXIMATE)
1 ounce	28 g
2 ounces	57 g
5 ounces	142 g
10 ounces	284 g
15 ounces	425 g
16 ounces (1 pound)	455 g
1.5 pounds	680 g
2 pounds	907 g

Appendix 2 Air Fryer Cooking Chart

Beef

Item	Temp (°F)	Time (mins)	Item	Temp (°F)	Time (mins)
Beef Eye Round Roast (4 lbs.)	400 °F	45 to 55	Meatballs (1-inch)	370 °F	7
Burger Patty (4 oz.)	370 °F	16 to 20	Meatballs (3-inch)	380 °F	10
Filet Mignon (8 oz.)	400 °F	18	Ribeye, bone-in (1-inch, 8 oz)	400 °F	10 to 15
Flank Steak (1.5 lbs.)	400 °F	12	Sirloin steaks (1-inch, 12 oz)	400 °F	9 to 14
Flank Steak (2 lbs.)	400 °F	20 to 28			

Chicken

Item	Temp (°F)	Time (mins)	Item	Temp (°F)	Time (mins)
Breasts, bone in (1 ¼ lb.)	370 °F	25	Legs, bone-in (1 ¾ lb.)	380 °F	30
Breasts, boneless (4 oz)	380 °F	12	Thighs, boneless (1 ½ lb.)	380 °F	18 to 20
Drumsticks (2 ½ lb.)	370 °F	20	Wings (2 lb.)	400 °F	12
Game Hen (halved 2 lb.)	390 °F	20	Whole Chicken	360 °F	75
Thighs, bone-in (2 lb.)	380 °F	22	Tenders	360 °F	8 to 10

Pork & Lamb

Item	Temp (°F)	Time (mins)	Item	Temp (°F)	Time (mins)
Bacon (regular)	400 °F	5 to 7	Pork Tenderloin	370 °F	15
Bacon (thick cut)	400 °F	6 to 10	Sausages	380 °F	15
Pork Loin (2 lb.)	360 °F	55	Lamb Loin Chops (1-inch thick)	400 °F	8 to 12
Pork Chops, bone in (1-inch, 6.5 oz)	400 °F	12	Rack of Lamb (1.5 – 2 lb.)	380 °F	22

Fish & Seafood

Item	Temp (°F)	Time (mins)	Item	Temp (°F)	Time (mins)
Calamari (8 oz)	400 °F	4	Tuna Steak	400 °F	7 to 10
Fish Fillet (1-inch, 8 oz)	400 °F	10	Scallops	400 °F	5 to 7
Salmon, fillet (6 oz)	380 °F	12	Shrimp	400 °F	5
Swordfish steak	400 °F	10			

Vegetables

INGREDIENT	AMOUNT	PREPARATION	OIL	TEMP	COOK TIME
Asparagus	2 bunches	Cut in half, trim stems	2 Tbsp	420°F	12-15 mins
Beets	1½ lbs	Peel, cut in ½-inch cubes	1Tbsp	390°F	28-30 mins
Bell peppers (for roasting)	4 peppers	Cut in quarters, remove seeds	1Tbsp	400°F	15-20 mins
Broccoli	1 large head	Cut in 1-2 inch florets	1Tbsp	400°F	15-20 mins
Brussels sprouts	1lb	Cut in half, remove stems	1Tbsp	425°F	15-20 mins
Carrots	1lb	Peel, cut in ¼-inch rounds	1 Tbsp	425°F	10-15 mins
Cauliflower	1 head	Cut in 1-2-inch florets	2 Tbsp	400°F	20-22 mins
Corn on the cob	7 ears	Whole ears, remove husks	1 Tbps	400°F	14-17 mins
Green beans	1 bag (12 oz)	Trim	1 Tbps	420°F	18-20 mins
Kale (for chips)	4 oz	Tear into pieces,remove stems	None	325°F	5-8 mins
Mushrooms	16 oz	Rinse, slice thinly	1 Tbps	390°F	25-30 mins
Potatoes, russet	1½ lbs	Cut in 1-inch wedges	1 Tbps	390°F	25-30 mins
Potatoes, russet	1lb	Hand-cut fries, soak 30 mins in cold water, then pat dry	½ -3 Tbps	400°F	25-28 mins
Potatoes, sweet	1lb	Hand-cut fries, soak 30 mins in cold water, then pat dry	1 Tbps	400°F	25-28 mins
Zucchini	1lb	Cut in eighths lengthwise, then cut in half	1 Tbps	400°F	15-20 mins

Appendix 3 Index

Z

Printed in Great Britain
by Amazon

81109865R00102